Philosophy and Community

Also Available at Bloomsbury

Socially Just Pedagogies: Posthumanist, Feminist and Materialist Perspectives in Higher Education, ed. Rosi Braidotti, Vivienne Bozalek, Tamara Shefer, Michalinos Zembylas

Problems in Philosophy of Education: A Systematic Approach, James Scott Johnston

Philosophy and Community

Theories, Practices and Possibilities

Edited by:
Amanda Fulford
Grace Lockrobin
Richard Smith

BLOOMSBURY ACADEMIC
LONDON · NEW YORK · OXFORD · NEW DELHI · SYDNEY

BLOOMSBURY ACADEMIC
Bloomsbury Publishing Plc
50 Bedford Square, London, WC1B 3DP, UK
1385 Broadway, New York, NY 10018, USA
29 Earlsfort Terrace, Dublin 2, Ireland

BLOOMSBURY, BLOOMSBURY ACADEMIC and the Diana logo are trademarks of
Bloomsbury Publishing Plc

First published in Great Britain 2020
This paperback edition published in 2021

Copyright © Amanda Fulford, Grace Lockrobin, Richard Smith, and Contributors, 2020

Amanda Fulford, Grace Lockrobin, and Richard Smith have asserted their right under the
Copyright, Designs and Patents Act, 1988, to be identified as Editors of this work.

For legal purposes the Acknowledgements on p. vii constitute an extension of this
copyright page.

Cover image © Karel Nepraš / National Gallery Prague, 2019

All rights reserved. No part of this publication may be reproduced or transmitted in
any form or by any means, electronic or mechanical, including photocopying,
recording, or any information storage or retrieval system, without prior permission
in writing from the publishers.

Bloomsbury Publishing Plc does not have any control over, or responsibility for, any
third-party websites referred to or in this book. All internet addresses given in this
book were correct at the time of going to press. The author and publisher regret any
inconvenience caused if addresses have changed or sites have ceased to exist, but
can accept no responsibility for any such changes.

A catalogue record for this book is available from the British Library.

A catalog record for this book is available from the Library of Congress.

ISBN: HB: 978-1-3500-7340-1
PB: 978-1-3502-6098-6
ePDF: 978-1-3500-7341-8
eBook: 978-1-3500-7342-5

Typeset by Deanta Global Publishing Services, Chennai, India

To find out more about our authors and books visit www.bloomsbury.com and
sign up for our newsletters.

Contents

Foreword: Community-engaged philosophy for lifelong learning
Eric Thomas Weber   vii

Preface: 'In all things of nature there is something wonderful'
Amanda Fulford   xii

List of Contributors   xvi

List of Abbreviations   xxii

Part One Philosophy and Community: Theories   1

1. Understanding philosophy in communities: The spaces, people, politics and philosophy of Community Philosophy *Steve Bramall*   3

2. Relocation and repopulation: Why Community Philosophy matters *Grace Lockrobin*   15

3. Registers of community: Policy discourse, subjectivity and coming to terms with our conditions *Naomi Hodgson*   38

4. Keeping the conversation going: A pragmatist assessment of the value of public philosophy *William C. Pamerleau*   56

5. Community Philosophy and social action *Graeme Tiffany*   69

6. Philosophy, dialogue and the creation of community *Amanda Fulford*   91

7. Beyond walls: The redemption of philosophy *Richard Smith*   103

Part Two Philosophy and Community: Practices   115

8. In philosophical conversation with: Art audiences *Grace Lockrobin*   117

9. In philosophical conversation with: Professionals *Jim Baxter*   131

10. In philosophical conversation with: New and beginning teachers *Janet Orchard, Ruth Heilbronn and Carrie Winstanley*   145

11. In philosophical conversation with: Learning-disabled performers *Nick Wiltsher and Aaron Meskin*   163

12. In philosophical conversation with: People in prison – beyond rehabilitation *Andy West and Kirstine Szifris*   177

vi   *Contents*

13   In philosophical conversation with: Philosophy Ireland – Building a
national P4C network *Charlotte Blease*   189

14   In philosophical conversation with: A diverse group of adults –
'Dwelling Together in Diverse Spaces' *Darren Chetty, Abigail Bentley
and Adam Ferner*   203

15   In philosophical conversation with: Undergraduate students and a
local school community *Elizabeth Watkins*   216

16   In philosophical conversation with: Adolescents in a behavioural
health unit *Alissa Hurwitz Swota and Michael De La Hunt*   229

Part Three   Philosophy and Community: Possibilities   241

17   Coda *Amanda Fulford and Richard Smith*   243

Afterword: Thoughts on moving philosophy outside *Graeme Tiffany*   248

Index   255

Foreword: Community-engaged philosophy for lifelong learning

Eric Thomas Weber

John Dewey often noted that schooling is not the same thing as an education. Schooling is typically only of focus for a short period of people's lives. We often think of it as preparation for life, but Dewey insisted that education is democratic life itself. Dewey is without doubt one of the greatest exemplars of public philosophy, yet since his day there has been a significant decline in publicly engaged philosophy. I am one of the truly lucky people to have studied with John Lachs of Vanderbilt University, who has worked for fifty years on the revitalization of public philosophy in the United States.[1] Lachs has been a teacher, a mentor and a friend. He serves as Chairman of the Board of Trustees of the Society of Philosophers in America (SOPHIA), an organization for which I began serving as Executive Director in 2010 and whose mission is of central relevance to the subject of this volume.

In 2015, SOPHIA leaders got together to revise the organization's long-standing yet vague mission – to complete a strategic planning initiative, envisioning the future of the organization. We found that there were many examples of particular public philosophers, especially in some venues like The Stone of *The New York Times*,[2] or any number of excellent local newspaper columns. Isolated individuals engaged in various kinds of public philosophical endeavour, and SOPHIA's efforts accomplished some very rich growth in local conversations in many parts of the United States. What we found was missing at the time, however, is precisely what this volume emphasizes: community. After SOPHIA received a number of grants and held individual events, we were left wondering what was left over from all of the hard work that went into their execution. What lasted from the fleeting yet rich local conversations that we held? The trouble was that, prior to 2015, we were not emphasizing the building of community in our mission. We came to recognize that community was essential. First, it is what can be left over from rich, philosophical conversation. In addition, our emphasis on conversation was philosophically rooted as well. One of the odd findings at our meetings was that participants were genuinely surprised that our intention of holding conversational meetings was sincere. We were not simply going to meet people and have someone deliver a lecture, after which the quiet audience members might each get to ask a single question. SOPHIA has long aimed to foster conversations as a core element of our mission, but when people saw that we meant it, they were surprised.

Leaders in our strategic planning effort noted that trust is essential for community engagement and growth.

People need to believe that you mean what you say, that their intelligence will be respected, and that learning is a two-way street, or can be, in public intellectual engagements – all tenets of SOPHIA's values. With this insight in mind, SOPHIA's new mission statement was established: 'The mission of the Society of Philosophers in America (SOPHIA) is to use the tools of philosophical inquiry to improve people's lives and enrich the profession of philosophy through conversation and community building.' Community is essential. That is important, I believe, because other volumes could be written presenting an outlook on public philosophy that fails to recognize this need. Michael Sandel's great collection of essays, *Public Philosophy*,[3] is precisely a series of one-way proclamations from a great moral philosopher to a curious readership. Public philosophy is often thought of in terms of the 'sage on the stage', who will descend upon the ignorant public to inform the plebeians about their misconceptions. Such would not be a fair characterization of Sandel, who is quite Deweyan in important ways; yet the traditional model for the public philosopher and the public intellectual is to have an influential scholar set aside his or her technical research for a spell to write the occasional opinion editorial, address or trade book. That is one valuable contribution that scholars can make, but today the public has access to an enormous quantity of thoughts. What is profoundly needed today is the cultivation of greater thoughtfulness. And, I argue, such a development will not take place until scholars and the public recognize that education is more than schooling, and should be understood as lifelong. Community-engaged public philosophy is essential, furthermore, for nurturing the philosophical attitudes and habits of mind that democracy today so desperately needs.

In aiming to build communities of philosophical conversation – a briefer statement of SOPHIA's new mission – we discussed the ideas of launching a journal and a podcast, though we did not know yet how. Eventually, the journal became *Civil American*,[4] an open-access, peer-reviewed journal published on SOPHIA's website for general audiences. The podcast opportunity arose in a less conventional fashion. When I moved to the University of Kentucky from the University of Mississippi in 2016, and reached out to people to get to know my new colleagues around campus, it turned out that one had a radio show on WRFL Lexington, 88.1 FM, the college's radio station. He suggested that he interview me on his show about my latest book, an opportunity that I welcomed and enjoyed. After the programme, he suggested that I pitch a radio show for the station. I had never considered this before. I had begun my own podcast a year earlier, but had only recorded four episodes, as academic life is very busy and it was primarily a labour of love. The podcast I had started was based on a speech I delivered in Jackson, Mississippi, in accepting the Mississippi Humanities Council's 2015 Public Humanities Scholar Award. I called the address 'Philosophy Bakes Bread.' The title was inspired by a famous line from the poet Novalis, who wrote that 'philosophy may bake no bread, but she can procure for us God, freedom, and immortality. Which, then, is more profitable, philosophy or economy?' Of course, the part people remember is that philosophy bakes no bread. Novalis's point was that philosophy is of even deeper practical importance than bread baking. That said, however, there are profound contributions that philosophical thinking can make in many areas of life, such that it is time, I believed then, and still believe now, that we start acknowledging all the myriad ways in which philosophy most certainly does metaphorically bake bread.

The first episode of the original Philosophy Bakes Bread podcast, which I later referred to as a pilot episode by the radio show of the same name, was an initial background episode featuring my speech in Mississippi that was recorded with my cell phone in my jacket pocket.[5] The next one was an episode on the ways in which Stoicism has helped me to be happy despite my daughter's very difficult start in life, medically speaking.[6] My wife and I had achieved many of our far-reaching goals, when our first child was born and suddenly suffered a stroke, leading later to debilitating epilepsy with lifelong consequences. We are happy today in large part because of the help of Stoic philosophy, at least that was the tradition most helpful to me at the time. On our podcasting service, I later called the first four podcast-only episodes the 'pilot season' of the radio show and podcast that a friend and I developed later.

When my family moved from Mississippi to Kentucky, I decided to launch myself deeper into the public philosophical work that I had been doing before. For this reason, it seemed like a good idea to propose a radio show and podcast for WRFL Lexington, as a production of SOPHIA, if I could run it with a co-host especially, to be more dynamic, and preferably as an interview show, as there is much more to philosophy than what I have to say about it. I designed a basic sketch of the kind of show that I would most want to listen to, which would start with questions about who the guest is. We so often begin the story of philosophy with the maxim inscribed at Delphi, 'Know thyself', as it was instructive for Socrates. He learnt thereby that when he was called the wisest man in Athens, it was because he realized that he was ignorant, unlike his fellow Athenians who thought themselves knowledgeable. The plan was to begin the show autobiographically, therefore, as it tells us something also about where ideas come from and why ideas appeal to some people and not others. It also contributes to understanding the pragmatic value of ideas. After that, we would have two substantive, fifteen-minute segments, because the radio station requires announcements roughly every fifteen minutes. Then, the last segment would include final big picture questions: the guest's view or response about whether philosophy bakes bread and how, as well as some humour and a question for listeners for the episode's conclusion.

In thinking about with whom to collaborate on the show, I asked myself which philosopher was the most fun to talk to in all of my years studying and teaching philosophy. That question arose because such a person would be the most inviting and the greatest help in building community with others about the topics we talk about. My wife deserves the credit for suggesting the ideal choice: Anthony Cashio. Anthony and I were graduate school colleagues at the greatest place to study John Dewey's philosophy at the time, Southern Illinois University in Carbondale, IL. We launched the show in January 2017, not knowing much yet about best practices, but we had fun and learnt a lot quickly. Within the first six months, we experienced bumps in the road, found significantly better tools to do what we wanted to do, in terms of audio quality, and had launched the show on a podcasting platform and SOPHIA's Web site, shared via social media. By the start of July 2017, we had witnessed over 10,000 downloads of the show and nearly a total of 30,000 by January 2018. In our first year we released a new episode every week, which was an incredible challenge to manage, but somehow we did it. In 2018, we scaled back and released a new episode every two weeks, airing a rerun in our weekly radio timeslot from the prior year's episodes. Despite the slowdown in production, today we have data revealing nearly 60,000 downloads of the show from over 100 countries, which does not count radio listeners, of course. The Philosophy Bakes Bread Facebook page has almost 100,000 followers,[7] and the show is now syndicating on KBLU LP Logan, 92.3 FM in Logan, Utah. Syndicating with one station is not much harder than syndicating with many more, so we are beginning to explore the possibility of offering syndication to many more stations around the United States. We also have listeners from around the world who have reached out to us with kind and generous feedback, from Australia to Portugal and from the United Kingdom to Venezuela.

All along the way and earlier, I have been developing my own social media presence and engagement, furthermore, which has grown far larger than I could have anticipated. Today, my own Facebook author page has over 230,000 followers.[8] Of course, this does not mean that such figures imply anything like meaningful public engagement. People follow inane profiles as well as meaningful ones. Nevertheless, I believe that if the great American public philosopher, John Dewey, were alive today, he would revel at what is possible, both for better and for worse, by means of social media. In one sense, we all have much to fear about the potential for stupidity, mass hysteria, and the rapid spread of false or damaging information, which can stoke fears and hatred. On the other hand, abstaining from engagement on such social platforms only leaves us powerless, not immune, to the harmful effects of social media manipulation. Given that, more and more scholars should be encouraged, I believe, to offer themselves as resources, as well as listeners, to their communities via social media. In addition, consider that radio and television have long been one-directional media for communications. Today, the internet and social media blast open barriers to communicative access. Even a radio show and podcast, as Anthony and I note in every episode, can be mechanisms for two-way communications. And we relish each voicemail we receive, that we can then use and respond to in future episode segments that we call 'You Tell Me!' Such public engagements are fun and enriching, as well as time-consuming. But today one of our problems is that they are undertheorized.

More than ever, academia and the public have a need for philosophical thinking about the nature of public philosophy and its role in and with community. Volumes like the present one are desperately needed to enable scholars and institutions to understand, support, and evaluate public philosophy as a vital and vibrant endeavour. I therefore congratulate the editors of this fine volume for their hard work and success and encourage them, the authors whose works appear herein, and the scholars and administrators out there who just need some more encouragement, to continue in the essential work that must be done in the wake of democratic instabilities in the United States, the United Kingdom and around the world today.

* * *

Notes

1 See, for example, Lachs (1995)
2 'A forum for contemporary philosophers and other thinkers on issues both timely and timeless' – see https://www.nytimes.com/column/the-stone
3 Sandel (2006)
4 See http://CivilAmerican.com
5 Weber (2015b)
6 Weber (2015a)
7 See https://www.facebook.com/philosophybakesbread/
8 See https://www.facebook.com/EricThomasWeberAuthor/

References

Lachs, J., (1995), *The Relevance of Philosophy to Life*, Nashville, TN: Vanderbilt University Press.

Sandel, Michael J., (2006), *Public Philosophy: Essays on Morality in Politics*, Cambridge, MA: Harvard University Press.

Weber, E. T., (2015a), '"Acceptance and Happiness with Stoicism", – Podcast Philosophy Bakes Bread', Pilot Episode 0.1, 4 March 2015, [Online], Available at: https://www.philosophersinamerica.com/2015/03/14/0-1-ep0-1-acceptance-happiness-with-stoicism-pilot/

Weber, E. T., (2015b), 'Background for "Philosophy Bakes Bread", Award Acceptance Speech – Podcast Philosophy Bakes Bread', Pilot Episode 0.0, 16 February 2015, [Online], Available at: https://www.philosophersinamerica.com/2015/02/16/0-0-background-for-philosophy-bakes-bread-award-acceptance-speech/

Preface: 'In all things of nature there is something wonderful'

Amanda Fulford

So one must not be childishly repelled by the examination of the humbler animals. For in all things of nature there is something wonderful. And just as Heraclitus is said to have spoken to the visitors who wanted to meet him and who stopped as they were approaching when they saw him warming himself by the oven he urged them to come in without fear. For there were gods there too – so one must approach the inquiry about each animal without aversion, since in all of them there is something natural and beautiful. (Aristotle 2001: 645a 17ff.)

*   *   *

This volume begins with a number of questions: why? what? and how? This seems just the right approach in a book about public or community philosophy, which often begins in puzzlement, or with questions which act as the starting point for our reasoning together. In public philosophy, these tend to be questions about ourselves; our place in the world; how we create, order and sustain the communities in which we live and about how we might live a good life together. Such questions are not new; they are ones that have been asked, discussed, resolved and reopened, both in and outside philosophy for millennia. They are still as pertinent and fresh now as when the Presocratics began to inquire into the world, and the place of human beings in it. They are also questions over which philosophers have long argued, and which have resulted in such a diversity and number of texts, that one person could not hope to tackle them all, even in a lifetime of reading. But they are also questions that are not reserved for professional philosophers nor for the hallowed halls of the academy. They are ones that we can, and do, all ask, and where in the most ordinary of places we can find something natural and beautiful; we too can find the gods there.

The questions with which this book opens are of a different kind, but are, nevertheless, important. In this preface we consider *why* we think that a volume like this is needed, and what motivated us to write it. We then turn attention briefly to *why* we consider that this volume is important to readers now, and *who* we hope will find the chapters interesting. Finally, this preface lays out *what* this volume is, what it

Preface xiii

is trying to achieve and what readers should *not* expect of it. So, some may get to the end of this preface, and stop reading. We hope that this is not the case, since whatever the inadequacies of this short section might be in explaining what we have tried to achieve in this volume, what follows in Parts One to Three represents a rich diversity of scholarly thinking and critical reflection on the theories, practices and possibilities of community and public philosophy. It is, to our knowledge, the first time that such a volume has been published. Our hope is that this book will not only inform but also inspire others to engage in philosophy with others outside the academy, and to find gods in doing so.

Why, then, did we write this book? Part of the answer is in the tangible growth of interest, particularly over the last half-century or so, in different forms of public and community philosophy, but also in the notable absence of scholarly writing on the subject. The innovative work of Matthew Lipman and his colleagues in the early 1970s at the Institute for the Advancement of Philosophy for Children at Montclair University in the United States was the start of the philosophy for children movement – often known by the acronym P4C. Since then, there has been a significant growth both in this kind of work and in associated publications, from academic work justifying, critiquing or evaluating P4C, to how-to guides and resource kits aimed at practitioners. But while there has also been growth in public and community philosophy with *adults* in a range of settings, very little is written on these practices, especially in the academic literature. This volume attempts to address this both through analyses of the ideas that underpin public philosophy and through critical reflection on its practices.

It is not only the scope and the originality of aim that we hope makes this volume attractive to a broad readership; it is also in its timeliness. This addresses another question: *Why* did we write this book now? We are living though an unusual – some might say unprecedented – period in our history. Donald Trump's election and presidency in the United States and the United Kingdom's momentous vote to leave the European Union are just two examples of events that could hardly have been imagined a decade ago. Both events have initiated extensive public debate, much of it acrimonious, and divisive. But while these affairs have undoubtedly got people talking, it seems that they have led, to a great extent, to an entrenching of views. Perhaps then there has never been a better time for a careful consideration of what it means to reason together about the views that we hold; to listen to and take seriously the views of others; and to re-evaluate our own positions, or at least to find that there are better reasons for holding those positions. This is what it means to do public philosophy: to enter into reasoned conversations together about the matters that are central to our lives and to work out how we might go on together, even when we might have profound disagreements.

As the title of this volume suggests, there are two concepts that are central to it: philosophy and community. These concepts also help to answer a further question: To whom is this book addressed? Philosophers may be interested to read how our understanding of what philosophy *is* might be affected by the idea and the practices of public philosophy. Those working in local government, as well as community workers and activists may want to read how different groups have engaged with community philosophy, and what the implications of this are for ideas about philosophy and community. Those involved in diverse forms of public philosophy practice will find in the volume ideas that they will recognize, but also new ways of conceptualizing this work, and its future possibilities. And those involved in formal and in informal education will read here about the educative possibilities of the type of dialogue and reasoning together that are at the heart of many iterations of public philosophy.

The volume is deliberately international in scope; it draws on thinking about public philosophy and its practices from different regions and contexts in order to illustrate the diversity in such work. Our contributors have similarly broad backgrounds. Some are academics in philosophy, education, medicine and health, ethics and bioethics, aesthetics and policy evaluation. Others are teachers, trainers, teacher educators, community philosophers and consultants. They all share an interest in the practices of public philosophy and in critical evaluation and theorizing of this work.

The volume is structured in three parts. Part One contains chapters which address conceptual and theoretical concerns in public and community philosophy. In Chapter 1, Steve Bramall outlines the history and development of public philosophy in order to provide the general context for the volume as a whole. In Chapter 2, Grace Lockrobin considers what it is to do philosophy with different communities, and what this might reveal about philosophy itself. In Chapter 3, Naomi Hodgson traces how the language of community in contemporary forms of governance has been repositioned. In Chapter 4, William C. Pamerleau argues that the value of public philosophy might be understood in relation to the philosophical tradition of pragmatism, since this shows us that conversing about our beliefs broadens perspectives and increases our sensitivity to the humanity of others. Chapters 5 and 6 have a focus on the purposes of public philosophy: Graeme Tiffany looks at how community philosophy is a form of social action, and Amanda Fulford considers the educative possibilities of forms of dialogue that are central to public philosophy. In the final chapter of Part One, Richard Smith draws attention to the complex and ambiguous tradition that community philosophy inherits.

In Part Two, contributors who are working in the field critically reflect on their practice. They introduce and outline their work with particular groups and discuss the implications of this for how we think about both philosophy and community. Each chapter has some focus on the dialogue that is characteristic of many different forms of public and community philosophy. The chapters here highlight this in their titles which all begin 'In Philosophical Conversation With'. The chapters illustrate the diversity of work in the field, and the contexts in which public philosophy and dialogue takes place: with museum and art gallery audiences (Grace Lockrobin); professionals (Jim Baxter); new and beginning teachers (Janet Orchard, Ruth Heilbronn and Carrie Winstanley); learning-disabled performers (Nick Wiltsher and Aaron Meskin); people in prison (Andy West and Kirstine Szifris); in a national network (Charlotte Blease); with diverse groups of adults (Darren Chetty, Abigail Bentley and Adam Ferner); and with undergraduate students (Elizabeth Watkins).

In Part Three we conclude with a Coda that reflects briefly on what the chapters in the volume reveal about philosophy and the idea of community. The volume concludes with an Afterword that looks beyond current practices to what the possibilities might be for public philosophy, and how this work might develop in original ways. In doing

Preface

this, Graeme Tiffany provides one example of how we might rethink the practices of Community Philosophy spatially by walking together in the outdoors.

But what exactly *is* this book? It is easy to say what it is not. We have not written a definitive 'how to' guide to doing philosophy in different community settings (as if such a guide were even possible or desirable). Rather, our aim has been to bring together, for what we think is the first time, contributions to a scholarly edited collection on public and community philosophy. We use the terms 'public' and 'community' interchangeably – as we do with 'philosophical inquiry' and 'philosophical enquiry'; this not only acknowledges how individual and groups perceive their work, and prefer to write about it, but also recognizes its diversity.[1] Our intention is that this volume not only informs those who are new to the field but also offers established colleagues a different perspective on thinking about what constitutes philosophy, and the concept of community. As such, we anticipate that it will be an important text not only for scholars working in the academy but also for those involved in all different forms of community involvement, from local government to grass-roots activists. Above all what this volume shows is that through public philosophy, and its concern with reasoning together, we are, in the words of the American philosopher, Stanley Cavell, 'educations for one another' (1990: 31).

*   *   *

Note

1   The terms 'community philosophy', 'Community Philosophy' and 'public philosophy' are used in this volume. The difference between these terms is not always clear, though community philosophy tends to be understood as the practices of philosophy with particular groups or more discrete communities, whereas the idea of public philosophy is suggestive of a more general audience. Rather than keep to a single term that we use consistently in this volume, we have made the decision to retain the different usages. We take the same approach to the use of 'philosophical enquiry' and 'philosophical inquiry'. While the former may simply suggest 'asking', whereas the latter tends to be used to describe a more formal, systematic investigation, both usages reflect the practices of community and public philosophy. By using all these terms, we draw attention deliberately to the diversity of work in the field of community and public philosophy. We also wanted to give contributing authors the freedom to describe their practices in ways that they consider reflect the work that they do.

References

Aristotle, (2001), *De Partibus Animalium I - IV*, Translated with an Introduction and Commentary by J. G. Lennox, Oxford: Clarendon Press.

Cavell, S., (1990), *Conditions Handsome and Unhandsome: The Constitution of Emersonian Perfectionism*, Chicago: University of Chicago Press.

Contributors

Jim Baxter is Professional Ethics Consultancy Manager for the Inter-Disciplinary Ethics Applied Centre at the University of Leeds, UK. He manages a small team of consultants, carrying out commissioned research projects and providing continuing professional development, working with professional bodies, private and public-sector organizations. Jim's PhD, completed in 2017, was on the subject of moral responsibility and psychopathy. He has research interests in theories of moral responsibility, psychiatric ethics, integrity and professional ethics. He lives in Sheffield with his partner Bella and their son Elijah, and he likes to sing, sometimes in front of other people.

Abigail Bentley is a doctoral researcher at the Institute for Global Health, University College London. Her current research focuses on gender-based violence and mental health in Mumbai, India. Originally trained as a biomedical scientist, Abigail has since transitioned over to public health and has spent the last six years working on maternal and child health in the UK and India. Abigail has a keen personal interest in exploring the topics of multiculturalism, identity and racism. In 2017 she co-led the 'Dwelling Together in Diverse Spaces' project at University College London alongside Darren Chetty.

Charlotte Blease is a philosopher of medicine and interdisciplinary health care researcher based at the Beth Israel Deaconess Medical Center/Harvard Medical School in Boston, United States. Born in Belfast, she has held academic appointments in the United Kingdom, Europe, Ireland and the United States. She is currently a Fulbright Scholar and Marie Curie Research Fellow at Harvard Medical School. In 2015 she co-founded and was first Chairperson of the all-island network Philosophy Ireland, which promotes philosophy in the community and in schools. She was appointed Patron of the Society for the Advancement of Philosophical Enquiry and Reflection in Education (SAPERE) in 2016. She has published widely in academic journals, and also in the media, including for *The Guardian* and *The Irish Times*.

Steve Bramall is lead trainer and project manager in community philosophy at SAPERE, a national charity promoting philosophy for children, colleges and communities. Since leaving academic teaching, Steve has spent fifteen years in practical philosophy promoting and supporting philosophical engagement and action in schools, museums, galleries, community groups, charities and pubs. Steve has published articles and books in philosophy of education, philosophy for children and community philosophy. He chaired SAPERE's Community Philosophy Advisory

Group and headed an Esmée Fairbairn funded community philosophy project. He serves on the Philosophy of Education Society of Great Britain's (PESGB) development committee and SAPERE's Professional Standards Board.

Darren Chetty is a teacher, writer and researcher with research interests in education, philosophy, racism, children's literature and hip-hop culture. He is a former recipient of the 'Award for Excellence in Interpreting Philosophy for Children' from the International Council for Philosophical Inquiry with Children (ICPIC) for his paper 'The Elephant in the Room: Picturebooks, Philosophy for Children and Racism'. In 2011 Darren launched the UK #HipHopEd Seminar series. He is a contributor to the bestselling book, *The Good Immigrant*, edited by Nikesh Shukla and published by Unbound. Darren tweets at @rapclassroom

Michael De La Hunt is the Medical Director of paediatric mental health services at Wolfson Children's Hospital, Jacksonville, Florida, and Division Chief, Division of Psychiatry at Nemours Children's Specialty Care, Jacksonville, Florida – a comprehensive paediatric multispecialty clinic. He earned a master of health science degree in Maternal and Child Health at The Johns Hopkins School of Hygiene & Public Health. He then attended the University of Minnesota Medical School studying for a medical degree before completing his residency training at Brown University/Rhode Island Hospital's Hasbro Children's Hospital in Providence, Rhode Island, where he earned a triple board degree in paediatrics, general psychiatry and child and adolescent psychiatry.

Adam Ferner has worked in academic philosophy both in France and the UK, but prefers working outside the academy in alternative learning spaces. He has written two books, *Organisms and Personal Identity* (2016) and *Think Differently* (2018), along with the co-authored *Crash Course: Philosophy* (forthcoming) with Zara Bain and Nadia Mehdi. He has published widely in philosophical and popular journals, and is an associate editor of the Forum Essays. He created and runs the collaborative writing project 'Changelings' at the Platform youth hub in North London.

Amanda Fulford is Professor of Philosophy of Education and Head of the Department of Professional Learning at Edge Hill University, Ormskirk, UK. She teaches postgraduate students in professional learning and supervises doctoral students. Her research interests are in philosophy of education, the philosophy of higher education and public and community philosophy. Her publications include *Philosophy and Theory in Education: Writing in the Margin*, with Naomi Hodgson (Routledge 2016) and the forthcoming *Philosophers on the University* with Ronald Barnett. She is co-editor of the 'Debating Higher Education' series with Springer, and has published numerous articles in international, peer-reviewed journals. She currently serves on the Executive Committee of the Philosophy of Education Society of Great Britain and on the Governing Council of the Society for Research into Higher Education (SRHE).

Ruth Heilbronn researches and lectures at UCL Institute of Education, London, UK, where she gained her PhD and led teams engaged in teacher education. She has previously held senior posts in schools. She writes on issues related to induction (DfE Report 338, 2002), ethical teacher education, values education, reflective practice and ethical deliberation. Relevant publications include *Teacher Education and the Development of Practical Judgement* (Continuum 2008) and co-edited books: *Research-Based Best Practice for Schools* (Routledge 2002); *Critical Practice in Teacher Education* (IoE Press 2010); *Philosophical Perspectives on Teacher Education* (Wiley Blackwell 2015); and *Dewey in our Time* (UCL IoE Press 2016). She is an executive member of the Philosophy of Education Society of Great Britain (PESGB).

Naomi Hodgson is Senior Lecturer in Education Studies at Liverpool Hope University, UK, where she teaches and researches in philosophy of education. Her research focuses on the relationship between education, governance and subjectivity. Her publications include *Philosophy and Theory in Education: Writing in the Margin*, with Amanda Fulford (Routledge 2016); *Citizenship for the Learning Society: Europe, Subjectivity, and Educational Research* (Wiley 2016); *Manifesto for a Post-Critical Pedagogy*, with Joris Vlieghe and Piotr Zamojski (Punctum Books 2018) and the forthcoming *Philosophical Presentations of Raising Children: The Grammar of Upbringing*, with Stefan Ramaekers (Palgrave 2018).

Grace Lockrobin is a philosopher working in the community and academia. In the community she is the Founder of Thinking Space, a non-profit that creates opportunities for people to philosophize together. She is also a teacher-trainer with SAPERE, an associate of the Philosophy Foundation and a board member of SOPHIA. In academia she is a teaching fellow at the University of Leeds, UK, where she leads a project that brings together philosophy students, teachers and children in weekly philosophical enquiry. She also consults with other UK universities, helping to set up similar programmes. Grace is currently finishing a PhD in Philosophy of Education at Institute of Education, University College London thanks to a studentship awarded by the Economic and Social Research Council. She lives in Sheffield with her husband Joe and their sons Otto and Ebbe.

Aaron Meskin is Associate Professor of Philosophy and Director of the Centre for Aesthetics at the University of Leeds, UK. He works on a variety of issues in aesthetics, the philosophy of food and philosophical psychology. He has authored numerous articles and chapters and co-edited five books, including *The Routledge Companion to Comics* (2016), *Aesthetics and the Science of Mind* (2014) and *The Art of Comics: A Philosophical Approach* (2012).

Janet Orchard has been a teacher educator in London, Oxford, and latterly at the School of Education, University of Bristol where she directs the EdD and MSc Education (Hong Kong) and contributes to the secondary Postgraduate Certificate of Education (PGCE). Her research interest is the contribution of philosophy to teachers' professional judgement. She co-edited *Learning Teaching from Experience* (2014, Bloomsbury) with Viv Ellis, and IMPACT 22, *What training do teachers need? Why Theory is Necessary to Good Teaching* with Chris Winch (2015, Wiley Blackwell). Her most recent work is on the 'Philosophy for Teachers' project with partners in England, Hong Kong and South Africa.

William C. Pamerleau is Associate Professor of Philosophy at the University of Pittsburgh at Greensburg, United States. He publishes in the areas of American pragmatism, existentialism and the philosophy of film. He is the author of *Existentialist Cinema* (Palgrave Macmillan 2009), a frequent contributor to the journal *Film and Philosophy*, and has published various articles on pragmatism, including the implications of pragmatism for public philosophy. He also organizes and moderates philosophical discussions for the general public.

Richard Smith is Professor of Education at the University of Durham, UK. He has recently served as Vice-Chair and Chair of the Philosophy of Education Society of GB. He was editor of the *Journal of Philosophy of Education* (1991–2001) and founding editor of *Ethics and Education* (2006–2013). In 2014 he served on the UK's Research Excellence Framework Panel 25 (Education). His current interests are in the epistemology of educational research, in the moral psychology of self-belief and in virtue epistemology. He is especially interested in aspects of not knowing, in what might be called the quieter qualities such as humility and diffidence, and in the place of irony in education. His *Understanding Education and Educational Research*, jointly written with Paul Smeyers (Universities of Ghent and Leuven, Belgium), was published by Cambridge University Press in 2014.

Alissa Hurwitz Swota is the bioethicist for Wolfson Children's Hospital/Baptist Health System and holds a courtesy appointment in the Department of Pediatrics at the University of Florida, Jacksonville. Previously, she was an associate professor of philosophy at the University of North Florida. She received her PhD from the University at Albany and completed a postdoctoral fellowship in clinical and organizational ethics at the University of Toronto Joint Centre for Bioethics. Her research focuses on ethical issues at the end of life, paediatric bioethics, humanities in healthcare and the connection between culture and ethical issues in the clinical setting. Her research has resulted in a book, numerous book chapters and journal articles. She delivers talks and workshops on ethical issues in medicine. Most importantly, she is mom to Hannah and Max.

Kirstine Szifris works as a researcher at the Policy Evaluation and Research Unit (PERU) at Manchester Metropolitan University, Manchester, UK. She completed her PhD at Cambridge University, 'Philosophy in Prisons: An Exploration of Personal Development' in March 2018. Her work involved teaching philosophy to prisoners in England serving long sentences. She focused on the role of philosophical conversation in the lives of prisoners, exploring its relevance to identity and self-understanding. Her work primarily involves researching prison education with a focus on prison sociology and desistance research. Her most recent publications include 'A Realist Model of Prison Education, Growth, and Desistance: A New Theory' with colleagues, Chris Fox and Andrew Bradbury, and two papers related to her philosophy work: 'Socrates and Aristotle: The Role of Ancient Philosophers in the Self-understanding of Desisting Offenders' and 'Philosophy in Prison: Opening Minds and Broadening Perspectives through Philosophical Dialogue'.

Graeme Tiffany is an informal and community education consultant, lecturer and researcher who writes about his work at http://www.graemetiffany.co.uk/. His pioneering community philosophy work includes the innovative 'Thinking Village' project (with the Joseph Rowntree Foundation), which brought philosophy to all aspects of life in a community, and informed social action. Later (with the Esmée Fairbairn Foundation) he was instrumental in developing a national training programme for community philosophy facilitators. Graeme now trains and supports practitioners and activists in the use of philosophical tools in a wide range of contexts, including research – notably in a European study of street violence.

Elizabeth Watkins is a freelance philosophy practitioner at Thinking Space CIC who has worked in a wide range of community settings since 2014. She is based in Nottingham and has worked across the East Midlands, Yorkshire and the North East areas of the UK. Elizabeth trained in philosophy at the Universities of Bristol and Leeds and taught for three years on the undergraduate community philosophy module, 'Philosophy Exchange' at the University of Leeds. Elizabeth has presented at the annual conference for the European Foundation for the Advancement of Doing Philosophy with Children (SOPHIA), and maintains a special interest in philosophy in arts and science settings.

Eric Thomas Weber is Executive Director of the Society of Philosophers in America (SOPHIA), co-host of the award-winning and syndicated Philosophy Bakes Bread radio show and podcast, and Associate Professor of Educational Policy Studies and Evaluation at the University of Kentucky, United States. He has authored *Rawls, Dewey, and Constructivism* (2012), *Morality, Leadership, and Public Policy* (2013), *Democracy and Leadership* (2015) and *Uniting Mississippi* (2015). He chaired the American Philosophical Association's Committee on Public Philosophy from 2011 to 2014. In 2011, he received the Cora Lee Graham Award for Outstanding Teaching and in 2012 the Thomas F. Frist Student Service Award at the University of Mississippi. In 2015, he was recognized with the Mississippi Humanities Council's Public Scholar Award. WRFL Lexington, 88.1 FM named Philosophy Bakes Bread the station's 'Favorite Talk Show' in 2017 and 'Overall Favorite Show' in 2018. Additionally, SOPHIA was honoured with the 2018 American Philosophical Association and Philosophy Documentation Center's Prize for Excellence and Innovation in Philosophy Programs. Finally, Weber has grown an active following of over 200,000 people at Facebook.com/EricThomasWeberAuthor.

Andy West lives in London where he teaches philosophy in prisons and primary schools with the Philosophy Foundation and King's College. His writing has featured in *3AM*, *The Millions*, *The Guardian*, *Tes* (formerly *The Times Educational Supplement*), *Storgy*, *Boundless*, *Open Democracy* and other publications. Previously he was a conflict mediator for Camden Council in London, UK. He can be found on Twitter at @AndyWPhilosophy

Nick Wiltsher is a postdoctoral fellow at the University of Antwerp's Centre for Philosophical Psychology in Belgium. He has previously worked in Leeds, Porto Alegre, and Auburn, Alabama. His PhD is from the University of Miami, United States. He works on imagination, aesthetics and philosophy of race and gender, and has published papers on these topics in a variety of philosophy journals.

Carrie Winstanley is Professor of Pedagogy at Roehampton University, London, UK, with a particular responsibility for learning and teaching, working with undergraduate and graduate students and with higher education staff. She has taught in schools and higher education for more than twenty years. She is particularly keen to encourage learners to embrace museum, gallery and outdoor education activities, and is also committed to fostering challenge in education. Carrie is a long-standing Executive Council member of the Philosophy of Education Society of Great Britain (PESGB), working on broadening diversity and encouraging learners at every level to engage more fully with the philosophy in education.

Abbreviations

ACE	Adult and Continuing Education
ALP	Adult Learning Project
CIC	Community Interest Company
CoE	Community of Enquiry
CoP	Community of Practice
CP	Community Philosophy
CRELL	Centre for Research on Lifelong Learning
CPD	Continuing Professional Development
CPI	Community of Philosophical Inquiry
HEA	Higher Education Academy
NIACE	National Institute of Adult Continuing Education
P4C	Philosophy for Children
P4T	Philosophy for Teachers
PHP	Partial Hospitalization Programme
PESGB	Philosophy of Education Society of Great Britain
PGCE	Post Graduate Certificate in Education
PIPs	Philosophy in Pubs
PI	Philosophy Ireland
PLC	Professional Learning Community
PwC	Philosophy with Children/Philosophy with Communities
RIA	Royal Irish Academy
SAPERE	Society for the Advancement of Philosophical Enquiry and Reflection in Education
SOPHIA	Society of Philosophers in America

Part One

Philosophy and Community: Theories

1

Understanding philosophy in communities: The spaces, people, politics and philosophy of Community Philosophy

Steve Bramall

Socrates was the first to call philosophy down from the heavens and to place it in cities, and even to introduce it into homes and compel it to inquire about life and standards and goods and evils. (Marcus Tullius Cicero, *Tusculan Disputations* V.10-11)

Introduction: How we philosophize

Always and everywhere, philosophers of all stripes have practised with others in philosophical communities. Ancient Athens had its many schools; India had orthodox and heterodox schools; China, the 'Hundred Schools'. In hindsight, we look back and skim off the best of what remains from these communal practices. We take out and take on the ideas, the questions, positions and challenges. We extract and apply the arguments, analyses and reflections. We sift out the methods and tease out the methodologies. We employ these intellectual goods to interrogate ourselves; use them to form and challenge our thinking; call on them to reconstruct our knowledge; improve our methods and generate our understandings. We enter disembodied conversations that transcend space, culture, language and time.

This engagement with philosophical histories is selective and abstracting. We choose a few outstanding thinkers and writers to stand for groups and traditions, to represent ideas and exemplify positions. There's too much to include all the small stuff and the detail, so what we want are the big questions from the big thinkers. But philosophy, as a history of big ideas and big thinkers, is a pretty thin account, and it can give a misleading view of what lived philosophy is like and how it works. A thicker history of philosophy would tell multiple stories, big and small, from particular voices, about groups of people coming together, sharing spaces, developing common interests, building collaborative relationships and growing social sentiments. A thicker history of philosophy would be a many-tongued history of groups of people finding ways of thinking together. And finding ways of *thinking* together means finding ways of *being* together. A history of philosophy as social practice would weave together the places, people, politics and philosophy into a holistic account: a story of the where and the who and the how and the why of our communal philosophical thinking.

Being together and thinking together, a complex unified practice, is how philosophy in communities is experienced. And being and thinking together means that communities of philosophers, particularly in their early days, need to make practical decisions. They must decide where to be, how to attract, who's in and who's out, how to get started, what to talk about, what their purposes are, what to do about food and drink and money and getting on and falling out. All raise philosophical questions; all affect the quality of thinking.

The social, spatial and political dimensions of philosophical practice can be seen in accounts of all contemporary grass-roots philosophy groups. The Café Philo movement in Paris in the 1990s saw Marc Sautet trial his brand of philosophy for communities with different sets of participants and spaces, before he hit upon the popular formulation of 'café pour Socrates', at the Café De Flores. In the 1990s in the United States, Christopher Phillips, founder of 'Socrates Cafés', found that they work best in public spaces like public squares or libraries, as 'some people, particularly homeless people, are put off by cafés' (Phillips 2002 quoted in Evans 2012: 42).

Where practice is more established, the social, spatial and political decisions require less attention, but are, whether explicit or not, integral to practice. Professional philosophers in modern universities have developed accepted ways of going about their business, but university philosophy is communal, social and political. It has established traditions pertaining to the use of space, indicators of success and how people get involved. It comprises communities of teachers, scholars and researchers who pool their varied knowledge, expertise, enthusiasms and commitments in the pursuit of good thinking and arguing. It proceeds according to particular, though contested, conceptions of philosophy.

So we might say that the practice of philosophy, whether in ancient China, the University of Chicago or a Paris café, is by nature communal, just as surely as it is by nature linguistic and conceptual. But if this is the case, that all philosophy involves communities of particular people in particular places, doing philosophical things together that bring about changes, then what is distinctive about philosophy in communities? Why is there a story to be told? What changes does the upsurge in philosophy in communities signify?

One way to think about the meaning, value and development of philosophy in communities would be to begin with an analysis of the concepts 'philosophy' and 'community' and their relationships to each another. I'm going to leave that to others, and here I'll take a different approach. To generate a useful account, one aimed at helping us to better understand the rise of philosophy in communities, I will explore and problematize philosophy in communities through considering philosophical communities as groups of people and philosophy as engagement in social, spatial and political as well as linguistic practices. This methodological move makes the task of describing and analysing philosophy in communities somewhat complex as it involves sociology, geography and politics as moments in philosophical practice. And this is not the only complexity. As this volume shows, philosophy in communities comprises a wide range of related practices that fit loosely, perhaps uneasily, and sometimes with resistance under the umbrella term 'philosophy in communities'. Philosophy in communities groups have different views and expressions concerning the place of practical and political action, about their relationship to academic philosophy traditions, about their purposes, about how they should be characterized as well as about the meaning and value of philosophy itself.

The quotation from Cicero that prefixes this chapter, about Socrates's contribution to the development of philosophy, asks us to appreciate his role in getting us to consider philosophy in relation to places, persons and purposes. I think that this sort of approach will help best in capturing the most important characteristics of philosophy in communities groups, and in generating some analytic insight into the special goods therein. In order to tell the story, I will begin from the perspective of one of the family members – Community Philosophy – a brand of philosophy in communities that is playful with places, characterful in people, ambitious in politics and pro-social and countercultural in purposes. It is a version of philosophy in communities that has some roots in the UK in the recent past, but is not restricted to these islands. I will give Community Philosophy practitioners the first words through an insider's description taken from a recent project.

Community Philosophy: Participatory philosophical engagement in the Socratic tradition

Community Philosophy is collaborative and philosophical thinking, reflection and action by members of voluntary groups who meet and think together in civil society's informal learning spaces. It is a growing grass-roots movement that is connecting people together in new associations and with novel aims and in altered spaces. The community groups formed and developed are characterized by democratic agenda-setting and decision-making, communitarian mutual support and challenge and productive, action-oriented dialogues. It is more street philosophy than academic philosophy, and it aims to change people, places and practices. It seems to be helping to change conceptions of philosophy too (Bramall 2013).

We get a first sense here that Community Philosophers are, in general, not satisfied with making academic philosophy accessible to those who would otherwise not be able to join in. They're not content to help with what one might term 'the redistribution of traditional philosophical goods'. Community Philosophers tend to be, rather, people who are committed to public philosophizing with others, and about the concepts and concerns that matter to participants. Community Philosophy aims to be, as does every other philosophy in communities group, a transforming practice, with its own particular intellectual and practice roots. One way to understand the specificity of Community Philosophy is to explore the relation between its practices and those of academic philosophy. How are they related? How do they compare and contrast?

I was listening recently to some academic philosophy colleagues who were talking about the problems of generating public understanding of, and public engagement with, philosophy. One made a distinction between two aspects of philosophy. He said: on the one hand, we can see philosophy as a body of knowledge; on the other, we can understand it as set of skills. I think 'body of knowledge' is a bit loose, as included in the body are things like the concepts, concerns and questions located in academic philosophical traditions, as well as the thinkers, books and arguments; but it is precise enough to make the distinction count. The skills aspect, in contrast, indicates philosophical capacities or abilities, like how to analyse concepts, how to use logic, or how to construct or critique an argument. Perhaps, more broadly, we might call these philosophical capacities or abilities, the methods of philosophy.

Using this distinction, it may be tempting to think of Community Philosophy as inducting non-professional philosophers into the methods of philosophy – a sort of practical introduction to 'philosophizing', developing the skills but leaving out the knowledge tradition. And this might be very valuable. After all, the tools and moves of academic philosophy seem to be generally useful for those wishing to argue and reflect, with respect for logic and reason, about matters of meaning and value. But to characterize Community Philosophy this way would be to miss a very important point; indeed, it would be to miss the very nature of Community Philosophy.

Community Philosophy is not merely public philosophizing, and it is not 'philosophy lite'. It is a particular, complex, embedded social philosophical practice. Community Philosophy has its own peculiar combination of roots, practices and aims. It has its own particular goods, processes and traditions, its own ways of evaluating and developing practice, actions and contributions. To get a feel for the uniqueness of Community Philosophy, we might usefully go again to its Socratic roots.

Community Philosophy is a mode of participatory public engagement in the Socratic tradition. The Socratic dialogues are set in non-standard learning spaces, like markets and fields and dinner parties. Socrates invited those with whom he conversed into conversations about the meaning and value of issues and concerns that mattered to them. He helped them to identify and problematize the significant concepts involved. Socrates provoked and disrupted. He encouraged people to question accepted wisdoms, meanings, authority and power relations. Socratic philosophy is a philosophy of street and marketplace rather than of the academy, and its effects are judged by actions in people's lived worlds. Socratic philosophy is a risky political venture; it opens up enquiries and actions where the outcomes are uncertain and unclear. It can ruffle feathers, as Socrates found out all too well.

Community Philosophy draws heavily on this tradition; in particular it draws on the Socratic conception of philosophy. The philosophy of Community Philosophy is a redistributed and redistributing philosophy, powered by the energy of purposeful community engagement. It is a critical, disruptive practice, nourished by academic philosophy, but at the same time a critical friend of the academy. Community Philosophy questions and challenges some limiting conceptions of philosophy – the sort that see philosophy as a canonical study of writers by scholars or as synonymous with critical thinking. It offers an alternative, or additive conception, one that aspires to be a practice fit for the purposes of critical active engagement by any, and all, people. In common with academic philosophy traditions, it is reflective, thought-provoking and understanding-generating, but it is not adequately described as a body of knowledge or skill set. Community Philosophy is a way of being and doing with commitment and with others, as thoughtful reflective agents.

UK Community Philosophy in the wider context of philosophy in communities

Community Philosophy in the UK developed as a particular practice through the dedicated work of a handful of pioneers who had the philosophical insight and moral drive to seek to refashion and repurpose academic philosophy into a community-based practical philosophy. But these pioneers did not develop Community Philosophy in a vacuum. The pioneer UK Community Philosophers drew on the ideas and practices of critical thinkers and activists like bell hooks in the United States (hooks 2003) and Paulo Freire in Brazil (Freire 1970). They developed practices from multiple sources including youth and community work and in dialogue with academic philosophers, particularly in philosophy of education. It also developed through dialogue with existing non-standard and community-based philosophical practices, foremost among these being Philosophy for Children (P4C).

We can trace some of these influences in current philosophy in communities groups. Philosophy for Teachers – a model of practitioner group ethical reflection currently developing in South Africa – draws on P4C and Pieter Mostert's Socratic Dialogue methodology to uncover and rethink key concepts in teachers' ethical dilemmas (see Orchard, Winstanley and Heilbronn 2016).[1] Patricia Hannam and Eugenio Echeverria (2009) developed philosophy for intercultural understanding with teenagers in Mexico. Graeme Tiffany's work with Community Philosophy in Ireland, Sweden and the UK combined critical philosophy with action research.

Where the Philosophy for Teachers initiative seeks to empower teachers through developing communities of reflective professional discourse, the Community Philosophy of Graeme Tiffany's work develops spaces, resources and expertise to enable local people to join, form and sustain their own self-determining, democratic philosophical communities. These groups have helped individuals and communities develop their thinking skills and dispositions, deepen their own thinking and that of others, and explore thinking as a practical tool for engagement in community and cultural life. Community Philosophy here is not a professional skillset; it is a moral, political and social movement, one that brings diverse people together and gives them a chance to access practical, transformational philosophy, to develop a thoughtful, purposeful voice, and to take pleasure in these collaborative activities. Its work on

Philosophy for Children and philosophy in communities

Perhaps the most important contributor to all of the practices described so far, one that influenced all of the pioneers of Community Philosophy, is Philosophy for Children (P4C). P4C was enormously influential in its early days in the 1970s in establishing philosophy as something of universal practical value. By insisting that even young children can think rationally and abstractly and that they can benefit from philosophical engagement, P4C helped to dispel some negative perceptions of philosophy – that it's only for clever people, is inconsequential, exclusive or elitist.[2]

Philosophy for children began with the work of Professor Matthew Lipman and others, who founded the Institute for the Advancement of Philosophy for Children at Montclair State University, United States in 1974. Lipman's work helped show that even young children are able to think philosophically together. This was supported by the writings of Gareth Matthews (1994) who did much to establish a conception of the child, such that children could be understood as having the capacities of rational agent philosophers. This resulted in P4C setting out to foster abilities and inclinations in children towards concept problematization, where participants in enquiry identify, challenge and co-reconstruct enabling and unsettling ideas. The model of philosophical learner here is of a person who, with others, is encouraged to generate challenging questions and set agendas – an important strand in Community Philosophy.[3]

The democratic politics of Community Philosophy also finds some of its roots in Philosophy for Children, which built on the conception of democracy found in the works and practices of John Dewey (see, for example, Dewey 1938). The early movers in P4C embraced a consciously countercultural politics. They were, in their support for democratic agency, like Dewey, prepared to question the *status quo* and to both champion and critique democracy. Lipman's popularizing and democratizing philosophy of critical thinking, informed by Dewey's pragmatism, is now a global phenomenon, a brand of purposeful philosophy, practised in over sixty countries, with most of these linking through the International Council of Philosophical Inquiry with Children (ICPIC).

Alongside the development of the political dimension of practical philosophy, P4C has been an innovative force in developing the pedagogies of practical philosophy that inform Community Philosophy. P4C developed the practices of learning collaboratively in the Community of Inquiry. It was Lipman and colleagues who helped transpose this learning ecology from its earlier scientific application into philosophical pedagogy. This social thinking model, used for planning, evaluation and development, continued to develop when, in the UK, Roger Sutcliffe and colleagues developed 'Collaborative Thinking' as a complementary to the 'caring thinking' articulated by Ann Sharp and others. These joined 'caring thinking' and 'creative thinking' to form the four pillars of the Society for the Advancement of Philosophical Enquiry and Reflection in Education's (SAPERE) P4C thinking model.[4]

Philosophy for Children in the UK: The role of SAPERE

SAPERE is the UK national charity for P4C (Philosophy for Children, Colleges and Communities). It continues to grow as a disruptive and innovative force in pedagogy, teacher-pupil relations and learning environments. Over more than twenty years in the UK, SAPERE's P4C has been used to reconstruct power relations in the classroom, create new thinking spaces and enable questioning and agenda=setting by young people. SAPERE has, throughout its history, been committed to communal learning relationships, critical pedagogies and altered learning environments; it has long been a champion of learning through the philosophical Community of Inquiry.[5]

In contrast with Community Philosophy, much of SAPERE's P4C works in traditional formal educational spaces and with traditional learners. But even here, the work aspires not simply to improve learning and teaching. It seeks to be transformational. This is evidenced by the recent innovation of the SAPERE school awards system. Schools are encouraged through this to involve pupils in disciplinary decision-making and self-evaluation, to help teachers to become more autonomous and philosophically reflective, and to build relationships with communities and other schools.

This approach has done much, indirectly, to influence the growth of Community Philosophy. The early UK Community Philosophy pioneers were SAPERE-trained and developed their approach, in part, through engaging with and adapting SAPERE's Philosophy for Children model. In Community Philosophy groups, a stimulus is normally used to provoke thinking and questioning. Group members are obliged to support and challenge one another in a Community of Inquiry. Philosophical dialogue is facilitated with the aim of exploring and analysing the concepts that emerge. Knowledge and understanding are collectively co-constructed. Like P4C, the ethos of Community Philosophy is one of critical, creative, caring and collaborative participation. But, whereas P4C aims for transformative action from *within* traditional formal learning contexts, Community Philosophy seeks to open up non-formal educational spaces and to include non-traditional learner groups. SAPERE has also supported the development of Community Philosophy in the UK directly. In 2013 SAPERE developed Community Philosophy training and support with bespoke training courses, networks, resources and guided practice.[6]

Community Philosophy: Diverse people, spaces and actions

The practice models developed by Community Philosophy go significantly beyond those used in schools. Community Philosophy is more political, flexible and experimental. Though drawing on the works of John Dewey and Matthew Lipman, it is equally influenced by the radical intellectual and practice traditions of Paulo Freire and bell hooks. Community Philosophy is more radical in its aims to engage the disengaged and to promote social action. In its pedagogy, it draws on the democratic engagement practices of transformational community work. It seeks out spaces and places in which diverse people can meet, think and act. It aims to develop the potential for group self-determination through intelligent democracy. It invites focus on the local, on what can change. Community Philosophy aims to advance a new paradigm in thoughtful political engagement in the civic realm, engagement where the outcomes are changed people, changed spaces and changed practices.

Community Philosophy brings together unusual combinations of people, including those who might, at first, appear to have little in common, but who, through conversation, find new interconnections and commonalities. Diversities of ethnicity, gender, age, background, voice and experience are both common and celebrated in Community Philosophy groups. Samira Bakkioui integrated Community Philosophy into international youth work through the European exchange programme with British and Swedish youth and community workers. Lawrence Darani employed Community Philosophy with groups in London using Community Enquiry with a lifelong learning group of older people. Katy Spendiff brought young people from diverse local groups together through Community Philosophy for the 'Big Conversation' in Wales.

Community Philosophy thrives in non-traditional and non-institutional settings like pubs, cafés, galleries and libraries and in housing associations and outdoors. Graeme Tiffany has developed philosophical cafés, philosophical street work and philosophical walks. He writes, 'Philosophical Walks take that most fundamental human movement – walking – and couple it with an opportunity to take part in a Community of Enquiry with your fellow walkers.'[7] Kay Sidebottom uses Community Philosophy with local authority councillors: 'I facilitated a meeting of new local authority Councillors, who were reflecting on the induction programme they had taken part in after election. Unlike the traditional methods we used in six-monthly reviews, the Community Philosophy approach enabled them to think more deeply about their experiences.' A question they chose to discuss was, 'How can the Council make better use of a Councillor's existing skills and experience?'

Community Philosophy results in unexpected and diverse actions. These range from pubs and cafés finding regular slots for philosophy meetings, to arts groups repurposing art spaces for community gatherings and to the transformation of institutional and recreational spaces. After leading a Community Philosophy arts group at the Turner Contemporary Gallery in Margate, UK, Keiko Higashi used Community Philosophy to transform a museum gallery such that it might better engage with different sectors of the public. Community Philosophy-derived plans were used to redesign gallery spaces to support a trusting interactive relationship with the public.

Four dimensions of philosophy in communities groups

Community Philosophy has been presented here as one member of a global family of related practices of Philosophy in Communities. In this wider family, Community Philosophy is a particularly playful, active, inclusive, experimental and ambitious member. It is but one of very many diverse examples of philosophy in communities groups that continue to emerge and develop.

The particular description of Community Philosophy has been presented here to help develop an analytic framework, a useful way to analyse and understand the growing number and the growing complexity of philosophy in communities groups more generally. Each group is particular, and has its own unique history, personnel and character, but all must engage with a common set of problems and possibilities that attach to coming together, to being together, as well as to thinking together. All philosophy in communities groups must take a position somewhere along the four dimensions that Community Philosophy articulates.

The first dimension is space. This spectrum stretches from more formal and traditional learning spaces, to non-formal and experimental learning environments. At one end of the scale are traditional colleges, schools, universities and sites of workplace learning. Here, community of enquiry pedagogy can be built into provision for the purposes of enhancing mutual mental stimulation, developing a more democratic, engaged and supportive ethos and generating philosophical questions, dialogue, knowledge and understanding. Towards the other end of this scale are a wide variety of repurposed places: rural spaces, squares, cafés, streets, churches, public houses, housing associations and many more. Philosophy in communities repurposes and revitalizes spaces. It reconstructs meeting spaces as informal learning spaces and asks us to consider the social and political suitability of novel spaces as sites for philosophical dialogue.

The second dimension stretches from less to more action, or, perhaps, from less to more politically and practically engaged. All philosophy brings about change, not only changes in thought and belief, but also in personal and professional power. But some philosophy in community groups seek explicitly and deliberately to bring about social and political change. A common feature of many such groups is relationship-building, generating intellectual engagement between people who might otherwise not engage. Towards the more radical end of the spectrum, philosophy in communities takes the form of campaign. Practice can aim at reforming school teaching, teacher formation and curriculum. Groups can influence public provision and decision-making. Philosophy in communities can help group members to develop their voice, to become influencers and civic leaders.

The third dimension is that which describes the sort of participants in the different groups of philosophy in communities. Towards one end of this scale are those who fit more traditional philosopher profiles: students in universities, public speakers, conference attendees and authors. A little further along this spectrum are vast numbers of people who hitherto may not have been in the privileged position of being encouraged and enabled to philosophize, and people who might never have thought that philosophy was for people like them, or that they might become or already be philosophers. Along this spectrum are, potentially, all people. After all, everyone is to some degree philosophical and able to do more. Philosophy in communities groups have a question then about who to include and exclude. In practice, however, the more common questions addressed are those concerning how to engage with people, perhaps how to make first contact with people for whom mutually beneficial philosophical engagements may be possible.

Philosophy in communities emerges in the places where people are and helps those people to come together to become more philosophical in the ways that they wish, for the purposes they choose, and in the philosophical manner they themselves develop. It might be argued, then, that philosophy in communities is philosophy developing a new set of places and ways for satisfying a philosophical desire, novel opportunities for scratching the philosophical itch. It does appear to satisfy a desire for philosophical voices to be developed, heard, amplified and given effect. It helps too to satisfy a public desire for connecting thoughtfully with others, for taking responsibility, for being together in reflective, conceptual, purposeful thinking, for more meaningful conversation and more thoughtful action.

But, at the same time as satisfying desires, philosophy in communities generates dissatisfaction. It is unsettling, it fosters disagreement and uncertainty. Philosophy in communities helps articulate alternative possibilities and invites critical commentary on our ways of living together, our localities, our policies, our leaders, ourselves and our world. It opens dialogues that have no clearly defined endpoints, that cross academic disciplinary boundaries, that can stray over unexpected intellectual territories and lead participants into unintended places. Philosophy in communities invites questions of how we should live together and, in so doing, opens a conversational space for thinking deeply and reflecting differently about how we are in fact living together.

The unsettling and critical dynamic of philosophy in communities extends to what we might think of as the intellectual roots of all groups; this is the fourth dimension, the understanding of philosophy itself. As with space, people and politics, philosophy in communities groups must take positions on philosophy, not least because philosophy in communities relies on academic philosophy. 'Without street philosophy, academic philosophy becomes irrelevant. Without academic philosophy, street philosophy becomes incoherent' (Evans 2012: 35). There is some truth here, but in developing the idea and practices of a philosophy of transformation for all, philosophy in communities is developing philosophical voices that are increasingly helping to articulate diverse conceptions of philosophy. And philosophy in communities groups, by their nature, are not merely accepting of characterizations and definitions handed down. They are speakers as well as listeners, teachers as well as learners.

Philosophy in communities is overwhelmingly appreciative of academic philosophy, especially of the applied philosophy of ethics, political philosophy and philosophy of education. But as philosophy in communities groups articulate more of their understanding of what they do and why and how, novel possibilities for collaborative conversations arise. Philosophy in communities groups are increasingly philosophically literate and articulate. They generate questions as what the purposes of philosophy are, what it means to 'do' philosophy, how we should understand the value of philosophy in our current moral, political and natural environment, who should be involved in defining philosophy. They have a decreasing need to judge their practice against the yardstick of an academic discipline or seek to ascertain fidelity by checking with a university department. They can conceive philosophy differently, dynamically, holistically and variously.

Perhaps it is unsurprising that an introductory characterization of philosophy in communities ends by returning to reflections and questions about the meaning and value of philosophy. Is the quality of human relationships a part of philosophy or a precondition? Is philosophy in the home or the street the same practice as philosophy in the academy? How do we know when philosophy in communities becomes something other than philosophy? To do justice to such reflections is beyond the scope of this chapter. But, maybe, as the practices of philosophy in communities help reinvigorate the philosophical dimensions of the public, professional and civic spaces, reflections on the practices of philosophy in communities may in turn help us rejuvenate our understanding of academic philosophy, and perhaps of philosophy itself.

Last words

Philosophy in communities is a hugely rewarding practice that can bring about wonderful transformations, but it is an endlessly challenging enterprise. Because the spaces, people, politics and philosophy are integral to the development and character of practice, they demand ongoing attention, commitment, rethinking and adjustment. Because the decisions about how to think together are bound up with decisions about how to be together, thinking with others about these matters can be complex and contentious. Positions and actions need to be taken concerning meaning, value, purpose and development; they require philosophical understanding and reflection. These decisions are made in situ, by participants, in a spirit of constant renewal. In this sense, philosophy in communities is experimental, a kind of ongoing action research. The combination of growth, experience, action and reflection in philosophy in communities suggests that it is, perhaps, the closest we have to Dewey's ideal of participatory democratic practice.

Notes

1 Philosophy for Teachers is a Philosophy of Education Society of Great Britain (PESGB) initiative that brings together P4C with Socratic Dialogue to support early stage teacher ethical reflection. For further reading see Orchard, Winstanley and Heilbronn (2016).
2 For a fuller discussion of the arguments, see Lipman (1988).
3 Gareth Matthews did much through his writings to establish that children are capable of abstract thinking and engagement with concepts. For a fuller discussion see Matthews (1994).
4 SAPERE's 4C thinking model is a development of Matthew Lipman's thinking model. An account of the SAPERE model can be found in the *SAPERE Level 1 Handbook* available from SAPERE enquiries@sapere.org.uk
5 For further details, see the SAPERE website at www.sapere.org.uk
6 Further details of the film produced by the project can be found at: https://www.you tube.com/watch?v=spN0Cw-7V
7 See Graeme's Community Philosophy web page for further details at: www. graemetiffany.co.uk

References

Bramall, S., (2013), 'Why Don't We Do It in the Street?' *The Philosophers' Magazine*, 62–3, London: Apeiron.

Cicero, M. T., (1877), *Tusculan Disputations*, trans. C. D. Yonge, New York: Harper and Brothers Publishers.

Dewey, J., (1938), *Experience and Education*, New York: Collier Books.

Evans, J., (2012), 'Connected Communities: Philosophical Communities', *A Report for the Arts and Humanities Research Council*, [Online], Available at: http://www.philosophy forlife.org/wp-content/uploads/2012/11/Grassroots-Philosophy.pd, Accessed 27 January 2019.

Freire, P. (1970), *Pedagogy of the Oppressed*, New York, Continuum.

Hannam, P., and Echeverria, E., (2009), *Philosophy for Teenagers: Nurturing a Moral Imagination for the 21st Century*, London: Continuum.

hooks, b., (2003), *Teaching Community: A Pedagogy of Hope*, New York: Routledge.

Lipman, M., (1988), *Philosophy Goes to School*, Philadelphia: Temple University Press.

Matthews, G., (1994), *The Philosophy of Childhood*, Boston: Harvard University Press.

Orchard, J., Winstanley, C., and Heilbronn, R., (2016), 'Philosophy for Teachers (P4T) – Developing New Teachers' Applied Ethical Decision-Making', *Ethics in Professional Education*, 11 (1): 42–54.

Phillips, C., (2002), *Socrates Cafe: A Fresh Taste of Philosophy*, New York: W. W. Norton & Co.

2

Relocation and repopulation: Why Community Philosophy matters

Grace Lockrobin

A confined conversation

Despite the encouraging examples of philosophizing discussed in this volume, philosophy in its most recognizable form is largely a conversation that takes place between a small number of people in an even smaller number of places. Given that the value of philosophy is not self-evident, we might legitimately ask what difference does it make who philosophizes and where they do it. This question is central to my account of the value of Community Philosophy and is the subject of this chapter.

Locating Community Philosophy

Before we can set out, some clarification is needed. 'Public Philosophy' has been described – in typically academic-centric terms – as 'publicly engaged and/or explicitly publicly relevant scholarship, action, and teaching' (Meagher 2013: 5). Here 'public' refers both to the content of academic work that is concerned with philosophical issues of public interest and to a particular method of doing philosophy 'with general audiences in a non-academic setting' (Weinstein 2014: 1). My interest here is with Public Philosophy in the second sense and I use the term 'Community Philosophy' because it connotes a dual sense of community as people and place. When I speak of Community Philosophy, I do so as a self-styled Community Philosopher, someone who has developed a way of working – in conversation with colleagues – that embodies certain theoretical ideas and is responsive to the many practical challenges this work presents. I refer to purposeful conversations, between people who live, learn, work or play together, on philosophical matters of mutual concern. These conversations constitute a philosophical *enquiry* insofar as they are motivated by an apprehension of a conceptual problem and are driven by questions that encapsulate these problems in a form that participants find both interesting and important. These enquiries aim at a deeper understanding of the issue in question, but participants may also seek – through disciplined and regular practice – a more general improvement in the quality of their own thinking and the thinking of their co-enquirers, as well as the emotional and social benefits associated with good conversation. Without denying the value of reading and writing philosophy in solitude, Community Philosophy is decisively social, being both participatory and dialogic in method. While there is some practice that takes place online among spatially and temporally disconnected people, Community Philosophy is most satisfying when conducted in person, in real time and in the places people feel most at ease. Doing philosophy this way permits non-verbal communication and creates a sense of connection between interlocutors that shapes the content and ethos of philosophy in positive ways. Proximity is significant for human beings, as is evident when we consider the insensitivities shown and insults slung in online arguments.

The conversation that emerges in these settings takes as its substance the contributions of the community group – specifically their interests, experiences and puzzlements. Sometimes these conversations will draw on philosophical expertise derived from canonical texts, professional speakers or expert facilitators; occasionally the discussions may yield written or recorded 'products', but crucially, don't depend on these antecedents or consequents for their legitimacy. Though its benefits are myriad, Community Philosophy, like other forms of amateurism, is often a practice pursued for its own sake.

Community Philosophy is a broad church with examples found in the philosophical work in schools and other educational settings (such as the practice promoted by the IAPC in the United States,[1] FAPSA in Australia[2] and SAPERE in the UK[3]); within informal adult educational and recreational settings such as cafés and pubs (including Café Philo in France,[4] Socrates Cafés in the United States[5] and Philosophy in Pubs in the UK[6]); in the informal education of children as part of after-school clubs and summer camps (e.g. the Brila Youth Project in Canada[7] and The Philosophy Club[8] in Australia); at public and commercial philosophy talks, festivals and conferences (such as 'How the Light Gets In' in the UK[9]); in cultural settings such as museums, galleries, libraries, theatres and cinemas (as can be seen in work of UK-based Thinking Space[10]); as part of public broadcasting on television, radio, podcasts and blogs (as in the work of US philosopher Michael Sandel with the BBC[11]); among group of professionals (as in Philosophy for Teachers projects in the UK, Hong Kong and South Africa[12]); in health care settings such as hospitals, hospices, care homes, mental health services and self-help groups (such as the meeting of professionals organized by the UK's Maudsley Philosophy Group[13]) and meetings of patients such as those organized by the UK charity the Philosophy Foundation[14]); in prisons and detention centres (such as the work of Princeton Universities Prisons Teaching Initiative in the United States[15] and The Philosophy Foundation[16]); in work with businesses and in professional contexts (such as the professional ethics training provided by the IDEA centre in the UK[17]); in work with marginalized groups such as homeless people (e.g. the work of Philosophy in the City in partnership with Sheffield's Archer project in the UK[18]); and in politics, local government, community projects and grass-roots activism (including the intergenerational work done in the UK-based Thinking Village Project[19], work with children at the US-Mexico border[20] and work by protesters such as Tent City University in London[21] at the height of the worldwide Occupy movements). Crucially, while the setting is significant, it is not the location alone that determines whether

Relocation and Repopulation: Why Community Philosophy Matters 17

the philosophical work in these contexts constitutes Community Philosophy. What is fundamental here is the idea of the community participating *as philosophers*. An academic philosopher may occasionally give a lecture for a public audience in a public place, but if the event leaves little room for active enquiry among participants, it is not Community Philosophy – at least not in the sense that interests me.

Inevitably my account of Community Philosophy is constructed with reference to a particular understanding of the notion of philosophy. Though I consider this problematic, the archetypal contemporary view of philosophy is that of the academic discipline practised by professional philosophers within university philosophy departments. Community Philosophy, in my view, is philosophy of *another kind* with its own content and methods that closely resemble, but do not seek to replicate, those of academic philosophers. The designation of certain kinds of activity as 'Community Philosophy' is an attempt on my part to draw the boundaries of the concept of philosophy more generously, and to suggest that the work of western professional academics does not exhaust the legitimate ways in which philosophy can be practised. My notion of philosophy is not restricted to the canon of great philosophical ideas suspended in text. It is a more dynamic view of philosophy as an ongoing and open-ended exchange. If the reader is sympathetic to this view, they will begin to appreciate why the matter of who philosophizes and where they do it makes *all the difference.*

Relocation and repopulation

Community Philosophy represents the relocation and repopulation of philosophy, motivated by the conviction that the benefits of philosophy should be distributed more equitably. When this happens, our understanding of the nature, purpose and value of philosophy cannot remain unchanged, and this is a good thing for philosophers, the wider population and the problems we explore. Metaphors of 'relocation' and 'repopulation' reflect the fact that philosophy is typically at home in academia and is characterized by the daily activity of a small group of professionals who read, converse, lecture, teach and write – typically for a specialist audience of peers and students. While these academics address a diversity of topics that may be of interest to the non-expert, the resonance of all of this urgent thought is barely felt beyond the institutional walls. The direction of travel evoked by this language is from academia outwards into the world. But this talk of philosophy 'inside' and 'out' presents a false dichotomy: in reality the boundaries are more blurred and some philosophers operate between academic departments and the outside world, guiding medical decision-making or contributing to political debates and producing journalism. One example of a philosopher who did all three was Mary Warnock: moral philosopher, Chair of the UK Committee of Inquiry into Human Fertilisation and Embryology, crossbench life peer and regular contributor to the *Guardian* newspaper, as well as author of numerous books on philosophy. Even without such exceptions, plainly traditional academics are themselves a community of people rooted in a place: much like any community they have shaped the methods and content of their practice to serve their ends. Within the academic community – and in response to the needs, desires, experiences, interests

18 *Philosophy and Community*

and abilities of individual academics as well as the many external pressures they face – philosophy has evolved into a discipline which uses highly technical language, offers esoteric examples and encourages myopic specialization. Not all of these developments have been wholly good for the discipline.

Communities breed convention

Within any community conventions take hold. As these conventions pervade, they appear increasingly inevitable and, eventually, invisible. Martha Nussbaum observes that the conventional style of philosophical prose in Anglo-American academic writing has been 'correct, scientific, abstract, hygienically pallid' (Nussbaum 1990: 19) and that this dominant style 'which seemed to be regarded as a kind of all-purpose solvent in which philosophical issues of any kind could all be effectively disentangled' (ibid) became second nature, shaping the very way in which philosophy – within this community – is understood, valued and practised. While there might be other ways of 'being precise, other conceptions of lucidity and completeness' (ibid) within an inward-looking academic community, these alternatives are often overlooked. The academicization and professionalization of philosophy, argues Nussbaum, 'leads everyone to write like everyone else, in order to be respectable and to be published in the usual journals' (ibid). Bryan Magee characterizes the 'publish or perish' culture of academic philosophy as one in which academics who wish to prosper face limited options:

> They can write about other people's work, the path which most of them pursue. If they are bent on producing original work of their own they can choose an area which has been neglected, so that almost anything they say will constitute a contribution. Or they can stay on familiar territory and draw hitherto undrawn distinctions: this results in the writing of more and more about less and less – the ever-increasing specialisation with which we are so familiar. All of these options are being pursued not primarily because of their own inherent value, but to advance the career of the writer (Magee 2000).

The unintended consequence of the philosophical culture that has been created within the academic community is an unhealthy exclusivity. At best, it is difficult for outsiders to participate in the conversation; at worst it results in outsiders failing to see that the work of philosophers has any value, or insiders regarding the philosophical efforts of others as inadequate. The benefits of philosophy, insofar as they are realized at all, are not widely distributed under such a model.

Philosophy's historical home

The academic department was not always the home of philosophy, nor were philosophers themselves always academics. Plato famously described Socrates, in the

Athenian market place, engaging the public in conversations that connected to their everyday concerns. Such descriptions epitomize – and perhaps also romanticize – the publicly engaged philosopher. Yet despite the veneration of Socrates by many academics, the typical department has strayed so far from these beginnings that Socrates wouldn't stand a chance of landing tenure in most faculties today (Frodeman and Briggle 2016). For hundreds of years the academy was not the natural home of philosophers, many of whom were located outside of the universities and did not teach philosophy at all. Hobbes, Descartes, Spinoza, Leibniz, Locke, Berkeley, Hume, Rousseau, Schopenhauer, Kierkegaard, Marx, Nietzsche were not academics, nor was Mill – and as Schopenhauer himself expressed it – 'Very few philosophers have ever been professors of philosophy, and even relatively fewer professors of philosophy have been philosophers' (Schopenhauer cited in Magee 2000). In fact, the problematic sequestration of philosophy and philosophers within the research university is a fairly modern phenomenon which can be traced to developments in the late nineteenth century. During this period the natural sciences and later the social sciences first made their appearance, bringing with them a culture of increasing specialization. By replicating this model, philosophy evolved into a 'disciplinary creature' adopting the same modus operandi of making progress rather than insight. Consequently, it was doomed to fall short (Frodeman and Briggle 2016: 8–9). One of the many problems associated with the institutionalization of philosophy is the separation of the acquisition of philosophical knowledge from the virtues that philosophizing once necessitated. Among these virtues is a love of wisdom and a commitment to the pursuit of the good life. Philosophy became a technical enterprise and 'having become specialists [philosophers] lost sight of the whole' (ibid: 10).

Philosophy and its close relations

When we compare philosophy to the other humanities it is perhaps unsurprising that we are more likely to find philosophy resident in academic departments than the local shopping centre. After all, the same is true of archaeology, anthropology or linguistics. These are subjects that stand on the shoulders of previous research and require a solid general education to furnish would-be students with the requisite skills and knowledge to make sense of them. Viewed this way, it is difficult to imagine any other home for philosophy but the academic department, where it may draw on a concentrated pool of mature thinkers and operate alongside – and in conversation with – its disciplinary cousins. However, the status quo is not inevitable, especially when we consider that philosophy is less like these discrete academic disciplines than we might think. Notably, it differs in terms of its *fundamentality*, its *accessibility* and in its *necessity* for human well-being.

During the course of an ordinary life one might conceivably avoid the central themes of archaeology, anthropology or linguistics. Philosophy, however, is concerned with *unavoidable* fundamental questions at the heart of human experience. In fact, philosophical questions are so fundamental that we often encounter them before we leave childhood.

In his early work, drawing on observations he had made of his own son and the children of his friends and colleagues, Gareth Matthews (1980) made observations that support such a claim. In one such example, Tim (about six years), while busily engaged in licking a pot, asked a question with a striking Cartesian resonance: 'Papa, how can we be sure that everything is not a dream?' (ibid: 1). Such examples have been met with some sensible scepticism. Taken in isolation, such 'philosophical one-liners' (Kitchener 1990: 426) do not establish that children are well equipped to address these questions. John White argues that we lack good reasons to conclude that children as young as Tim are typically driven by 'doubts of a categorical sort about the distinction between appearance and reality' (White 1992: 75). Instead he suggests that such utterances, amputated from any deeper desire to investigate the concept itself, could be motivated by the desire to use language appropriately. The breadth of these examples, often in the context of extended dialogue, makes this scepticism seem unwarranted (Pritchard 1996; McCall 2009; Wartenberg 2014; Shapiro 2012 and Sowey 2018). But even where we can be confident of the speaker's intention, asking questions is only part of the picture. It is what one does with these questions that determines whether it is genuine philosophizing that appears to emerge at such an early age. In the view of Michael Hand, 'To be competent in any form of inquiry is not just a matter of asking questions of a particular kind: it is a matter of *answering* questions by means of *appropriate methods of investigation*' (2008: 5; emphasis in original). Here philosophy differs from the academic humanities on the grounds of its *accessibility*: its methods of investigation are within the grasp of ordinary people. One might begin to philosophize without a prohibitive degree of prior knowledge, experience or equipment. While acknowledging this, Hand, however, sounds a note of caution which we ought to heed:

> While all manner of questions come naturally to the minds of children, the methods of investigation required to answer them typically do not. This is perhaps especially true in the domain of philosophy. A characteristic feature of philosophical questions is their intractability to those unfamiliar with the techniques of philosophical inquiry. It is easy enough to ask how we can be sure that everything is not a dream … but not at all easy to see how these questions can be satisfactorily answered. The problem is not that the evidence required to settle them is particularly hard to come by, or collectable only with the aid of specialist equipment, but rather that gathering evidence does not seem to help here: the questions remain even when all the facts are known. In the absence of philosophical training, the natural response to such questions is to dismiss them as unanswerable (Hand 2008: 5).

This concern does not undermine my claim that philosophy is both fundamental and accessible, but it does support the claim that Community Philosophy can benefit from the support and guidance of professional philosophers, particularly when they are able to facilitate the development of the necessary skills and strategies required to investigate the questions that people find curious. However, counter-intuitively, this support does not require expert philosophers to flex their muscles *as experts*, at least not in the sense of speaking at length on subjects about which they might know a great deal. In fact Community Philosophy – both with children and with adults – shakes up the very notion of philosophical expertise creating opportunities for the philosopher to act as facilitator rather than traditional teacher. To philosophize does not require us to marshal various facts about the history of ideas. We philosophize when we identify conceptual problems, articulate our curiosity in the form of questions, develop hypotheses that may constitute answers and then analyse, synthesize and evaluate the results together. It is 'more narrowly a quest for truth, more broadly a quest for meaning' (Lipman 2011: 8). With practice, these exercises in critical, creative, caring and collaborative thinking are attainable for ordinary people, but expert guidance can help this process succeed.

What philosophy has in common with football

While the fundamentality and accessibility of philosophy means that we often *do* philosophize within the course of a normal life, there is a further reason to think that we *must*. Unlike other specialist humanities subjects – the study of which is life-enhancing for some, but not necessary for all – there is an urgent need for philosophical enquiry. Whether or not we are properly equipped to answer it, we all face the philosophical question of how to live a good life. What might it mean to be properly equipped to address such a question? The ability to philosophize is one credible answer.

There are two respects in which philosophy, in general, and Community of Enquiry, in particular, are conducive to human flourishing in my view. First, the subject matter of Community Philosophy often directly addresses the question of how we should live. To philosophize within a community, about matters of common interest and in the face of reasonable criticism from our peers, is a highly plausible way in which one might explore the constituents of a life worth living. When we ask, Should a banker be paid more than a nurse? Do borders matter? or Why vote?[22] the ensuing conversations illuminate what we ought to value. Second, even when questions of value are not the explicit subject of an enquiry, *eudaimonia* is fostered by Community Philosophy's methods: the iterative process of coming together to explore ideas is not just intellectually demanding, but morally developmental too. Participants must be courageous enough to make mistakes and propose ideas that may be rejected. They must also listen patiently, tolerating frustration, boredom and incomprehension. Matthew Lipman described the ethos of a community of enquiry as one in which rationality develops tempered by judgement or *reasonableness* (Lipman 2011: 10). This is an exercise in the cultivation of courage, patience and justice as well as many of the other virtues that make flourishing a possibility according to Aristotle (Aristotle 1955: 104). For these reasons I believe that philosophy, along with a varied diet of other worthwhile human practices such as art and sport, can help people flourish.

In my attempt to articulate why it matters who philosophizes and where they do it, I have arrived at the conclusion that philosophy has less in common with the other academic humanities than we might assume. It differs in its fundamentality, accessibility and necessity for human flourishing. It is perhaps more helpful to think of philosophy and other academic humanities as distant cousins and look instead at philosophy and its other close relations.

There are other fundamental, accessible, necessary human practices that might provide a new way of thinking of philosophy as something connected to everyday life and open to everyone. Philosophy has much more in common with participation in a local park run or community choir than one might think. Sport, music and art, like philosophy, are pursued professionally, but, unlike philosophy, they are also embodied in a well-populated and widespread culture of amateurism. While weekend football leagues, art clubs and brass bands are all familiar ways in which people might spend their free time – the philosophical equivalent, despite the examples I have already mentioned and the case studies offered in this volume, are exceedingly rare. This is a great pity.

The notion of an amateur often has pejorative connotations denoting a lack of expertise, skill or finesse. Yet there is also a sense of amateurism that reveals the contribution of philosophy to human flourishing. An amateur values a practice for its own sake; theirs is a labour of love rather than remuneration. Amateurism is also associated with a culture of informality and enjoyment, and while philosophy often feels like very hard work, these connotations cast that effort in a new light. Usually, those who run or sing together do so because they think such practices are inherently valuable. They also form part of a person's conception of a good life as something that involves a healthy body, betterment, beauty, creativity or communality. We spend our precious leisure time on these pursuits because they make life worth living. Philosophy belongs here too. When we see the similarity between philosophy and football, the former is liberated from its intuitional walls, free to take root in communities.

The strange products of professionalization

So far I have argued that philosophy can be practised recreationally as well as professionally, but there is more to be said in defence of the claim that amateur philosophy can constitute a substantial social good. If philosophy brings any benefits to the public whatsoever, one might assume that these benefits will come about thanks to the work of experts. However, on examination, we see that the geography of philosophy impedes this. When philosophers speak only to each other, strange things happen. Consider, for example, the remarkable cottage industry that has arisen around the 'Trolley Problem' – a thought experiment originally devised by philosopher Philippa Foot, in which one must decide whether to divert a runaway train (or trolley) saving five lives but killing a sixth (Foot 1967). Dubbed 'Trolleyology' by Kwame Anthony Appiah, the persisting discussion of this dilemma and its numerous variants with their weird and wonderful names such as the Fat Man Case and the Loop Case (Thomson 1985), the Extra Push Case, the Roller Skates Case, the Trap Door Case, and the Lazy Susan Case (Edmonds 2014), have occupied half a century of philosophical thought. It is easy for non-professionals to poke fun at areas of academic research that may seem silly in the

Relocation and Repopulation: Why Community Philosophy Matters   23

absence of knowledge of their context. Historically, these examples have been designed to examine whether certain variables are morally relevant, variables such as killing one versus killing many, or intending versus foreseeing harm. Philippa Foot almost certainly embarked on her original defence of abortion – written in living memory of the indiscriminate killing of the First World War – in all seriousness and with the real world clearly in view. However, what the contemporary phenomenon of Trolleyology shows us is that as these esoteric examples multiply, along with the scholarly discussion they generate, the conversation is in danger of mutating from one sincerely concerned with pressing ethical concerns into something far more impractical and impenetrable. New examples mimic the conventional two-horned dilemma structure of the original and, while they introduce new elements, they still eliminate 'irrelevant' detail. This approach to ethics apes the scientific method widespread in analytic circles, but in doing so, makes certain kinds of assumptions about what matters in ethical enquiry, thereby distorting the texture of ethical problems as we naturally encounter them. Factors such as time pressure, uncertainty about the outcome, panic at the moment of decision-making or one's own tangled history of loyalties and sympathies have no place in the Trolleyology game. Conversations that play by these rules direct those who participate towards conclusions that may be more thorough and nuanced, but also more distant from the very phenomena they seek to investigate. The result of these kinds of philosophical subcultures is that many contemporary discussions of the Trolley Problem read much more like an intellectual in-joke than an earnest ethical enquiry.

The fruits of academic labour

In defence of this particular example academics may highlight the fact that in this case, unlike the majority of philosophical ideas buried in published papers, the Trolley Problem is a thought experiment that is widely known among the public where it has even been the focus of empirical research (Petrinovich, O'Neill and Jorgensen 1993) and the topic of various popular philosophy publications (Edmonds 2014). Perhaps the Trolley Problem is *precisely* the kind of philosophical output that can help philosophy relocate and repopulate, since all anyone needs for superficial engagement with the literature is an intuition and the willingness to consider the reasons that might justify it. However, when the movement of philosophy from the professional to the public sphere amounts to little more than the new-found popularity of a handful of famous thought experiments, this can undermine the project I have in mind. Their ubiquity may suggest that this approach is the gold standard in ethical enquiry and that when it comes to ethics, only questions about killing, explored using pared-down puzzles, count. Consequently, novice philosophers may not realize that they needn't start with these strange cases at all. It might serve them better to begin with a newspaper article about self-driving cars[23] or a podcast about the allocation of healthcare resources during natural disasters[24] – both contemporary issues that open up the same issues with the messy immediacy of real life. There has been much fresh discussion of trolley problems recently, with philosophers employed to write algorithms for autonomous vehicles based on various ethical theories (Goldhill 2018). But even if Trolleyology may occasionally cast light on real-world problems, this hardly amounts to the redistribution of the benefits of philosophy.

Trolleyology is a specific example of the unbeneficial trajectories that philosophy has taken. There are more mainstream candidates for the claim that philosophy bears fruit that benefits the public. Academic philosophers such as Bertrand Russel,[25] John Dewey,[26] Peter Singer[27] and Martha Nussbaum[28] have been particularly successful in addressing matters of public concern – often in publicly engaging ways. The interdisciplinary work of other philosophers including Mary Warnock and Michael Sandel – both within academia and in partnership with public institutions – demonstrates how philosophers can work beyond the Philosophy department. Their efforts have undoubtedly helped to bring philosophical perspectives and practices to bear on world problems. This work is 'Public Philosophy' in the former sense outlined in the introduction of this volume. Insofar as it benefits the public by stimulating intellects and stimulating change, it is to be celebrated. But it is no substitute for Community Philosophy in the sense that I have in mind, since it proceeds from the basic assumption that there is no need for transformation within philosophy as it stands (Meagher 2013). This kind of work assumes that philosophy needn't relocate nor repopulate for its benefits to be felt more widely and that the ball is in the professionals' court: where they are willing, they can keep doing what they've always done but simply get a little better at communication and collaboration. This view involves an impoverished conception of what the benefits of philosophy might be.

Further examples of publicly beneficial philosophy can be found within the relatively new sub-disciplines of applied philosophy, environmental ethics and bioethics. Here there has been some progress made towards distributing the benefits of philosophy more equitably, but these attempts have had less obvious impact on the public than their proponents might have hoped. Applied philosophy and environmental philosophy both fall prey to a culture of academic publishing in which the approval of one's academic peers, rather than uptake by professionals or policy makers, is a marker of success. Only bioethics provides a more helpful model of how relocation into new settings and repopulation with new people can transform the philosophical landscape and help the benefits of philosophy to be felt more widely. Philosophical conversations in bioethics routinely involve doctors, patients, scientists, lawyers and policy makers as well as philosophers. There is still great potential for further movement.

A more promising model for the redistribution of philosophical goods comes in the form of 'Field Philosophers', a proposal in which academically trained philosophers, housed within the university, 'help excavate, articulate, discuss and assess the philosophical dimensions of real-world policy problems as defined by the stakeholders involved. Using case-based methodology and a context-sensitive approach they would address their findings at both academic and non-academics alike' (Soames 2016: 124). Examples that might satisfy this model can be found in the work of organizations such as The Institute for Philosophy in Public Life[29] and the Public Philosophy Network.[30] Undoubtedly, Field Philosophers are allies in the struggle to distribute the benefits of philosophy more widely. However, Community Philosophy does not simply recreate this proposal, but represents something distinct and important. To appreciate this, it may help to recognize that Field Philosophy is a proposal that has grown out of a certain dissatisfaction with academic culture and an acknowledgement of the economic, political and ethical problems this has created for philosophy as a praxis and for professional philosophers themselves. Perhaps as a consequence, Frodeman and Briggle still assume a particular role for the philosopher in which their own philosophical thinking takes centre stage. What *is* radical in their account is the changes they propose to both the methods of production and the audience for this work. Field Philosophers think within organizations on particular projects, assimilating the insights of those they find there. The products of their philosophical thinking are disseminated within those organizations – as well as to fellow academics – and are designed to be useful to those grappling with those problems, while enriching the academic philosopher with a more vivid sense of real-world philosophical problems. I welcome this work, but I think Community Philosophy has a different objective achieved by different means.

It is a mistake to assume that Community Philosophy must be supported by someone housed within a university. A great many Community Philosophy initiatives are grass-roots, self-organized groups, operating from pubs and cafés, led by volunteers and attended by interested amateurs. The rise in such initiatives is well documented in the work of Jules Evans, co-founder of the London Philosophy Club,[31] the biggest philosophy club in the world (Evans 2012). When Community Philosophy does make use of academic support, the academic participates as a *facilitator*. Facilitators of Community Philosophy are not Field Philosophers in my view. What they contribute in these conversations is their philosophical skill and sensitivity in drawing out the thoughts of others and reflecting them back to the group for closer examination. Though they may benefit enormously through this process as I have done, the development and communication of their own ideas is not their central objective. They are instead in the service of the philosophical development of others. We might think of academic philosophers as operating on the 'macro level', hoping that their ideas will somehow disseminate; Field Philosophers work at the 'meso' level, attempting to directly affect policy or organizations. By contrast, Community Philosophers work at the 'micro' level, focusing on the cultivation of individuals and communities of thinkers (Frodeman and Briggle 2016: 125).

Of course, Field Philosophers might also contribute to Community Philosophy enquiry as facilitators, participants or co-enquirers. Here the boundaries between these roles become quite blurred, but one ethical consideration in particular preserves the distinction. Participation in Community Philosophy requires the philosopher to speak clearly and persuasively without relying on canonical ideas with which one's interlocutors may be unfamiliar. Above all they should avoid playing the 'expert' card as this is a move that discourages people from thinking for themselves. Philosophers betray Socrates's legacy if they cast themselves as authority figures, argues Martha Nussbaum (2010). What Socrates brought to Athens was an example of truly democratic vulnerability and humility; class, fame and prestige count for nothing and the argument counts for all (ibid).

The benefits of philosophizing for ourselves

While we may benefit when experts philosophize on our behalf or when they communicate their ideas to us, philosophy is most potent when it is practised by the individual within a community of thinkers; when she considers what to believe or what to value and by doing this exercises the intellectual, emotional and social dispositions that help her live well. The absence of philosophy *as something widely and diversely practised* affects the well-being, dignity and power of those excluded from the conversation and the state of a wider society in which the goods of philosophizing are not well distributed. These kinds of conversations are part of what gives life meaning and helps us flourish.

When thinking of what the public misses out on when they lack the opportunity to philosophize together, I am reminded of a series of conversations I had with communities following a terrorist attack in the UK in May 2017. In the weeks that followed the bombing of a pop concert at Manchester Arena which resulted in the death of twenty-two people, I facilitated philosophical enquiries with schoolchildren, teachers, museum visitors, artists and academics in separate projects across the north of England. For a period, despite the diverse focus of these projects, the topic of the bombing was raised again and again. It found its way into disparate conversations about the value of art and the nature of friendship and was discussed by young people and adults. My enduring impression of this time was that this event had made such an impact on communities in the north of England that they were compelled to explore it philosophically, even when it wasn't the theme of the event that had brought us together. During this period I found no new writing by professional philosophers in response to the issues of home-grown terrorism and what it meant for our sense of safety, freedom and community. I remember wondering why it was that academic philosophers so often failed to speak on the topics that affect people most deeply. But I was also conscious that even if the journals, newspapers and blogs had overflowed with philosophical analysis of terrorism, as they did post on 11 September (Primoratz 2018), this would have been no substitute for the deeply personal labour of investigating this matter for oneself and in conversation with one's community. Only these conversations allow us to ask, What does this tragedy mean for my life?

Restoring the ancient philosophical project

I have claimed that philosophy is mostly practised in the same institutional places by the same academic faces. This is a problem if you share my view that those who philosophize benefit from doing so, since it suggests that these benefits are not well distributed. However, this line of argument does not imply that the philosophical interests of professionals and the public should converge entirely. Though a mutual exchange of ideas and practices would likely benefit both academics and amateurs, a significant overlap seems both impractical and undesirable. As Bertrand Russell persuasively argued in his essay *Philosophy for Laymen*, 'Not only in philosophy, but in all branches of academic study there is a distinction between what has cultural value and what is only of professional interest' (Russell 1946: 40). Academic philosophy can only achieve its most original, persuasive and wise insights if professionals are free to pursue the lines of enquiry they consider to be most pressing, using the kind of practical expertise it takes a lifetime to accrue. I am arguing for something far more modest: a relaxation of the border controls, more freedom of movement and a resulting landscape in which philosophers – new and experienced, novice and expert, amateur and professional – mix, contributing their perspectives and approaches, both inside universities and beyond in hospital wards, residential homes and art galleries. Such a shift would restore what Russell regarded as the ancient philosophical project which had as its dual aims seeking knowledge of the natural world along with the wisdom required to use it in pursuit of a good life (ibid: 41). This view of philosophy, as simultaneously theoretical and practical, offers an appealing vision of a possible philosophical landscape of the future. Without assuming that the 'layperson' can spare a great deal of time for study, philosophical enquiry can still bring enormous value to the individual and to society:

> [Philosophy] can give a habit of exact and careful thought, not only in mathematics and science, but in questions of large practical import. It can give an impersonal breadth and scope to the conception of the ends of life. It can give to the individual a just measure of himself in relation to society, of man in the present to man in the past and in the future, and of the whole history of man in relation to the astronomical cosmos. By enlarging the objects of his thoughts it supplies an antidote to the anxieties and anguish of the present, and makes possible the nearest approach to serenity that is available to a sensitive mind in our tortured and uncertain world. (ibid: 48)

The promise of Community Philosophy

Community Philosophy is not philosophy *for* the wider community; it is philosophy *by* the community. Since philosophy is inherently active not passive, meaningful participation in philosophical practice is necessary to fully realize its intellectual, emotional and social benefits. Consequently, Community Philosophy is not the business of academics addressing issues of public interest, even where they may make intellectual breakthroughs that trickle down into ordinary life. Nor is Community Philosophy a project that aims at enhancing the research or the reputation of academics who work with the public. Community Philosophy is more than public talks by philosophers or popular philosophical publications – both cases where audience interaction can be minimal. These may be side effects of Community Philosophy, but they don't achieve the redistribution the benefits of philosophy that I would like to see.

Community Philosophy is committed to enabling communities to philosophize *for themselves* about topics *that matter to them*. This is the case because it rests on a concept of philosophy as a living praxis. While this work may occasionally inspire philosophical research at the most elite level, or result in a larger readership of philosophical publications, its greatest value resides in the transformative effect that thinking has on the individual thinker. Here comparisons with sport, art and music again prove useful. While we may benefit from watching an exciting 100-metre sprint, standing in front of a transcendent painting or listening to a virtuosic live performance, these benefits are quite distinct from the good that is ours if we actually run, paint or play. This does not replace or diminish the value of engaging with the work of professionals, but it does represent something uniquely important. When we engage with a practice repeatedly over weeks, months and years, especially when we do so with others learning and teaching as we go, we accrue habits, skills and that special kind of un-articulatable wisdom: *phronesis*. Where the practice is conducive to living a good life, we step closer to flourishing as a result. This is true of Community Philosophy.

Some criticisms of Community Philosophy

Having described with great optimism the potential of Community Philosophy, I will now anticipate some of the criticisms my view might attract. Chief on the list is the claim – commonly addressed to philosophers working with children – that philosophical enquiry by non-experts is simply not philosophy at all.

Community Philosophy is not really philosophy

Some readers may worry that Community Philosophy, as I have described it – driven by questions that arise spontaneously and without scholarly context; pursued without the rigorous training that makes them answerable and resulting in conclusions that may be naïve or faulty – will lack the right kind of intention, discipline and outcomes to qualify as real philosophy.

I have previously described some of the sensible concerns we might have about the significance of intention in the questions of young children or any philosophical novice. We are right to designate as 'philosophy' only those conversations that are driven by conceptual and contestable philosophical questions and oriented towards philosophical answers using appropriate methods of critical and creative thinking. It is also reasonable to expect only those capable of using philosophical methods to be able to arrive at these kinds of answers in the right kind of way. Doubtless we all agree that pre-linguistic babies don't yet philosophize, and adults in the end stages of dementia don't philosophize any more. However some objectors make the mistake of exaggerating what it takes to *start* philosophizing.

The philosophical questions we ask needn't be canonical to count. A question such as 'Is it fair to split the restaurant bill equally when some at the table are unemployed?'[32] is a legitimate *philosophical* question when it is accompanied by philosophical intentions and pursued using philosophical methods. While robust training will typically make us more disciplined in our examination of it, such training is not an entry requirement. The basic tools of Community of Enquiry are the intellectual abilities to think critically and creatively, accompanied by the socio-emotional abilities to do so caringly and collaboratively. These dispositions can be cultivated through practice.

Community Philosophy needn't be professionally polished to count as philosophy either. It is sufficient for it to resemble its counterpart in content and methods. Academic and Community Philosophy *do* resemble one another in several key respects: both ask non-empirical, intractable questions about the fundamental concepts that we use to understand ourselves and the world around us. Both use a process of critical thinking, understood as an iterative practice of 'active, persistent and careful consideration of any belief or supposed form of knowledge in the light of the grounds that support it and the further conclusions to which it tends' (Dewey 1933: 9). And both arrive at answers that represent the contributors' best attempts at understanding the problem, but that are also always open to revision.

Community Philosophy is bad philosophy

Even if Community Philosophy sufficiently resembles some broader notion of philosophy to bear the name, some may think it best understood as bad philosophy. Given that Community Philosophy does not rest on a comprehensive knowledge of the history of thought and is less systematic and more prone to errors in reasoning and logical fallacies, we might see the appeal of such a view.

While this assessment certainly holds in some cases, the implication of this criticism – that less sophisticated philosophy is not worthwhile – is unfair. In our assessment of Community Philosophy, what we ought to attend to is the quality of the philosophical practice relative to the level of practitioner expertise. We grant that novice seven year-olds grappling with fractions for the first time are doing maths, and not some other activity. Furthermore, we do not regard them as bad mathematicians simply because they cannot yet recognize fractions when expressed as decimals. We have built into our concept of the highly demanding, technical and abstract practice of maths, an idea of mathematical *progress* accrued with practice over time. In part, this idea comes from having been systematically introduced to maths throughout our formative education, something not true of philosophy. As with maths, the philosophy we see in schools in the form of Community of Enquiry must start where the children are at. So too must the Community of Enquiry we see in communities of adults. In some respects, it is necessarily less sophisticated than its academic counterpart, but it is not inferior as a result. Community Philosophy represents a foundation on which more careful thinking can be built. Yet, despite what I have said so far, the relationship between community and academic philosophy should not be understood *exclusively* in terms of greater and lesser sophistication. Among amateurs or novices in any area of human practice, we sometimes see embodied ways of operating that are superior to those expressed by their professional or expert counterparts. Consider the impact of exorbitant levels of pay received by professional footballers on the way in which they regard themselves and their conduct on and off the pitch. In contrast, we may think that the self-discipline and commitment of unpaid amateurs represents a form of sportsmanship that is preferable. Or consider instead the way in which seven-year-olds often understand mathematics as all-pervading, and how this often erodes by the time they reach the end of compulsory education as maths becomes something firmly contained within disciplinary boundaries. Community Philosophers can certainly learn from the experts, but the experts have something to learn too, especially when it comes to the resourcefulness, connectedness, relevance, urgency, sincerity and pleasure with which philosophy can be practised within communities.

Community Philosophy undermines the value of philosophical expertise

An objector who regards Community Philosophy as suffering from a lack of sophistication, but grants this novice practice is a necessary stage through which those who wish to become competent philosophers must pass, may still argue that this process could be accelerated by soliciting experts to teach on subjects of interest or consulting a philosophical text. Why advocate a practice in which the blind lead the blind? One might worry that this is a practice that in some way undermines the value of philosophical expertise.

I will happily concede that reading philosophical texts and listening to philosophers speak is a valuable part of one's philosophical education. Similarly in art, sport, music or academia, many novices seek the assistance of experts. The hunger for this kind of input is evident in the format of many grass-roots philosophy clubs where there are often invited speakers (Evans 2012). We generally assume those who have dedicated their lives to honing a certain set of knowledge and skills are more knowledgeable and skilful as a result and rightly so, but we must take care when thinking of philosophical 'expertise' as it is a notion that arises out of disciplinary specialization more befitting of the sciences. Philosophy is a domain in which there is much disagreement among philosophers and the public alike. Furthermore, much of this disagreement is reasonable and 'not readily attributable to woolly thinking or ignorance or inattention to relevant considerations' (Hand 2017: 14). As Michael Hand (speaking here about morality) puts it, 'Sensible and sincere people armed with similar life experience and acquainted with roughly the same facts come to notably different conclusions about the content and justification of morality [or other philosophical issues for that matter]' (ibid). Philosophers, like any member of the public, do not have the last word on philosophical matters. Philosophy requires all of us to grapple with the problems ourselves. To do this, we need to hone our skills over time and Community Philosophy allows for this.

It is not that Community Philosophy has *no role* for the academically trained philosopher. Of crucial importance to Community Philosophy is the idea of a facilitator, someone who helps manage the dialogue through a subtle balance of intervention and restraint. Within a Community of Enquiry, the facilitator drives progress using sensitive questioning that, for the most part, 'doesn't offer any new ideas or information to the group but simply attempts to make visible, clarify, or connect what has already emerged' (Kennedy 2004: 755). When the facilitator does introduce new information, ideas, questions, or lines of enquiry, these contributions are not designed to lead the group to a particular conclusion (Robinson 2016). Instead the facilitator follows the discussion 'wherever it may lead but without letting the enquiry drift or lose the agreed focus' (Murris and Haynes 2009: 3). In my view someone with philosophical training is well suited to the role of facilitator where their input is welcome. This is not necessarily so, because such a person possesses knowledge of a particular scholarly area of debate, as one might assume. Instead I suggest that their training is useful because of the way in which a good philosophical education provides a person with a degree of sensitivity to what constitutes a philosophical problem, and a strong sense of the kinds of methods that might enable thinkers to begin to construct their own response. While the facilitator should intervene to ensure that the group thinks carefully and critically about the subject and makes progress towards satisfactory answers, their own knowledge of what has previously been written on the subject, or their own carefully considered views on the subject, does not generate any extra entitlement to be heard in this context. Nor can this knowledge be used to provide the group with a shortcut to the answer. Community Philosophy is, in the Deweyan sense, an enquiry stimulated by the groups' confrontation *and conceptualization* of a problem and explored by those learners with solutions devised according to terms they agree (Dewey [1938] 1991). Philosophical answers simply cannot be handed down fully formed by experts. Where the expert does offer ideas – where appropriate – these are invitations to the group to explore rather than to accept uncritically. This is a decisively humble role for the philosopher to take in which they will likely listen more than they speak, but it is also immensely valuable. Over the years in which I have facilitated and observed Community Philosophy in its many guises, I have consistently noticed the ways in which the philosophical sensitivity of experts enhances the quality of dialogue and gets the best out of people. While it is true that experts can simply become better communicators of their own research, publishing blogs and magazine articles alongside their papers, they can also contribute something of enormous value when they facilitate discussion while relinquishing their own agenda. By noticing, examining, amplifying, connecting and reflecting what is said, the more-experienced can help the less-experienced explore the subjects that matter to them, in ways that are deeply life-enhancing.

Community Philosophy creates echo chambers

More of a legitimate worry, in my view, is the claim that Community Philosophy risks the creation of echo chambers in which participants' own perspectives are reinforced through a process of reverberation and repetition within a closed environment in which opposing views are absent. The emphasis I have placed on enquiring with those with whom we live, learn, work or play may suggest that it is somehow intrinsic to Community Philosophy that we enquire within a pre-existing or self-identifying community. Communities of peers may share the same limited experiences, prejudices or values. We only need to consider the way in which social media presents us with palatable political and cultural morsels, to see how conversations of this kind could be extremely self-limiting.

This final objection allows me to highlight something of great importance. Community Philosophy presents the opportunity *to create* communities of enquiry out of the connections and conflicts we experience in everyday life. Neighbours, classmates or colleagues do not automatically constitute a community. Community is something cultivated over time through the development of trust. When genuine communities are created, even those that appear homogenous from the outside, they will still contain enormous diversity. When a community develops in a hospitable environment, this kind of difference can freely emerge. However, while philosophy requires us to assume a critical stance to our most fundamental views, this often does not happen until someone explicitly challenges us. Mindful of this, communities may seek to diversify their membership, but even when this is impossible, it is still quite possible to seek out diverse perspectives and to welcome these ideas into the conversation, even when those that hold them are absent.

Community Philosophy is not a panacea

Advocates of Community of Enquiry both in schools and in communities can sometimes sound almost evangelical about its benefits. This can be seen in the way in which a 2015 study of the benefit of philosophical enquiry in schools was reported by the UK and International press with headlines that included 'Primary children learn faster and fight less if they study philosophy' (Woolcock 2015; Gorard, Siddiqui and Huat 2015). Those who are inclined to remind us that Community Philosophy is not a panacea are wise to do so. Any contribution philosophy makes to the pursuit of human flourishing must be viewed within the context of those other things that make life worth living. Community Philosophy might be good for us, but so is singing and squash.

Conclusion

So what difference does it make who philosophizes and where they do it? In my view, it makes all the difference. Philosophy is good for us; it is a fundamental, accessible and necessary human practice that promotes flourishing. Its benefits may be felt when ideas trickle down from the macro-level, or when philosophers influence organizations at the meso-level; but it is at the micro-level where its impact can be felt most profoundly in the lives of the wider public. Along with a varied diet of other worthwhile human practices, the iterative process of coming together within a Community of Enquiry enables us to examine what a good life means to us while practising the intellectual, emotional and social habits that help us achieve it.

When philosophy resides in the same old places, practised by same old faces, this shapes the very nature of philosophy, forming it around the needs, desires, experiences, interests and abilities of the few, to the exclusion of the many. When academic philosophers do connect with the pressing issues of our time, or go out into the community to share their ideas, this goes some ways towards addressing this problem, but not far enough. The benefits of philosophy cannot be fully realized as long as we think of philosophy as something that is done on behalf of the public or done to them. People must philosophize for themselves if they are to share the benefits. This is the central conviction of Community Philosophy as I understand it. Community Philosophy relocates philosophy in cafés, libraries and prisons, and repopulates it with new voices, including some that have been historically marginalized. In these new settings, new speakers shape the philosophical agenda around the concerns of real communities and devise accessible and engaging approaches to their exploration. This is good news for the public, good news for professionals and good news for the pursuit of the problems of philosophy in which we all have a stake.

Notes

1 The IAPC is the Institute for the Advancement of Philosophy for Children. It is the world's oldest organization devoted to young people's philosophical practice. See https ://www.montclair.edu/cehs/academics/centers-and-institutes/iapc/

2 FAPSA (The Federation of Australasian Philosophy in Schools Associations) is an umbrella organization supporting the interests of its nine affiliated associations. Through professional development and advocacy initiatives, FAPSA seeks to enrich and expand philosophy education in primary and secondary schools in Australasia. See https://fapsa.org.au/

3 SAPERE (The Society for Philosophical Enquiry and Reflection in Education) promotes Philosophy for Children throughout the UK. See https://www.sapere.org. uk/

4 Café Philosophique (or café-philo) is a grass-roots forum for philosophical discussion, founded by philosopher Marc Sautet in Paris, in 1992. It now has variants worldwide and, along with the work of Matthew Lipman, influenced the format of both the Socrates Café and Philosophy in Pubs movements.

5 Socrates Cafés are gatherings around the world where people from different backgrounds get together and exchange philosophical perspectives based on their experiences using the version of the Socratic Method developed by founder Christopher Phillips. See https://www.socratescafe.com/

6 Philosophy in Pubs is a UK grass-roots philosophy initiative where people come together in community venues and share ideas about life's big questions in a friendly, relaxed atmosphere. See https://philosophyinpubs.co.uk/

7 Brila is a youth-driven charity that promotes critical thinking, shapes social responsibility and enhances self-efficacy through creative philosophy projects and the production of digital magazines. See http://brila.org/

8 Based in Melbourne, Australia, The Philosophy Club partners with schools and communities to build a culture of critical and creative thinking through collaborative philosophical enquiry. See https://thephilosophyclub.com.au/

9 The UK Festival 'HowTheLightGetsIn' is the world's largest ideas and music festival and takes place in Hay-On-Wye, UK. See https://howthelightgetsin.org/hay/

10 Working from Sheffield, UK, Thinking Space is a non-profit whose members create community philosophy projects for everyone, often in cultural settings. See: http://thinkingspace.org.uk/

11 'The Public Philosopher' is a UK BBC radio programme and associated podcast in which Harvard Philosopher Michael Sandel is joined by a live audience to discuss ethical and political philosophical problems. See https://www.bbc.co.uk/programmes/b01nmlh2/episodes/guide

12 Supported by the Philosophy of Education Society of Great Britain (PESGB) Philosophy for Teachers uses Community of Enquiry to support early stage teacher ethical reflection. For further reading see Orchard, Winstanley and Heilbronn (2016).

13 The Maudsley Philosophy Group is a seminar that meets regularly on the grounds of the Maudsley Hospital, Britain's largest mental health teaching hospital affiliated with the Institute of Psychiatry at King's College London. Sessions are attended by an interdisciplinary group of professionals interested in the theory and practice of Psychiatry and Philosophy. The group also offers a series of lectures for the public that include interactive discussion. See http://www.maudsleyphilosophygroup.org/

14 Founded in 2007, The Philosophy Foundation conducts philosophical enquiry in schools, communities and workplaces. They have worked with the Children's Hospital School at Great Ormond Street Hospital UK since 2012. See https://www.philosophy-foundation.org/hospital-schools

15 The Prison Teaching Initiative (PTI) offers credit-earning college courses to inmates at three New Jersey correctional facilities. See https://www.princeton.edu/news/2013/12/05/second-chance-through-princetons-prison-teaching-initiative

16 The London-based Philosophy Foundation also works with prison communities. Some of this work has taken place in Manchester at Thorn Cross prison in collaboration with Kirstine Szifris, whose PhD is on philosophy in prisons. See https://www.philosophy-foundation.org/philosophy-in-prisons. Founder of The London Philosophy Club, Jules Evans, has also done philosophy in Low Moss prison. See http://www.philosophyforlife.org/further-thoughts-on-philosophy-in-prisons-from-a-rank-amateur/

17 Inter-Disciplinary Ethics Applied Centre is a specialist unit for teaching, research, training and consultancy in applied ethics based in Leeds, UK. Their work blends in-depth theoretical enquiry and real-world experience to address the most complex ethical issues facing the world today. See https://ahc.leeds.ac.uk/ethics

18 Philosophy in the City (PinC) is an award-winning outreach project, where student volunteers from the University of Sheffield's Philosophy department go into schools and other institutions to teach philosophy, to encourage engagement with philosophical issues and ways of thinking. In 2018, they collaborated with The Archer Project, a charity run by the Cathedral to help homeless people in the city. See https://www.sheffield.ac.uk/philosophy/news/philosophy-in-the-city-teams-up-with-archer-project-and-sheffield-cathedral-1.697335

19 Working in the UK, the 'Thinking Village Project' looked at how Community Philosophy can open community conversations within and between generations about 'nuisance' behaviours and the fear of crime. Find out more at https://www.jrf.org.uk/report/promoting-intergenerational-understanding-through-community-philosophy

20 In 2014, local school teachers, professors and students of philosophy at the University of Texas El Paso (UTEP), and several community organizations teamed up for a bilingual project called Philosophy for Children in the Borderlands. See https://youtu.be/mnt-XFg90Jk

21 Initiatives such as 'Tent City University in London' made headlines in the UK at the height of the Occupy protests around the world. See, for example, https://www.the guardian.com/uk/2012/jan/19/occupy-london-tent-city-university

22 These are examples of questions asked during public philosophy sessions conducted by Michael Sandel for the BBC. See https://www.bbc.co.uk/programmes/b01nmlh2/episodes/guide

23 In 2018, new technological developments around self-driving cars – along with several high profile fatal accidents – led to numerous discussions of the Trolley Problem in the media, for example, https://www.economist.com/science-and-technol ogy/2018/10/27/whom-should-self-driving-cars-protect-in-an-accident

24 The Podcast Radio Lab deals with these kinds of real life philosophical dilemmas. In the episode 'Playing God' producers Simon Adler and Annie McEwen follow *New York Times* reporter Sheri Fink as she searches for the answer in a warzone, a hurricane, a church basement and an earthquake. Find out more at https://www.wny cstudios.org/story/playing-god

25 For example, through the invention of symbolic logic, Bertrand Russel has been credited as helping to establish the set-theoretic foundations of mathematics and gave us the formal theory of computation and ushered in the digital age. For further reading see Soames (2016).

26 Influential figures in Pragmatism, in particular John Dewey, envisaged philosophy as 'a form of social practice that engaged with the social problems of the age' (Evans 2012: 41). Dewey's ideal was of a 'Great Society' in which neighbours would meet up for face-to-face ethical and civic discussions (Dewey 1927). This vision of grass-roots ethical philosophy influenced later community philosophers like Matthew Lipman who were instrumental in the development of Philosophy for Children (Lipman 1991).

27 For example, Peter Singer founded The Life You Can Save, a non-profit that promotes 'high impact philanthropy – giving that is informed, intentional, and impactful.' Find out more at https://www.thelifeyoucansave.org/

28 Since 1990, the United Nations Development Programme has been publishing Human Development Reports based on the 'capability approach' devised by of economist Amartya Sen and philosopher Martha Nussbaum. See http://hdr.undp.org/en/content /capability-approach-and-human-development-some-reflections

29 Based in the United States, The Institute for Philosophy in Public Life bridges the gap between academic philosophy and the general public, cultivating discussions between professional philosophers and those with an interest in the subject, regardless of their experience or credentials. See https://philosophyinpubliclife.org/

30 The Public Philosophy Network is a US-focused online social network for philosophers, community-based practitioners, policy makers and other constituents interested in thinking critically about public issues. Find out more at http://publicphilosophynetwork.ning.com/

31 The London Philosophy Club holds free talks from some of the leading contemporary philosophers. They organize debates, socials and a regular reading group – events described as fun, accessible and interactive and guided by the belief that philosophy improves people's lives and should be open to all. See https://www.meetup.com/lo ndonphilosophers/

32 This was a question that we explored over several hours in a Community Philosophy session with a group of educators led by Community Philosopher Pieter Mostert. Further details can be found at https://za.linkedin.com/in/pieter-mostert-438a942b

References

Aristotle, (1955), *The Ethics of Aristotle: The Nicomachean Ethics*, revised edn, trans. J. K. Thomson, New York: Viking.

Dewey, J., (1933), *How We Think: A Restatement of the Relation of Reflective Thinking to the Educative Process*, Lexington, MA: D.C. Heath.

Dewey, J., ([1938] 1991), 'Logic: The Theory of Inquiry', in J. A. Boydston (ed.), *John Dewey: The Later Works, 1925–1953*, Vol. 12, Carbondale, IL: SIU Press.

Edmonds, D., (2014), *Would You Kill The Fat Man?: The Trolley Problem and What Your Answer Tells Us About Right and Wrong*, Princeton: Princeton University Press.

Evans, J., (2012), *Connected Communities: Philosophical Communities - A Report for the Arts and Humanities Research Council*, [Online], Available at: https://philosophypa thways.com/download/Connected-Communities-Philosophical-Communities2.pdf, Accessed 6 November 2018.

Foot, P., (1967), 'The Problem of Abortion and the Doctrine of Double Effect', *Oxford Review*, 5: 5–15.

Frodeman, R., and Briggle, A., (2016), *Socrates Tenured: The Institutions of 21st-Century Philosophy*, London: Rowman and Littlefield.

Goldhill, O., (2018), 'Philosophers are Building Ethical Algorithms to Help Control Self-driving Cars', [Online], Available at: https://qz.com/1204395/self-driving-cars-trolley-p roblem-philosophers-are-building-ethical-algorithms-to-solve-the-problem/, Accessed 1 March 2018.

Gorard, S., Siddiqui, N., and Huat, B., (2015), 'Philosophy for Children Evaluation Report and Executive Summary', [Online], Available at: https://educationendowmentfoun dation.org.uk/public/files/Projects/Evaluation_Reports/Campaigns/Evaluation_Repo rts/EEF_Project_Report_PhilosophyForChildren.pdf, Accessed 1 March 2018.

Hand, M., (2008), 'Can Children be Taught Philosophy?', in M. Hand and C. Winstanley (eds), *Philosophy in Schools*, 5–17, London: Continuum.

Hand, M., (2017), *A Theory of Moral Education*, London: Routledge.

Haynes, J., and Murris, K., (2009), 'The Wrong Message: Risk, Censorship and the Struggle for Democracy in Primary School', *Thinking*, 19 (1): 2–12.

Kennedy, D., (2004), 'The Philosopher as Teacher: The Role of a Facilitator in a Community of Philosophical Inquiry', *Metaphilosophy*, 35 (5): 744–65.

Kitchener, R. F., (1990), 'Do Children Think Philosophically?', *Metaphilosophy*, 21: 416–31.

Lipman, M., (1991), 'Rediscovering the Vygotsky Trail', *Inquiry*, 7 (2): 14–16.

Lipman, M., (2011), 'Philosophy for Children: Some Assumptions and Implications', *Ethics in Progress*, 2 (1): 3–16.

Magee, B., (2000), 'Sense and Nonsense', [Online], Available at: https://www.prospect magazine.co.uk/magazine/bryan-magee-profundity-obscurity-bad-writing, Accessed 2 January 2019.

Matthews, G., (1980), *Philosophy and the Young Child*, Harvard: Harvard University Press.

McCall, C., (2009), *Transforming Thinking: Philosophical Inquiry in the Primary and Secondary Classroom*, London: Routledge.

Meagher, S., (2013), *Public Philosophy: Revitalizing Philosophy as a Civic Discipline*, Kettering Foundation, [Online], Available at: https://publicphilosophynetwork.nin g.com/page/kettering-report-1, Accessed 18 January 2018.

Nussbaum, M. C., (1990), *Love's Knowledge: Essays on Philosophy and Literature*, Oxford: Oxford University Press.

Nussbaum, M. C., (2010), *Not For Profit*, Princeton: Princeton University Press.

Orchard, J., Winstanley, C., and Heilbronn, R., (2016), 'Philosophy for Teachers (P4T) – Developing New Teachers' Applied Ethical Decision-Making', *Ethics in Professional Education*, 11 (1): 42–54.

Petrinovich, L., O'Neill, P., and Jorgensen, M., (1993), 'An Empirical Study of Moral Intuitions: Toward an Evolutionary Ethics', *Journal of Personality and Social Psychology*, 64: 467–78.

Prichard, R., (1996), *Reasonable Children*, Lawrence, KS: University Press of Kansas.

Primoratz, I., (2018), 'Terrorism', *The Stanford Encyclopedia of Philosophy*, [Online], Available at: https://plato.stanford.edu/archives/win2018/entries/terrorism/, Accessed 15 December 2018.

Robinson, G., (2016), 'Feeling the Pull: Ethical Enquiry and the Tension it Creates for Teachers', *Analytical Teaching and Philosophical Praxis*, 36 (1): 44–54.

Russell, B., (1946), 'Philosophy for Laymen,' *Universities' Quarterly*, 1: 38–49.

Shapiro, D., (2012), *Plato Was Wrong: Footnotes Doing Philosophy with Young People*, New York: Rowman and Littlefield.

Soames, S., (2016), 'Philosophy's True Home', [Online], Available at: https://opinionator. blogs.nytimes.com/2016/03/07/philosophys-true-home/, Accessed 15 February 2018.

Sowey, M., (2018), 'Strengthening Dialogic Argument: What Teachers Can Learn from Authentic Examples of Student Dialogue', *Journal of Philosophy in Schools*, 5 (2): 54–78.

Thomson, J., (1985), 'The Trolley Problem', *Yale Law Journal*, 94 (6): 1395–415.

Wartenberg, T., (2014), 'Assessing an Elementary School Philosophy Program', *Thinking: The Journal of Philosophy for Children*, 20 (3/4): 90–4.

Weinstein, J. R., (2014), 'Public Philosophy: Introduction', *Essays in Philosophy*, 15 (1): 1–4.

White, J., (1992), 'The Roots of Philosophy', *Royal Institute of Philosophy Supplement*, 33: 73–88.

Woolcock, N., (2015), 'Primary Children Learn Faster and Fight Less if they Study Philosophy', [Online], Available at: https://www.thetimes.co.uk/article/primary-ch ildren-learn-faster-and-fight-less-if-they-study-philosophy-tswzlzn833n, Accessed 10 March 2018.

3

Registers of community: Policy discourse, subjectivity and coming to terms with our conditions

Naomi Hodgson

Introduction

It is often at times of political crisis and upheaval that calls for community, and academic interest in it (Walkerdine and Studdert 2012), are particularly pronounced. In the 1950s, Robert Nisbet noted that the 'fears of the nineteenth century conservatives in Western Europe, expressed against a background of increasing individualism, secularism, and social dislocation, have become, to an extraordinary degree, the insights and hypotheses of present-day students of man in society' (Nisbet 1953: 3, cited in Noddings 1996: 245). This, it seems, is a perennial concern; what has changed perhaps are the identified sources of dislocation and the material conditions in which community is constituted. In the 1960s, community was posited by sociologists as an antidote to the increasingly individualized 'mass society', and in social politics it presented a form of resistance to centralized bureaucracy (Rose 2000: 175). While decentralization has taken place in the intervening period, notably in the move to New Public Management in the 1970s and subsequent shifts in governance, appeals to the notion of community remain: often not as a form of resistance, however, but within the language of policy itself. In the late twentieth century, community became a particular focus of policy as states began to resituate themselves as competitive actors in a global knowledge economy. Practices of government were recast in terms of cohesion, empowerment and transparency, opening up the parameters of accountability to include individuals themselves.

Appeals to community in the name of achieving stability and cohesion are seen not only in policy but also in scholarship. Nel Noddings has drawn attention also to the way that community, in the educational literature, 'is put forward again and again as a redemptive solution. Educators speak and write with enthusiasm – sometimes with obvious longing – about communities of learners, professional communities, schools as communities, and community partnerships' (Noddings 1996: 246). Kathleen Knight-Abowitz, however, finds the discourse of community to be both 'essentialized' and 'dichotomized', citing Shane Phelan's (1996) assessment that 'the summoning of the ideal of community signals an identitarian politics of sameness, unifying and fixing individual selves in order to construct stability and order in a disorderly world' (ibid: 143). By contrast, to think more broadly of philosophy as thinking – as an educative practice, borne in conversation, in which we put ourselves and our societies to the test of their own disappointments and ideals – we can see why philosophy is more likely to be found today among informal learning communities in bookshops, festivals, pubs and online than in the formal institution of the university (Evans 2012). This marks a radical point of departure from the discourse of sameness in relation to community identified here, evident today not only in the language of education and social policy but also in consumer marketing, where subscribing to a service provider or signing up to an app are also referred to as joining communities, emphasizing the 'like-mindedness' of fellow users. Take Facebook and Instagram, for example:

> Share updates and photos, engage with friends and Pages, and stay connected to communities important to you (Facebook).

> Join the community of over 1 billion people and express yourself by sharing all the moments of your day – the highlights and everything in between, too (Instagram).

Downloading and signing up to an app is a form of choosing and joining a community. Like trying a new grocery store, if you don't like it, you no longer have to shop there, or use the app; it is a form of community based on shared interests, an identification based on one's self-understanding, a lifestyle choice.

The sense of urgency around the need for community seems to have been exacerbated, or at least recast, as we have moved further away from a welfare state model of government and the implicit sense of solidarity this entails. Since the UK voted to leave the European Union, existing divisions, perhaps previously unrecognized or unacknowledged, have been exposed. In the United States, Donald Trump's presidency has been characterized by a toxic rhetoric over immigration. A period characterized by opening borders and taking down walls has passed, to be superseded by the very opposite. Voters on all sides appear to feel disenfranchised, in conflict with each other about what democracy is, and yet calls 'to move beyond division and come together. To move beyond uncertainty into a brighter future' (May 2019) seem to pose agreement as the morally responsible thing to aim for. The existence of division is seen to be an affront to democracy, freedom and sovereignty, rather than evidence of it.

The current political context arguably requires more than appeals for cohesion and integration and guidance on how local organizations can be supported to facilitate these (as given in, for example, the Government's Integrated Communities Strategy Green Paper, HM Government 2018). And while further critiques of such policies might be instructive, and indeed cathartic, there is a risk that they too seek an (eternally deferred) ideal of community.

In philosophy and philosophy of education, responses to crises of community have commonly drawn on political liberalism or communitarianism for conceptions of what form of community we ought to pursue in Western liberal democracies (see, for example, Kymlicka 2005; Arthur and Bailey 2000; McLaughlin 1995). Since the linguistic and progressive turns of the mid-twentieth century, informed by critical pedagogy, feminism and poststructuralism, however, some have argued that these are insufficient conceptualizations of community for pluralist democracies. Duck-Joo Kwak, for example, has argued that both Alasdair MacIntyre's communitarian response and John Rawls's liberal response seem 'too simplistic and not quite responsive to the sense of uneasiness we feel today' in our fluid, postmodern condition (Kwak 2010: 405). Feminist and postmodern conceptions of power, self, other and society have led to new approaches being proposed that emphasize plurality, voice, embodiment and the primacy of relations rather than structure, often turning to literature rather than traditional philosophical sources (see, for example, Noddings 1996: 60; Knight Abowitz 1999).

Although offering important correctives to the exclusive and subordinating effects of universalizing grand narratives (cf. Lyotard 1979), postmodern accounts have also been criticized for a fetishization of difference. Nicholas Burbules and Suzanne Rice have argued that 'the celebration of difference becomes a presumption of incommensurability, a denial of the possibility of intersubjective understanding' (1991: 401). A similar point has been made recently in relation to critical accounts rooted in a political conception of education oriented towards emancipation, often informed by critical pedagogy (Freire 1993). Respect for otherness has become an 'assumption that we can only act and speak if we first have the certainty that we fully understand and really respect the other', a hermeneutics that constitutes 'an unsolvable problem: we will never find the common ground – today expressed, for example, as mutual respect, cohesion, tolerance, intercultural understanding – from which we could begin' (Hodgson, Vlieghe and Zamojski 2018: 12). This unsolvability places notions of freedom, democracy and representation as eternally deferred ideals against which to debunk the status quo (ibid). The approach taken in this chapter does not focus on these critical approaches to the relationship between community and education; a critique of critique is not what is sought here. Rather, I seek to draw out what is often left out of view by policy accounts, and some educational research accounts, of community, as constituted in community philosophy or indeed in our daily practices.

In what follows I will look first at the shift from the welfare state to the facilitating state, taking the UK as an example of how the language of community in contemporary forms of governance has been repositioned within a discourse of autonomy, choice and empowerment. Broadening out to the wider western European context, I will then consider the form of individuality that this notion of community requires. Seen in terms of a shift from a historical self-understanding, characteristic of the telos of the citizen of the nation state, to an environmental self-understanding, the individual today is asked to understand herself as needing to optimize her own performance by investment in a continual cycle of learning and self-monitoring (cf. Simons and Masschelein 2008; Simons and Hodgson 2012). This mode of subjectivation, in which a particular rendering of citizenship as active citizenship is mobilized, has been subject to critique for the individualized, depoliticized notion of community that this seems to constitute.

Rather than setting out how education might foster a repoliticized notion of citizenship elaborated in view of achieving cohesive communities, this chapter aims to draw out what is left out of sight in governmental notions of community. Drawing on Robert Esposito and Stanley Cavell, I draw attention to notions of community and subjectivity that acknowledge partiality and indebtedness as existential elements of our living together. Shifting away from a notion of community understood in relation to the modern reference points of 'state-citizen-society', Bruno Latour offers a different way to consider our current crisis and our disappointment in, and cynicism towards, politics – or the political establishment at least. Latour's conception of political community encourages us to see what we have in common beyond that defined by statements of values or measures of active citizenship. The reference point instead becomes what we care about, around which a community gathers. To illustrate this, I conclude by considering what this means for our coming to terms with our current conditions and indicate what might be seen as instantiations of community today – outwith its formal institutions.

Community as an object of government: From the welfare state to the big society

In the late 1970s, the welfare state model of government, established in the UK after the Second World War, began to be challenged. It was seen to be top-heavy, bureaucratic, elitist, conservative, male-dominated. The main rationale and impetus for reform, however, came from what has been referred to as the New Right (Clarke, Gewirtz and McLaughlin 2000: 3): centralized public provision of services was seen as an impediment to the economy and as fostering a culture of dependency. The New Right rhetoric created a stigma around those 'on benefits', still powerful and evident in the media today, who were seen to be getting money for nothing. The reformed system introduced responsibilities to be fulfilled in order to earn such rights. In line with wider shifts towards neoliberalism, the Conservative government, led by Margaret Thatcher, began to move away from universal welfare provided by state-centred, publicly funded institutions, to privatization of utilities and infrastructure, with individuals positioned as active choosers taking responsibility for their own welfare, with options facilitated by the state (for a more detailed account of the move towards individual responsibility, see Hodgson 2018; Tuschling and Engemann 2006).

Following the election of Tony Blair's Labour government in the UK in 1997, community and individual responsibility began to take a more prominent role in strategies of government. Home Secretary Jack Straw, in an echo of a famous speech by Thatcher, claimed that there was 'no such "thing" as society, not in the way Thatcher meant it but because society is not a "thing" external to our experiences and responsibilities. It is us, all of us' (cited in Rose 2000: 1395). New Labour's Third Way rationality of government, developed by the sociologist Anthony Giddens (1998), combined neoliberalism 'with a basic commitment to the social welfare programme and the idea of the responsible state' (Delanty 2003: 75). This commitment to social welfare was not a return to 'the welfare state'; rather, the individual was addressed as a citizen/consumer, in terms of their responsibility and the possibility of access to knowledge, a source of empowerment for the individual to shape their own life (ibid: 76).

Nikolas Rose identifies in Straw's speech an important reframing of society, in which the relationship between individual and community is emphasized: 'no longer external and constraining, but an aspect of "all of us"' (Rose 2000: 1395). Tony Blair would articulate the Third Way in terms of its championing of four values. The first pair – equal society, opportunity for all – Rose suggests, 'harks back to the obligations of left-of-center politics down the ages'. The second pair – the values of responsibility and community – though not new, is distinctive, as it 'identifies the reciprocal obligations of the subjects of government' (ibid: 1397). While 'those who exercise power ... must provide the conditions of the good life' (ibid: 1398), those subject to it 'must deserve to inhabit it by building strong communities and exercising active responsible citizenship' (ibid). The governmentality of the Third Way, then, operates through 'a community-based ethics that shapes the values that guide each individual' (ibid). Governance of the individual in terms of their freedom and individual autonomy (cf. Barry, Osborne and Rose 1996) means not an atomized form of individualism, but fostering a particular understanding of the individual as responsible for the health of the community, empowered to shape it according to local needs and interests. Individuals, Rose writes, 'are understood as citizens, not of societies as national collectivities, but of neighbourhoods, associations, regions, networks, subcultures, age groups, ethnicities, and lifestyle sectors – in short, communities' (Rose 2000: 1399).

The principles of decentralized power, increased localism and individual responsibility were central to a 2010 speech given by then conservative prime minister, David Cameron, during which he set out three key principles of the notion of the Big Society:

1. More power to local government and beyond local government, so people can actually do more and take more power.
2. Open up public services, make them less monolithic, say to people: if you want to start up new schools, you can; if you want to set up a co-op or a mutual within the health service, if you are part of the health service, you can; say to organisations like [The] Big Issue [Foundation]: if you want to expand and replicate yourself across the country, we want you to.
3. More philanthropic giving, more charitable giving, and more volunteering in our country (Cameron 2010).

Government is positioned here as facilitating these opportunities. The idea of making public services more open and less monolithic casts the modern institutions of government departments as outmoded for today's challenges. Cameron later refers to the civil service, for example, as requiring a culture change, since it doesn't understand social enterprise. Community-based social enterprise has become not only increasingly possible due to such policy shifts but also increasingly necessary, as cuts to public funding and pressures on businesses, such as economic downturn and competition from online retailers, have seen the closure of, for example, libraries and small post offices. The continuation of these services relies instead on volunteers, the charity sector, or the incorporation of services into existing businesses.

A notable aspect of the governmental use of the notion of community is its pluralized form: as Rose notes, it is a compartmentalizing of different communities that, in the current context, individuals can identify with based on shared interests, attitudes, values, tastes and allegiances. It positions the individual as needing to make explicit his or her interests and allegiances. This has been criticized by both Charles Taylor and Alasdair MacIntyre for the 'instrumental (or bureaucratic) attitude and the narrow pursuit of self-expression and self-fulfillment' it entails (Noddings 1996: 250). This focus on particular aspects of ourselves rather than on collective interest points to the non-referentiality – or perhaps self-referentiality – on which our participation in community is seen to be based, that a focus needs to be taken into account when rethinking how community is constituted today.

As Henrik Enroth states, theory has not kept pace with the manner of the shift from nation state governing to globalized, late neoliberal governance, characterized by the lack of fixed referents, and there remains a presupposition of the 'existence of subjects and objects of governing embedded in a nation-state-society constellation' (Enroth 2014: 64). Such reference points are no longer fixed in the current rationality of governance that operates beyond the level of the nation state. This non-referentiality is felt in various ways in our condition today: for example, in moral relativism, in discourses of quality and excellence, in the rise of populist, 'post-truth' politics, and, as we shall consider here, in individualized notions of community. This raises issues for the role of the educator, too. As Duck-Joo Kwak notes, there is a 'lack of a common source of authority on the basis of which we invoke community' (2010: 406), something that applies to community philosophy as well as other forms of community. It is little wonder that the need to come to terms with, to find a way to articulate, what it means to be in community, seems highly urgent, and yet highly problematic today.

The emergence of communities – plural – as an object of government is, then, in part constitutive of the late twentieth-century shift from the welfare state and centralized government to New Public Management, privatization and, with it, responsibilization (Lemke 2001; Foucault 1991), steered by the facilitating state (Rose 2000: 1400; cf. Donzelot and Estebe 1994). Moving away from the bureaucratic, 'top-down' decision-making of modern government, communities became involved in decision-making over local resources in the name of a more representative, accountable and efficient form of government. This pluralized use of the term 'communities' has, in the last two decades, become a catch-all for identity- and interest-based groups, formed on the basis of shared interests, that is, what those who choose to participate have in common. While this could be treated critically as a (mere) symptom of the consumerization of citizenship, or positively as a form of democratization, the notion of community has, as Noddings has noted, a 'dark side' (Noddings 1996: 245), marking out those who don't belong. Historical examples abound, but more recently we have seen a resurgence of this in political speech. The way in which community operates as a discourse of shared interests, however, changes the rationale. Take, for example, Donald Trump's appeal with regard to the building of a wall along the United States–Mexico border: 'Some have suggested a barrier is immoral. Then why do wealthy politicians build walls, fences, and gates around their homes? They don't build walls because they hate the people on the outside, but because they love the people on the inside.'[1] Living in a gated community or having a garden fence becomes a sign of a parent or partner doing their moral duty to protect their loved ones, equated with the imposition of physical barriers between countries: both are about the protection of the private, autonomous individual from possible future danger from those whom we assume to have nothing in common.

The change of the mode of governance, illustrated in the previous section with reference to the UK, but indicative of a more general trend, increasingly brings local communities and their constitutive parts into focus as objects of governance and self-governance. This entails a particular self-understanding of individuals in relation to community, which we explore in the next section.

Citizenship for the knowledge economy: From historical to environmental self-understanding

These shifts in the mode of governance are by no means limited to the UK context. They are, to an extent, a response to straitened economic conditions in light of the global economic crisis of 2008, but also part of longer-term shifts in the position of the nation state in conditions of globalization. As we have seen earlier, in the speeches by Straw and Cameron and in Rose's analysis, the relationship between the individual and the state has also changed, and so too has the self-understanding required of members of society. The shift in the self-understanding of the individual in these conditions has been analysed by Maarten Simons and Jan Masschelein with particular reference to the significance that learning has come to have in governance and self-governance. In the shift from the welfare state to the facilitating state, the freedom of the individual and their capacity to choose and be self-determining has been cast in terms of the need and opportunity for lifelong learning. The conditions of globalization and the shift in the role of the nation state lead Simons and Masschelein (2008) to argue that there has been a shift in our experience of time and space. The self-understanding this constitutes is recounted here in order to further elaborate on the ways in which the governmental invocation of community set out in the previous part shapes our relationship to ourselves and community. The educational context referred to here shows how a particular use of 'learning' forms part of our understanding of this; the context of community philosophy is one dimension of it.

In Simons and Masschelein's account, the educational institution is typified by the modern school in which duration was divided 'into successive or parallel segments, where they add up in a cumulative series of temporal stages, towards a terminal stable point' (ibid: 690). Time is thus a 'linear process that is characterized as "progress"' (ibid). At this time (late eighteenth/early nineteenth century), 'analytic pedagogy' emerges and 'establishes educative procedures dividing the process of learning into several levels, and hierarchizing each step of development into small cumulative steps' (ibid). Homogenization in terms of age groups effects a normalization in which regular measurement establishes a norm, an average, in relation to which pupils understand themselves. A particular, evolutionary individuality is produced: one is situated within a linear temporality in which progress is measured against others and on the basis of one's age.

While aspects of this remain familiar today, the rationality according to which we organize space and time in relation to education and work, and understand ourselves, has shifted: the discourse of learning and the casting of a variety of spaces – not only schools and universities but also museums, cities, online space and, of course, the hired rooms, Socratic cafés, pubs and other venues of community philosophy – as learning environments not only renames these spaces but also changes our orientation to them and to ourselves. Learning is now the focus, adapted according to individual needs as we navigate our learning journeys. In their analysis of recent Flemish policy, Simons and Masschelein show that, rather than being taught, didactically, a fixed body of knowledge, 'pupils should be regarded today as the subjects of learning and no longer merely objects of teaching (methods)' (ibid: 692). This is illustrated in the notions of personalized learning and 'learning to learn', a process by which the skills and competencies, the 'learning behaviours', are developed by the individual in order that she can take ownership of her learning process. Rather than a linear trajectory towards a pre-determined end or standard, the learner is situated within a field of opportunities, and any point is a provisional point at which to gauge learning needs and aspirations.

The spaces in which this learning takes place – be it the school, the university, the MOOC, the self-care app – must then provide stimulation, resources and opportunities (ibid). Think of the classroom wall: once a space on which completed work and achievements were displayed, now a 'learning wall' in which resources and stimulus materials are regularly updated according to the learning needs of the class, in order to provide support and challenge. Or the library that has been renamed a learning resource centre: no longer positioned as a repository of canonical knowledge accessed on the authority of the teacher, it is a space in which the individual, empowered to progress their own learning, can access and benefit from the resources – physical or virtual – according to their own learning needs, with the space designed to accommodate a variety of modes of learning.

The teacher facilitates and creates the stimuli for learning, which consists of not only the physical or virtual learning environment but also the provision or facilitation of regular feedback: 'In her unique trajectory the learner is no longer in need of surveillance and normalising instruction [as in the modern school], but is in need of permanent monitoring, coaching, and feedback' (ibid: 693). This enables the individual learner to continue her learning journey across different learning environments, knowing her position and needs at all times. Simons and Masschelein refer to this self-understanding as an environmental self-understanding, a responsive, adaptable relation to the here and now, based on current needs and resources. No longer situated on a linear trajectory between past and future as in the historical self-understanding of the modern period, the individual today is oriented in relation to an 'atemporal' present with the past judged only 'in terms of the opportunities (and resources) it offers today to face present challenges' (ibid: 695).

The shift to the language of learning environments not only marks a change in terminology to reflect where we learn today, but also invokes the environment itself as learning. In the digitized classroom, with online platforms as sources of learning and behaviour management tools, and the 'big data' that these generate, the feedback may not be provided by a teacher but by the material, digital devices themselves. This is by no means limited to formal educational contexts; apps developed for parents and families are a widespread source of information and advice and thus also of data on those individuals' engagement in learning activities and their locations (see Ramaekers and Hodgson forthcoming). This digital and virtual element in the constitution of community also needs to be taken in to account when we are trying to come to terms with what it means to be in community today.

Simons and Masschelein situate their account in relation to sociological accounts of the individualized society (cf. Beck 1992), as it describes a self-understanding in which one is positioned not in relation to others but in relation to one's own past performance, learning needs, skills and competencies. The notion of 'personalized learning' is an apt illustration. This self-understanding does not derive directly from a particular pedagogy or a fixed sense of what is being progressed to, but rather, and in conjunction with the influence of progressivism and child-centredness, is shaped by wider political and economic change in which learning has become a key component. The learning disposition is required of us throughout our lives, in the context of education, work, family life, friendship and leisure. It has also been shown to shape contemporary understandings of citizenship: no longer related solely 'to legal rights and to residence and birth in a sovereign territory, but to a disposition towards or orientation to a set of values relating to learning and self-improvement in a particular environment' (Hodgson 2016: 3).

The recasting of citizenship as 'active citizenship' captures the shift from the association of citizenship with political and legal status, to its more mobile, globalized form, in which one's citizenship is a matter of individual expression of particular attitudes and values. In the European context in particular, active citizenship becomes an object of measurement and an aspect of ourselves that we could improve. It emerges in the context of a shift to societal success now being assessed on the basis of its citizens' participation and well-being, rather than purely economic measures such as GDP.[2] Active citizenship indicators (Hoskins et al. 2006) not only monitor the levels of participation of particular nations or regions and the effect of interventions to foster citizenship, but also provide a way to engage the individual in the desired citizenship behaviours. Developed by the Centre for Research on Lifelong Learning (CRELL), the definition of active citizenship 'includes new and less conventional forms of active citizenship, such as one-off issue politics and responsible consumption, as well as the more traditional forms of voting and membership in parties and NGOs' (Hoskins 2006: 11). As we saw previously in relation to community, previously taken-for-granted aspects of living together are now parts of ourselves to be made explicit and worked upon. The individual responsibility for community, not only in terms of political participation but also how we behave as autonomous choosers in terms of consumer behaviour, is evident in this conception. We see a move towards taken-for-granted notions of citizenship relating to legal rights, determined by place of birth, to the need to make visible and measurable the extent to which we participate.

The opening up of space through processes of globalization and the mobility that this encourages and necessitates is often expressed in terms of global citizenship, shared goals, and opening up economies through trade agreements and liberal deregulation. Environmental self-understanding is constituted in this shift, and in the technological developments that enable and accompany it, as the individual is asked to see themselves as entrepreneurial, adaptable, innovative, and as needing to permanently monitor their skills and competencies in order to respond proactively to economic conditions. This globalized space or society is 'a space or society in which we all have a stake' (Masschelein and Simons 2002: 601). It is 'defined by what members have or should have in common: enterprising capacities, communicative and learning skills and competencies, the ability to define and come to agreements about needs and about what should be done, and finally the ability to *participate* (society being conceived as the "unity of units")' (ibid).

It is not that we are encouraged to collaborate, find shared interests and so on that is at issue here, but that these indicators of active citizenship are taken as proxies for political participation and, moreover, that what it means to participate – politically – is pre-determined. It could be argued that this is a form of solidarity, that is, that we are all steered towards activities beneficial for the greater good. What this 'greater good' is, however, is not up for discussion. The political aspect of the governmental invocation of community is brought in to question in the next section.

Depoliticization, immunization, negation

This particular form of individualization, in which the individual is given greater responsibility for determining her own learning needs, and the ways in which this has shaped our understanding of our citizenship, has been described in terms of a depoliticization (Biesta 2009; Frazer 2007), as it marks a further shift away from collective concern, the solidarity implicit in the welfare state, to individual responsibility steered by a facilitating state. The personalization of learning and the depoliticization of citizenship, accompanied by a focus on individual social and emotional learning behaviours (from the early years, to the workplace, to our free time), leads to concerns as to what sense of democracy and community we are passing on. In relation to current conceptions of citizenship education, for example, Duck-Joo Kwak (2010) writes that we 'may end up fostering, at best, our future citizens' ability to choose and confirm their ways of life, rather than to contest and live up to them, because they are carefully designed to avoid political controversy over "comprehensive" values of the good life in the name of "civic" values' (ibid: 407). The idea that democratic community is necessarily a site of contestation seems absent in their current rendering. Responses to this from the field of education are often critical – revealing how policies or curricula perpetuate inequalities and create passive, consumer-citizens (Giroux 1999), articulating the need for moral education or character education as a way to regain the lost normativity (Alexander 2005, Arthur, Davies and Hahn 2008), or calling for 'deep philosophical reflection' (Kwak 2010) in order to address this democratic deficit through education.

The response to the depoliticization characteristic of renderings of individual and society in the age of consumerization, privatization and 'learnification' (Biesta 2009) takes a different direction in the work of Masschelein and Simons (2002). Rather than comparing a compromised form of democracy to an ideal or previous form, their account draws attention to what is overlooked in our current conceptions. Following Roberto Esposito, Masschelein and Simons (2002) question the notion of the collectivity (society, community) that is characterized by what is held in common and at the same time enables expression of individuality. We see this not only in policy discourses of community but also in the commercial sector, as seen earlier in the marketing blurbs for social media apps. Instead, Esposito invokes 'the original meaning of *munus* (void, debt, gift) in *communus*', which is 'exactly the opposite of this conception … community is not a matter of "having" something in "common", something that we share with others, but of the opposite: it is not a matter of "having" but of "lacking"' (ibid: 601). Hence, Masschelein and Simons continue, 'the very notion of community includes an infringement of subjectivity and individuality' (ibid: 602).

They suggest, therefore, that rather than the opening up associated with globalization, the rendering of multiple aspects of ourselves as visible, measurable and calculable, including our relations with others – the thorough accounting for ourselves that constitutes an environmental self-understanding – effects an 'immunization': 'This is not only about transforming human subjects into discrete individuals; immunisation is in addition a shield against the passivity and void within the subject itself' (ibid). The identification with an app, or the seclusion of one's self in an echo chamber of news and shared opinion, can be seen as instantiations of this 'shield against … the void': in apps, in wearable technologies, in positive psychological programmes for well-being, we are offered the sense of knowing ourselves, and accounting for ourselves in totality. The only excess is when we exceed yesterday's number of steps, or feel more energized; the only void is the gap between current performance and the next learning milestone.

Esposito's account – and Masschelein and Simon's use of it – is not an appeal to an ideal community: a political version to be contrasted with, and used to critique, a depoliticized form as such. Rather, it is an illustration of existential conditions of living in community with others that an individualized, immunized, account denies. Thus it helps us to further articulate what is left out of notions of community that emphasize coherence and agreement, and political discourses that invoke communities as an explicit expression of pre-defined forms of political participation. Turning to Stanley Cavell, we find a different articulation of responsibility than we find in the rendering of active citizenship, invoked by our very living together in common, rather than as a specific evidencing of participation.

Cavell refers to the community as unstable – not in a pejorative sense, but in its changing nature, in the need for constitutive parts to find ways to go on together – and, hence, to the need to continually search for and maintain a communal life. This maintaining is an ongoing investment of ourselves into common practices, a shared way of life, one that pre-exists us and in relation to which we understand ourselves: our very subjectivity is constituted in relation to others. In the moral perfectionist account of democracy that Cavell elaborates, drawing on Ralph Waldo Emerson, democratic community is always in the making. Not as something external to us but constituted by our very investment in it. For Cavell, this investment is most profound in our shared use of language. In what we say, we are representative of a culture, of a set of criteria that amount to an agreement, perhaps only at a minimal level, about what our words mean (Cavell 1979).

In his recasting of Plato's allegory of the cave (Cavell 2004), Cavell presents democracy and education not as teleological, linear processes, a transition from dark to light, ignorance to enlightenment, but a series of nexts, always in the making. Cavell describes 'the path from the *Republic*'s picture of the soul's journey (perfectible to the pitch of philosophy by only a few, forming an aristocratic class) to the democratic need for perfection' as 'a path from the idea of there being one (call him Socrates) who represents for each of us the height of the journey, to the idea of each of us being representative for each of us – an idea that is a threat as much as an opportunity' (Cavell 1990: 9). The idea of each of us being 'representative for each of us' offers a way to think of autonomy and the individual in line with the notions of 'lack' and 'infringement' that we find in Esposito's and Masschelein and Simons' account of subjectivity and community. Our existential condition of living with others not only renders perfectibility and perfect cohesion an unachievable ideal at the social level, but our very understanding of ourselves as individuals is constituted in our relations to others. Cavell refers to this in terms of our partiality; the polysemy of the term draws attention to a number of interrelated aspects. Our partiality refers to that to which we are partial; though such desires and preferences are often sidelined or repressed by the need for conformity, a term used particularly by Emerson to refer to our unthinking ways of going on (Emerson 2003). Partiality also refers to our existential incompleteness; we can never fully know ourselves, and our sense of self is indebted to our thrownness into pre-existing community. This is captured by the idea of the self as a series of nexts, expressed by Emerson as our attained and unattained self. For Cavell, this refers not to having 'one unattained/attainable self we repetitively never arrive at, but rather than "having" "a" self is a process of moving to, and from, nexts' (Cavell 1990: 12). Thus, our very existence, as a process of growth, education, experience and change, is characterized by loss – perpetual loss of a previous self. As Cavell puts this, 'One way or the other a side of the self is in negation – either the attainable negates the attained or vice versa' (ibid).

In our representativeness, Cavell writes, we are educations for one another. Not in the sense of an accrual of learning in a positive, optimizing sense: education challenges us, changes us, confronts us, pulls us up against our own and others' assumptions about how things are and how things should be. This is not a matter of arguing the

50   *Philosophy and Community*

point to seek a final resolution; community and democracy rather are constituted in our freedom to and willingness to test the degree of our agreement. This is not, however, a denial of the issue of our ability to test ourselves in this way today when political debate – or at least debate in general in the public sphere – seems to be characterized by division, aggression, misunderstanding (wilful or otherwise), driven by ideological rhetorics rather than reasoned debate. Drawing on Cavell, Kwak refers to the weakening of this agreement, in terms redolent of our current political debate: 'The weakening of community so pervasive in our daily life today is manifested in the crisis of our communication, and … the crisis of our communication threatens the authority my words hold for others to whom I speak' (Kwak 2010: 408).

From Cavell's account we gain a sense of community as something that is not visible, both in the sense that we find in, for example, active citizenship indicators or engagement with social media and in the sense that it is such a part of our everyday that we don't recognize it, at least perhaps not until a particular instance of its coming together or its dissolution. In drawing our attention to language, our partiality and our representativeness, Cavell helps us to bring out those mundane aspects of what it means to live in community that go unnoticed, either due to their mundanity or because they cannot be captured in metrics of societal well-being. He also warns what is at stake if the authority of our words, our very ability to speak representatively, is in crisis. In the moral perfectionist notion of democracy he offers, we also gain a sense of democratic community as always in the making, always still to come. By existing in a plurality of communities gathered around singular tastes we are immunized from the plurality – and partiality – of community.

In states of crisis, as we have seen, we hear the call for cohesion, and often the search for educational solutions: lack of political participation is a learning problem; political literacy is a learning problem; not conforming to Fundamental British Values is a learning problem. This is not to deny that education plays no part in the health of our democracy (the history of philosophy and philosophy of education is largely the pursuit of answers to the question of how it ought to do so). Rather, in the face of non-referential notions of community and citizenship, post-truth politics and a populism that derives its support from emotional appeals to fear, nostalgia and idealism, it seems time to question what we – as grown-ups, perhaps as academics – care about when we care about community, and just what we practise when we practise community philosophy.

Affirming community

As noted earlier, we still situate our notions of community in relation to modern reference points of state-society-individual (and arguably educational institutions are prominent reference points on this), even though teleological accounts, as we see in the historical understanding of self and nation state, do not currently shape the logic of governance (cf. Enroth 2014). They do however still hold some symbolic power when we try to make sense of apparently intractable issues. Cavell refers to 'the democratic need for perfection' and the state of holding one (individual, idea) as 'the height of the journey' (Cavell 1990: 9). Might it be that, so dominant is the association of community with cohesion and totality, and with the responsibility of state institutions for its surety, only now are we facing the realization, in some Western democracies – and writ large in the UK's current Brexistential crisis – that there is no 'height of the journey', to use Cavell's phrase? It is not only that changes in governmental rationality offer non-referential notions of community and citizenship (cf. Enroth 2014) but also that we need to come to terms with the notion that the sense of Western democracy we have inherited is, in fact, groundless without our willingness to invest in it, and in the name of democracy?

Latour proposes what he terms a more 'realist' politics that might offer a way out of binary, and state-centric, conceptions of community. In the reassessment of notions of public and private necessitated by sociopolitical change – from the decline of the welfare state, privatization, individualization and so on – a recasting of the notion of the public, beyond its public–private binary has been offered by the field of Science and Technology Studies, and most notably in the work of Latour. We have seen so far that the telos of the nation state, conceptualized around the state-society-individual triumvirate, no longer provides the reference point for postmodern governance (cf. Enroth 2014) but also that the critical responses to this, crucially radical as they were in the late twentieth century, have 'run out of steam' (Latour 2004). They no longer gain purchase on the way in which community is – and is not – constituted. Hence, Latour proposes – indeed made manifest through an art exhibition – a thing-centred politics: literally, a politics that gathers us around what matters. 'The general hypothesis is so simple that it might sound trivial – but being trivial might be part of what it is to become a "realist" in politics. We might be more connected to each other by our worries, our matters of concern, the issues we care for, than by any other set of values, opinions, attitudes or principles' (Latour 2005: 4).

Latour situates our desperation with the current political situation precisely in the transparency and openness with which governance works:

> Columnists, educators, militants never tire of complaining of a 'crisis of representation'. They claim that the masses seem no longer to feel at ease with what its elites are telling them. Politicians, they say, have become aloof, unreal, surrealistic, virtual and alien. An abysmal gap has opened between the 'political sphere' and the 'reality that people have to put up with' (ibid: 16).

The cynicism and distrust is a situation all too familiar in the wake of expenses scandals and austerity cuts. But the crisis may also be due, Latour suggests, to the promise of transparency: 'We are asking from representation something it cannot possibly give, namely representation *without* any *re*-presentation, without any provisional assertions, without any imperfect proof, without any opaque layers of translations, transmissions, betrayals, without any complicated machinery of assembly, delegation, proof, argumentation, negotiation and conclusion' (ibid; emphasis in original).

This is not an argument that politicians shouldn't be expected to tell the truth, or a claim that they don't anyway because we are in a post-truth era. Rather, it points to

52   *Philosophy and Community*

the impossibility of any representation ever being complete. Nor is this a depoliticizing move that only points us to a relativistic notion of truth. It is, however, a comment on the nature of knowledge and an acknowledgement that we have a responsibility for our democracy:

> There might be no continuity, no coherence in our opinions, but there is a hidden continuity and a hidden coherence in what we are attached to. Each object gathers around itself a different assembly of relevant parties. Each object triggers new occasions to passionately differ and dispute. Each object may also offer new ways of achieving closure without having to agree on much else. In other words, objects – taken as so many issues – bind all of us in ways that map out a public space profoundly different from what is usually recognized under the label of 'the political' (ibid: 5).

Rather than see Latour's conception as another ideal form against which to judge our current reality, I close this chapter by considering the instantiation of a thing-centred politics, as a gathering around shared concerns precisely in order to differ and dispute. We see this, arguably, in practices of community philosophy. While some such practices might be seen as instrumentalized by a university accountability system that requires 'engagement' and 'impact', they can be (less cynically) seen as a form of gathering that creates public space, discussion, the possibility to think about matters of concern. The traditional view might see philosophy as an elitist practice situated in universities, and in its disciplinary form this is partly correct. As I wrote at the beginning of this chapter, to think more broadly of philosophy as thinking, as an educative practice, borne in conversation, in which we put ourselves and our societies to the test of their own disappointments and ideals, we can see why philosophy is more likely to be found today among informal learning communities in bookshops, festivals, pubs and online than in the formal institution of the university (Evans 2012). It has, albeit through formal programmes, gathered people in conversation who ordinarily are the object of political or philosophical judgement, not involved in it themselves. Aislinn O'Donnell's work in prisons in Ireland provides a good illustration. Such programmes are not founded on a need to 'teach' philosophy for the moral improvement of those involved, but to talk and to think. Drawing on Jacques Rancière and Plato, O'Donnell states,

> My position is this: let's presuppose without evidence or justification that anyone can be a philosopher, and engage in dialogue and discussion on the basis of that presupposition. And let's also assume that everyone has the right to a philosophical and intellectual life and to be part of that long conversation and tradition. After all, everyone asks philosophical questions, even if they don't necessarily think philosophically about those questions (O'Donnell cited in Humphreys 2018).

It would be easy to offer a critical account of such programmes: they are aligned with government agendas and do their bidding for them, and again let them off the hook for the lack of cohesion and the issues that cause such tensions. In some cases, perhaps this is warranted, but that is not the focus here. These examples are drawn upon as an affirmation that people can and will speak together, in ways that acknowledge uncertainty, and so as a sign of hope in the present.

* * *

Notes

1 See: https://www.cbsnews.com/live-news/trump-primetime-address-to-nation-speech-announcement-border-wall-fight-government-shutdown-today/
2 See: http://ec.europa.eu/environment/beyond_gdp/index_en.html

References

Abowitz, K. K., (1999), 'Reclaiming Community', *Educational Theory*, 49 (2): 143–61.
Alexander, H. A., (2005), 'Moral Education and Liberal Democracy: Spirituality, Community, and Character in an Open Society', *Educational Theory*, 53 (4): 367–87.
Arthur, J., and Bailey, R., (2000), *Schools and Community: The Communitarian Agenda in Education*, London: Routledge.
Arthur, J., Davies, I., and Hahn, C., (2008), *SAGE Handbook of Education for Citizenship and Democracy*, London: Sage.
Barry, A., Osborne, T., and Rose, N., (eds), (1996), *Foucault and Political Reason: Liberalism, Neo-Liberalism and Rationalities of Government*, Chicago: University of Chicago Press.
Beck, U., (1992), *Risk Society: Towards a New Modernity*, London: Sage.
Biesta, G., (2009), 'What Kind of Citizenship for European Higher Education? Beyond the Competent Active Citizen', *European Educational Research Journal*, 8 (2): 146–58.
Burbules, N. C., and Rice, S., (1991), 'Dialogue Across Differences: Continuing the Conversation', *Harvard Educational Review*, 61 (4): 393–416.
Cameron, D., (2010), 'Big Society speech', [Online], Available at: https://www.gov.uk/g overnment/speeches/big-society-speech, Accessed 6 February 2019.
Cavell, S., (1979), *The Claim of Reason: Wittgenstein, Skepticism, Morality, and Tragedy*, New York: Oxford University Press.
Cavell, S., (1990), *Conditions Handsome and Unhandsome: The Constitution of Emersonian Perfectionism*, Chicago, IL: Chicago University Press.
Cavell, S., (2004), *Cities of Words: Pedagogical Letters on a Register of the Moral Life*, Cambridge: The Belknap Press of Harvard University Press.
Clarke, J., Gewirtz, S., and McLaughlin, E., (2000), *New Managerialism, New Welfare?*, London: Sage.
Delanty, G., (2003), 'Citizenship as a Learning Process: Disciplinary Citizenship Versus Cultural Citizenship', *International Journal of Lifelong Education*, 22 (6): 597–605.
Donzelot, J., and Estebe, P., (eds), (1994), *L'Etat Animateur: Essai sur la Politique de la Ville* [The animator state: Essays on the politics of the city], Paris: Esprit.
Emerson, R. W., (2003), *Selected Writings of Ralph Waldo Emerson*, ed. W. Gilman, New York: Penguin.

Enroth, H., (2014), 'Governance: The Art of Governing after Governmentality', *European Journal of Social Theory*, 17 (1): 60–76.

Evans, J., (2012), 'Connected Communities: Philosophical Communities, A report for the Arts and Humanities Research Council', [Online], Available at: https://philosophypa thways.com/download/Connected-Communities-Philosophical-Communities2.pdf, Accessed 6 February 2019.

Foucault, M., (1991), 'Governmentality', in G. Burchell, C. Gordon and P. Miller (eds), *The Foucault Effect: Studies in Governmentality*, 87–104, Chicago: University of Chicago Press.

Frazer, E., (2007), 'Depoliticizing Citizenship', *British Journal of Educational Studies*, 55 (3): 249–63.

Freire, P., (1993), *Pedagogy of the Oppressed*, London: Penguin.

Giddens, A., (1998), *The Third Way: The Renewal of Social Democracy*, Cambridge: Polity Press.

Giroux, H. A., (1999), 'Schools for Sale: Public Education, Corporate Culture, and the Citizen-Consumer', *The Educational Forum*, 63 (2): 140–9.

HM Government, (2018), *Integrated Communities Strategy Green Paper*, London: Ministry of Housing, Communities and Local Government.

Hodgson, N., (2016), *Citizenship for the Learning Society: Europe, Subjectivity, and Educational Research*, Oxford: Wiley.

Hodgson, N., (2018), 'The Entrepreneurial Subject', in P. Smeyers (ed.), *International Handbook of Philosophy of Education*, 1201–21, Dordrecht: Springer.

Hodgson, N., Vlieghe, J., and Zamojski, P., (2018), 'Education and the Love for the World: Articulating a Post-Critical Educational Philosophy', *Foro de Educación*, 16 (24): 7–20.

Hoskins, B., Jesinghaus, J., Mascherini, M., Munda, G., Nardo, M., Saisana, M., Van Nijlen, D., Vidoni, D., and Villalba, E., (2006), Measuring Active Citizenship in Europe. Luxembourg Office for Official Publications of the European Communities. [Online], Available at: https://ec.europa.eu/jrc/sites/jrcsh/files/jrc-coin-measuring-active-citizenship-2006_en.pdf, Accessed 6 February 2019.

Humphreys, J., (2018), 'Why we Need "Community Philosophy"', *The Irish Times*, 20 February 2018, [Online], Available at: https://www.irishtimes.com/culture/why-we-nee d-community-philosophy-1.3390995, Accessed 6 February 2019.

Kymlicka, W., (2005), 'Education for Citizenship', in J. M. Halstead and T. McLaughlin (eds), *Education in Morality*, 79–102, London: Routledge.

Kwak, D.-J., (2010), 'Teaching to Unlearn Community in Order to Make a Claim to Community', *Educational Theory*, 60 (4): 405–17.

Latour, B., (2004), 'Why Has Critique Run out of Steam? From Matters of Fact to Matters of Concern', *Critical Inquiry*, 30 (4): 225–48.

Latour, B., (2005), 'From Realpolitik to Dingpolitik: Or How to Make things Public', in B. Latour and P. Weibel (eds), *Making Things Public: Atmospheres of Democracy*, 4–31, Cambridge, MA: The MIT Press.

Lemke, T., (2001), '"The Birth of BioPolitics"– Michel Foucault's Lecture at the Collège de France on Neoliberal Governmentality', *Economy and Society*, 30 (2): 190–207.

Lyotard, J.-F., (1979), *The Postmodern Condition: A Report on Knowledge*, Manchester: Manchester University Press.

Masschelein, J., and Simons, M., (2002), 'An Adequate Education in a Globalised World? A Note on Immunisation Against Being-Together', *Journal of Philosophy of Education*, 36 (4): 589–608.

May, T., Prime Minister, (2019), 'PM's Brexit speech in Stoke-on-Trent: 14 January 2019', [Online], Available at: https://www.gov.uk/government/speeches/pms-brexit-speech-in-stoke-on-trent-14-january-2019, Accessed 6 February 2019.

McLaughlin, T., (1995), 'Liberalism, Education and the Common School', *Journal of Philosophy of Education*, 29 (2): 239–55.

Nisbet, R. A., (1953), *The Quest for Community*, New York: Oxford University Press.

Noddings, N., (1996), 'On Community', *Educational Theory*, 46 (3): 245–67.

Phelan, S., (1996), 'All the Comforts of Home: The Geneology of Community', in N. J. Hirschmann and C. DiStefano (eds), *Revisioning the Political: Feminist Reconstructions of Traditional Concepts in Western Political Theory*, 235–50, Boulder: Westview Press.

Ramaekers, S. and Hodgson, N., (forthcoming), 'Parenting Apps and the Depoliticisation of the Parent', in C. Faircloth and R. Rosen (eds), 'Childhood, Parenting Culture, and Adult-Child Relations in Transnational Perspectives', Special Issue of *Families, Relationships, and Society*.

Rose, N., (2000), 'Community, Citizenship, and the Third Way', *American Behavioural Scientist*, 43 (9): 1395–411.

Simons, M., and Hodgson, N., (2012), 'Learned Voices of European Citizens: From Governmental to Political Subjectivation', *Teoría de la Educación*, 24 (1): 19–40.

Simons, M., and Masschelein, J., (2008), 'From Schools to Learning Environments: The Dark Side of being Exceptional', *Journal of Philosophy of Education*, 42 (3–4): 687–704.

Tuschling, A., and Engemann, C., (2006), 'From Education to Lifelong Learning: The Emerging Regime of Learning in the European Union', *Educational Philosophy and Theory*, 38 (4): 451–69.

Walkerdine, V., and Studdert, D., (2012), *Concepts and Meanings of Community in the Social Sciences*, Discussion Paper, AHRC Connected Communities Programme.

4

Keeping the conversation going: A pragmatist assessment of the value of public philosophy

William C. Pamerleau

What is the value of public philosophy – that is, philosophical discussions undertaken by people not formally trained in philosophy? My own observations suggest that discussions in public philosophical forums do not usually end with much resolution of the issues at hand, nor are people likely to change their beliefs on substantive issues. So what good comes of it for the participants, and how might professional philosophers judge the value of this activity? I suggest that the pragmatist perspective can show us why public philosophy is indeed worthwhile and why it ought to be of interest to professional philosophers. In this chapter, I argue that pragmatism's anti-essentialist nature shows us the value of conversations that are not expected to discover the one right way of understanding things. Philosophers like John Dewey, but especially Richard Rorty, argue that these conversations broaden our individual perspectives while increasing our sensitivity to the humanity of others. They edify individuals and promote group solidarity, then, even if they aren't effective in problem-solving or reaching consensus, and that is reason enough to keep the conversations going.

Public philosophy

I will begin by relating my experiences with public philosophy. For about fifteen years I have been moderating a local chapter of Socrates Café, an international initiative begun by Christopher Phillips (2002) aimed at forming local philosophy discussion groups. The gathering I moderate meets monthly, with discussion based around a philosophical (or related) theme, usually articulated in the form of a question. Discussions I have recently moderated include 'What is art?', 'What is democracy?' and 'What is the value of honesty?' While politics and current events are popular topics (and conversations often get sidetracked on these issues), my goal is to pursue the ideas that underlie our taken-for-granted beliefs – that is, to get to discussants to become aware of and examine the deeper philosophical issues on which their practical concerns are based.

These meetings are not typically about analysing particular texts read in advance. They involve people stating their own views and challenging others. Often participants will cite the views of various authorities on a particular topic, but more often than not they are simply trying to explain and justify their own views, or to respond to the views of others. But the discussions are an opportunity not just to share ideas, but to explore *why* people hold the ideas that they do. A philosophical discussion, academic or public, has always been characterized by the desire to investigate the reasoning that supports a belief.

Since meetings are open to the public, they attract a wide spectrum of people from the local community, who differ widely in levels of education, sorts of work experience, political persuasion, religious views and so on. These differences mean that the conversation will go in many directions, reflecting different world views and values. Most have anecdotal experiences that inform their opinion, and these are often the most interesting contributions to the discussions.

The meetings almost always end without any resolution of the topic discussed, which is not surprising given that even professional philosophers have reached no consensus on these sorts of questions. And there is seldom any drastic change in anyone's position. At the end of a recent discussion, one of the participants blurted, 'Did anyone change their mind on any of this stuff? Of course not!' Despite differing opinions, however, it is understood that the nature of the discussion requires a willingness to let other speak and to treat them respectfully, which they usually do. Sometimes discussions get heated, but it never stoops to insults or name-calling. The prevailing understanding is that the discussion isn't about winning a debate, but about exploring perspectives. In fact, I believe this is the great value of a philosophical discussion as opposed to, say, a political debate: the focus is on the argument, or at least the perspective behind the belief, and is not a debate to see. The goal isn't to *win* but to *understand*.

There is a core number of people who return to these discussions, month after month. What is the attraction? I have often asked that question, and most of the time people reply that they like hearing what others have to say. They feel like they're learning something, though they may not be able to articulate just what they are learning (certainly not the answers to the questions that instigate the topic). In fact, some people regularly attend and say nothing the entire time. They simply like listening to others.

In sum, people show up, express a variety of opinions, examine a variety of arguments and explanations, pursue a fair number of unrelated tangents and finish with little convergence of views or increase in the level of agreement. But most are willing to return in a month and do it all again. These sorts of exchanges are what I refer to in the rest of the paper as 'public philosophy'. Again, it is philosophy, and not mere discussion, because the entire goal is to gain insight into the line of reasoning or perspective behind the beliefs that we either take for granted (if they are our own) or perhaps too hastily dismiss (if they are our opponents).

In addition to Socrates Café, I've also moderated similar discussions with student groups – meetings held outside of any particular class and open to all students and faculty. I've also engaged in open discussions as part of various public lectures, and to a lesser extent have followed online discussions. Much of what I have described earlier applies equally to these other forums, so while the characteristics I am

58 *Philosophy and Community*

attributing to public philosophy are based primarily on my own experiences that have emerged from Socrates Café, admittedly anecdotal in nature, I am reasonably sure it holds in many situations where the public engages in discussions on philosophical topics.

Is this endeavour worthwhile? I think the best perspective from which to appreciate the value of public philosophy is that of the pragmatists, whose views I next investigate.

Pragmatism and the value of conversation

In this section, I will explain the essentials of pragmatism with regard to its relevance to public philosophy. I will begin with arguably the most important figure in the pragmatist tradition, John Dewey, but I devote more attention to Richard Rorty, whose nuanced views on conversation are particularly relevant to the issue at hand.

The classical pragmatists, especially Charles Sanders Peirce, William James and John Dewey, sought to critique various assumptions within the tradition of philosophy and offer a new way forward for a discipline they viewed as having lost its way. They believed that the tradition's search for truth, particularly as it was embodied in rationalist philosophers like Descartes, was overly abstracted from real-world concerns and irrelevant to our lives. Instead, philosophers like Peirce and Dewey thought we should take a lesson from the comparative success of science in retooling philosophy to solve real-world problems. They suggested we develop an experimental method by which we establish beliefs, keeping our thinking rooted firmly in consequences. Just as with a scientific theory, our values and beliefs ought to be seen as fallible and open to revision based on how well they actually serve us in understanding the world and improving it. Dewey notes,

> But what serious-minded men not engaged in philosophy most want to know is what modifications and abandonments of intellectual inheritance are required by the newer industrial, political, and scientific movements. ... Unless professional philosophy can mobilize itself sufficiently to assist in this clarification and redirection of men's thoughts, it is likely to get more and more sidetracked from the main currents of contemporary life (Dewey 1917: 4).

In his social philosophy, Dewey was committed to democracy: 'Regarded as an idea, democracy is not an alternative to other principles of associated life. It is the idea of community life itself' (Dewey 1927: 328). And in the Western world of the twentieth century Dewey found democracy to be compromised by increasing social isolation and professional specialization, which were undermining a communal understanding of our condition and its possible solutions. He wanted to restore connections by allowing us to talk to one another again – to allow our specialized knowledges to inform one another and coordinate goals and actions.

Not only does conversation help restore community, but, according to Dewey, the participants themselves are able to enlarge their experience. He refers to these exchanges as 'genuine conversations' and notes that the effect of the conversation isn't due to the outcome – it's due to the conversation itself:

> In genuine conversation the ideas of one are corrected and changed by what others say; what is confirmed is not his previous notions, which may have been narrow and ill-formed, but his capacity to judge wisely. ... Even if previous ideas are in the main confirmed, yet in the degree in which there is genuine mutual give and take they are seen in a new light, deepened and extended in meaning, and there is the enjoyment of enlargement of experience, of growth of capacity (Dewey 1994: 190).

But for Dewey, pragmatism also has the potential to provide tangible results to our most pressing problems. I think Robert Frega's interpretation of Dewey's vision of inquiry gets to the essential point: 'The idea of political inquiry as collaborative practice aimed at solving problems emerging in the course of associated life offers the preliminary basis for a pragmatist theory of public reason' (Frega 2010: 48). A key point here is the idea of 'practice aimed at solving problems': the idea is to correct our beliefs and activities as we see their effectiveness in action. The pragmatist philosopher can contribute by articulating the method, goals and means, but Dewey had hoped that adoption of this method in the public realm would lead to real changes in what people believed and did.

Richard Rorty's contemporary pragmatism is more sweeping in its indictment of traditional philosophy and less optimistic about what pragmatism can deliver. Like Dewey, he emphasized the need for conversation, but he did not think that discourse would necessarily, or likely, result in common understandings and values through which we could move in unison towards solving problems. Conversation is nevertheless valuable, for Rorty, both because of the sort of benefits Dewey describes as 'genuine conversation' and for reasons of his own that I will soon explain.

Rorty's principal attack on the tradition of philosophy stems from a rejection of the correspondence theory of truth and the resulting anti-essentialism. Words and sentences do not neatly map onto an external world in a one-to-one correspondence that would make them true. That means there is no one way of talking about the world that is the true picture of reality. Following James's more holistic approach, Rorty asserts, 'There are no essences anywhere in the area. There is no wholesale, epistemological way to direct, or criticize, or underwrite, the course of inquiry' (Rorty 1982: 162). What we have instead are various vocabularies – a way of defining, explaining and making sense of things. Some vocabularies are developed by scientists, others by social policy makers, others by philosophers investigating the meaning of life and so on. But none of these correspond to the world as it is in itself, since language just is not the sort of thing that *can* correspond to some non-linguistic reality. We adopt vocabularies because they *work*; they help us cope with the world, not because they are *true*. Of course, different vocabularies work for different situations: we want to use the vocabulary of the medical doctor in addressing a physical ailment and not that of the artist, because the former works better for the issue at hand (and not because it describes reality better).

The task of philosophy, on pragmatist grounds, should not be to discover the single best vocabulary, then, but to expand our current vocabularies or be open to new ones. In the early work *Philosophy and the Mirror of Nature*, Rorty describes the latter goal of philosophy as 'edification', the 'project of finding new, better, more interesting, more fruitful ways of speaking' (Rorty 1979: 360). Like Dewey's genuine conversation, Rorty suggests that we become more effective at developing our ability to enlarge our own possibilities as well as become sensitive to the plights of others through open-minded discourse. This, and not the search for essences or metaphysical foundations, ought to be the business of philosophy. 'To see keeping a conversation going as a sufficient aim of philosophy, to see wisdom as consisting in the ability to sustain a conversation, is to see human beings as generators of new descriptions rather than beings one hopes to be able to describe accurately' (ibid: 378).

In a more recent work, Rorty gives a nuanced examination of the different perspectives people bring with them to conversations. He notes that everyone has a 'final vocabulary': 'The set of words which [human beings] employ to justify their actions, their beliefs, and their lives' (Rorty 1989: 73). Final vocabularies aren't final in the sense that we're done developing vocabularies and this one is the best; they're final in the sense that we don't know how to do better, at present. 'Those words are as far as he can go with language; beyond them there is only helpless passivity or a resort to force' (ibid). 'Ironists' doubt that their final vocabulary is better than others or that their final vocabulary is closer to reality than others. ('Ironists' is used in this later work in lieu of 'pragmatists', but it is a continuation of the same position Rorty had previously ascribed to pragmatism.) They see their vocabulary as contingent, that it could have been otherwise had they been differently socialized, and they are therefore wary of judging others. The contrary of irony is 'common sense' – those who take their final vocabulary for granted and are comfortable judging others from within it. Ironists do not think that there is a vocabulary out there that corresponds to reality, and so they don't try to 'infer' whose view is more rational or truer than another's; instead their method is 'redescription', by which they seek to replace one description with another that works better (ibid: 78). Ironists, therefore, are opposed to common sense, on the one hand, and a traditional form of philosophy which seeks a theoretical grounding of our views, on the other. One can imagine the value of having public discussions populated by ironists, then, who will tolerate and even welcome discussion with those who offer different vocabularies. As I will discuss in the next section, this may turn out to be an issue for public philosophy as I've described it earlier, since many of the discussants are decidedly not ironists.

One final point that will have a bearing on the discussion later in this section stems from Rorty's insistence, in his later works, that philosophizing under the assumption that there is a single best vocabulary for understanding the world should be relegated to the private sphere. We may want to pursue that kind of philosophy for our own, private benefit. But our public policies, specifically those regarding a free and open democracy, should have no such theoretical grounding, and Rorty thinks we need none. In the Western world, we all already share the conviction that democracy is the best form of social organization, a conviction shaped by our cultural history.

We are committed to democracy because we know of no other arrangement that works better (Rorty 1991: 175–7). In fact, we should avoid seeking any philosophical basis for democracy, including pragmatism, because democracy is better off without a theoretical grounding. If we do insist on such grounding, then we create the possibility that democracy can lose its legitimacy if the theory does, and worse, the theory can be used as a source of tyranny and exclusion with respect to those who do not agree with it. The public sphere, then, should be based only on a sense of solidarity with other human beings, which amounts to little more than saying that we should avoid cruelty, humiliation and exclusion. It should not be 'justified' on the basis of any one best vocabulary. In addition to the anti-essentialist views that emerge from Rorty's critique of the correspondence theory of truth, this refusal to insist on a theoretical grounding for democracy furthers the position that there is no one way of arbitrating disagreements, no method or criteria for measuring whose arguments are best. We just have to let these conversations play out and see what comes from them, and our justification for doing so is simply that we know of no better conditions to produce helpful vocabularies than the ideally uncoerced conversations that constitute democracy.

Many have pointed out difficulties with Rorty's public–private distinction, however. As Andrew Smith has argued, and I think he is right, some forms of discourse that Rorty would delegate to the private sphere can help the public conversations along by showing how intellectual traditions might be impeding the goal of solidarity. Pragmatism itself is one of them, according to Smith: unlike other forms of philosophical discourse, it doesn't favour a single best vocabulary. More importantly, pragmatists might also encourage the emergence of 'prophets' who 'engender social hope' that the future can be better than the past (Smith 2014: 161). And these prophets, particularly well exemplified by feminist philosophers, can help us expand our sense of who is being excluded and new ways of understanding each other, thereby enlarging our community and averting the erosion of solidarity. That makes them useful for the conversation even if Rorty would relegate them to the private sphere. 'The pragmatist therefore aims to assist the prophet to develop both a common vision with regard to our hope for the future and a sense of how to refashion our practices and institutions to achieve it' (ibid: 165–6). That means that intellectual pursuits in the private sphere can expand the scope of our sense of solidarity, positively impacting the basis of the public sphere. Tracey Llanera makes a very similar point: 'It is thus incoherent for Rorty to valorize the divide between the private and the public, particularly when he admits that their interaction is critical for human development' (Llanera 2016: 326).

To sum up this issue: Rorty thinks that public conversations that ground our political views must rest on a shared sense of solidarity and not on any single vocabulary or theory, in order to keep the public free from the tyranny of a particular vocabulary. He concludes, then, that we should relegate discussions about such vocabularies to the private sphere. This might be at odds with the sort of public philosophy I described in the previous section, since discussants certainly do bring their own theories to the discussion. But as Smith and Llanera point out, Rorty fails to recognize that some of those views can help foster solidarity. Furthermore, as we will see in the next section,

62 *Philosophy and Community*

the dynamics of these public distinctions mitigate much of Rorty's concern: their inherent diversity and disconnection from direct public policy creation insulate them from the consequences he fears.

The value of public philosophy

Public discussants versus public discussion

I began this chapter by inquiring about the value of public philosophy, both for its participants and for professional philosophers. We are now in a position to answer those questions. But first of all we must characterize the nature of public philosophy in light of the discussion of pragmatism.

There are two perspectives to keep in mind: that of each individual participant in a public philosophy conversation, and that of the interaction as a whole – the discussion itself. From the perspective of the individual discussants, I think it's fair to assume a thorough pluralism with regard to their epistemic expectations. Some participants are what Rorty would consider ironists – those who are willing to entertain beliefs while realizing their contingency and non-privileged status. Some embrace what Rorty calls common sense – they think their final vocabulary is the best and have no qualms judging others from its perspective. Most, however, embrace a degree of contingency without being full-blown ironists – they admit a certain degree of fallibility and recognize cultural conditioning while still thinking their own final vocabulary has an advantage over others. In short, discussants enter conversations with different final vocabularies and different expectations about the effectiveness of those vocabularies. But they also *know* that others differ from themselves in this way. Newcomers to Socrates Café, for example, quickly learn to expect different sorts of responses from different participants. They know that they are separated by some fundamental differences in their final vocabularies (though obviously they would not express that fact in those terms). That means they know they are going to be unlikely to find a way of arbitrating disagreements that all will find acceptable: there is no agreed upon measure of right. I argue, then, that while the discussants may themselves be diverse, the discussion effectively conforms to the pragmatist description of what constitutes public conversation. Even if the discussants think there is a right way to think about the world, most will acknowledge that the public discussion cannot deliver it, because the discussion isn't playing by any one person's set of rules or criteria. Even if participants outside of the discussion usually interact with groups or media sources that bolster their own final vocabulary, they know they cannot expect that from the public philosophy discussion because of its diversity of opinion. In short, the discussion has no common metaphysical or epistemological bases, even if the individuals participating in it do have strong convictions.

Discussants have no qualms about grounding their public discussion in views that Rorty thinks should be relegated to the private sphere (e.g. specific religious beliefs). How should this element of Rorty's position affect our appraisal of public philosophy?

First of all, I tend to agree with philosophers like Smith and Llanera that Rorty's split between the public and the private is too severe, that solidarity-building attitudes can blossom from private intellectual pursuits. But the purpose of public philosophy discussions is not to establish policies or provide for them a theoretical foundation; they serve to benefit the self-understanding of the discussants. The fact that they are inefficacious is a virtue here: there's no fear that out of these discussions will arise a theoretical grounding for public, democratic practices that might become a tyranny, determining who has the right thinking about society and whose voice must be silenced, which is the real fear driving Rorty's insistence on the separation between the public and private.

Why converse?

Having articulated the nature of public philosophy in pragmatist terms, we are now in a position to consider the value of these discussions. I will first approach this from the perspective of professional philosophy, which will give us the conceptual means to understand the value of public philosophy to the non-professional discussants themselves.

Whether you think something valuable will come from public philosophical discussions depends largely on what you think philosophy itself is capable of. I will consider three positions: non-pragmatist philosophers who think philosophy is about discovering answers to metaphysical and epistemological queries, pragmatists in the Deweyan tradition that expect philosophy to solve problems and generate a communal will, and pragmatists like Rorty who think that keeping the conversation going is reason enough to pursue a decidedly post-metaphysical form of philosophy. These are, of course, points along a continuum, and I do not claim to have canvassed the opinions of all professional philosophers. My purpose is simply to highlight the appeal of the pragmatist position as set against a more traditional form of philosophy.

If you are a philosopher who does champion the traditional view – that philosophy ought to be about discovering essences or first-principles or, at least, determining the best possible theory – you may well decide that public philosophy is useless. This might be the view of those who maintain something like the Enlightenment's expectation of the power of philosophy, the way Descartes did; but even Peirce himself, considered a founder of pragmatism, argued that a science-minded approach to philosophical inquiry would produce a convergence of belief – the one best picture of reality (Peirce 2000: 74). Public philosophy would seem a waste of time, from this perspective. Discussions advance on a topic and then recede before any resolution is achieved. Tangents are frequent. The discussants often do not even agree on the questions being asked, let alone the means by which they can be answered. In short, if you're looking for fruitful conclusions to the conversations – a theoretically viable answer to the question on the table, the nature of the discussion would make it seem extremely unlikely that the endeavour will end successfully.

If you're a pragmatist, your view will be considerably different. Since you don't think that philosophy is about finding enduring answers, that there is no one best vocabulary to be discovered, then the fact that a conversation about philosophy holds little promise of finding one is no immediate count against it.

Let's first consider Dewey's view. I think in one way Dewey would approve of the practice of public philosophy, and in another he would find it lacking. He would approve of it to the degree to which it is a genuine conversation, and there are many ways in which it is. Recall that Dewey thinks this conversation, even if it doesn't change minds, results in deepening and extending understanding, and 'there is the enjoyment of enlargement of experience, of growth of capacity' (Dewey 1994: 190). When I ask people why they come to Socrates Café it is usually for this reason: that it benefits their understanding of why people think the way they do, to understand where people are coming from. This is perhaps the most important value of philosophical conversations, both public and academic, the insight into *where people are coming from* intellectually. In other forms of discourse, say political or legal discourse, the discussants have as their goal to make their view prevail – that is, to win the argument. They may not much care why others think the way they do, nor are they particularly keen on a critical investigation of their own views. But in philosophical discourse the goal is to understand why people think the way they do, and in public contexts like Socrates Café there is no expectation that one side will win, be proved right, or have the final word. It is this increase in understanding the self and others that I think Dewey has in mind when he refers to 'enlargement of experience', and it is what Rorty has in mind in his earlier work when he refers to philosophy as 'edification'. But Dewey sometimes talks as if he wants more from discourse. He wants us to overcome separations that keep us from being an integrated community and to *effectively* pursue the problems that face us as such a community. His problem with the tradition of philosophy was that it proposed values and beliefs that were irrelevant to the problems we face. He considered pragmatism a way to make philosophy more efficacious, and the inability of public philosophy to unite us into a common, democratic will might have irked him. For example, Dewey thought it was vital to consider the physical means of achieving our goals while we are determining what those goals are – that we cannot shape ideals apart from careful attention to the real-world conditions that they seek to inform. 'The ineffectiveness in action of "ideals" is due precisely to the supposition that means and ends are not on exactly the same level with respect to the attention and care they demand' (Dewey 1929: 279). Public philosophy is decidedly not grounded in a mindful consideration of material conditions, at least not in any systematic way.

But it shouldn't surprise us that a public philosophy discussion lacks a grounding in empirical study or that it doesn't solve problems. It's not intended to. It's intended to be *only* a conversation, not a policy meeting. Might it be expanded to provide more substantive conversation, *results-oriented* conversation? Perhaps, but there is no institutional arrangement for such discussions currently. John Stuhr has pointed out that the reception of Dewey's pragmatism is dependent upon causes lying outside of philosophy, not inside of it. 'Dewey noted that any pragmatic reconstruction of philosophy, like any broader pragmatic reconstruction of culture, requires a cultural climate unfavorable to old traditions, value, and attitudes, and instead favorable to new experiment and experience and many maybes' (Stuhr 2003: 177). In the current political climate throughout much of the globe, the trend seems towards more sectarianism and a staunch defence of tradition; and social media, along with the rise of politically aligned news sources and internet sites, only fuels these flames. Stuhr, reading Dewey, thinks that society has to meet pragmatism halfway before it can be realized, and it seems doubtful that our society is ready to embrace the main suppositions of pragmatism on the institutional level in the foreseeable future.

So if there is a value to public philosophy, it looks like we're stuck with the conversation itself. This makes Rorty's position an attractive one as a means of recognizing this value, since Rorty so thoroughly undermines the effectiveness of philosophy to produce anything more than effective conversations. But there are strong objections to Rorty's view that philosophers must be content with the conversation itself, and it's important to consider whether they undermine his views on this issue.

Among the strongest criticisms of Rorty's position is that he sets up a false dichotomy between an untenable, essentialist philosophy, on the one hand, and the sort of free conversation described earlier, on the other. Susan Haack describes the dichotomy as follows: 'The characteristic stamp of Rorty's This-or-Nothingism: either we accept this particular composite, a certain conception of the role of philosophy within culture, of the role of epistemology within philosophy, of the role of "foundations" within the structure of knowledge, this "neo-Kantian consensus", or we jettison the whole lot and take "carrying on the conversation" as our highest aspiration' (Haack 1995: 127). Haack claims that there are other options, and she offers a number of ways to classify epistemological positions between these options that do not fall victim to Rorty's anti-essentialist arguments. Her critique goes beyond the scope of this chapter, but if she is right, then professional philosophers need not resort to merely carrying on the conversation; they have a basis to continue pursuit of theoretical grounds for belief.

Frank Farrell attacks Rorty on a related point, arguing that merely comparing vocabularies without a connection to how those vocabularies relate to the real world robs vocabularies of a grounding in the world which most of us do, in fact, assume to be the case. 'For when we examine our discourse in detail according to the criterion of usefulness, the everyday realist vocabulary seems very useful indeed, useful enough to have survived very well the Darwinian clash of vocabularies in history. So as a non-philosophical pragmatist, he ought to be a realist without qualms' (Farrell 1995: 164).

Rorty has replied to Farrell's argument by insisting that it is his (Rorty's) position that is being unfairly characterized here. He does not deny that the world impacts what we believe, only that we cannot specify how the connection takes place in a way that would reveal direct connections between the world and our claims about it, couched as they are in a historicized vocabulary (Rorty 1995: 194).

However, I do not think we need be overly concerned about these objections to professional philosophy when considering the value of public philosophy, to which we can now turn our attention. If Rorty is right, then professional philosophers are more likely to agree that carrying on the conversation is important, for it will be all that is left. However, if he is wrong, then philosophers can pursue a deeper philosophical grounding to their beliefs with an easy conscience, but that doesn't discredit Rorty's points about the benefits of conversation as described earlier. Rorty's views may offer us a way to appreciate the value of public philosophy *whether or not* he is successful in his critique of professional philosophy.

Let me develop this point. In my reading of Rorty, he is offering us two things: (i) a critique of philosophy as an academic discipline – the business of the professional philosopher – and (ii) an argument for the value of keeping conversations going both in and out of academia, even where it might lack any possible closure such as demonstrating the right answer, reaching a consensus or determining the one best way to understand a position. Certainly, the success of the first makes it much easier to appreciate the second. But what if we reject the first and insist that Rorty has not demonstrated our inability to get substantive solutions to problems in metaphysics and epistemology? Would that affect his argument that there is value in keeping the conversations going when they have no expectation of resolution? I think not. Even if professional philosophers expect their conversations will get somewhere or solve some issues, it could still be the case that we can appreciate *public* philosophy for all the things Rorty says of conversation. You wouldn't expect it to be efficacious qua philosophy, but you might agree that it has value for the participants because it 'enlarges experience' or 'edifies'. That's why I think it's important to note that public philosophical discussion *effectively* takes a pragmatic position. If you think Rorty's pragmatism is wrong with regard to the purpose of philosophy as a discipline, you can still admit that Rorty has a point about the value of conversations which cannot hope to achieve resolution about the issues they discuss.

In claiming that Rorty's views best allow us to appreciate the value of public philosophy, I do not by any means claim that public philosophy as I have been describing it constitutes Rorty's ideal form of conversation. Note, for example, his description of how people would converse in his 'liberal utopia'. (Note also that 'liberal' here does not refer to the left-leaning political ideology sense of 'liberal'. Rorty is using the term in its classic sense to refer to societies that insure a large private sphere in which people can pursue their concept of the good without imposition from public institutions.) 'To sum up, the citizens of my liberal utopia would be people who had a sense of the contingency of their language of moral deliberation, and thus of their consciences, and thus of their community ... people who combined commitment with a sense of the contingency of their own commitment' (Rorty 1989: 61). But as I pointed out earlier, the individuals who engage in public philosophy are not necessarily cognizant of the contingency of their language or values. In fact, Rorty himself has pointed out that 'metaphysics is woven into the public rhetoric of modern liberal societies' (ibid: 87). People *do* argue by reference to what are for them religious or ethical absolutes, and sometimes there is even some degree of mild coercion which detracts from the positive aspects of the conversation. However, a utopian ideal is, of course, ideal, and as such is not likely to ever exist. The fact that public philosophy isn't ideal shouldn't distract us from its strengths. As mentioned earlier, its members do perceive the plurality of views and the fact that their own views are not granted special status by the other participants, which, to point out once more, makes it essentially pragmatic in character even if the individuals within it are sometimes absolutist adherents of 'common sense'. In addition to the enlargement of perspective of those individuals as the result of hearing how others might offer alternatives or critiques of their final vocabularies, such discussions bolster solidarity, according to Rorty. As participants in such a discussion, we come to see the humanity in the views of those that we might have dismissed as 'other'. In fact, in a social environment throughout much of the world where political discourse is perceived in terms of winning and losing, and political opponents are caricatured and perceived as other, an opportunity for people to come together to exchange views and examine arguments simply for the sake of learning what others have to say – and not to win the argument or secure your advantage – offers a refreshing reprieve from the predominant political discourse. Public philosophy forums, I would contend, are one of the few places that actually encourage the growth of solidarity among thinking persons who disagree with one another on core issues.

Finally, if one *is* a pragmatist, there is a value to public philosophy beyond admitting that it's good for its participants. We can learn from them what their concerns are, how they think about important issues, what they count as reasons for or against some position and what they don't – and so on. If Dewey's hopes that pragmatism can make a difference are justified – if there is ever a chance that we can shape institutions in the way he envisions – then we must understand the means and methods of achieving goals. Surely understanding how people are thinking is important in understanding what is needed to inform public opinion and to promote community in a divided society. Listening to how people converse in public philosophical forums then becomes an important source of information. And it goes without saying that philosophers who want to join the public discussion can offer means of contextualizing, clarifying and offering new ways of discussing topics that can move those discussions forward in positive ways.

In sum, the reality of public philosophy is that it is generally ineffective in offering concrete solutions to the topics discussed. But pragmatists show us why the conversation itself holds value. Even non-pragmatist philosophers should appreciate that Dewey and Rorty demonstrate the value of *public* philosophy, even if they think that their professional discourse can do more. Either way, I hope to have provided justification for why professional philosophers should support keeping this conversation of public philosophy going – perhaps even joining it themselves.

References

Dewey, J., (1917), 'The Need for A Recovery of Philosophy', in J. Dewey (ed.), *Creative Intelligence: Essays in the Pragmatic Attitude*, 3–69, New York: Holt.
Dewey, J., (1927), *The Public and Its Problems*, Athens, OH: Swallow Press.
Dewey, J., (1929), *The Quest for Certainty*, New York: Minton Balch.
Dewey, J., (1994), *The Moral Writings of John Dewey*, ed. J. Gouinlock, New York: Prometheus Books.
Farrell, F., (1995), 'Rorty and Antirealism', in H. Saatkamp, Jr (ed.), *Rorty and Pragmatism: The Philosopher Responds to His Critics*, 154–88, Nashville: Vanderbilt University Press.
Frega, R., (2010), 'What Pragmatism means by Public Reason', *Etica & Politica/Ethics & Politics*, XII: 28–51.

Haack, S., (1995), 'Vulgar Pragmatism: An Unedifying Prospect', in H. Saatkamp, Jr (ed.), *Rorty and Pragmatism: The Philosopher Responds to His Critics*, 126–47, Nashville: Vanderbilt University Press.

Llanera, T., (2016), 'Redeeming Rorty's Private-Public Distinction', *Contemporary Pragmatism*, 13: 319–40.

Peirce, C., (2000), 'The Fixation of Belief', in J. Stuhr (ed.), *Pragmatism and Classical American Philosophy*, 2nd edn, 67–76, New York: Oxford University Press.

Phillips, C., (2002), *Socrates Café*, New York: W. W. Norton & Company.

Rorty, R., (1979), *Philosophy and the Mirror of Nature*, Oxford: Blackwell.

Rorty, R., (1982), *Consequences of Pragmatism*, Minneapolis: University of Minnesota Press.

Rorty, R., (1989), *Contingency, Irony, and Solidarity*, Cambridge: Cambridge University Press.

Rorty, R., (1991), *Objectivity, Relativism, and Truth: Philosophical Papers*, Cambridge: Cambridge University Press.

Rorty, R., (1995), 'Response by Rorty', in H. Saatkamp, Jr (ed.), *Rorty and Pragmatism: The Philosopher Responds to His Critics*, 189–96, Nashville: Vanderbilt University Press.

Smith, A., (2014), 'Solidarity as Public Morality', *Contemporary Pragmatism*, 11 (1): 153–70.

Stuhr, J. J., (2003), *Pragmatism, Postmodernism and the Future of Philosophy*, London: Routledge.

5

Community Philosophy and social action

Graeme Tiffany

Introduction

In describing the development of Community Philosophy in Chapter 1 of this volume, Steve Bramall compares Community Philosophy with Philosophy for Children (P4C). While both practices might engage with the concept of action, he suggests that action is a specific intention of Community Philosophy, and the same cannot be said of P4C.

Bramall is careful in suggesting the need for an expansive account of 'action', including even the simple act of 'changing one's mind'. Likewise, I'd say, 'Talking *is* a form of action', in a deliberate attempt to push back at the popular adage that suggests otherwise. In this sense we might say dialogue is a prerequisite of the thinking that propels action.

This chapter aims to develop this account, by considering particularly the role Community Philosophy plays (and might play) in imagining, informing and catalysing the wider notion of 'social action'.

A starting point is to recognize that relatively little has been written about Community Philosophy, at least in comparison to P4C. Of course, this book seeks to address this issue. We might conclude Community Philosophy is relatively new, whereas the history of P4C, from its origins in the work of Matthew Lipman in the 1960s and 1970s (see also Lipman 1991), is both well developed and well documented. And yet, accounts of 'social action'-oriented work predate both, having long been an important part of the lexicon of community workers, including youth workers, adult educators and social workers (Twelvetrees 2017). Such references tend to mark these social practitioners as 'radical' and 'progressive' and as 'political actors' (Alinsky 1971; Coady 1980; Lovett 1988; Thompson 1980), whereas other educators – typically school teachers – are cast more in a neutral light. In the interpretation of these practices, the emphasis is typically on 'action': it is this that shapes it as political. It is much less common for the 'social' to be ascribed political value, which is precisely what I want to do here.

'Social' is a relational concept, which implies a moral and ethical context. Therein, social action is a process in which groups of people (rather than individuals) engage, to determine what might, could and should be done, whether through informal or bureaucratic means. It is the social that renders it political, albeit in the broadest sense

70   *Philosophy and Community*

of the word – politics with a small 'p', as some may say. This further invokes questions about participation and democracy, which are particularly pertinent to Community Philosophy.

Philosophy and social action: Freedoms and constraints

Community Philosophy emerged as a critical response to a number of issues identified by informal and community educators and community development workers interested in the practices of P4C, and those of (the much less common) Philosophy for Communities and Philosophy *with* Communities movements. A concern for participation and democracy motivated much of the work undertaken by many in developing Community Philosophy.

We might start with what's implied by the word 'with'. It would seem to suggest a more concerted commitment to the development of a participatory culture, even though P4C and Philosophy for Communities are routinely articulated in participatory terms. In linking participatory practices to social action (or at least the potential for social action) it becomes necessary to evaluate the claims made about working in a participatory way. Here, geography provides a tool for analysis, in the sense of the freedoms and constraints engendered by the space in which philosophical practices occur. We might think of 'institutional' and 'non-institutional' settings, and appreciate then the profound distinction between places of formal education (in the case of P4C, typically schools) and the myriad sites of informal and community education, from cafés and community centres to the street, and so on.

Obviously enough, these spaces function differently. Whereas (albeit with the notable exception of those home-schooled) children and young people have to go to school (which in turn validates curriculum-based models of learning), no such compulsion exists in non-institutional settings, either to be present or to engage in the activities organized therein. The context is one of voluntary association: what happens, by necessity, is subject to negotiation. Conversely, those seeking to develop philosophical practices in institutional settings are constrained not just by the compulsory context, but also by its practical manifestations (which are both geographical and temporal in character). Think of the symbolic effect of walls, and contrast this with the provocation provided by French street social workers, who deliberately aim to work '*sans murs*' – without walls.

These thematics provide a further and important contrast: institutional contexts tend to have defined spatial boundaries and prescribed temporalities. The most obvious example is, again, school, which is typically understood as a building, with a regimen of time, from the 'school day' to defined lesson times. For those working in non-institutional settings, practices are much more fluid in terms of time, the epitome of which is street-based youth work and social work, which both tend to happen *when* clients need it. Practitioners in these fields also aim to be geographically mobile; they move around, in view of the fact that those with whom they seek to engage and work are similarly mobile. For them, effective practice relies on flexibility; it needs to be as free of constraint as possible. As such, it is described as 'low threshold': everything possible is done to make the workers, and therefore the services they offer, accessible and so remove barriers to engagement.

The parallels with social action are obvious: for it to be possible, the context in which it sits needs to be as free of constraint as possible. Equally, the fact that P4C is so often physically and temporally bounded, and Community Philosophy is often not, raises questions beyond the possibility of philosophy-inspired social action: How can the value claims of such practices, whether to equality, social justice or democracy, be realized; and, practically, what form should these practices take for social action to become possible in the first place?

What follows is an attempt to chart the emergence of Community Philosophy based on my own experience, and that of Community Philosophers with whom I have worked. I am well aware others have done similar things: see, for example, Evans and Dixon's wide-ranging review of grass-roots philosophy (2012). And yet my aim here is to expand on the notion of Community Philosophy-inspired social action and to show how thinking about the issues raised above has informed its practice. I am selective on this basis alone. The examples given will consider constraints, challenges and the conditions necessary to advance the values identified. Philosophically inspired pedagogies and methodologies are given particular prominence, as is the argument that all philosophical practices need to be grounded in a wider conceptualization of democratic practice. This prompts wider observations, about what might influence change at a local, societal (and perhaps even global) level.

I hope all this has resonance for other educators and social practitioners in its conclusion that the theory and practice of Community Philosophy 'shines a light' on substantive questions in the philosophy of education, and especially those relating to education for equality, social justice and democracy.

Community philosophy: Background and borrowings

In 1994, having been influenced by my experience of working with the Adult Learning Project (ALP)[1] in Edinburgh, Scotland, I wrote a paper for the National Institute of Adult and Continuing Education (NIACE) (Tiffany 1994a). On an occasional basis, NIACE produced special editions, in this case dedicated to 'Young Adults Learning'. The paper described efforts to create and employ a practice, inspired by Paulo Freire, in youth work settings. Of concern at the time (and a concern I hold to this day) was to create an educational experience that did not invoke the response: 'It's like school.' I can say with conviction that, as a youth worker, I have rarely worked with young people for whom such a statement implied something good. I have always wondered what it is about school that leads to such negativity among so many.

To my mind, the crux of the matter then (and now) is the lack of a participative culture, in which young people have at least some power to inform decisions as to what, and how, they learn. So often they are cast as consumers of education, rather than creators or co-creators of learning. Mark Smith's seminal little book *Creators and*

Consumers (1982) undoubtedly influenced generations of youth workers, as did Freire's work. The premise is clear, and teased out in Jeffs and Smith's (1990, 1999) defence of working without the framework of a 'curriculum', at least in the sense of a 'course to be run'[2] (i.e. determined by others).

Inspired by my experience of working at ALP, I designed a range of Freire-influenced, question-focused methodologies for use in my work with young people. I was struck by how often those who experienced them stated, appreciatively, 'We never get asked questions like this at school.' Indeed, some said they never got asked questions at all. However, there were more than a few who were sceptical about the process: these young people seemed to think this was just another form of the manipulation they believed they had been subjected to in school. This became apparent to me when, having offered the young people the opportunity to decide upon questions about an image I presented to them (obtained from a friend who, as a photo-journalist, took pictures for the local newspaper), they queried the choice of image. I realized that despite the freedom extended to 'ask anything' they sensed that there was something 'going on'.

Smith's influence on my and other youth workers' practice was such that we aimed to treat young people's perceptions respectfully, as forms of truth. I resolved to offer multiple images and invite a choice of these in advance of any discussion about the questions we might explore. I placed thirty or so photographs face down on the floor and asked the group to select one of them. That I had to do this to demonstrate I wasn't trying to manipulate them seemed extraordinary, but necessary given the extent of their negative experiences. I became even more convinced that what I have since called a 'generative phase' is essential in Community Philosophy; that simply being involved in generating the questions to be enquired into is, in and of itself, a form of social action.

The same can be said of talking. Community Philosophy contests the criticism: 'all talk and no action'. Voicing, and testing, our ideas and aspirations – in conversation – actively subjects them to criticism and stimulus. It helps us think about decisions made, and those we intend to make; and sometimes we change our mind:

> There does seem to be a strong cultural resistance to the idea that talking is a form of action: we reached conclusions. From the project's perspective, talking supports thinking and thinking is a precondition to changing one's mind: it is the foundation for behavioural change. And reasoned behaviour change (based on critical, creative, caring and collaborative thinking) must be considered a form of action (Tiffany 2009: 13–14).

These are all forms of action, and constitute territory conducive to social action. In *Freire for Young Adults*, I provided an example to show the connectedness of these forms of action:

> By facilitating dialogue on common themes, contentious issues and conflicting opinions, people's perspectives on everyday situations would not only become apparent to others but would become clearer to the participants themselves. My

Community Philosophy and Social Action

intention was to stress the need to link thinking with action, in such a way that the group would seek further discussion, learning or an experience in order to act on their deliberations. We would work cyclically; one session would be spent on reflection, dialogue, and deciding on a form of action. The following week we would participate in this action and then reflect in and on this action (Tiffany 1994a: 65).

In the same piece, I spoke about how I'd placed the photographs, face down, on a table and invited a young person to choose one. To me, the photograph was of two boys wearing singlets and waist ribbons, garb I associated with boxing. I asked the group to come up with words that the image brought to mind. They responded with, among others, 'fighting', 'violence', 'aggro', 'fear' and 'getting a good hiding'. Then I asked if the responses they'd generated had anything in common. It became clear that what they said was based on shared experiences, of situations they'd been in where they were exposed to violence, felt in fear and had come to harm. A number of these stories related to 'going down town' where they would often come into contact with groups of young people from other neighbourhoods. Our discussion moved on to the factors that might lead to violence, and to how those present dealt with fear. Comments included: 'It depends on how much you've had to drink' and 'It depends on if you are with your mates.' Soon we were talking about decision-making in a context of fear. The group agreed this was something we should discuss further, and that it would be interesting to do so. Having already explained that the design of the project included identifying activities that would help us to learn, it was suggested that we might do something adventurous, something that felt risky enough to frighten people. And so we decided to go sea-cliff climbing [the young people lived next to the sea, and were aware these cliffs existed]. The article related what happened:

The experience was strangely different from other outdoor activities we had undertaken together. There was a tangible air of purpose: we were going climbing for a particular reason. It was part of a whole, the second half of something we had begun the previous week. Throughout the day we talked about fear, about how we dealt with it ourselves, how we behaved towards others who were fearful themselves, and how all this affected our attitude to self and others (ibid).

While what I wrote then is now a quarter of a century old, I continue to think it was an important experiment in what I'd later describe as 'philosophy-inspired social action'. It certainly meant I was receptive when I later discovered the world of P4C. And yet, as a youth worker, my experience of P4C generated more questions than answers. Among these were those relating to the autonomy of participants, and the sense in which autonomy – as self-determination – is a fundamental expression of action: what processes, what pedagogies and what methodologies were needed if the autonomy of participants was to be respected, encouraged and facilitated? And then there was the issue of *social* action: how might the actions of individuals marry with those of a community? I've grappled with this particular question for a number of years, drawing

74   *Philosophy and Community*

at least tentative conclusions in a critique of the value of personal autonomy, in which I theorized the self as a socially constructed identity, necessarily lived out through social action (Tiffany 1994b). There are elements here I'm sure that are relevant to the practice of Community Philosophy.

Autonomy, self-determination, action and social action

Accounts of P4C often refer to a series of steps, or stages, in the use of a Community of Enquiry methodology (see, for example, Dialogueworks' 4 Phase Inquiry Method). In this, enquiries typically culminate with 'Last Words'.[3] Arguably, what participants learn through the experience of this methodology changes them: they may have acquired additional knowledge, have developed further skills or new and enhanced values and virtues. All are important. However, while learning is reasonably equated with change, it is something else to say it constitutes action. This would require the application of such knowledge and/or skills and the active demonstration of these values and virtues. Where the end of an enquiry constitutes an end in and of itself, we can only hope that this learning reveals itself later, and manifests itself in action. It seems only logical to employ methodology that deliberately creates space and time for action to occur. In maintaining a commitment to 'community', this logic extends to *that* community being encouraged and supported in taking action *as a community*: implying *social* action. What are the methodological implications? Shouldn't we build in the question 'How might our deliberations inform and catalyze social action (and in the sense of real and practical change)?'

With these thoughts in mind, I'd want to argue that Community Philosophy adds a step, or stage, in which time is set aside to explore what action that community might take, on the basis of the conclusions drawn from its enquiry. We might go even further: where the taking of this action, and subsequent reflection on it, constitutes and becomes further 'steps'.

Again, we might reflect on the impact of institutional settings. Take school: How often are the conclusions drawn by pupils in P4C translated into social action, or even imagined as being able to inform social action? Is this even encouraged? Fundamentally, what changes do they effect? Could we imagine, for example, an enquiry into the reasonableness of school uniform ever leading to its abandonment?

Intriguingly, the enquiries I have facilitated with young people (a label I give them on the basis of engagement in non-institutional settings) have often concluded that pupils (as they are referred to in school) are virtually powerless, precisely because of the institutional context in which they are present. And this is despite the fashionable talk of 'pupil voice' and 'participation', and the existence of structures such as school councils.

It becomes obvious then that the institutional context has a profound influence on the potential and possibility of Community of Enquiry methodology to inform, catalyse and indeed facilitate social action. Indeed, the institutional context appears to actively constrain it. Or perhaps not?

The case of the wandering prisoner

I've certainly observed (what I've argued constitutes) the most basic form of action in schools: pupils changing their minds. Schools seem to exert little or no constraint on that. If viewed in the sense of 'self-correction', changing one's mind, on the basis of a rigorous process, of evidence-gathering, and enquiry into reasonableness, is undoubtedly valuable. But what of other inhibitors, and the constraints they present? Of these, one only came to mind given an experience of working in a prison.

I had been facilitating an enquiry among inmates involved in a philosophy-inspired prison education programme. All seemed well, and our conversation appeared of interest to all present. And yet, after around half an hour or so, one of the inmates got up and, without a word, simply walked out of the room. No one batted an eyelid, including the two prison educators present. So, I and those remaining, continued our discussion. A short while later, the inmate returned. Again, there was no reaction; the group simply carried on.

This case of the wandering prisoner contributed a nuanced perspective and greater understanding of how institutional environments affect enquiry-based methodology. It seems to me (an analysis if you like) that here was someone expressing his autonomy, taking action in a tangible way.

I found out later that the philosophy sessions were one of a series of choices that existed within the time set aside each day for prisoners to engage in educational activities. These were not mandated: inmates chose to engage with these activities, or not. There was no obligation to participate, or indeed to be present for the entirety of the time these sessions lasted. What struck me later was the near impossibility of a school pupil not so much behaving in this way, but being allowed to. The question then is to what extent is action (whether autonomous, freely chosen, individual, or social) possible within institutional settings, where respect for autonomy is clearly not a given. More fundamentally, can there be action without such autonomy?

P4C and the 'captive audience' versus the freedom of community

Whether disenchanted school teachers trying to rekindle the values that brought them into teaching in the first place, educators for whom democracy is all-important, or those more therapeutically minded who see benefits to self, others and society from people saying what they feel and think, there are many aspirant facilitators of philosophical enquiry. Schools, naturally, become an attractive place to practice in: there are children aplenty to practise on.

The opportunities in school would seem abundant, and yet, as we have seen, there are constraints. We might add to these the pressures of the curriculum, which often mean there are few opportunities for philosophical enquiry. Likewise, for the 'external' facilitator, gaining access can be hard enough, especially when so little time exists for doing something 'different'. So why do so many advocates of public philosophy persist in trying to get into schools? Perhaps there is a cultural assumption that school is the obvious place to be: it is where young people are, after all. Perhaps also it's assumed that engagement is going to be unproblematic; that the setting will see to that.

It takes a comparison with work in non-institutional settings to reveal some of the tensions. A provocation comes in reflecting on the voluntary context that defines such settings. In community settings access cannot be taken for granted. Nor engagement. There are no captive audiences. The Community Philosopher has to work for their relationships; community work skills become as important as the philosophical. The prize though is that certain freedoms follow on. It's as if there is an inversion of effort: while in institutional settings the philosopher might be able to embark on their activities quite soon, but be faced with untold work to facilitate action, in community settings the effort comes first, and life and the possibility of action is easier thereafter.

Working in the street is the quintessential metaphor. I've asked teachers, 'If the walls of your classroom fell down (if it became like the street), what would you do, and would you [have to] teach differently?' A common conclusion is that acting upon pupils – 'doing to' – is very different from 'working with'. Few teachers advocate the former, and yet few are immune to the pressures on them to 'deliver' the curriculum. They appreciate that a tension (to say the least) exists between directing pupils and facilitating their autonomy – helping them take action in terms *they*, either as individuals or as a community, determine.

What emerges are further questions, many of which continue to have spatial and temporal dimensions: Might other spaces be better suited to philosophical enquiry? Is there somewhere other we can escape from the time-controlling bell? Might then philosophical practices in non-institutional, perhaps public, settings actually have greater potential for informing, catalysing and facilitating social action? Among a range of intentions, 'The Thinking Village' project aimed to tackle these questions. Its activities are examined next.

'The Thinking Village': An experiment in Community Philosophy-informed social action

'The Thinking Village' project was funded by the Joseph Rowntree Foundation[4] and ran from 2006 until 2009. The three and a half-year experimental 'Demonstration Project' used Community Philosophy to promote conversations and develop positive relationships between different groups of people and professional groupings across a distinct geographical community. That said, decisions as to where the work took place were influenced by the rationale that

> critical to the process is the educator not being in control of the setting: the work happens in places that people freely choose to be in. This does not preclude working in institutional settings (including schools) but the space used should be a 'social' space, free from the prescription of a curriculum (Tiffany 2009: 9).

There was a particular emphasis on inter-generational work and on creating 'a conversational bridge between the young people in the community and the decision-making structures with which they were rarely directly involved' (ibid: 14). These conversations were to provide a medium for learning, to enable groups to work together and to examine problems (including those related to conflict and controversial issues), and act as a stimulus and catalyst for action and the 'democratisation of community life' (ibid: 5). In particular, they broadened the base of participation and generated 'enough momentum to enable dialogue to become self-sustaining' (ibid: 10). It is important to state that action took place where considered appropriate, and this was freely chosen.

In practice, the issues were identified through the careful analysis of community concerns, illustrating the significance of the 'community' dimension of the Community Philosopher's work. The topic of antisocial behaviour was at the forefront of concerns in the early days of the project. Shortly after the arrival of the project, a Dispersal Order was served on the neighbourhood. This gave police the power (in a designated area) to disperse groups of two or more people 'where their presence resulted, or is likely to result, in a member of the public being harassed, intimidated, alarmed or distressed'.[5] The order proved controversial in many aspects: it was seen to be a product of the lobbying of a small section of the community and was routinely vilified by many young people who saw themselves as being discriminated against because of it. However, the order certainly provoked what was arguably much-needed community conversation. The tensions around antisocial behaviour in general, and the Dispersal Order in particular, were the topic of a great deal of debate, and proved fertile ground for philosophical enquiry. A range of issues were revealed and subjected to analysis. These included how the media portrays young people, what actually constitutes antisocial behaviour, and the extent to which a person's judgement is widely held and can be reasonably claimed as a community norm. A series of enquiries took place which identified that a key issue for young people was how they were policed on the streets: many felt they were unfairly treated. When the dialogue turned to what action might be taken, the group came up with the idea that they might have similar dialogues with police officers in a non-conflict situation. A number of meetings were planned, one involving a 'speed-dating' event at which a series of quick-fire questions were posed to a range of stakeholders (including the police) who had been involved in the discussions about antisocial behaviour. A participating police officer said they were very constructive:

> The questions put to us by young people were challenging and informative. Challenging because they questioned our basic rights as police officers to do our job and informative because the questions themselves spoke of the thoughts young people have of the police (ibid: 12).

The success of this work achieved recognition further afield and the young people were invited to facilitate discussions with other groups of young people in other parts of the city. Buoyed by their achievements, they went on to form an active philosophy group, 'P4U'. The group met fortnightly and took part in a wide range of activities including inter-generational dialogues.

Some reflections

The project found a relationship between controversial issues and high levels of community engagement and involvement. Local people welcomed Community Philosophy as a means to discuss these issues, and contrasted it with community meetings that had turned into 'shouting matches' about who was to blame for the problems experienced. Many recognized that these meetings often exacerbated existing fractures in the community, and even created new ones. Of note were the comments made about social action; discussing what local people could do, as part of the process of enquiry, was regarded a progressive alternative to investing faith in others to sort things out. The latter was seen as weakening a community's ability to solve its own problems (Tiffany 2009).

This emphasis on discussing the possibility of social action (and what form it might take) became a central part of the project's work. Many of these discussions led to conclusions about what practical action was needed. A particular example was of the action catalysed by an enquiry into 'antisocial behaviour':

> Some of the work did have outcomes that fit a more conventional view of action in the practical sense. For example, street-based work led to relationships with a group of young people who were keen on basketball but faced playing on a local court that was potholed and substandard. The project worked to bring different parties together to discuss the issue in order to gain agreements and resources to create new opportunities (ibid: 14).

Elizabeth Alley, a participant in the project, mentions Community Philosophy (and makes specific reference to social action) in her reflections on life in the village (Alley 2009):

> At the discussion on community spirit held by the Community Philosophy Project we considered how life is breathed into communities when there is something to celebrate. This conclusion had been drawn from time invested in concept-analysis (as important a role as might be imagined for philosophy): 'How should "spirit" be defined? Its derivation from the Latin *spirare* is useful in this context. For what characterizes the 'real community' is its breath of life, its animation' (ibid: 163).

Later, Elizabeth describes her own and others' enjoyment of activities organized by the project, such as a series of inter-generational activities, including excursions. It's important to note that the decision to organize these activities emanated from the enquiries community members participated in, as in the example in the section 'Thinking Village' as to what constituted 'community spirit'. The facilitators deliberately included a social action element in their methodology, and asked, 'On the basis of our discussions, what actions might we take?' Subsequent discussions concluded the need for activities, with the hope that they'd animate community life. Project workers then worked alongside members of the community to organize these activities. Many were followed by further enquiries into the experience participants had had, in further attempts to draw out community learning and make links with social action.

Further examples of Community Philosophy-inspired social action can be found in the project report. For now, what's important is to reiterate the process by which action becomes possible:

> In Community Philosophy, time is often also invested in a concluding phase. Participants are invited to identify the things they think they have learnt and the action, if any, that they imagine might be taken to integrate this new learning into everyday life. This might lead to a further enquiry on a particular issue that has emerged; it might mean recognising the need to develop some new knowledge or access some particular information, or it might be concerned with organising a campaign or some other form of practical action that the group is motivated to pursue (ibid: 26).

And it is this that acts as provocation to the wider world of public philosophy: What happens to the conclusions generated through Community Philosophy and Communities of Enquiry?

With this question in mind, it's worth reflecting on the social action that the project as a whole catalysed. Certainly, the report proved a stimulus for discussion within a loose network of people interested in Community Philosophy and its future. Significantly, there was a realization that the potential existed for others to learn from 'The Thinking Village' project such that they might work in similar ways. The idea of developing a Community Philosophy Facilitator training course emerged from this discussion.

Community Philosophy Facilitator training: Promoting social action elsewhere

In 2012, a group of people with a shared interest in public philosophy came together with the aim of developing a training course for those wishing to facilitate Community Philosophy. This work was supported by the Esmée Fairbairn Foundation,[6] administered by SAPERE[7] and informed by what had been learnt from 'The Thinking Village' project.

The process of creating a course involved a thorough review of the philosophical and practice-based foundations of Community Philosophy, the development of a trial training course and subsequent participatory evaluation with course participants who had attempted to integrate what they'd learnt into their practice. Their comments further refined the detail of the course. Graduates of the course went on to use Community Philosophy in a wide variety of ways and in a range of community settings. A good deal of their work demonstrated a social action dimension. Examples of this were written up in the form of case studies, so as to provide a resource for others to learn from. One in particular showed how significant this social action dimension could be.

The Powell-Cotton Museum case study

One of those who undertook the Community Philosophy Facilitator training course was Keiko Higashi. Keiko described her experience as a project manager at a museum in 'Tea, Cake and Conversation: Creating a Community at the Powell-Cotton Museum' (Brown and Higashi 2015). Her paper provides a wonderful example of how Community Philosophy informed and initiated social action and shaped the very fabric of a museum and its activities.

Keiko's account details attempts to increase access to the museum, develop awareness of its collection, diversify its audience and highlight research. First, conversations were initiated with staff. These (and commentary from a past review of the museum) highlighted poor communication and coordination. This was seen as hampering the progress of projects, creating distrust and a lack of sustainability.

Keiko and another project manager, Sarah Brown, resolved to create a sense of community, ownership, sustainability, collaborative working and positive developments in the museum. They viewed Community Philosophy as a means to support both thinking and action. A series of philosophical discussions was held about how a particular gallery (due for a make-over) could and should be used, and might be made to feel and look. Transcripts of the discussions were shared with designers, and these fundamentally influenced the design of the gallery. Keiko recalls what happened in her paper:

> From early discussions with staff and volunteers, the project Managers realized that there was a real fear that the new contemporary design would lose the identity and essence of the museum's history. These concerns were taken on board and fed back to the designers as something that needed to be considered. As a result, a key visual aspect of the design was to reuse and restore the old cabinets and storage crates that had been kept behind the scenes at the museum since its opening over a century ago. When revealed at a progress briefing, there was a great response from staff and volunteers, who could see that their concerns and ideas had been listened to.

> One particular discussion, 'Are we here to entertain or to educate?' proved seminal. Staff and volunteers spoke of their perception that the museum had a bias for educated people, and the assumption that the new gallery would be used by academics and scientists. Thoughts turned to what was needed to create a space where anyone can be a researcher without a hierarchy of learning styles. In other words, learning through touch and play would have the same priority as scientific study (ibid: 110–11).

Not only had the design of the gallery been substantively informed by Community Philosophy, but a philosophical approach had 'spread into the day-to-day life of the museum and [is] used to raise sensitive topics or resolve conflicting opinions' (ibid).

It's clear that this and the previous examples illustrate well the capacity of Community Philosophy to catalyse both tangible and practical action and cultural change. It's clear also that time has to be invested in thinking specifically about what actions might be taken and this should be informed by the conclusions that communities draw from their enquiries. The reference to cultural change is important. Keiko's account repeatedly mentions the significance of Community Philosophy's emphasis on collaboration as a driver for change and action. She speaks a lot of sharing (especially knowledge, and how this knowledge transfer should be a 'two-way experience'), and of ensuring that people's concerns and ideas were listened to. This involved the existence of feedback loops, the building of trust (undeniably, a relational concept) and a sense of ownership, and ultimately the idea that all participants (whether professionals, volunteers or visitors) were co-curators. Pertinent also were efforts to establish an egalitarian environment; this is perhaps best evidenced by a comment on the museum's Facebook page which spoke of volunteers and staff being 'pro-children'. A wonderful anecdote exists of parents complaining that it was difficult to extract their children from the new gallery; such was the children's enthusiasm for it. And that this was reflected in unprecedented 'dwell time', a metric for measuring visitor engagement.

A series of tentative conclusions can be drawn: Community Philosophy appears to validate participatory activities, even among cynics, who come to see its capacity to dig deeper, reveal truths and build community, which, in combination, foreground real and lasting change in both practical and cultural terms. We might start to consider now social action and the question of scale.

Action that changes the world: A question of scale?

It's implicit that the aim of social action is to effect change, whatever the form that might take. It's easy to be sceptical, and even cynical, here in doubting whether such action can lead to change, and especially change that it is meaningful and valuable. The risk is in concluding that social action is impossible or meaningless and not worth pursuing. Concern for scale can be the most significant inhibitor, especially when, as Henningsen (2010) suggests, a 'Romantic ethic' can exist, in which workers and activists are intent on 'changing the world'. This is where earlier references to Freire's ideas can act as inhibitors too, given his many references to tackling social justice and emancipatory politics, which can seem to many too grand an aspiration to warrant serious commitment. This might explain why there is a general fondness for Freire's ideas, but relatively few examples of deliberate attempts to put his philosophies into practice.[8] What if we were to consider first a different scale of endeavour?

Thoughts on this are offered by de St. Croix in her study of youth work as community action (2016), which, notably, used Community Philosophy as a research methodology. She references Holloway's (2002) treatise on practical anarchism, which argues that it's possible to change the world without taking power, and recognizes this in her observations of the often minor ways in which youth workers take action. For her, these are not insignificant actions; rather these workers' practice demonstrates everyday forms of resistance, including deliberate inaction.

This practice does not only encompass mass collective forms of action such as large demonstrations and occupations; it includes what is sometimes referred to as 'everyday' or 'micro' resistance (Weitz 2001; Thomas and Davies 2005a, b). My aim here is not to privilege everyday resistance over more ambitious and collective forms of activism, but rather to acknowledge the importance of localized and subtle actions and inactions at a time when workers are governed in decentralized ways. In everyday forms of activism, people use the tools at their disposal to speak or act for what they believe is right and against what they see as wrong. It could be that 'these everyday, apparently trivial, individual acts of resistance offer the potential to spark social change and, in the long run, to shift the balance of power between social groups' (Weitz 2001; de St Croix 2016).

De St. Croix's work is relevant here as it paints a powerful picture of the multiplicity of behaviours that can constitute action and the different levels at which it can occur.

Another way to look at this, and in keeping with Community Philosophy's democratic roots, is that the facilitator should steadfastly *not* make any assumptions about the form of action communities should take, or even whether action is appropriate or valuable in the first place. Rather, their role is to support enquiry into this possibility, such that it is freely determined and chosen by that community, or indeed even rejected. This role extends to encouraging those involved to test the ideas generated. The ethic is one of autonomy enhancement: which in and of itself can be understood through the prism of action.

There are inevitable ethical questions, risks perhaps, in working in this way: What if the community determines it wants to engage in action that goes against the facilitator's principles? It seems reasonable to say that philosophical enquiry – and particularly Community of Enquiry – methods inherently offer a range of safeguards and protections.

Anecdotally at least, those working with Community Philosophy have never reported experiences of groups that contemplated anything oppressive. Far from it; in emphasizing the caring and collaborative thinking commonly associated with the method of Community of Enquiry, the process appears robust enough to withstand manipulation. Furthermore, the intensely participatory nature of Community Philosophy functions to ensure critique of whatever action is imagined. This notion of Community Philosophy as a participatory process lends itself, as de St Croix shows, to the wider world of participatory action research.

'The Touch Project' and Community Philosophy as participatory action research

'The Touch Project' was a two-year European research project into youth violence. It represented an opportunity to test the use of Community Philosophy as a form of participatory action research (PAR) and extend the scope of what might be possible in terms of promoting social action. Community Philosophy was used as a research methodology, in which young people affected by youth violence were encouraged to generate questions they thought were important in seeking to better understand the phenomenon of violence. Necessarily, this involved their considerable efforts to define violence, prompted by essential philosophical questions about meaning and value. Six topics emerged: 'taking responsibility', 'loyalty', 'respect', 'having a sense of purpose', 'money' and 'public space', each of which was subject to further enquiry. Many reported that, even though they had been subject to a wide range of juvenile justice interventions, this was the first time they had ever been asked what violence was, what role it played and what value it was ascribed. It's clear, at least from this group's experience, that psycho-social models of intervention dominate, and those using philosophy are extraordinarily rare.

Again, we can see how the 'generative' dimension of Community Philosophy proved important: trusting young people to determine their own philosophical endeavours. We become aware that the knowledge they possess and create is noticeably absent from the policy and practice discourses relating to the prevention of youth violence. Might this be testament to the failure to value 'knowledge on the ground' and context-appreciative practice? A subsequent session saw young people working together to articulate the themes that had emerged from their enquiries through the use of mapping technologies and model-making. The things they designed and built shed further light on issues of public space, surveillance and violence (and in the myriad forms they had come to realize it existed). Challenged to explain their maps and models to others, their responses added further texture to what both they and the researchers learnt. It seems clear also that these technologies and geographical tools have a particular value in Community Philosophy, as they support reflection into the role of space and place in community life and how the environments we live in are controlled and affect us. When coupled with the use of these tools as a stimulus for philosophical enquiry, the value of Community Philosophy as a research tool becomes abundantly clear.

It is easy to say involving communities in research constitutes action, but this needs some qualification, and especially within this (or any other) example of university-led research where the demands to work in a rigorous way are ever-present. In the foreword to the book about the project (Seal and Harris 2016), John Pitts suggests that making and sustaining contact with young people affected by violence is essential to understanding it, as is engaging them in a 'crucial conversation about the kinds of adults they want to become and the kind of world they want to bring into being' (2016: vi.). Research methods, he suggests, should utilize social practices that aim at helping young people become 'active, reflective, citizens, confident in their abilities and ready to play a part in making the world a better place' (ibid). This, of course, constitutes the discourse of participation and social action.

It is through these means we can better understand the relationship between critical enquiry and action and, as for Paulo Freire, that between reflection and action. Indeed, Freire's work makes clear the need to think in a more nuanced way about how these two concepts are related. In *The Politics of Education* Freire alludes to a 'fundamental problem that has preoccupied philosophy – especially modern philosophy' (1985: 153): the 'relationship between subject and object, consciousness and reality, thought and being, theory and practice'. His contribution is to demand appreciation of the 'dialectical unity' between these concepts: one cannot be regarded independently of the other, as if a dualism exists. In practice, this means reflection and action must be seen as related, in *praxis*:

> That means, and let us emphasize it, that human beings do not get beyond the concrete situation, the condition in which they find themselves, only by their consciousness or their intentions, however good those intentions may be. ... It is only as beings in praxis, in accepting our concrete situations as a challenging condition, that we are able to change its meaning by our action (ibid: 154).

As Freire says, a simple verbal denunciation of social justice is not enough; and the same can be said of any 'mechanicalism' that bypasses a rigorous analysis of reality. The essential point here is that processes that aim at participation and action demand participants' involvement in critically examining their realities *and* the action this informs. No separation of reflection and action can take place if the process is to be authentic, pedagogical, democratic and transformative.

'Working with' as against 'doing to'

Participatory research emphasizes 'working with', as against 'doing to' – where the latter might, for example, involve gathering data about participants without their involvement in that process. In emphasizing the social action dimensions of Community Philosophy as a form of PAR, there is a need then to imagine research as both a collaborative process (involving researchers and community members) and potentially a form of autonomous social action that a community might undertake in order to examine its own needs and interests, and potentially act upon them. The involvement of academic or other researchers is not implied. It appears then that the collaborative nature of Community Philosophy must have a participative character if social action is to be possible and meaningful. We have seen also that participatory practices offer protection from manipulation and a means to empowerment.

Furthermore, Community Philosophy seems to suggest a need to revalue participatory methodologies that have long traditions, but are scarce in their application outside the world of international development, as if they are appropriate for others but not ourselves. The criticisms levelled at development work, by the proponents of participation, that it gave (and continues to give) insufficient attention to people's local knowledge (Petty et al. 1995; Cooke and Kothari 2001; Kumar 2002) become pertinent to the advancement of philosophy in the community. This valuing of 'knowledge on the ground' contributes not just to the ongoing challenge to traditional research paradigms (Chambers 1994, 1997) but, as Seal and Harris suggest, 'a desire to break with positivistic, scientific approaches, and the belief that many phenomena are socially constructed' (2016: 47–8) (see also Cohen, Manion and Morrison 2000). This suggests that PAR, participatory learning, and action informed and influenced by participation need to become mainstream.

Community Philosophy thus can be seen to contribute to the active creation of knowledge in a way that gives it a particular moral stance. In so doing, it can make public unheard voices, and encourage interaction between these and other voices, such that communities are empowered to contribute to an analysis of their own conditions (Seal and Harris 2016). What's imagined can clearly change these voices, and inform and catalyse social action.

Concluding themes

In recognizing the parallels between participatory research and Community Philosophy, particular themes emerge. We see their similarities extend beyond an orientation towards action: the processes are similar, specifically in terms of having an evolutionary character – in the same sense as the 'generative' dimension referred to in the section 'Action that changes the world'. In this, a commitment to participation goes further than asking questions, in a narrowly consultative fashion: it extends to communities deciding which questions to explore rather than being asked to respond to those determined by external actors.

Similarly, Community Philosophy shares the common principles identifiable in participatory approaches (see Petty et al. 1995). These include ensuring the design of the process and its evaluation is influenced by those who are most likely to be affected: a valuing of negotiation and consensus-building and broader collaborative activity, and a focus on cumulative learning as the stimulus for making change and taking action, including continually developing the capacity of people to initiate action of their own. The aim here is to deliberately privilege local actors and work in a way that is responsive to local conditions, and changes in these conditions. Thus Community Philosophy aims to go beyond a view of participation as merely 'taking part'; rather, it makes a commitment to 'the principle that those who will be substantially affected by decisions made by social and political institutions must be involved in the making of those decisions' (EEC, in Bullock, Stallybrass and Trombley 1977).

There is important nuance in the terms in which social action is informed: the freedoms made possible in working in non-institutional settings need to be grasped. For example, what constitutes 'data' can be re-imagined, as something internally generated and locally evaluated, rather than externally demanded and controlled. Then there is the possibility of working in a context-appreciative way, especially temporally: taking account of what came before, and what might come next, and being able to determine how much time is invested in the process of enquiry rather than having this dictated by an institutional domain. The contrast with P4C in school is stark, with its emphasis on 'clock-time', where philosophical activity is typically fitted into the 'timetable' and its segmented lessons. This inhibits the possibility of what's learned informing what follows, of taking action on the basis of the conclusions drawn (including, simply, continuing a dialogue). In contrast, non-institutional community settings make possible work that is flexible and responsive, developmental, sustainable and autonomy-enhancing, albeit there is much work to do in developing the relationship-based foundations for it.

A further contrast is an emphasis on the 'social': seeing the concept of community in strongly collaborative terms. There is an emphasis then on sharing; and reflection becomes a group rather than an individual process; and 'personalisation' and 'differentiation' are resisted in favour of working together in joint endeavour. Kumar's (2002) social 'attitudes' offer an interesting template for what's needed for this to happen:

> Self-critical awareness of one's behaviour, bias and shortcomings: respecting others: not interrupting, not lecturing: but being a good, active listener: not hiding but embracing error: passing initiative and responsibility to others: having confidence in the ability of others and open-ended flexibility (ibid: 45).

In practice,

> Participants are asked to make links to wider issues, but without resorting to generalized statements about 'we' and 'they'. The method is Socratic, in that it asks the group to build an argument together, question its own assumptions and statements, and expand on ideas. The group tries to logically and rationally build an idea or argument, and then interrogate it. It is the role of the facilitator to keep the group on track (Seal and Harris 2016: 51).

Likewise, for Seal and Harris, 'these components are integral to the development of a learning environment as a precursor to, and the context in which, open, critical and democratic dialogue are fostered' (ibid: 49). Further, they argue, this creates the potential of liberation 'from any external authority that imposes a predetermined process' (ibid: 50), which is a reality few would dispute exists within institutional contexts.

Care must be taken not to read this as an account of absolute freedom, as if the Community Philosopher is without responsibility. Rather, in non-institutional settings, responsibility is manifested differently. Whereas a teacher, for example, is governed by accountability and performance regimes, working in civil society settings depends less on bureaucracy and more on a negotiated values context. Honesty, integrity, reliability and trustworthiness matter more. In essence, trust and credibility replace accountability, and informal relationships supplant formal authority; power resides in the community, and deliberate efforts are made to ensure this. Davies's commentary on youth work is pertinent when he asks, 'Is the practice proactively seeking to tip balances of power in young people's favour?' (2005: 11). Broadly then, a principal aim of Community Philosophy is to facilitate action in a manner that affects self, other and community, and perhaps even beyond.

While there's hope here, this is no panacea for wider structural violence and inequality, and prevailing oppressive hegemonies. But it is an attempt to value Community Philosophy-inspired action in all its forms, accepting that structural change can be hard, even impossible, to achieve in the context of the work done. Equating action to social change, and only social change, can lead to disillusionment. Attempts then to change anything can wither on the vine, unless, that is, a more nuanced view of action – as has been suggested in terms of scale – is adopted. Hickey and Mohan's (2004) reconceptualization of participation, empowerment and development, as we have seen, helps greatly: seeing power as stratified and differentiated, rather than in binary terms, recognizes that many people have a limited capacity for action but this is not a reason not to encourage it at a local level.

To return to 'The Touch Project' as an exemplar, we can recognize the value of using Community Philosophy not just as a research methodology, but as one capable of maximizing 'the transformative and pedagogic potential of the research process' (Seal and Harris 2016: 51); that Community Philosophy is a form of community learning, which uses philosophical enquiry as

> the basis for a deep conceptual analysis and exploration of the issues affecting participants ... [in which] participants determine the questions to be examined and are encouraged to engage with each other in a critical and collaborative manner. The method lends itself to social action, and is thus allied to the interests of participatory researchers (ibid).

This fits well with previous reflections from an earlier time in Community Philosophy's development:

> Community Philosophy as an intervention is capable of stimulating critical reflection on community issues and problems. An aim is to use the understanding that emerges – the learning – to inform action: hence the methodology's 'practical' orientation and its aspiration to act as a 'transformational practice' (Tiffany 2010: 3).

It becomes clear then that the 'process' of Community Philosophy takes on an extraordinary significance.

A last word: Community Philosophy and social action – from process to a new kind of politics

Together these ideas inform an understanding of Community Philosophy as a resolutely political project, albeit one, unusually perhaps, intent on advancing a commitment to particular processes rather than particular outcomes. Importantly, these processes are found to facilitate rather than dictate social action, and action that is freely chosen by communities, as distinct from the prescribed outcomes they are so often directed towards by policy and practice.

There are important process-oriented parallels to be found in the work of recent commentators, especially George Monbiot who, in *Out of the Wreckage: A New Politics for an Age of Crisis*, advances a view that would not be out of place in Community Philosophy: 'To ask how participatory culture can revive political life is, in one respect, to miss the point: it is political life' (2017: 83). Monbiot's entire premise rests on a contestation of the view that humans are an inherently competitive species, a view of the world that validates a range of cultural and political pressures seemingly intent on individuating all facets of human existence. He writes,

> We are extraordinary creatures, whose capacity for altruism and reciprocity is unmatched in the animal kingdom. But these remarkable traits have been suppressed by an ideology of extreme individualism and competition. With the help of this ideology, and the story used to project it, alienation and loneliness have become the defining conditions of our time. Far from apprehending them as threats to our well-being, we have been induced to see them as aspirations (ibid: 182–3).

So, we return again to the need to elevate the status of the social, and, in practice, methodologies that support collaborative thinking and social action – action undertaken *with* others. For Monbiot this constitutes a 'politics of belonging', in which 'community projects proliferate into a vibrant, participatory culture that transforms the character of our neighbourhoods' (ibid). Transformation, of course, implies action; and, in the context of community, this implies social action. Furthermore, 'a flourishing community stimulates our innate urge to cooperate. It helps immunize us against extremism and demagoguery, and it turns democracy into a daily habit. Community is the place from which new politics begins to grow' (ibid: 184). Likewise, cooperation, like collaboration, implies action. And, again, this is implicitly *social* action. Perhaps Community Philosophy is at least one of the means by which this might occur.

Notes

1   The Adult Learning Project, then based in Gorgy-Dalry in Edinburgh, Scotland, was one of the earliest attempts to put the ideas of Paul Freire into practice in a European context. See Tiffany, G. (1994a) *Freire for Young Adults*, National Institute of Adult and Continuing Education (NIACE) special edition on Young Adults Learning.
2   From the French *currere*.
3   A 'Last Words' activity is typically used as the culmination of the '12-step model'. In this, participants are encouraged to give a final thought about, say, their experience of the process; something they found interesting; what they have learnt; what they think now; or a thought they will ponder on, in the future.
4   The *Joseph Rowntree Foundation* is an independent organization working to inspire social change through research, policy and practice. See: *https://www.jrf.org.uk/*
5   UK Government's Respect and Dispersal Powers. Home Office. Available at: https://webarchive.nationalarchives.gov.uk/20100408122626/http://www.asb.homeoffice.gov.uk/uploadedFiles/Members_site/Documents_and_images/Enforcement_tools_and_powers/RespectAndDispersal_Guidance_0018.pdf.
6   The Esmée Fairbairn Foundation is one of the largest independent grant-makers in the UK. It aims to improve the quality of life for people and communities throughout the UK both now and in the future by funding the charitable work of organizations that are building an inclusive, creative and sustainable society: https://www.esmeefairbairn.org.uk/

7 SAPERE: https://www.sapere.org.uk/
8 Living Adult Education being a notable exception, see Kirkwood and Kirkwood (1990).

References

Alinsky, S. D., (1971), *Rules for Radicals: A Pragmatic Primer for Realistic Radicals*, New York: Random House.

Alley, E., (2009), *Discovering New Earswick: Essays from the New Earswick Bulletin 2000 – 2007*, York: Ebor Press.

Brown, S., and Higashi, K., (2015), 'Tea, Cake and Conversation: Creating a Community at the Powell-Cotton Museum', *Journal of Museum Ethnography*, 28: 107–21.

Bullock, A., Stallybrass, O., and Trombley, S., (eds), (1977), *Fontana Dictionary of Modern Thought*, London: Fontana Press.

Chambers, R., (1994), 'The Origins and Practice of Participatory Rural Appraisal', *World Development*, 22 (7): 953–69.

Chambers, R., (1997), *Whose Reality Counts? Putting the First Last*, London: Intermediate Technology Publications.

Coady, M., (1980), *Masters of their Own Destiny*, Nova Scotia: Formal Publishing.

Cohen, L., Manion, L., and Morrison, K., (2000), *Research Methods in Education*, London: Falmer-Routledge.

Cooke, B., and Kothari, U., (2001), *Participation: The New Tyranny*, London: Zed Books.

Davies, B., (2005), 'Youth Work: A Manifesto for Our Times', *Youth and Policy*, 88: 11.

de St Croix, T., (2016), *Grassroots Youth Work: Policy, Passion and Resistance in Practice*, Bristol: Policy Press.

Dialogueworks: 4 Phase Inquiry Method, [Online], Available at: https://dialogueworks.co.uk/philosophy-for-children-p4c/, Accessed 10 January 2019.

Evans, J., and Dixon, T., (2012), 'Philosophical Communities. Bristol: Arts and Humanities Research Council Connected Communities programme', [Online], Available at: https://ahrc.ukri.org/documents/project-reports-and-reviews/connected-communities/philosophical-communities/, Accessed 10 January 2019.

Freire, P., (1985), *The Politics of Education: Culture, Power and Liberation*, New York: Bergin & Garvey.

Henningsen, E., (2010), 'The Romantic Ethic in Outreach Work', [Online], Available at: http://journals.openedition.org/sejed/6615, Accessed 10 January 2019.

Hickey, S., and Mohan, G., (2004), *Participation: From Tyranny to Transformation?*, London: Zed Books.

Holloway, J., (2002), *Change the World Without Taking Power: The Meaning of Revolution Today*, London: Pluto.

Jeffs, T., and Smith, M., (eds), (1990), *Using Informal Education: An Alternative to Casework, Teaching and Control*, Buckingham: Open University Press.

Jeffs, T., and Smith, M. K., (1999), *Informal Education: Conversation, Democracy and Learning*, Ticknall: Education Now.

Kirkwood, G., and Kirkwood, C., (1990), *Living Adult Education: Freire in Scotland*, Milton Keynes: Open University Press.

Kumar, S., (2002), *Methods for Community Participation: A Complete Guide for Practitioners*, New Dheli: Vistaar Publications.

Lipman, M., (1991), *Thinking in Education*, New York: Cambridge University Press.

Lovett, T., (ed.), (1988), *Radical Approaches to Adult Education*, London: Hutchinson.

Monbiot, G., (2017), *Out of the Wreckage: A New Politics for an Age of Crisis*, London: Verso.

Petty, J., Guijt, I., Scoones, I., and Whompson, J., (1995), *Participatory Learning and Action: A Trainer's Guide*, London: International Institute for Economic Development.

Seal, M., and Harris, P. (2016), *Responding Meaningfully to Youth Violence through Youth Work*, Bristol: Policy Press.

Smith, M. K., (1982), *Creators not Consumers: Rediscovering Social Education 2e*, Leicester: National Association of Youth Clubs (NAYC) Publications (now Youth Clubs UK).

Thomas, R., and Davies, A., (2005a), 'Theorizing the Micro-politics of Resistance: New Public Management and Managerial Identities in the UK Public Services', *Organization Studies*, 26 (5): 683–706.

Thomas, R., and Davies, A., (2005b), 'What Have the Feminists Done for Us? Feminist Theory and Organisational Resistance', *Organization Studies*, 12 (5): 711–40.

Thompson, J. L., (1980), *Adult Education for a Change*, London: Hutchinson.

Tiffany, G., (1994a), 'Youthwork as an Educational Process: Freire for Young Adults', *Journal of Adults Learning*, 6 (2): 64–6.

Tiffany, G., (1994b), 'What Is Personal Autonomy? What, If Anything, Is Its Value?', Unpublished.

Tiffany, G., (2009), 'Community Philosophy: A Project Report', York: Joseph Rowntree Foundation, [Online], Available at: https://www.jrf.org.uk/report/community-philo sophy-project-report, Accessed 10 January 2019.

Tiffany, G., (2010), *Community Philosophy: A Transformative Youth Work Practice*. Sociétés et Jeunesses en Difficulté (SEJED): Bruxelles, http:// sejed.revues.org/6650

Twelvetrees, A., (2017), *Community Development, Social Action and Social Planning*, 5th edn, London: Red Globe Press.

Weitz, R., (2001), 'Women and their Hair: Seeking Power through Resistance and Accommodation', *Gender and Society*, 15 (5): 667–86.

6

Philosophy, dialogue and the creation of community

Amanda Fulford

Philosophy, it seems, is big business. This is not seen in oversubscribed philosophy courses in universities, but rather in moves towards the popularization of philosophy with the general public, or perhaps more correctly, a move towards popular philosophy. There are now philosophies of just about everything; but what this tends to mean is that you merely have a view on the way things are, or should be. Such philosophies are often touted in popular literature. These texts are humorous, tongue-in-cheek or just plain gimmicky, as in the case of Sgarbi's (2013) *The Philosophy of Cats: The Meowsings of Feline Wisdom*. But others attempt to address an issue systematically or to suggest philosophical understandings of popular topics, as in Barry Smith's (2009) *Philosophy of Wine*, Dan O'Brien's (2010) *Gardening: Philosophy for Everyone*, Michael Austin's *Running and Philosophy: A Marathon for the Mind* and David Kaplan's (2012) *Philosophy of Food*.

The popularization of philosophy opens up a whole range of questions about what philosophy is, and what it means to call oneself a philosopher. To hear the answer, 'I'm a philosopher' in answer to the question 'What do you do?' tends to elicit one of a number of responses. Perhaps the most common is surprise; this seems reasonable – there are relatively few who would identify themselves as philosophers when compared with the number of workers in the retail, technology or hospitality sectors, or with the number of qualified doctors, lawyers and teachers. Another response tends to be admiration; philosophy has a reputation for being a difficult discipline, and so those who 'do' it must be regarded as knowledgeable, even highly intelligent. Perhaps a frequent reaction is bafflement arising from an uncertainty over what philosophers actually spend their days doing, and why people would pay money for them to do so (surely it's just thinking?). And, of course, there's the reaction of amusement, usually accompanied by nervous laughter. 'What's the point in philosophy?' tends to underlie this response. 'Why do they bother with what is just abstract thinking?' These are, of course, broad generalizations, and my aim is neither to caricature philosophers, nor to ridicule those who might ask such a question of philosophers out of a genuine interest or from a desire to engage sincerely with another person. Some of the responses, though, may be related to a difficulty in seeing what the philosopher 'does' in contexts outside the academy, since her work as an academic tends to take place wholly within the confines of the academy. University-trained economists work in commerce as accountants; those qualified with a university chemistry degree work in industry; and those having completed university courses in sociology and anthropology often work in our communities. But the philosopher is much less often thought of as a professional who works outside the academy, though there are some notable exceptions such as philosophers in residence in some elite (i.e. independent) public schools. But it seems odd, to say the least, to think about having a formal role for a (professional) philosopher on the factory floor, or in the boardroom of a large corporation. While the term 'philosopher' might be used of an employee, it is most likely to be a humorous, tongue-in-cheek reference to their liking for reflective thinking, or for what might be regarded as deep and meaningful aphorisms.

Philosophy, then, is strongly connected with the university, and with research in all the different fields of philosophy (philosophy of mind, of science, epistemology, moral philosophy and so on), and with the work of professional philosophers. To study philosophy in the academy tends to be concerned with developing an acquaintance with a significant body of philosophical literature, and with demonstrating skills in reasoning, and in logic, in order to pursue and defend arguments that stand up to the most rigorous examination. But the tendency is that professional philosophers working in the academy often pursue their research and writing as a solitary activity. Unlike much research in the social and applied sciences, where published research often shows evidence of sustained collaboration and joint writing ventures, research in philosophy more often tends to result in the publication of sole authored work. As Peters et al. state, in a paper that emerged from an Editors' Collective a rare collaborative writing project in the fields of education and philosophy: 'Publications are often thought of in terms of ... a radically individualized idea of the creative, innovative and meritocratic individual. Even writing collaborations are usually given kudos for originality and one is privileged over others as the "lead author"' (Peters et al. 2016: 1405).

But putting aside the matter of writing – and publishing – philosophy, the *practice* of philosophy has, from its most ancient roots, also been marked by dialogue. In thinking about philosophy and dialogue, it is not only that philosophers, theologians and thinkers have written about dialogue (Saint Augustine encouraged conversation with God; Edmund Husserl wrote about the fundamental role of intersubjectivity; and, for Martin Buber, dialogue is the foundation of the kind of relationships that we might have with another person). It is also that the *doing* of philosophy is dialogic. We see this, of course, when professional philosophers present their ideas at academic conferences and seek to engage the audience with the aim of defending and improving their argument. Here, philosophy is marked by its experts testing their ideas through dialogue, or to put it another way, their philosophy is mediated *by* dialogue. But there is another way of thinking here, one that suggests that philosophy itself *is* dialogue. That this is a bold claim is reflected in Richard Smith's comment: 'It can be taken for granted, of course (some will suspect irony here), that philosophy is to be written and read, rather than spoken or argued aloud, in a dialogue between or among embodied persons, among friends, in the university seminar or tutorial, in the café or bar' (2016: 129).

Philosophy, Dialogue and the Creation of Community 93

To forge this link between philosophy and dialogue is to make the claim that philosophy can arise out of our encounter with others in dialogue. Of course, not every dialogue counts as philosophy; this would be a ludicrous claim, and any such requirement would be almost impossible to live with. When I say 'Hello' to my neighbour, and ask how they are, the inquiry is merely a pleasantry. Indeed, such spoken exchanges are simply part of how we go along together in the world. But to posit the idea of philosophy-as-dialogue, as co-constructed through encounter and conversation with others, changes our view not only of who does – or can do – philosophy, but also of the very nature of philosophy itself. In this sense, the emphasis on philosophy as a body of knowledge to be attained, or a set of texts to be read, shifts towards an idea of the love of wisdom that is developed through our conversation (our turning together) with others. Such conversation is driven by matters of import to the members of the community who choose to converse together. And these conversations typically happen in locations outside of the university – in community centres, libraries, cafés, pubs, to name a few. Part Two of this volume demonstrates not only the diversity of settings in which these philosophical conversations take place, but also the range of communities who engage in community philosophy. But the conversation that takes place in these settings is not simply idle chatter. It is marked not only by taking the opportunity to say how we see the world, but also by an openness to having those ideas tested by others, and so to reach more reasoned conclusions about our lives, and about how to live together well. To recognize that philosophy outside of the academy is particularly marked by this kind of reasoned dialogue with others in public settings is also to say that, in one sense, there can be no philosophy without community. In this sense, to do philosophy requires that we come together with others in dialogue. The very idea of community philosophy, therefore, not only alters our perception of what counts as philosophy, but also informs our ideas of what it means to be in community through dialogue.

The American philosopher Stanley Cavell (1926–2018), in writing about language, touches on some of these same ideas. While his work is not directly concerned with community philosophy, his writing on what it means to be part of a language community helps us to understand what is at stake in the practices of philosophy with the public. Commentators on Cavell's work have drawn attention to his interest in the criteria that underpin and sustain all our human practices, and how we develop judgement in relation to them (see Standish 2013). Paul Standish illustrates the everyday nature of criteria by using the example of a chair. There are, he notes, criteria that govern the appropriate way to sit, on a chair, for example. In such cases, the criteria require no explicit articulation, as they are inextricably part of the fabric of our everyday practices. But there are also criteria at play when we use language; these criteria are essential for the effective operation of language, and for mutual understanding. When, for example, we think about the specific circumstances in which we would use one word – as opposed to another – we are thinking about criteria. Criteria come into play when we consider the contexts in which we might we use the word 'serviette', and when it would be appropriate to use 'napkin'. So we are able to claim that when we use the word 'serviette', we mean something in particular; we tend to think of it as something cheap, often made of paper and disposable. But to use the word 'napkin'

94   *Philosophy and Community*

refers to something more expensive, commonly made of linen or damask, and that can be washed and reused. To take another, arguably more significant, example, we might ask what is at stake in the difference between 'freedom', 'independence' and 'liberty'. If language is to be a means of communication, then it makes sense that we should agree in criteria. Such agreement, claims Cavell, signals community. In his seminal work, *The Claim of Reason*, Cavell puts it like this: "The philosophical appeal to what we say, and the search for our criteria on the basis on which we say what we say, are claims to community' (1979: 20). When we agree in criteria, we are, for Cavell, 'mutually voiced … mutually attuned top to bottom' (ibid: 32). What we consent to is, for Cavell, an indication of our membership in a community. It is about what *we* say.

This is important for community philosophy where groups often come together, and where the focus of the dialogue is about seeing to what extent there can be mutual attunement with regard to particular concepts. Community philosophy sessions, as our colleagues show in their contributions to Part Two of this volume, often begin with a focus on a particular concept, for example, 'friendship', 'justice' or 'identity'. The aim of such sessions is not to reach some kind of generalization, or accord, based on a majority view. Nor is it the case for Cavell that in our use of language, the aim is to arrive at an agreement. It is rather that, through dialogue, we might agree in criteria – we say that the world seems this way for us; or indeed, we might dissent in criteria – we refuse to acknowledge that the world is this way for us. For Cavell, this process is a deeply educative one. It is through our agreement and disagreement in criteria (and I would also argue, through the practices of dialogue in community philosophy) that 'we are educations for one another' (Cavell 1990: 31).

Philosophy as educative: Epictetus and Seneca

The idea that the practice of philosophy is educative, that a person can be educated (i.e. brought out and led forth) through its doing, is an ancient one. But there is an important distinction to be drawn here between the teaching of philosophy in formal educational settings, and the idea of doing philosophy as being educative. The former is commonly the preserve of academic courses in universities and of professional philosophers; the latter, however, is more congruent with the practices of community philosophy. Seen in the latter way, philosophy has an audience beyond the academy, and, we might say, is returned to the wider community. The idea of 'return' is used deliberately here to recall some of the ancient Greek practices of philosophy and, in particular, the public practice of philosophy, and the practice of philosophy with the public. This idea is ineluctably linked to Stoicism – the school of Hellenistic philosophy founded in Athens in the early third century BCE. The school's name can be traced to the public colonnade, the *Stoa Poikile*, on the edge of the Athenian *agora*, where Zeno of Citium, the founder of the Stoic school, would walk up and down, lecturing and discussing philosophy in this public space. In this respect, his engagement with the public was an emulation of the practice of Socrates who pursued philosophical dialogue through the use of the *elenchus*, a refutation of invalid arguments that is central to most of the Platonic dialogues.

Philosophy, Dialogue and the Creation of Community

This engagement with the public that was a notable feature of Zeno's approach to philosophy is not an isolated example. In the same way, Gaius Musonius Rufus, and his pupil, Epictetus – both notable Stoics – undertook philosophical lectures in public.[1] This kind of public discourse is not education (for the public) in terms of the systematic learning of philosophy through formal schooling, but rather signals a broader idea of philosophy as educative. It is a plea for a kind of self-education, for the development of attitudes and habits of virtuous and rational behaviour. Epictetus's philosophy was not only for the learned Stoic scholar, but also for the public, and for anyone who would be 'wise and good'. Arrian reports Epictetus as saying: 'The chief concern of a wise and good man is his own Reason. … In this manner ought everyone chiefly to train himself' (Epictetus 1865: 200).

Just as public discourse was one of the means by which Epictetus sought to emphasize the public nature of philosophy as a form of education on the self, so Seneca, the Roman Stoic philosopher and statesman, also engaged in a form of educative dialogue when he wrote 124 letters to his friend and Procurator of Sicily, Lucilius. The approach Seneca took to philosophy in the *Letters* was to proceed through a form of dialogue with his friend. It is clear from what is written that this kind of dialogue was profoundly educative for both correspondents. We could also say that, for the attentive reader, Seneca's letters remain similarly educative today. The contemporary American philosopher, Martha Nussbaum, finds the same educative possibilities for both the interlocutors of the Platonic dialogues and for those reading them. She argues that, rather than 'education' comprising a set of conclusions about a particular issue, or arrival at the 'truth', we might see it in different terms: 'The dialogue, in its open-endedness, sets up a similarly dialectical relation with the reader who is invited to enter critically and actively into the give-and-take' (2000: 126). In particular, these dialogic forms of encounter demand of the reader that she gives reasons for her own position on any subject: 'The dialogue reader is asked by the interaction to work through everything actively and to see where he really stands, who is praiseworthy and why' (ibid: 127). I argue that such practices can also be considered as a work on the self – a form of care of the self. In their introduction to Seneca's *Letters*, Margaret Graver and A. A. Long point to this same more public audience for the letters (2014). While Roman tradition might have led Seneca to dedicate the letters to an individual, this was, they argue, a mere compliment, and should not detract from what was a wider intended audience for Seneca's philosophy. Moreover, central to Stoic ethics was the requirement to serve the community. While this might seem at odds with a life lived in philosophical reflection (a point Seneca discusses in his essay, 'On Leisure'), Graver and Long quote Seneca's *Letters* to illustrate the public nature of the audience for his philosophy. As Seneca writes: 'The work that I am doing is for posterity: it is they who can benefit from what I write. … The right path that I myself discovered late in life when weary from wandering, I now point out to others' (VIII, #2).

The style of Seneca's *Letters* suggests that his philosophical approach was both dialogic and mutually educative, aspects largely reflected in the later Epictetus's *Discourses*. Most of the letters open with an observation of a specific, often mundane, incident (about health, clothing, travel, celebrating etc.) that allow Seneca to conduct a far broader exploration of an issue or a principle, all with the aim of helping himself,

96   *Philosophy and Community*

and Lucilius, to become better Stoics and to live a life of virtue. But the letters do not comprise anything like a formal curriculum for a Stoic education, or amount to a systematic discussion of Stoic theory. There are occasions where Seneca gives specific advice on, for example, how to read philosophical texts (Letter II). He also provides a more detailed exposition of the rules of moral reasoning (Letters XCIV and XCV), and introduces more substantive philosophical discussions later in the letter series when he perceives that Lucilius has made progress in philosophy, and in virtue. But by more consistently drawing on the mundane, and in using examples from daily life, Seneca ensures that the collection remains attractive to a broader audience with little prior knowledge of, or experience in, philosophy (Graver and Long 2015). The letters seem almost 'like the conversation of two people walking together' (ibid: 10). For Seneca, the benefits of such dialogue are clear. He writes to Lucilius in the *Letters*:

> You are right when you urge that we increase our mutual traffic in letters. But the greatest benefit is to be derived from conversation, because it creeps by degrees into the soul. Lectures prepared beforehand and spouted in the presence of a throng have in them more noise but less intimacy. Philosophy is good advice; and no one can give advice at the top of his lungs. Of course we must sometimes also make use of these harangues ... but when the aim is to make a man learn and not merely to make him wish to learn, we must have recourse to the low-toned words of conversation. They enter more easily, and stick in the memory; for we do not need many words, but, rather, effective words (XXXVIII, #1).

That such dialogue is educative is clearly reflected here. Graver and Long refer to Seneca's use of oral and written forms of discourse as modes of education – as eliciting *mutual* transformation. The *Letters* show that Seneca himself was changed through the dialogue, through the engagement with the philosophy that he espoused. In letter VI, on the subject of sharing knowledge, Seneca wrote of the benefit to his own philosophical thinking and virtuous living of the ongoing dialogue with his friend:

> I feel, my dear Lucilius, that I am being not only reformed, but transformed. You cannot conceive what distinct progress I notice that each day brings to me. ... I am glad to learn in order that I may teach. ... No good thing is pleasant to possess, without friends to share it (VI, #1, 3).

Seneca's role is to guide both his reader *and* himself through the processes by which progress could be made in Stoic virtue, while avoiding those attitudes and habits that would impede such progress. Indeed, these were the very aims of his *Letters*. This approach calls to mind what Michel Foucault, in his lectures at the Collège de France between 1981 and 1982, outlines as a way of understanding the relations between the self and the truth in the Hellenistic cultural phenomenon of *epimeleia heautou* – commonly translated as 'care of the self' (Foucault 2005). In tracing this idea through Hellenistic and Roman society, Foucault understands it in various ways: as an attitude towards the self, the world and others; as a form of attention and attending to what takes place in our thought, as well as the taking of action by the self on the self, which is

Philosophy, Dialogue and the Creation of Community   97

a form of education through which the self is transformed (pp. 10–11). He summarizes the care of the self as 'the idea of education, but of education that is also generalized: the whole of life must be the individual's education. … And the *epimeleia heatou*, now that its scale encompasses the whole of life, consists in educating oneself. … There is now something like a spiral between education and a form of life' (ibid: 439). Thinking for oneself with others is an educative practice; in Foucauldian terms, it is a work on the self. Philosophy is not a sterile exercise in thinking, but rather a form of care of the self. The subject implied in the idea of the care of the self is one that is understood as capable of transformation and modification, but not only as a subject in isolation; care of the self also entails the care of others. As Frédéric Gros puts it:

> Care of the self … was exercised in a largely communal framework: it is the school of Epictetus … addressing itself to a large public of disciples or itinerant students; it is Seneca practising care of the self by engaging in a correspondence with his friends. … Foucault ceaselessly insists on it: care of the self is not a solitary activity … but rather constitutes, on the contrary, an intensified mode of social relation. It is not a matter of renouncing the world and others, but of an alternative modulation of this relation to the other by the care of the self (Gros 2005: 701–2).

Philosophy and Community through dialogue

The philosophy of Seneca's *Letters*, through which both participants are to make progress in virtue (we might say, are educated or, in Seneca's words, are 'transformed'), is mediated through dialogue – a mutual exchange of ideas that open up from the very practical concerns of daily life. This is philosophy far removed from how we tend to understand it in terms of the published outputs from academics in contemporary philosophy departments. Richard Smith addresses this very point when he makes the distinction between philosophy as something that is written down (in the 'standard format' of the academic journal article or monograph chapter), and philosophy as something that we do – particularly through forms of conversation, reasoning or dialogue with each other. He turns to Plato's dialogue, *Phaedrus*, to illustrate his point, showing that the interlocutors in such dialogues comprised members of the public – 'flesh-and-blood people who might be met with anywhere, at any time' (2010: 159). Indeed, Socrates's dialogues were with just such people: Euthyphro (who is travelling to the law courts to have his father prosecuted for manslaughter), Theaetetus (a talented young geometrician) and Ion (a rhapsode). What characterizes the dialogue between Socrates and these interlocutors is, as Smith notes, that when they

> give themselves over fully to the process of dialectic, to the to-and-fro of question and answer, none of them will be quite the same at the end of the dialogue. What characterizes these encounters is that each will have been *educated* a little, or perhaps a lot, by the philosophy they have engaged in. … For this reason it seems fair to call these dialogues exercises in philosophy of education (ibid: 160).

It seems that the commitment to philosophical dialogue and mutual transformation in Seneca bears strong lines of connection with the very ideas at the heart of community philosophy. The practices of community and public philosophy that our colleagues outline in Part Two of this volume are all founded on forms of dialogue. But, just as many of Seneca's *Letters* begin from the shared interests of the two interlocutors, dialogue in community philosophy similarly proceeds from matters that are of significance and concern for the communities themselves. Those in dialogue within the prison system may begin from concepts of justice and fairness, and those in diverse community settings may have concerns relating to identity, responsibility and citizenship. But in all of these contexts, and whatever subject might be taken as the starting point, dialogue is central.

Philosophical dialogue with others is both educative, then, and a form of care of the self. But such dialogue is not to be understood merely as the rehearsal of precise linguistic behaviours or as the demonstration of a particular set of skills. It is rather an opportunity that requires us to be 'mutually under interrogation', and one in which we experience the 'deconstructive and transformative power of the question itself [which] calls both my and the other's assumptions to account' (Kennedy 2004: 751). This is not philosophy *for* the community, in the sense that it is undertaken with the express purpose of transmitting knowledge, improving social cohesion, increasing tolerance and so on. It is rather philosophy *with* – or perhaps even between – members of the community, where the locus of control for the dialogue lies with the community itself. Such philosophical dialogues have ends that are not strictly determined; they remain resolutely open-ended. Engaging in such dialogue is not undertaken with a view to arriving at a consensus on an issue, or indeed in sorting out the messiness of the world in which we live. It is rather an open-ended process of the development of the self – an ongoing education with others through conversation. The philosopher John Dewey puts it like this:

> In genuine conversation the ideas of one are corrected and changed by what others say; what is confirmed is not his previous notions, which may have been narrow and ill-formed, but his capacity to judge wisely. What he gains is an expansion of experience; he learns; even if previous ideas are in the main confirmed, yet in the degree in which there is genuine mutual give and take they are seen in a new light, deepened and extended in meaning, and there is the enjoyment of enlargement of experience, of growth of capacity (1994: 190).

Why community philosophy?

In 2012, on appointing Angie Hobbs as the UK's first professor for the Public Understanding of Philosophy at The University of Sheffield, the Vice-Chancellor, Professor Keith Burnett, said:

> This appointment reflects our belief that the thinking which takes place in universities can and should reach out beyond the academic realm and make a difference in

Philosophy, Dialogue and the Creation of Community 99

the wider world. This is as true of philosophy as it is of research in medicine or engineering. In fact, on many levels, our society has a profound need for the kind of deep thinking about how we live which is found in philosophical discourse.[2]

But while this kind of statement might be considered admirable, it suggests two things. First, there seems to be reference here to a kind of external engagement agenda, in which the role of the academic philosopher in the university is to reach out and to share philosophy's insights for the benefit of the general public. Of course, this is in many senses right and proper, especially where the research that the academic undertakes has the benefit of public funding. Indeed, the emphasis on the impact of academic research is increasingly measured in terms of its effect outside the academy, and on society, culture, on quality of life and on public policy.[3] Second, there is a risk that, in stating that society has a 'profound need ... for deep thinking', Professor Burnett, along with policy makers and pressure groups, sees the potential of thinking together as some kind of panacea for a whole range of perceived social ills. There is a strong sense in such statements, that engaging with philosophy should be done for particular ends that often relate to wider community, or national, priorities – increased social cohesion being just one example. In 2008, the Joseph Rowntree Foundation reported the success of using community philosophy to increase intergenerational understanding of nuisance behaviours and fear of crime (Porter and Seeley 2008). This is by no means an isolated example: Michele Moses et al. have also written about the achievement of greater mutual understanding as a result of a project to bring philosophical inquiry into communities. They state: 'We were able to put our own expertise in philosophy and race-conscious education policy to good use by purposefully creating opportunities for diverse community members ... to engage in dialogue and deliberation with each other over the issue of affirmative action' (Moses, Saenz and Farley 2015: 193). They also report other outcomes including participants changing their views, increasing their knowledge of affirmative action and increasing communication with others. Such ends are perhaps even more sharply focused in the movement to bring philosophy to children in schools, where philosophical inquiry through dialogue is used to support the development of personal responsibility and moral education (Cam 2014), critical thinking skills (Daniel and Auriac 2011) and self-esteem (Sasseville 1994). Nancy Vansieleghem draws attention to where such approaches risk the instrumentalization of philosophy for children, and argues for its richer possibilities in terms of dialogue within a community of inquiry:

> Is it not possible that the focus on dialogue and critical thinking in function of a future ideal has made us lose sight of ways in which the presence of the other is integral to its practices – that is, that it may have, concealed within it, the practices of a real philosophy for children? After all, does not the community of inquiry always imply thinking with the other, facing conflict with the other, searching for an answer with the other, doubting with the other? Do we not always in any case have to deal with and face the other? (Vansieleghem 2005: 33).

If the practice of philosophy – through dialogue and shared inquiry – is educative (as thinkers from Seneca to Nussbaum suggest), then it is not just a matter of securing a broader audience for the dissemination of philosophy from the academy, but rather a matter of the public themselves *doing* philosophy. And something further follows from this. The idea of 'community' that is at the heart of different forms of community and public philosophy is not just a matter of location, of where the philosophy takes place. The fact that the term 'community philosophy' is commonly used signals not only that the dialogue takes place in locations outside the academy, in libraries, prisons, hospitals, community centres, pubs and other public spaces, but also that it takes place with the different communities in these places. It is also that through philosophical dialogue with others, community is negotiated and created. It is through reasoning together that we create a community. We come to see as individuals where (to use Cavell's words) we agree in criteria, and where we must dissent. In doing this, we take the views of others seriously, and see to what extent we accept or reject these views, and how our own positions stand up to scrutiny by others. Through participating in a community of philosophical inquiry, David Kennedy argues, 'We come to understand that not just our belief systems but even our very selfhoods are under continual reconstruction, *and always in relation to others*. … What we can learn is to bear with the fundamental inquiry into who we are and what we might become that this form of dialogue represents, knowing that it will always be transforming' (2004: 748, italics mine).

If, as Kennedy argues, shared philosophical dialogue is transformatory in the ways that he suggests, then both local and national governments should take its potential more seriously. But philosophy in, and with, the community has, in the main, been a grass-roots concern. There is scant evidence that it has been taken seriously by university departments of philosophy, or of education, beyond ticking a box, as it were, in terms of a university's strategy for community engagement and outreach, or for generating 'impact' data. If philosophy with the community through inquiry and dialogue is a worthwhile pursuit, if philosophical dialogue with others is a form of care for the self that enlarges experience and grows capacity – in short, is educative – then it should be a concern not only for philosophers and educators but also for those with responsibility for civil life. Critical attention to philosophy with communities is needed because it is a practice that is itself educative, that goes to the heart of philosophy's concern with how to live well with each other. It is hoped that this volume makes an important contribution that much needed critical attention.

Notes

1 Epictetus's *Discourses* were largely written down by his pupil, Arrian.
2 See http://www.sheffield.ac.uk/news/nr/university-appoints-first-uk-professor-of-the -public-understanding-of-philosophy-1.174523, Accessed 4 November 2016.
3 The Research Excellence Framework (REF), the system for assessing the quality of research in UK Higher Education Institutions, defines impact as follows: 'an effect on, change or benefit to the economy, society, culture, public policy or services, health, the environment or quality of life, beyond academia'. See http://www.hefce.ac.uk/rsrch/ REFimpact/, Accessed 22 November 2016.

References

Austin, M., (2007), *Running and Philosophy: A Marathon for the Mind*, Oxford: Blackwell Publishing Ltd.

Cam, P., (2014), 'Philosophy for Children: Values, Education and the Inquiring Society', *Educational Philosophy and Theory*, 46 (11): 1203–11.

Cavell, S., (1979), *The Claim of Reason: Wittgenstein, Skepticism, Morality, and Tragedy*, New York: Oxford University Press.

Cavell, S., (1990), *Conditions Handsome and Unhandsome: The Constitution of Emersonian Perfectionism*, Chicago: The University of Chicago Press.

Daniel, M., and Auriac, E., (2011), 'Philosophy, Critical Thinking and Philosophy for Children', *Educational Philosophy and Theory*, 43 (5): 415–35.

Dewey, J., (1994), *The Moral Writings of John Dewey*, ed. James Gouinlock, New York: Prometheus Books.

Epictetus, (1865), *The Works of Epictetus*, trans. T. W. Higginson, Boston: Little, Brown, and Company.

Foucault, M., (2005), *The Hermeneutics of the Subject: Lectures at the Collège de France 1981–82*, trans. G. Burchell, New York: Palgrave Macmillan.

Graver, M., and Long, A. A., (2015), 'Introduction to the *Letters on Ethics*', in L. A. Seneca, *Letters on Ethics*, trans. M. Graver and A. A. Long, 1–24, Chicago: University of Chicago Press.

Gros, F., (2005), 'Le Souci de Soi Chez de Michel Foucault. A Review of *The Hermeneutics of the Subject: Lectures at the Collège de France, 1981 - 1982*', *Philosophy and Social Criticism*, 31 (5–6): 697–708.

Kaplan, D. M., (ed.), (2012), *The Philosophy of Food*, Berkeley: University of California Press.

Kennedy, D., (2004), 'The Role of a Facilitator in a Community of Philosophical Inquiry', *Metaphilosophy*, 35 (5): 744–63.

Moses, M. S., Saenz, L. P., and Farley, A. N., (2015), 'The Central Role of Philosophy in a Study of Community Dialogues', *Studies in Philosophy and Education*, 34: 193–203.

Nussbaum, M., (2000), *The Fragility of Goodness: Luck and Ethics in Greek Tragedy and Philosophy*, Cambridge: Cambridge University Press.

O'Brien, D., (ed.), (2010), *Gardening: Philosophy for Everyone*, Oxford: Blackwell.

Peters, M. A., Jandrić, P., Irwin, R., Locke, K., Devine, N., Heraud, R., Gibbons, A., Besley, T., White, J., Forster, D., Jackson, L., Grierson. E., Mika, K., Stewart, G., Tesar, M., Brighouse, S., Arndt, S., Lazaroiu, G., Mihaila, R., Legg, C., and Benade, L., (2016), 'Towards a Philosophy of Academic Publishing', *Educational Philosophy and Theory*, 48 (14): 1401–25.

Porter, S., and Seeley, C., (2008), *Promoting Intergenerational Understanding through Community Philosophy*, York: Joseph Rowntree Foundation.

Sasseville, M., (1994), 'Self-esteem, Logical Skills and Philosophy for Children', *Thinking*, 4 (2): 30–2.

Seneca, L. A., (2014), *Letters from a Stoic*, trans. Robin Campbell, London: Penguin Classics.

Sgarbi, F., (2013), *The Philosophy of Cats: The Meowsings of Feline Wisdom*, London: Gibson Square Books.

Smith, B., (2009), *Questions of Taste: The Philosophy of Wine*, Oxford: Oxford University Press.

Smith, R., (2010), 'Writing the Philosophy of Education', in R. Bailey (ed.), *The Philosophy of Education: An Introduction*, 158–66, London: Continuum.

Smith, R., (2016), 'Reading between the Lines', in A. Fulford and N. Hodgson (eds), *Philosophy and Theory in Educational Research: Writing in the Margin*, 129–38, Abingdon: Routledge.

Standish, P., (2013), 'Rethinking Democracy and Education with Stanley Cavell', *Foro de Educación*, 11 (15): 49–64.

Vansieleghem, N., (2005), 'Philosophy for Children as the Wind of Thinking', *Journal of Philosophy of Education*, 39 (1): 19–35.

7

Beyond walls: The redemption of philosophy

Richard Smith

Thou wall, O wall, O sweet and lovely wall,
Show me thy chink, to blink through with mine eyne.
William Shakespeare, *A Midsummer Night's Dream*
V. 1.174–77

Perhaps the only thing that can be said with certainty about Philosophy in the Community is that it does not take place where we have become used to finding it for the last few hundred years, in schools, colleges and universities and other sites of formal education, characterized by the conventions of curricula and teaching practices, including the studying of texts, and ending in examinations and the awarding of grades. It is worth pausing to reflect that if Western philosophy, starting with the Presocratics such as Heraclitus, Empedocles, Zeno and Parmenides, has developed over more than two and a half millennia, our modern conventions have applied to a fraction of that time. In going outside the walls of the academy and into the public world – the hired rooms, Socratic cafés, pubs and other venues described and explored in this book – Philosophy in the Community is, arguably, returning philosophy to its origins.

Another of those origins, perhaps, lies in the ambition to return philosophy to the everyday concerns of ordinary people. Here again the contrast is commonly made with academic philosophy, which is often characterized for being 'too theoretical, too specialized, too cut off from ordinary people and their concerns', forgetting the example of Socrates, who 'practiced philosophy out in the city, in informal dialogues, group discussions and symposia' (Evans 2012: 34). An overdrawn contrast is, as Evans notes (p. 35), particularly sterile in this context. It ignores the support that academic philosophy has often given to the many versions of philosophy outside the university, as well as the historical roots each has in the other. I would add that every department of knowledge has developed sophisticated and technical branches to deal with the problems and opportunities of the modern era. We do not expect a non-specialist to understand particle physics: why should philosophy be different? There is at the same time something odd about the idea of 'ordinary people', as if, say, Peter Higgs, who theorized the existence of the Higgs boson particle now named after him, was not an ordinary person. Or as if people outside of the academy, being more 'ordinary', were

104 *Philosophy and Community*

thus more 'real' than those inside – an ontological claim which the alert philosopher would be quick to dismiss. Somewhere here too there seems to lurk one of the puzzling tendencies of our time, the automatic suspicion of 'elites'.

The characterization of Philosophy in the Community as 'Socratic' captures something important about it, of course, which is that, like Socrates, philosophers working in the community do not for the most part operate in buildings designated for that purpose, any more than Socrates did. But it is misleading to think of Socrates wandering around Athens and engaging in spontaneous conversation with his fellow citizens. Most of the Platonic dialogues are far from spontaneous, and they are so far from being extramural, in the literal sense, that Plato has been careful to describe their settings – the walls within which they take place – and those walls often seem to colour the dialogues that take place within them.

Perhaps the best example of this is the most famous and influential dialogue of all: the *Republic*. It does not take place spontaneously, but under duress. Socrates and Glaucon have left Athens to see a religious festival taking place in the Piraeus, the area of the docks. When they start to return to Athens, but are intercepted. Polemarchus the son of Cephalus noticed them in the distance and told his servant to run after them and tell them to wait. Lee's (1968) translation captures the undertone of violence: 'The slave caught hold of my coat from behind and said "Polemarchus says you are to wait".' When Polemarchus and his friends catch up with Socrates and Glaucon the conversation goes as follows:

> 'Socrates', said Polemarchus, 'I believe you are starting out on your way back to town.' 'You are quite right,' I replied. 'Do you see how many of us there are?' he asked. 'I do.' 'Well, you will either have to get the better of us or stay here.' 'Oh, but there's another alternative,' said I. 'We might persuade you that you ought to let us go.' 'You can't persuade people who won't listen,' he replied. 'No', said Glaucon, 'you certainly can't.' 'Well, you can assume we shan't listen.' (trans. Lee 1968)

Socrates and Glaucon are taken to the house of Polemarchus and his father Cephalus. There were real people of this name, father and son, in Athens at the time when the dialogue is set (Nails 2002). They were successful businessmen whose slaves manufactured shields for the hoplites of the Athenian armies. These shields could be used as offensive weapons in fighting at close quarters, by being jabbed into an opponent's face or under his chin, as well as for defence against swords and spears. The euphemism of 'the defence industries' is nothing new.

It is Cephalus, old and approaching death, who has demanded Socrates's presence. As his capacity for enjoying the pleasures of the body diminish, his love of intelligent conversation, he finds, increases. This is what he wants from the famous philosopher. His idea of philosophy is perhaps revealed when Socrates asks him about his experience of being old. Cephalus's reply is evasive. Some people complain about the tribulations of old age, he says, while others are glad to put the passions of youth behind them. He tells an anecdote about the dramatist Sophocles that suggests he took the latter view. When Socrates asks him if his wealth is a consolation to him in his old age,

Beyond Walls

105

Cephalus replies with another anecdote, about the politician Themistocles. To Socrates's question about what he has gained from being rich, Cephalus replies that his wealth has made it easier for him to avoid unintentional wrongdoing or lying, failing to make due religious sacrifices, or leaving debts unpaid. He quotes some lines from the poet Pindar which he understands to make the same point. Having given Socrates the benefit of his philosophy of life, and demonstrated that he has rubbed shoulders with some famous Athenians in his time, he goes off – not to appear again in the dialogue – to make yet another sacrifice to his gods, leaving his son Polemarchus to take his place in what we are invited to think of as the properly philosophical discussion that follows and constitutes the bulk of *Republic*.

These walls, then, embrace a man who assumes he can converse with Socrates on equal terms. However he has mistaken sententiousness – and a passing knowledge of the words of famous Athenians – for philosophy. His voice is echoed today in that of (what some rather rudely caricature as) the Saloon Bar in a pub in one of the more prosperous parts of the UK: 'You're a philosopher, Mr Socrates. Now *my* philosophy is … .' Socrates's way of philosophizing is well equipped to deflate people like this, but Cephalus does not stay to take the risk. Like his son, he knows you can't persuade people who won't listen. This is the atmosphere in which that long dialogue, *Republic*, takes place and by which we can see, if we are alert to its location, the quality of its philosophizing is compromised.

The *Symposium* is also set in a place of privilege: a dinner– or drinking–party hosted by Agathon, a prize-winning tragedian (this dates the dialogue, with reasonable certainty, to the year 416 BCE). The guests at the party are prominent Athenians, including the comic dramatist Aristophanes, the politician Alcibiades and of course Socrates himself. They agree to forgo the usual entertainments at such parties (such as flute-girls and other female company) in favour of making speeches in praise of *erōs* ('love', but the word has a strong flavour of sexual passion). The speeches are generally light-hearted and, with the possible exception of Sophocles's, neither profound nor particularly philosophical, in the sense we expect of Plato's dialogues. They are, as Waterfield (2008: xxi–xxii) notes, entirely conventional: the speakers merely compete to find different ways of praising *erōs*, with hardly a word about its drawbacks.

The significance of the date of the party, which Plato has made sure we notice by placing it in the house of Agathon, is that the following year was calamitous for Athens. Its leaders, with the enthusiastic support of Alcibiades, decided to send an expedition against Syracuse, in Sicily, in the hope of securing a conclusive advantage in their war with Sparta. The Sicilian Expedition was indeed a turning point in the war with Sparta, but not in the way the Athenians had hoped. It was a disaster. Roughly 40,000 Athenian men and 200 ships were lost. The historian Thucydides gives a harrowing account of the defeat and of the sufferings of around 7,000 Athenian prisoners of war in the stone quarries of Syracuse. He describes it as 'the most calamitous of defeats; for they were utterly and entirely defeated; their sufferings were on an enormous scale; their losses were, as they say, total; army, navy, everything was destroyed, and, out of many, only few returned' (Thucydides, *History of the Peloponnesian War*, end of Book 7, trans. Warner, 1954).

The Sicilian Expedition is often regarded as the culmination of Athens's characteristic hubris: its arrogant assumption of superiority over the rest of Greece (let alone, we might say today, over non-Greeks). There were other signs of this at the time, including the desecration of the statues of Hermes that stood at crossroads and roadsides throughout Athens. The vandals were never caught and their motives never established, but they were widely supposed to be youths on their way home from parties not unlike that hosted by Agathon. Alcibiades himself was suspected of being involved, but nothing was ever proved against him or anyone else.

What, then, were the foremost citizens of Athens – its writers, philosophers, intellectuals (its elites, perhaps) – doing while the crisis of their city festered towards its climax? Plato shows them playing party-games in the house of one of their own, and uncritically sentimentalizing the wonders of *erōs*. Of course it is possible to regard the speeches at the feast as displaying the blithe artistic and intellectual sophistication that gives life meaning even as the lights of civilisation grow dim. It seems more natural however to see them as emblematizing irresponsibility: there is no hard thinking here about anything, least of all about the moral and political crisis descending on Athens. If this is Philosophy in the Community, what it shows that some kinds of communities – particular walls, we might say, are inimical to it, and even tend to corrupt it.

Other walls again in Plato's dialogues cannot be separated from what transpires within them. Socrates's *Apology*, his defence against charges brought against him of impiety and corruption of the young, takes place in a Court of Law. The *Crito* takes place in the prison cell where Socrates awaits the day of his execution: he explains to his friend Crito that the seriousness of his philosophical mission cannot be reconciled with Crito's proposal to bribe the gaoler to allow Socrates to escape into exile. The *Phaedo* is set in the same cell and supposedly records Socrates's conversation with his friends on the last day of his life, which ends with him drinking hemlock, as prescribed by the Athenian Court. Much of the dialogue is taken up with the question of the immortality of the soul and its ability to survive the death of the body. Here the confinement of the walls of the prison cell seem to confer an extraordinary solemnity on what is said within them; to the point where they distract, it might be said, from the weakness of Socrates's arguments for the soul's immortality. At the same time it is not clear whether we should read Socrates's arguments as an attempt to console his sorrowing friends. It is not clear whether the solemnity of the occasion guarantees its philosophical significance or reveals its marvellous, ordinary humanity. As if these two, of course, could ever be entirely separated.

* * *

Perhaps I should offer some explanation at this point for writing the next part of this chapter in autobiographical form. There is a reluctance on the part of philosophers to devote any thought to what we might call 'philosophy's walls': the physical setting in which the study of philosophy and philosophical discussion takes place or, to put it less abstractly, where the philosopher and the student of philosophy live, work and study. It is notable that those who are an exception to this, such as Montaigne – who writes about the dimensions of his study, the inscriptions on its beams, the lavatory situated by

Beyond Walls 107

the side of it, his cat – have never been fully accepted into the philosophical canon. No doubt this is at least partly due to the long philosophical tradition of separating intellect and reason from the body and its sensations, a separation that is particularly marked in the *Phaedo* itself, where it operates chiefly as part of the rather desperate argument that while the body may die, the soul will not. It would be ironic, if not dishonest, to argue for more attention to the physicality of philosophy while excluding oneself – one's *self* – from it in the manner of philosophy's conventional academic practitioners.

My own formal introduction to philosophy took place under the conditions of, so to speak, a double confinement. The text set for A-level study at my Grammar school[1] was Plato's *Phaedo*: the account, supposedly written by Phaedo of Elis (Plato being absent through illness), of the conversation between Socrates and his friends on the day that ended with his judicial execution by the draught of hemlock. The confines of the prison cell were strangely echoed by the room in which our lessons took place: it was a stockroom, made intimate, or claustrophobic, by the shelves of textbooks that lined its walls, and the absence of a window. Since the class consisted of just one other student and myself, it no doubt did not warrant the allocation of a proper classroom. The stockroom also enabled the teacher to smoke during the lessons: no one else ever seemed to use the room and in any case the smell of tobacco was soon overpowered by that of long-disused books, many of them speaking of the school's classical tradition of which my fellow-student and I were almost the last heirs. Here we grappled with Plato's Greek, as we encountered the frankly weak arguments for the immortality of the soul, tried to make sense of what some have regarded as Plato's Theory of Forms, and read the moving conclusion to the book:

> Raising the cup to his lips, quite readily and cheerfully [Socrates] drank off the poison. And hitherto most of us had been able to control our sorrow; but now when we saw him drinking, and saw too that he had finished the draught, we could no longer forbear, and in spite of myself my own tears were flowing fast; so that I covered my face and wept, not for him, but at the thought of my own calamity in having to part from such a friend ... he walked about until, as he said, his legs began to fail, and then he lay on his back, according to the directions, and the man who gave him the poison now and then looked at his feet and legs; and after a while he pressed his foot hard, and asked him if he could feel; and he said, No; and then his leg, and so upwards and upwards, and showed us that he was cold and stiff. And he felt them himself, and said: When the poison reaches the heart, that will be the end. He was beginning to grow cold about the groin, when he uncovered his face, for he had covered himself up, and said – they were his last words – he said: Crito, I owe a cock to Asclepius; will you remember to pay the debt? The debt shall be paid, said Crito; is there anything else? There was no answer to this question; but in a minute or two a movement was heard, and the attendants uncovered him; his eyes were set, and Crito closed his eyes and mouth.

> Such was the end, Echecrates, of our friend; concerning whom I may truly say, that of all the men of his time whom I have known, he was the wisest and justest and best. (trans. Jowett 1871)

Our teacher was a veteran of the Second World War: it was generally known (perhaps it was only a rumour, but I think not) that he had fought in Burma behind enemy lines. We also read with him Book 2 of Thucydides's *History of the Peloponnesian War*. When the narrative of the texts reached a climax – the death of Socrates, or the account of the Plataeans' slaughter of the Thebans who had bluffed their into their city ('One party managed to find a gate that was unguarded. A woman gave them an axe and they cut through the bar; but they were soon observed and only a few of them got away. Others were cut down here and there in different parts of the city': (Thucydides 2. 4, trans. Warner 1954) – he would take out a clasp-knife, pull up the blade, and stab it violently and repeatedly into his desk as we stumbled through our translation.

Perhaps it was the combination of respect for accuracy, if only at this stage in the matter of translation, in what I had been studying, together with its roots in ordinary experience, even if that was the experience of extraordinary times and people, that pushed me to apply to read (as it used to be put) philosophy at university. Perhaps the stockroom had a more subliminal effect, something stirred again by the monastic architecture of my prospective college, Merton, when I went there to be interviewed. It was impressive too that like most Oxbridge colleges founded in the Middle Ages, Merton was semi-fortified, divided into quadrangles: walls within walls and, on the south side, incorporating some of the original thirteenth-century city walls.

When I later came to study the philosophy of education, I was struck by the idea that any education worth the name must offer its pupils and students a 'place apart': somewhere removed from the clamorous demands of the world and an opportunity, almost to a requirement, to try some of the other ways of thinking – the 'languages of the curriculum', as it is sometimes put – that have from time to time been thought valuable. The phrase 'a place apart' is Michael Oakeshott's. He writes, of the school or university:

> Here, the learner is animated, not by the inclinations he brings with him, but by intimations of excellences and aspirations he has never yet dreamed of; here he may encounter, not answers to the 'loaded' questions of 'life', but questions which have never before occurred to him; here he may acquire new 'interests' and pursue them uncorrupted by the need for immediate results; here he may learn to seek satisfactions he had never yet imagined or wished for. (Oakeshott 1972: 25)

There is much to be said on behalf of this picture of education, not least as it applies to young people (and their families) who do not have enough 'cultural capital' to understand the importance of acquiring more of it. But it is – Oakeshott would not have denied it – a deeply conservative picture, one that too readily elides the privileged forms of understanding found in the academy with the assumption that the academy – universities in particular – exists primarily for the sake of replicating the forms of specialist knowledge possessed by its priestly caste.

Some of the kind of prejudice lurking here is illustrated by the philosopher Mary Midgley in her book, published shortly before her death in 2018, *What Is Philosophy For?* She describes her attempts in 1986 to rally support for beleaguered Philosophy departments in UK universities, of which eight were eventually closed, including her own department at the University of Newcastle. One of those whose support she canvassed was, as she describes him, the 'very distinguished Oxford Philosopher Michael Dummett'. In his reply to her letter he told Midgley that it was wrong to try to save the threatened provincial departments.

> Philosophy, he said, was a serious and highly technical subject which should only be studied at its own proper level. Any less professional approaches to it were useless and might even do harm. And what Dummett meant by the proper level is clear from a well-known passage in his writings where he said that 'the proper object of philosophy' had been finally established with the rise of 'the modern logical and analytical style of philosophizing'. This object, he said, was 'the analysis of the structure of thought, [for which] the only proper method [is] the analysis of language'. And, not surprisingly, he thought the business of linguistic analysis had now become a highly technical pursuit – something increasingly like nuclear physics – which could only be carried out by people specially trained in it. (ibid: 10)

Philosophy, as a 'highly technical subject', or what I referred to in p. 108 as the practice of a priestly caste, played a major role in the second half of my undergraduate degree. A substantial part of it was logic: it involved, among other things, examining the legacy of Bertrand Russell and the critique of it that had recently been mounted by Peter Strawson, then Waynflete Professor of Metaphysical Philosophy (a very High priest indeed), as well as his rejection of contemporary correspondence theories of truth and Quine's attempt to dismantle the analytic/synthetic distinction (the distinction between statements that true by virtue of their meaning and those that are true by virtue of some fact to be found in the world). Elements of these technicalities could be – and were – traced back to Kant and, beyond him, to Plato and Aristotle.

There was, I found, a certain kind of satisfaction to be had in getting to grips with this, much as there is a kind of satisfaction to be had in solving a cryptic crossword (I recall upsetting one of my tutors by making this comparison). And the attempts of Strawson and others to do justice to the richness and messiness of ordinary language in the face of those who favoured bringing highly formal kinds of logic to bear on it were, and are, important. But behind this there seemed to lie the assumption that no respectable philosophizing in other areas – political, aesthetic, ethical and so on – could possibly be done by anyone who had not sufficiently got to grips with the intricacies of logic; one sensed too that proficiency in logic was taken to be a general badge of intellectual merit.

What I have sketched here is a set of assumptions that have militated strongly, and undeservedly, against the emergence of anything so non-technical and walls-free as Community Philosophy. When I left university and began working as a secondary teacher in Birmingham I looked around for opportunities to engage with the broader kinds of philosophy that my undergraduate curriculum had not opened to me. I discovered that there were evening classes in Philosophy, at the Birmingham Midland Institute in the centre of the city. This was a much-respected institution. It traced its origins (not quite accurately) back to the Lunar Society, composed of scientists, intellectuals and industrialists (and many were all three) who met in private houses in Birmingham between 1765 and the early years of the nineteenth century. The Lunar Society took its name from the fact that meetings were held on dates when the light of the full moon made travel home at the end of the meeting safer for the participants. I mention this because the changing nature of the Society and its successor bodies in many ways reflects the changing nature of adult education outside universities and colleges. For the Lunar Society and similar associations there were of course no universities in England – apart from Oxford and Cambridge, so remote as hardly worth considering in respect of any contribution they might make – to draw on, define oneself by contrast with, or actively repudiate.

Those who gave the extramural courses, significantly so-called, that I enrolled on, by contrast with what might be called the community-based natural philosophers of the Lunar Society, were given by professional philosophers at the University of Birmingham. Although they were given outside the university and in premises and under the aegis of an organization independent of the university, there was little to distinguish them from lectures given in the university a few miles away. I believe that they were in fact based on the same notes as lectures given to second- and third-year undergraduates. This is by no means to criticize the lecturers, merely to note the continuing assumed connection between the university, as the natural home of philosophy, and the community outside it.

The classes I took were first on Wittgenstein and then on Chomsky. I still have my notes on the Wittgenstein classes, carefully written up. They chart the transition from the Wittgenstein of the *Tractatus*, and his treatment of problems about denotation and meaning, inherited from Russell and Frege among others, to the Wittgenstein of the *Philosophical Investigation* and his other late work such as *Culture and Value*. While my notes are not entirely coherent in places, they confirm my recollection that the lectures were of very high quality, not simply in terms of their academic content but also in terms of the patient good humour of the lecturer. They do not, in short, entirely support a simplistic contrast between the remoteness of conventional academic philosophy and the practices of the varieties of community philosophy today. And it was as true then as it is today that people went out to find philosophy for all kinds of reasons. For me these classes shed light on some of the philosophical problems that I had found obscure as an undergraduate. But, more than that, they confirmed my conviction that philosophical logic in the analytical mode was not only not the kind of philosophy I wanted to continue studying: it was not – despite assumptions widely made by highly respectable philosophers such as Dummett (above) – any kind of essential preliminary, or sort of universal key to the understanding of other branches of philosophy. Still less was it the essence of philosophy, compared to which environmental or medical ethics, or political philosophy, or philosophy of religion, or phenomenology could hardly expect to attract the attention of serious philosophical thinkers at all. But it seemed very telling that these were the only philosophy classes on offer at an institution whose mission was to reach members of the public with a broad interest in philosophy. Whether this was the decision of the Birmingham Midland Institute or of the University's Department

Beyond Walls 111

of Philosophy I was never able to discover. Perhaps they were indeed simply elements of the University Philosophy curriculum, and thought just by virtue of that to be the obvious thing to offer to the wider public.

In 1978 I left Birmingham for an appointment as lecturer in philosophy in the School of Education at the University of Durham. The job consisted largely of trying to persuade trainee and in-service teachers that there were interesting and significant issues in the practice of education: for example, what it is worthwhile to study, and why?; issues raised by classroom management and discipline; the moral content of education. The enthusiasm of the students was rather more variable than that of the students I had met in my Birmingham evening classes. My Durham students came in nearly all cases with no knowledge of philosophy at all, and were quite naturally distracted by how they were going to survive in the classroom during concurrent or impending teaching practicums. Certainly I was inexperienced in teaching students of this kind and at this level. But it did seem to me that they needed a 'place apart' in Oakeshott's sense if they were going to see what philosophy could offer, and that little was being gained by the well-meaning attempt to join theory and practice so closely together.

In these circumstances it was a pleasure – and a surprise – to be contacted by the University's Head of Adult and Continuing Education (ACE) and asked if I would like to teach an evening class in Philosophy. We met and talked at length. He had a sophisticated and wonderfully humane understanding of the work I would be doing. My classes would contain a mix of people across a broad spectrum of ability and grasp of philosophy, but a uniformly high level of motivation. They would come for all kinds of reasons, that might include dissatisfaction with their careers or marriages, the felt need to be part of a thoughtful and supportive community for one reason or other, or plain loneliness – and all of these motives and needs were legitimate and it was the job of ACE and its full- and part-time tutors to meet them as best we could. Some more oblique remarks suggested that colleagues in the university's Philosophy Department were quite ready to offer evening classes but – I was left to infer – they would resemble my classes in Birmingham in largely repeating what was taught to the full-time undergraduates. Behind this, I came to realize from further conversations with ACE colleagues over many years, was an unresolved and probably unresolvable tension. In order to be respectable in the wider university ACE's courses needed to be of the same quality, understood as meaning at the same level of rigour, as the regular undergraduate provision. However, at the same time ACE academics were completely committed to the idea that their students came to evening classes for the wide range of reasons that the Head of ACE had talked with me about. More than that: they and their colleagues in similar university departments in the UK and elsewhere in the Anglophone world were developing rich theories of what is sometimes called andragogy, the teaching of adults (as opposed to pedagogy, the teaching of children). These theories are familiar to practitioners of community philosophy today, having been in many cases been developed by them and in other cases informed them, in ways that are now difficult to disentangle. It seems strange that these theories had little impact on the teaching that went on in the wider university, where the students are of course adults, albeit

112 *Philosophy and Community*

usually young ones. It is perhaps too easy to conclude that ACE was seen as a threat to established practices, but it is the only conclusion that I could come to then, and that I can come to now.

Partly in the light of what I understood about these theories, and partly in the light of my conversations with the Head of ACE and his colleagues, I thought carefully about the title and content of my first evening class. The title I settled on was 'Philosophical problems in understanding ourselves and others'. It would begin with the question of how we can possibly understand people who are very different from ourselves: in gender, background, class, culture and even language. It would continue with a challenge to the idea that at least we understand ourselves, having privileged access to the inner core of our own being. I envisaged 'solipsism' as the only technical term that would be introduced in the first few sessions, and described, with deliberate vagueness to leave room for manoeuvre as the class and I got to know each other, the direction of travel as being towards the 'anti-psychiatry' of Thomas Szasz and R. D. Laing. I wanted, as far as possible, to honour what the members of the class brought with them, while providing the reassurance of a structure, and even a reading-list for those who wanted one.

The class that I met on the first evening numbered two dozen. They were as various as I had been led to expect. They included, among others, a crane-driver, a solicitor, a bricklayer, a published and performed playwright, a company director who had been a prisoner of war in Burma, a postman. There were two lecturers from a local teacher-training college that was in the process of closing down. Several people were ready to explain that they were in the process of a long journey of self-discovery; two told the group that they had from time to time been users of the mental health services. A substantial core of the group were regular extramural students who knew each other well and in some cases had supported each other through life crises. None came to these classes through the dark winter evenings in search of a qualification, since the course did not offer one. No one was looking for something to write on their resumé or to impress their friends with – in fact several said that their friends would have been less impressed than baffled. That this was specifically a university extramural class, carrying the word 'philosophy', seemed to be neither here nor there, beyond offering some guarantee that, in the words of one student, 'it wouldn't be a complete load of rubbish'. The consensus seemed to be that people came in the hope of meeting some interesting people and talking about some interesting ideas.

I taught an extramural evening class every year for the next twelve years. One clear and enduring message from the students was that they wanted books to read between the weekly sessions, but not technical philosophy texts. It was also clear that the crossover between philosophy and literature went down very well. The idea that literature and philosophy are distinct and separate has in any case always seemed to me misguided. (The technical philosophical logic that I have mentioned above might be thought of as creating its own particular literature.) So we took as themes Jane Austen's and George Eliot's treatment of virtues and vices; Platonic and Buddhist themes in the novels of Iris Murdoch; self-deception and wishful thinking in Ibsen's plays; the relationship between humankind and technology in Pirsig's *Zen and the*

Art of Motorcycle Maintenance; what it might mean for a novel to be 'postmodern'. I would introduce the topic in ten or fifteen minutes at the start of a session, and then the conversation would go where it went – with minimal steering on my part if, for example, I sensed that some people were disappointed that we had moved too far away from the text we had started from, or if, as in fact seldom happened, one person or group were taking over the discussion to the point where others felt excluded.

Were these classes successful? I don't know how to answer this question. Certainly many of the students came back year after year, and if that was often as much for the sense of community as anything else, then perhaps that is the best of outcomes, as we have learned to call them. It quickly came about too that at the end of the two-hour class a large subgroup, usually between six to ten students, and I would continue discussion at a nearby pub, until closing time. Here was true conversation: the turning to-and-fro of discussion, argument, anecdote, recollection, stories of personal experiences, reference to other books people had read or plays or films they had seen. There was, needless to say, no summing-up at the end. I recall a lot of laughter. One of the quieter members of the class who came for five or six years and always joined us in the pub afterwards, said to me (quietly) that it opened a world to her. I suspect many of us felt the same.

These classes – this community philosophy, though this title was not in use at the time – were brought to an end by the Conservative government of Margaret Thatcher. She regarded them as a leisure activity on a par with gardening or collecting stamps. In future they would continue only if they counted towards a qualification, and students would have to be assessed in much the same way as full-time undergraduates, and pay, in proportion, the same fees, which were many times more than the extramural students had been paying up to then. A second blow was what was called the 'equivalent level qualification': any extramural student who already held a first degree would have to pay 'full fees', that is, a very high fee, for taking a class at an equivalent level. Extramural education could only be understood as the pursuit of a qualification. Few of the extramural classes survived this attack. The Department of Adult and Continuing Education at my university, like many others throughout England (some of the other jurisdictions, for example, in Wales and Scotland, managed to soften the blow), was closed. Most of its full-time tutors were made redundant and their experience and wisdom thrown to the winds.

Such was the end of this particular practice of community philosophy, Echecrates, concerning which I may truly say, that of all the versions of philosophy that I have known, it was the wisest and justest and best. The revival of community philosophy described in this book is as extraordinary an achievement, I sometimes think, as its resurrection in Athens by Plato after the execution of Socrates.

Note

1   A-levels are taken, mainly in England, typically by sixteen- to eighteen-year-olds. A Grammar school was (and sometimes still is) a selective school in the state system of education.

References

Evans, J., (2012), *Connected Communities: Philosophical Communities*, London: Arts and Humanities Research Council.

Jowett, B., (trans.), (1871), *The Dialogues of Plato*, Oxford: Oxford University Press.

Lee, D., (1968), *Plato: The Republic*, London: Penguin.

Midgley, M., (2018), *What Is Philosophy For?* London: Bloomsbury.

Nails, D., (2002), *The People of Plato*, Indianapolis, IN/Cambridge: Hackett.

Oakeshott, M., (1972), 'Education: The Engagement and Its Frustration', in R. F. Dearden, P. H. Hirst and R. S. Peters, *Education and the Development of Reason*, 19–49, London: Routledge & Kegan Paul.

Thucydides, (trans. R. Warner, 1954), *History of the Peloponnesian War*, London: Penguin.

Waterfield, R., (2008), *Plato: Symposium*, Oxford: Oxford University Press.

Part Two

Philosophy and Community: Practices

8

In philosophical conversation with: Art audiences

Grace Lockrobin

Community Philosophy in museums and galleries

In theory, museums and galleries are an ideal setting for Community Philosophy. They are, after all, so public: often located in public places, publicly owned and – where entry remains free – open to all. Like few other places except libraries and religious buildings, their primary function is as containers of material loaded with meaning and ripe for enjoyment and exploration. The contents of museums and galleries promise to stimulate discussion about issues that concern everyone. Furthermore, while we might regard those who enter art spaces as a community insofar as they are members of society, they are a community in a more interesting sense: a group of people united by a common appreciation of art and ideas.

In practice, however, the problems that face those seeking to have philosophical conversations with – and in – the community are magnified in these settings. Many simply do not feel that art spaces are open *to them*: the contents seem alien, the atmosphere stifling. Often, those who do visit comprise a self-selecting group of disproportionately white, wealthy and well-educated people (Warwick Commission 2015). Furthermore, while art spaces may be centrally located in urban areas, they are not inhabited by a consistent and well-defined group of people. Although these spaces attract individuals within particular demographics, those who comprise 'art audiences' are likely to be a collection of strangers who don't regard themselves as a community. Finally, philosophy is often understood as something purely cerebral, whereas galleries are corporeal places that arouse the senses, engage the emotions and communicate by ambiguous and non-linguistic means. These features of the art environment may appear deeply *unphilosophical*, and this may cast doubt on the claims we make about the legitimacy of the work we do in museums and galleries.

So, if we envisage Community Philosophy as a practice that is potentially socially cohesive and intellectually challenging, then we have some work to do to address problems of access, diversity and sense of community that are evident when doing philosophy in museums and galleries. Philosophizing in this environment also requires that we rethink the philosophical methodology that we use in this context, and defend

118   *Philosophy and Community*

it as philosophy. So, of all the opportunities to engage in philosophical enquiry, why here and with these people? And what can this work tell us about community and philosophy? This chapter addresses these questions.

The social context of our work

For a little over a decade, through the work of Thinking Space, an organization I set up in 2008, I have been asking the question: What good can philosophy do in communities? A mixture of empirical evidence and professional experience so far suggests that philosophy can do a great deal of good, especially among communities where voices are sometimes marginalized – for example, among schoolchildren in receipt of free school meals (Gorard, Siddiqui and See 2017). Exploring this question has brought me the pleasure of philosophizing with people of all ages and backgrounds. These include schoolchildren, college and university students as well as adults in civic, cultural, professional, educational and recreational settings including libraries, boardrooms, conferences, woodland, theatres and parks. My co-enquirers have included preschoolchildren and their parents, learning-disabled people, refugees and asylum seekers, professionals – such as scientists and television producers – and older people, as well as fellow academics and educators. This has offered me insight into some of the ways in which philosophy enables people to explore the meaning and significance of foundational ideas – concepts such as existence, knowledge and value – on which we build our understanding of ourselves and the world around us. The benefits of exploring these matters in conversation, and of coming together to conduct these conversations face to face, are emotional as well as intellectual; they are also deeply social (Siddiqui, Gorard and See 2017).

The theoretical context of our work

Thinking Space's work is influenced by the notion of the Community of Enquiry first articulated by Charles Sanders Peirce (1877), then reworked by the educator, philosopher and social activist John Dewey (1938) before being finally operationalized in classrooms by Matthew Lipman (1988), originator of the Philosophy for Children (P4C) movement. The Community of *Philosophical* Enquiry is a group of people who come together to talk about the meaning of contested concepts that they share in common and are of central importance to human beings. Often supported by a facilitator, participants enter into deliberations together in which they will challenge assumptions and reasons in the expectation that new meaning or significance will arise as a result (Kennedy and Kennedy 2011). Although the Community of Philosophical Enquiry is sometimes understood in reductive terms as simply a set of procedures that include sharing a stimulus, generating questions and agreeing an agenda, it is much better understood as a regulative ideal: an articulation of the principles we aspire to when philosophize together. Among these aspirational ideas are the importance of puzzlement as the essential driver for enquiry; the centrality of the question as the means by which we frame that puzzlement; and the potential of distributed thinking, acts of 'wondering, questioning, inferring, defining, assuming, supposing, imagining, distinguishing and so on' that can be distributed within a group and can progress as a result (Lipman 2003: 95). Progress in an enquiry amounts to the emergence of new – or more nuanced – meanings, along with the internalization of dispositions that make us generally better at thinking.

A real example

In what follows, I discuss my work with 'art audiences' – by which I mean anyone willing to think philosophically about, and with the aid of, works of art. Such audiences do not merely comprise those who regularity visit art spaces, or love art. Over the last decade I have undertaken this work in partnership with museums, galleries and art departments in schools and universities, as well as with artists, curators, art educators and art students who have made use of an array of original artworks and artefacts and reproduced images, and the artistic creations of participants.

To provide some of the texture of a real workshop, I discuss in what follows examples from a 2017 project: 'Modern Visionaries: Van Dyck and the Artist's Eye' in collaboration with the Laing Gallery, Newcastle-upon-Tyne, UK, with the support of the National Portrait Gallery in London. This project was built around an exhibition of the same name, that had as its centrepiece Van Dyck's last known self-portrait (Van Dyck 1640). Painted in the mid-seventeenth century, it was an unusual image for the time in that it depicted the artist without any of the tools of the trade that would usually signify his status as a craftsman. Instead it presented someone who might be considered a public intellectual. Displayed alongside this work was a curated collection of painted, sculptural, filmic and photographic self-portraits as well as other depictions of artists from the twentieth century to the modern day. We were invited by the curator to devise four public workshops to run alongside the exhibition.

The setting for this conversation

Unlike many of our Community Philosophy projects in which a specific community is our starting point, and the venue is merely a practicality, our work with art audiences differs in that we begin with a decision about where the work will take place, identifying a particular aesthetically interesting environment such as a gallery, museum, sculpture park, or public art installation. We think of these projects as site-specific because of the way in which the surroundings and their contents influence the ethos of the enquiry and the substance and quality of thinking that takes place, as I will describe in what follows.

The communities taking part

When it comes to the crucial question of *who* participates in these conversations, we are often led by our gallery partners who have existing relationships with community groups, as well as strategic objectives to attract particular demographics such as older people or young families. Sometimes the subject of an exhibition will lend itself to working with a particular community such as students or special interest groups.

Our audiences for the four workshops that comprised 'Modern Visionaries' attended both open and closed workshops. The free open workshops attracted a mixed group of adults recruited from the city's two universities, the local Job Centre and the regional art educators' network. In our closed workshops we devised sessions for a specially invited group of young art students, and a group of paying secondary school teachers attending as part of their continuing professional development.

The subject of the enquiry

At the planning stage of a project like this we often work closely with an expert such as a curator – or in other cases with an artist, art educator, art academic or philosopher of art. Together we consider the artworks that will feature in the workshops and discuss the themes they illuminate, speculating on the resonances they may have for the audience we have in mind. During these discussions, we are looking for a conceptual hook – an irresistible idea that is both interesting and inclusive. Having learnt that dialogue is more focused and free-flowing when it is carefully framed rather than completely open-ended, we build our sessions around a central concept or concepts. These themes sometimes emerge from a conversation within our team, on other occasions our participants set the agenda.

Obvious starting points for these enquiries are aesthetic concepts like value, creativity and beauty. However, the appeal of Community Philosophy in galleries is the way in which art is pregnant with ideas on every aspect of human life: money, marriage and murder are all there. Consequently, the conversations we cultivate need not investigate the artwork itself, nor matters confined to the art world. This particular project initially provoked an analysis of the concept of self-portraiture and its rationale, value and ubiquity. But this theme gave way to a much wider discussion of self-image, self-knowledge and self-belief and, within these topics, representation, reputation, authenticity, vanity, celebrity, talent and genius.

The conceptual theme is a frame for the session, but the ultimate focus of discussion will be a problem that intrigues the group, eventually captured in the form of a question. For the enquiry to gain traction participants must enter a state of aporia or doubt. Confronting a seemingly impassable problem makes this necessary shift from certainty to uncertainty possible. However, participants must also feel that they have the resources required to make some progress. The chosen question represents a vision of progress would look like; it translates the inarticulate feelings of confusion experienced in the face of philosophical problems, into a task that can be tackled together. With this in mind, at the planning stage we are alert to the problematic nature of the chosen theme, for example the limits of self-knowledge and the question of whether one can be wrong about one's own nature, desires or beliefs. During some of these workshops we presented participants with explicit problems to help them experience the aporetic tension that signals the need to enquire. In other workshops, we encouraged the group to identify a problem themselves. In every case, we are always careful not to prejudge the issues that will capture their interest and refrain from attempting to map out the content of discussion in advance, or manipulate the discussion once it begins.

The form the enquiry takes

Rather than following a fixed format, our aesthetic enquiries combine multiple activities that promote a blend of curiosity, confusion and challenge with the aim of creating a hospitable atmosphere for philosophical thinking about a central question. Since it is likely that we arrive at these questions and facilitate the ensuing discussion using structures and strategies that are widespread in Community Philosophy, I have chosen not to elaborate on these aspects of a session here, but instead to describe those more distinctive exercises that explicitly bring together aesthetic appreciation and philosophical thinking. These exercises encourage an examination of the artworks and their organization, with the expectation that this will provide insights into the meaning of the central concept that we are exploring, ultimately supplying us with new ideas that will help us to answer our chosen philosophical questions.

Contemplative exercises: Looking for meaning in the artworks

In order to extract meanings from artworks, we encourage participants to slow down, looking more closely at artworks than they may be accustomed to doing. At the beginning of one of our enquiries on the theme of 'self-image', we spent an extended period of time in front of a single artwork, *Head of a Young Boy* by Pablo Picasso (1945). After a period of silence, we first invited the group to preface their contributions with 'in the artwork, I notice … ', documenting as many publicly accessible visual, auditory and tactile perceptions as possible. Our intention was that the group would point out features of the artwork that some may have overlooked, but that everyone could access. For example, 'I notice it depicts a child'; 'I notice he has large black eye'; 'I notice it is a lithograph print'; 'I notice there is a signature' and 'I notice the date'. We took our time over this task, allowing for lengthy periods of silent looking. Occasionally, participants would smuggle their own interpretations into the exercise such as 'I notice it is a brooding picture'. Where this happened, we would encourage them to treat the exercise as a game in which we must initially refrain from meaning-making, until everyone has enjoyed a shared experience of concrete features of the work.

Next we look for new contributions that begin with 'in myself, I notice…', collating all those privately accessible emotional, intellectual, imaginative, interpretative, critical and questioning ideas that respond to the things that we can all see. Here responses included 'I notice myself feeling melancholy'; 'I notice myself judging it as crude or childlike'; 'I notice myself imagining that it is fake'; 'I notice myself objecting that this is not *really* a self-portrait'. Here we encouraged participants to link their private responses to public features of the artwork, for example: 'Perhaps because the work features a child, I notice its childlike qualities.'

I have suggested that artworks can be allies in the search for meaning, but something that obstructs this is the tendency of audiences to treat their aesthetic experiences as entirely subjective and to talk about them in obscure, inaccessible or exclusionary ways. These attempts to 'show our working' during aesthetic experience help us to bridge the gap between the subjective and objective elements of enquiry. While the scaffolding of this activity might seem excessively elaborate or controlling, these exercises can actually emancipate the later extended dialogue from some of the problems caused by using opaque references to the stimulus. In an earlier iteration of the exercise, participants initially described the same painting with monosyllables like 'sad' and 'strange'. When asked to elaborate, they said self-conscious and unilluminating things about the colour and the use of line. However, after a period of careful looking, the group began to discuss whether it was appropriate to include this work in a collection of self-portraits. Some speculated that it could have been an image produced by Picasso in his childhood, before one participant pointed out the date which we noted was just at the end of the Second World War. Picasso was not a boy when this melancholy image was produced; he was a grown man. In fact, the participant speculated, Picasso's contemporaneous work – such as *Guernica* (1937) – reveals him to be someone deeply horrified by war, someone who had lost the innocence of childhood. This interpretation of the image as a nostalgic self-portrait attracted everyone's full attention stimulating a flurry of further questions: 'Must a self-portrait resemble the artist?'; 'Should we try to discern inner lives from outward appearances?' and 'Can one hope to manage their own image?' Here contemplation had been genuinely stimulating, allowing the group to uncover the kinds of problems that drive good discussion.

Exploratory exercises: Looking for meaning in the art space

People behave differently in art spaces: they whisper, wander, linger and examine – perhaps because they know they are surrounded by meaning. Besides the richness of the artworks themselves, even the architecture and organization of the gallery is meaningful. Art spaces invite viewers to move along various trajectories experiencing objects in a particular order, for example, by artist, chronologically or thematically. Exploring a gallery guided by this kind of curatorial direction can feel like a physicalized form of argument in which the space persuades us to see ideas in a particular way. But unlike a linear argument, a gallery is multidimensional and we needn't explore it by walking from one end to the other as the room insists. Instead we can wander through it drifting towards those artefacts that attract our attention and lingering in front of those that hold it. To work like this is not only a pleasure but a cerebral and somatic

Philosophy with Art Audiences   123

freedom that we rarely experience in traditional engagement with philosophical texts. Exploring gallery spaces freely sharpens our sensitivity to ideas that have philosophical potential, making us better equipped to identify our own philosophical interests. This is something I see as central to the autonomy of Community Philosophy. In our work, we promote exploration by giving participants permission to wander. Often at the beginning of the enquiry and periodically throughout, we move around at will, looking for the most beautiful, boring or banal work, the most insightful, impenetrable or interesting. Within our repertoire of exploratory exercises – as a result of this wandering – we pick favourites, describe them, name and rename them, compare and contrast them, sort and classify works, rank and order them, advocate for them and critique them and imagine them otherwise. In each case we make our own discoveries, and when we show other people what we have found, we all stand or sit in front of the artwork in order to contemplate it.

One of our Modern Visionaries workshops began with the request that everyone wander until they found a work they felt they could have made themselves – an exercise that anticipates a common criticism of bad art or non-art. The ensuing discussion of the candidates' shortcomings, and the lively disagreement this created, produced a working set of considerations for the evaluation of art.

Creative exercises: Looking for meaning in the artistic process

For the most part, our work positions members of the Community of Philosophical Enquiry as active participants when it comes to philosophy; yet – often for practical reasons – they remain passive observers when it comes to art. Yet it is not art appreciation but *art-making* that is the mirror image of philosophizing. If philosophizing brings unique personal insights in the search for meaning, it is plausible that art-making does this too. So, where possible, our workshops also invite people to paint, draw, write or otherwise create in response to a workshop theme. These activities serve a number of functions. The period of making is usually rather quiet, allowing participants time to think. Furthermore, the products of these activities, like the artworks in a gallery, are meaningful. However, during these exercises, we have the additional benefit of having the maker present to talk about what they have made. Finally, the proliferation of artistic responses to a particular a creative exercise gives us plenty of material to compare, contrast, classify, explain, exclude and so on. This can greatly enhance the breadth and depth of our conceptual analysis.

During one of our Modern Visionaries workshops on the concept of 'representation', one group of art students responded to the brief to produce self-portraits in numerous interesting ways. Some students dutifully used the mirrors that we provided, producing their own likeness in pencil or chalk. However, others proceeded without the use of mirror making more impressionistic images. Others drew inanimate objects that symbolized their nature or interests, while one produced an abstract form that attracted questions about whether it represented anything at all.

Exemplification exercises: Instrumentalizing art in the search of the meaning of concepts

I now hope to show how we use art in a different way. Rather than seeking to extract meaning imbued in the works by the intentions of the artist, the historical context or by curatorial placement, we also approach artworks as makers of meaning in our own right. One way we do this is to focus on the enquiry theme rather than the art, and to instrumentalize the artworks as a source of examples that can help us articulate our own ideas about the central concept we are exploring philosophically.

Examples are a crucial part of dialogic enquiry, but when novice philosophers draw examples from their wider experience – without a common point of reference – they can digress, talk past one another, or examples can proliferate beyond usefulness. Drawing examples from the artworks around us is a discipline that focuses the group on thinking *together*. Among the various activities we use to encourage exemplification, the most fruitful is the twin search for classic and controversial examples. With a concept in mind, in this case 'authenticity', participants working in pairs survey the gallery looking for that concept exemplified in an artwork in the most archetypical (or least controversial) way. Simultaneously they must also find a problematic case: an artwork that they are uncertain about how to classify: one that almost – or only just – conforms to their idea of the particular concept under scrutiny. So during the Modern Visionaries workshop we explored a gallery containing multiple possible examples of 'authenticity' including Sarah Lucas's *Eating a Banana* by the young British artist famous for sexually suggestive sculptures (see Lucas 1990); R. S. Lowry's *The Man with Red Eyes*, depicting a figure who has been weeping and produced at a time when his mother was dying (Lowry 1938); a relatively traditional self-portrait by Chris Ofili (see Ofili 1991); and *False Positive, False Negative* by Jane and Louise Wilson, sisters whose images appear in this conceptual piece with faces painted in geometric patterns that confound the facial recognition software used in CCTV (perhaps a self-portrait or a comment on surveillance culture or both?) (Wilson and Wilson 2012). Our participants were asked if there was a classic or controversial case of 'authenticity' among this set. From the diverse concrete examples this activity generated, we were able to extract more insightful thoughts on the abstract idea we were exploring together.

The challenges we face

Having set out the shape of our work with art audiences, revealing the philosophical and practical thinking that shapes our approach, I now turn to the problems highlighted in the introduction, followed by a discussion of some of the modest ways we have begun to address them.

It will by now be clear that our preference for locating our work in museums and galleries creates problems as well as opportunities. Our challenge is to devise opportunities for Community Philosophy that are broadly accessible and appealing, encourage diverse perspectives and represent diverse demographics, involve a genuine sense of community, but which are still robustly philosophical in approach. These challenges face anyone who wishes to create opportunities for the public to philosophize, but they are particularly acute for the outsider who organizes Community Philosophy on behalf of – instead of from within – a community. What is more, the wider context compounds these problems. Despite an enormous boost in visitor numbers (DCMS 2012) and incremental improvements in the diversity of visitors, the breadth of participation in the arts remains an enormous problem, especially in a UK culture where arts and cultural education is being devalued such that fewer people have the early experience with the arts that lays the foundation for lifelong engagement (Jeffreys 2018). Given the baggage philosophy already carries as an elitist activity that few encounter in their early education, we may assume that it is poorly placed to assist with this problem. If we wish to broaden philosophical conversations to include other voices beyond those with plenty of cultural capital, then there might be better places to look for new recruits.

These concerns rest on a number of assumptions about Community Philosophy that require unpacking. The first is that Community Philosophy ought to be accessible to all; the second is that diversity is necessary in Community Philosophy; the third is that Community is a solely social or spatial concept and the fourth is that Philosophy is an entirely intellectual practice.

The assumptions we make

Community Philosophy should be accessible

The Community Philosophy we practise is motivated by the view that one of the primary ways in which philosophy benefits people is through their participation in it and through the impact this has on how they think and act. While I acknowledge that the public might also benefit from professional philosophers effecting social change or communicating interesting ideas, I think that the inherently participatory nature of philosophy means that, if people never think philosophically for themselves, they miss out on a uniquely life-enhancing experience. Justice requires that these benefits be distributed as equitably as possible.

Clearly, not every opportunity can be open to all. For Modern Visionaries, we devised workshops for specific people with a common purpose. Our commitment to accessibility focuses on avoiding the exclusion of people for arbitrary, unwarranted reasons. There is simply no justification for the exclusion of black and ethnic minority participants, or those who have experienced economic or educational disadvantage – even if this exclusion is widespread in the art world for structural reasons that are difficult to overcome.

Diversity is necessary in Community Philosophy

Two senses of diversity are at play here and both are important: we may wish our sessions to be both demographically and intellectually diverse. Philosophy is often perceived as elitist and for good reason since more than 80 per cent of full-time positions in academic philosophy are held by men, compared with 60 per cent in academia overall (Wilson 2013). These is also much evidence to suggest that women of all races, and men of colour, disappear from the profession or have greater difficulty obtaining permanent jobs (Alcoff 2002). As Meager states: 'If public philosophical practices are to gain credibility with various publics, then it stands to reason that philosophy needs to become more inclusive and representative of those publics' (2013: 13). But there is more to demographic diversity than creating events that better represent wider society for its own sake. There are good reasons to think that the intellectual diversity necessary for incisive and imaginative thinking rests, to some degree, on whether a broad range of life experiences nourish philosophical conversations. Academic philosophy has been criticized for discriminating against minorities in ethically *and epistemically* damaging ways 'by excluding them from inquiry; denying them epistemic authority; denigrating their modes of knowledge; elaborating theories that depict them as inferior or deviant; devolving social theories that make gendered power relations invisible; strengthening gender bias and social hierarchies' (Tripodi 2017: 3). These are not problems we seek to reproduce in the relatively young practice of Community Philosophy.

Community is more than a social or spatial concept

The setting of museums and galleries in the heart of conurbations obscures the fact that art spaces are unlike some of their other institutional neighbours such as churches, schools or community centres: these tend to be inhabited by a consistent and well-defined community. Although valued by the public, museums and galleries do not necessarily occupy the same emotional or intellectual space within a town or city as markets or cafés. Visits are likely to be infrequent, quiet, solitary affairs – quite unlike visits to their public places like the pub. Consequently, our work in this setting does not constitute Community Philosophy on account of the location.

Our work doesn't constitute Community Philosophy by virtue of its attempts to connect with the people I have dubbed 'art audiences' either. This group is typically a randomly assembled collection of strangers rather than a pre-existing, self-identifying community. While they sometimes appear to be demographically similar, these individuals do not live, learn, work or play alongside one another; they do not identify in some common way, nor do they necessarily share an interest in philosophy or art. They are a community only in the loosest sense of being 'the public' or members of society. To compound matters, coming together to talk about philosophy brings with it certain anxieties: many people have never done this before and do not know what to expect. Naturally some people are afraid of making themselves vulnerable in public. When taken together, these considerations might make us regard the art space as inimical to community-building.

Yet the establishment of a community is foundational to our approach. In order to listen to one another, learn from one another, build on one another's ideas, respect one another's point of view and yet demand that claims be warranted by evidence and reasons (Lipman 1988), we need a sense of community. Our task then is to create fleeting but meaningful communities for the duration of our time together. This is not quite the obstacle it may seem, since we understand community as something more than a spatial or social concept it is a *pedagogical concept*. Consequently, the building of a community is work that must be done in any group, including groups of friends, clubs and classes. A Community of Philosophical Enquiry is bonded together by a shared interest in the philosophical issues that it identifies as important. Prior social familiarity or spatial proximity is no guarantee of commitment to following the argument wherever it leads. This shared commitment – which is the cornerstone of the Community of Enquiry – arises within the course of a typical discussion where effort is made to cultivate an ethos of criticality, creativity, collaboration and care.

What we've learnt

It is from these convictions that we have attempted to address the challenges of access, diversity and the creation of a sense of community. In what follows I outline some of the things we have learnt in this process.

Artworks are mobile

Despite our preference for site-specific enquiry, engagement in this work does not always depend on individuals crossing the threshold of an institution. Museums and galleries, with philosophers in tow, can bring these resources into community settings too. One such project of ours involved touring primary schools with artefacts from the handling collection of regional archives, allowing children to touch, draw and ask questions – experiences that provided the stimuli for philosophical enquiry. We were encouraged to see that such work preserves some of the audience attentiveness and intrigue that makes artworks a productive source and instrument of enquiry. Engaging communities in aesthetic enquiry beyond the gallery walls can also be a way of inviting them in. Our series of visits laid the groundwork for the classes to visit their local museum and to engage philosophically with the objects in the context of an exhibition. For some of the most deprived communities we visited, this was the first time they had visited their local museum.

Aesthetic experiences are everywhere

We also learnt that it is possible to move beyond traditional ideas of the art space and the artwork and into other environments in search of candidates for artistic appreciation. When done well, this requires us to identify meaningful aspects of our surroundings and to encourage within the participants the expectation that meaning can be extracted from their own surroundings and situation. Amid the familiarity and mundanity of the classroom or community centre, this is often difficult but not impossible. During one of our projects working with a professional photographer, we provided students with digital cameras to take into the school grounds and invited

128   *Philosophy and Community*

them to capture images that resonated with our theme. In this instance the cameras reignited the curiosity encouraged by an art space and students returned with images that revealed an aesthetic and intellectual attentiveness towards their otherwise humdrum school yard.

We can use a common language

By encouraging our participants to attend closely to draw examples from concrete artworks in front of us – rather than making references to other artworks, artists or concepts – we attempt to sidestep some of the problems created by the exclusionary historical, technical and theoretical language that can deter the uninitiated and even obscure the clarity of what they mean to say (Jones 2015). The problem of exclusionary language also arises in philosophical culture and it is something we seek to minimize. We explicitly encourage participants to use accessible language, to refer to examples drawn from shared stimuli and to prioritize their own intuitions, ideas and arguments before those of other, famous thinkers. Despite these conventions, we are sensitive to the fact that historical, theoretical or technical contributions can provide useful ideas and points of reference for the enquiry. Consequently, our sessions do not prohibit mention of the ideas of great thinkers or the use of specialist language. However, where used these should help the group make sense of shared problems. The use of historical, theoretical or technical references makes us sound knowledgeable, but it is no substitute for grappling with the problems we uncover in their raw inarticulate state.

Philosophy can be playful

We have also learnt the importance of celebrating ambivalence, suspicion and even antipathy towards art and the art world. Working with curators has enabled us to observe the sometimes problematic way in which art lovers can revere artworks and devalue the contributions of participants who may not see what all the fuss is about. Through irreverent and playful activities, we take care to ensure our sessions do not assume the values or meanings we are investigating. During *Modern Visionaries*, we asked a newly formed group of strangers to award the worst artwork in the exhibition with a rosette. These kinds of activities often involve a lot of laughter, as well as faux outrage and impassioned defence as participants criticize celebrated works of art. As a result, they can be enormously bonding.

Defending our approach as philosophy

The exercises we use in our work encourage contemplation, exploration, creation and exemplification. In our work these strategies supplement the extended philosophical dialogue typical of Community Philosophy. Some may regard these additions as enjoyable and engaging, but lacking in philosophical rigour. Philosophical enquiry

Philosophy with Art Audiences   129

is ultimately a linguistic, logical and truth-seeking practice: when we philosophize together we search for meaning and express our insights using words – as clearly and precisely as we can according to shared rules. The philosophical search for meaning, and ultimately for truth, depends on this language-bound, rule-governed conceptualization and communication. Operating in this way allows ideas to be privately understood and publicly evaluated. However, working out what we think, and saying what we mean in words, is enormously difficult, particularly when we discuss the meaning of contested concepts and our own vocabulary feels inadequate.

While acknowledging the differences between philosophical and artistic forms of meaning-making, we think artistic works, spaces and practices can help here. Art employs a wild and varied vocabulary: sensory stimulus, impressions, allusions, references and suggestions that together communicate multiple, often conflicting, meanings. The inherent ambiguity of art demands that the audience intuits, infers and imagines as well as intellectualizes. We have found that these tools for talking and thinking can assist us in our philosophical search for, and communication of, meaning. In this work we are bilingual and translation between one way of meaning-making and another helps us make connections that may have been previously invisible to us. Philosophical enquiry with art – especially with idea-laden conceptual, symbolic or representational forms of art – opens up additional channels of communication and reveals fresh ways of thinking, perceiving, responding, feeling and being. Engaging philosophically with artworks in aesthetically sensitive ways develops perception, discrimination and responsiveness that are not only useful to us as philosophers, in very modest ways and when regularly practised, but also help us become better people able to examine situations and extract the details that matter (Nussbaum 1990). The value of this kind of practical wisdom or know-how is often overlooked by philosophical methodologies that favour the achievement of propositional knowledge, but that is their loss.

References

Alcoff, L. M., (2002), 'Does the Public Intellectual Have Intellectual Integrity?' *Metaphilosophy*, 33: 521–34.

Department for Culture Media and Sport (DCMS), (2012), *Taking Part: The National Survey of Culture, Leisure and Sport Adult and Child Report 2011/2012*, London: DCMS.

Dewey, J., (1938), *Logic: The Theory of Inquiry*, New York: Henry Holt.

Gorard, S., Siddiqui, N., and See, B. H., (2017), 'Can "Philosophy for Children" Improve Primary School Attainment?' *Journal of Philosophy of Education*, 51 (1): 5–22.

Jeffreys, B., (2018), 'Creative Subjects Being Squeezed, Schools Tell BBC', BBC News, 30 January 2018, [Online], Available at: https://www.bbc.co.uk/news/education-42862996, Accessed 10 December 2018.

Jones, S., (2015), 'Galleries: Let's Ditch the Artspeak and Arty Bollocks', *The Guardian*, 30 July 2015, [Online], Available at: network/2015/jul/30/galleries-lets-ditch-the-artsp eak-and-artybollocks, Accessed 30 June 2018.

Kennedy, N., and Kennedy, D., (2011), 'Community of Philosophical Inquiry as a Discursive Structure, and Its Role in School Curriculum Design', *Journal of Philosophy of Education*, 45 (2): 265–83.

Lipman, L., (1988), *Philosophy Goes to School*, Philadelphia: Temple University Press.

Lipman, M., (2003), *Thinking in Education*, Cambridge: Cambridge University Press.

Lipman, M., (2011), 'Philosophy for Children: Some Assumptions and Implications', *Ethics in Progress*, 2 (1): 3–16.

Lipman, M., Sharp, A. M., and Oscanyon, F. S., (1980), *Philosophy in the Classroom*, 2nd edn, Philadelphia: Temple University Press.

Lowry, R. S., (1938), '*The Man with Red Eyes*', Oil on canvas, 535 mm × 435 mm, London: National Portrait Gallery, [Online], Available at: https://www.npg.org.uk/collections/search/portrait/mw60217/LS-Lowry, Accessed 10 June 2018.

Lucas, S., (1990), '*Eating a Banana*', Digital print on paper, 539mm × 596 mm, London: Tate Britain, [Online], Available at: https://www.tate.org.uk/art/artworks/lucas-eating-a-banana-p78443, Accessed 10 June 2018.

Meagher, S., (2013), 'Public Philosophy: Revitalizing Philosophy as a Civic Discipline', Kettering Foundation, [Online], Available at: https://publicphilosophynetwork.nin g.com/page/kettering-report-1, Accessed 18 January 2018.

Nussbaum, M. C., (1990), *Love's Knowledge: Essays on Philosophy and Literature*, Oxford: Oxford University Press.

Ofili, C., (1991), '*Chris Ofili*', Oil on canvas, 1019 mm × 442 mm, London: National Portrait Gallery, [Online], Available at: https://www.npg.org.uk/collections/search/por trait/mw132439/Chris-Ofili?LinkID=mp14611&role=sit&rNo=0, Accessed 10 June 2018.

Peirce, C. S., ([1877] 1958), 'The Fixation of Belief', in C. S. Peirce, *Selected Writings*, 91–112, New York: Dover Publications.

Picasso, P., (1945), '*Head of a Young Boy*', Lithograph on paper, 307mm × 227mm, London: Tate Britain, [Online], Available at: https://www.tate.org.uk/art/artworks/pic asso-head-of-a-young-boy-p11364, Accessed 10 June 2018.

Picasso, P., (1937), '*Guernica*', Oil on Canvas, 34900mm x 77007mm, Madrid, Museo Nacional Centro de Arte Reina Sofía, [Online], Available at: https://www.pablopicasso. org/guernica.jsp, Accessed 3 February 2019.

Siddiqui, N., Gorard, S., and See, B. H., (2017), 'Non-Cognitive Impacts of Philosophy for Children', Project Report, School of Education, Durham University.

Tripodi, V., (2017), 'The Value of Diversity and Inclusiveness in Philosophy: An Overview', *Rivista di Estetica*, 64: 3–17.

Van Dyck, A., (circa 1640), '*Sir Anthony van Dyck*', Oil on canvas, 560mm × 460mm oval, London: National Portrait Gallery, [Online], Available at: https://www.npg.org.uk/co llections/search/portrait/mw245199/Sir-Anthony-van-Dyck, Accessed 10 June 2018.

Warwick Commission on the Future of Cultural Value (2015), 'Enriching Britain: Culture, Creativity and Growth', Coventry: University of Warwick, [Online], Available at: https ://warwick.ac.uk/research/warwickcommission/futureculture/finalreport/warwick_co mmission_final_report.pdf, Accessed 20 July 2018.

Wilson, J., and Wilson, L., (2012), '*Jane and Louise Wilson*' ('*False Positive, False Negative*'), Screen print on mirrored acrylic, 650 mm × 965 mm, London: National Portrait Gallery, [Online], Available at: https://www.npg.org.uk/collections/search/portrait/mw232991/Jane-and-Louise-Wilson-False-Positive-False-Negative, Accessed 10 June 2018.

Wilson, R., (2013), 'Women Challenge Male Philosophers to Make Room in Unfriendly Field', *The Chronicle of Higher Education*, LIX: 19, January 18.

9

In philosophical conversation with: Professionals

Jim Baxter

Professions are commonly thought to be *communities of practice*. Wenger (2000) identifies three identifying conditions of a community of practice: First, there needs to be a shared *domain* of interest. This could be, for example, a TV programme, a football club or a type of artistic practice. Second, there needs to be a *community*. Members of the community interact with each other and engage in shared activities. This is facilitated through a shared space, physical or virtual (a message board or a social media network, for example), within which members of the community can gather to share ideas, comment on each other's practice, offer and seek encouragement and advice and so on. Finally, there needs to be a *practice*. Members of the community are engaged in the same type of activity: a particular style of painting, say, or domestic electrical work. By engaging in the community and interacting with their peers, practitioners develop a shared set of resources – knowledge, skills, understanding, stories, cases – through which they are able to improve their individual practice and thus the practice of the community as a whole. Professions fulfil all three criteria. The domain and the practice are defined by the type of work in which the profession is engaged. The community is realized through formal and informal networks of interaction among professionals. Many, though not all, of these are facilitated through the professional body, which runs training events, holds conferences, articulates responses to technical and social change on behalf of the profession and formalizes the ethical principles underlying the profession's work through a code of practice.

My own involvement with professionals comes through working, over the last ten years, as a consultant to a variety of organizations, including professional bodies and organizations employing professionals. The professionals with whom I have worked in this time have included accountants, insurance brokers and underwriters, actuaries, independent financial advisers, bankers, a variety of medical professionals, engineers (including electrical, software, mechanical, chemical, civil and nuclear engineers), intellectual property attorneys, town planners, chartered surveyors, ecologists and environmental managers.

The usual setting for conversations with professionals is in continuing professional development (CPD) courses, which are organized either through employing

132   *Philosophy and Community*

organizations, directly as open courses, or most commonly, through professional bodies. Thus, the setting for these conversations – when they take place face-to-face – might be in the workplace or the university, but is most commonly in a training room provided by the professional body, either at their own premises or in a hotel or other third-party meeting venue. Just as often, though, the courses take place online. Discussion is integrated into online courses either by arranging webinars using video-conferencing software or by using discussion forums. Whereas a webinar takes place synchronously, requiring participants to log in at a particular time and have access to the relevant software and some minimal hardware, discussion forums can take place asynchronously. For example, a cohort of fifteen professionals might be given a case study and asked to formulate a group response to it over a period of, say, three days. Participants can log in on several occasions during that time, giving both their own initial response to the case and reacting to others' comments. This has the advantage of flexibility, allowing professionals to fit the discussion around their working lives, but also allowing participants in different countries and time zones to take part in the same conversation. It also has another advantage which is less frequently noted: while some participants may prefer the directness of a face-to-face conversation, participants who are less socially confident may be more likely to express an opinion if they can consider and revise that opinion before submitting it, instead of having to speak spontaneously. My experience is that discussion forums are less likely to be dominated by a small number of confident participants than are face-to-face conversations.

The content of courses is designed, in part, to give participants an opportunity to practise thinking through ethical[1] issues and making ethical decisions in a setting in which the consequences of those decisions are only hypothetical. As well as developing ethical reasoning skills, however, a key aim of this process is to help participants to feel the *force* of ethical issues. For example, an engineer working on safety systems for self-driving cars may see her job as being simply to solve the problems she is presented with. However, the way in which she solves these problems may impact directly upon the public, significantly, in either a positive or a negative way. Encouraging her to see this, and by extension, encouraging professionals to see that they have ethical responsibilities which extend beyond the confines of their immediate job, is an important aim of ethics CPD.

Case studies are a key element of courses. Derived from real professional experience and typically identified through conversation with professional body representatives, these ensure that conversations remain grounded in professional practice. They are not used to illustrate simple points of principle, however, but rather to encourage participants to come to a better, more sophisticated understanding of the values underlying the case. By moving between the general and the particular, participants come to understand better what ethical values mean, by understanding what they mean *in practice*. For example, imagine a group of insurance professionals is asked to respond to a case in which they witness an apparent minor insurance fraud perpetrated by a friend. Should they confront the friend? Ask her to return the item for which she has fraudulently claimed? Report her to the authorities, or to the insurance company? A relevant consideration might be the potential impact that insurance fraud has on the public interest, for example by causing a general increase in insurance premiums. Given that, as professionals, the participants have a responsibility to safeguard and promote the public interest, does this make a difference to what they should do in the case? Answering this question might mean that the participants' response to the case is informed by a better understanding of the underlying issues, but it also might enrich their understanding of what the professional duty to the public interest requires *in general*, and how it relates to other ethical considerations, such as loyalty to friends or the need to treat people fairly and with respect.

Another key element of these conversations, and one on which I intend to focus in this chapter, takes the form of reflection on the nature of *professionalism*, and of the particular profession of which participants are members. Reflecting on these issues can affect the way participants see their own ethical relationships with clients, colleagues and wider society. For example, a central element of professional ethics is the requirement to maintain and justify the trust of the public (Bennion 1969, chapter 1; Friedson 1994, chapter 9). In a discussion with a group of actuaries, this might be brought to light by noting the disparity of power and knowledge between actuaries and the general public. Actuaries, through their decisions, can profoundly affect the well-being of a very broad swathe of the public: pension-holders, insurance policy-holders and so on. These members of the public, however, are unlikely to have anywhere near the sophisticated understanding of the decisions that affect them as do the actuaries who are making them. In most professions, these disparities are thought to ground the requirement of trust between professionals and the public. But actuaries must face the fact that, not only does most of the public not know as much about their work as they do themselves, very few of the public even have more than a very vague idea of what an actuary is. This marks them out as different from other professionals, such as doctors or lawyers. What does this then say about the relationship of trust? Can the public trust a group of people they barely know exist? Is their lack of visibility an ethical failing on the part of the actuarial profession? Do individual members have a duty to make their profession more visible? I include this example not to suggest a particular answer to these questions but to illustrate the way these conversations work in general. The intention is to highlight certain theoretical considerations, along with certain observable facts and, on the basis of these, to encourage participants to consider their normative implications for their profession and for themselves personally. This philosophical form of reflection, I believe, can be enlightening for professionals.

It is also, on the other hand, unfamiliar to most professionals and is often challenging for them. Relatively little of the reflection, idea-sharing and learning undertaken within professional communities, in the ordinary run of things, is philosophical in nature. More typically, professionals reflect on, and share ideas about, more technical aspects of their area of practice. While ethics is sometimes discussed, this is typically articulated in terms of regulation (of the content of the code of ethics, examples of unethical practice, disciplinary procedures and so on) or of organizational reputation and scandal. Despite this, it seems to me that philosophical reflection and discussion can be of value to professionals in helping them come to a better understanding of their domain of interest, of the practice in which they are engaged and of the

134 *Philosophy and Community*

community of which they are a member, in a way which helps them to become better professionals.

In this chapter I intend to explore some different ways in which valuable insights can come from reflecting philosophically on the nature of professionalism itself, and of the particular profession in which participants are working. Reflection of this kind crystallizes ideas which may be latent in the way professionals think about themselves and their work. Most professionals will be aware that they have responsibilities which arise from their being a member of a profession. They will have some sense that their work is 'more than just a job'. They will be aware that, in some sense, their conduct can reflect not just on themselves and their employer but also on their profession as a whole. They will typically feel something of a sense of pride in being a member of their profession. They will have an idea that there is such a thing as 'professional integrity', related to but distinct from ordinary integrity, which is, or should be, a central consideration in how they approach their work. Thinking philosophically about these ideas allows them to gain an understanding not just of what their ethical responsibilities are (which could be achieved largely by gaining familiarity with the code of ethics) but of how those responsibilities are generated by the nature of professional work itself and of their relationship with clients and the public. Thus, they come to a much better understanding of *why* they have these responsibilities, and of why they are important. Understanding why an ethical principle is important allows them to weigh it alongside other considerations when responding to situations and cases. For example, understanding why professional confidentiality is important helps professionals to understand its limits and to weigh it alongside other ethical considerations such as the public interest in deciding how to act in a particular case.

Another way in which philosophical reflection can help professionals is motivationally. A pre-reflective understanding of the professional's position – one which I have found to be prevalent in many professions – may be characterized as follows: professionals' primary responsibility is to their employer, derived from a contractual relationship in which the employer pays the professional a salary in return for their help in returning a profit to the employer. The professional has a responsibility to serve the client's interests because doing so is the primary means through which profit is delivered to the employer. Ethical constraints are set by law and regulation.[2] Through engaging philosophically with their profession, professionals can move away from this pre-reflective understanding, and instead come to see themselves as a member of a group with a broader social purpose and a set of fundamental values and principles, which are derived from the societal need for professions to exist and from the privileged position of professionals relative to their clients and the public. For many professionals at least, this understanding of the ethical framework in which they operate is a more effective motivator than the pre-reflective understanding outlined earlier. Professional pride is generated not only by the feeling of a job well done but also by the sense of a broader public value in the work. Moreover, being motivated in this way enables professionals better to fulfil their responsibilities to clients and the public. If the value of these responsibilities is seen as essentially instrumental and ultimately derived from the value of the employer, it is perhaps more likely to come under pressure

Philosophy with Professionals

in particular cases: if greater profit can be returned to the employer by acting against the client's interests, and there is little or no prospect of the action's reflecting negatively on the professional's or the employer's reputation, then why not act against the client's interest? In contrast, if that interest is seen as a more fundamental value derived from the nature of the work itself, it may be less likely to be disregarded.[3]

A final way in which philosophical reflection on professionalism can help professionals is in motivating and equipping them to be active, critical members of their own profession. A professional who comes to see their profession as an institution which exists to serve the public interest, for example, is likely to be more alert to the profession's success or failure in living up to that central purpose. More generally, engaging in discussion with some degree of philosophical rigour helps professionals to develop their reasoning skills. This is valuable to the professional community as a whole, as a community of reasoners.

In the remainder of this chapter, I will give attention to some further ways in which critically examining the nature and purpose of professional work and of individual professions can enlighten professional work. Along the way, I will also show how these raise philosophical questions themselves. First, I will raise the question of whether moral theory should be used in in teaching applied ethics to professionals. Second, I will turn to the idea of professional integrity, and the prospects for its inculcation and assessment. Finally, I will reflect on issues arising from the use of case studies in professional ethics training; in particular, the ethical and epistemological questions arising from the asking of questions without the expectation that participants will be able to agree on an answer. I will introduce each issue by describing how it arises in work with professional communities, then consider its philosophical implications and finally suggest ways in which critically examining professionalism can help.

Moral theory and applied ethics

The role, if any, that moral theory should play in both the teaching and the practice of applied ethics, is a question which arises quite frequently in work with professionals. Introductory ethics courses for non-specialists, perhaps especially when they are also taught by non-specialists, will often take as their starting point the usual trio of moral theories: consequentialism (typically utilitarianism), deontology (typically expressed simply as an emphasis on duties and rights, but perhaps drawing on Kant in more detailed courses) and virtue ethics (typically with some mention of Aristotle). Contractarianism is sometimes included as a fourth theory. Students will be introduced to these theories and will then examine cases in the light of them. When discussing potential ethics courses with professional bodies, there is sometimes an assumption that this kind of approach will be taken. This assumption is not restricted to training activities: it is not uncommon to hear someone from a professional body refer to their code of ethics as 'a deontological code', contrasted with a utilitarian code. (It is rarer to hear someone claim their code as being 'utilitarian' or 'virtue-theoretic' in character.)

The idea that applied ethics should be taught in this way came under effective attack in a paper by Rob Lawlor (2007). In fact, Lawlor's contention is not just that moral theories should not be given primacy, but 'that moral theories should not be discussed extensively when teaching applied ethics' (ibid: 370). Lawlor makes two arguments in support of this claim: one practical and one methodological. Practically, he argues that teaching moral theory boils down to a choice between, on the one hand, teaching a useless and distracting caricature of the theories and, on the other hand, teaching their true range and subtlety, including controversies among theorists, which is beyond the scope of applied ethics courses and unlikely to be properly understood by participants. In either case, participants may be vulnerable to various unfortunate pitfalls generated by a superficial understanding of moral theory. They may conclude either that moral theory is obviously wrong and silly (potentially also applying this conclusion by extension to the whole of moral philosophy) or they may conclude that answers to particular cases are only true relative to a particular moral theory – one answer may be 'true for utilitarians', another 'true for deontologists' and so on. Even if they do not fall prey to this form of relativism, they may conclude that answers to particular moral problems are only answerable if one first answers the much more difficult question of which moral theory is the right one. Understandably pessimistic about their chances of answering this question, they might conclude that they must give up on the specific problems too. This leads to Lawlor's methodological point, which is that they would be mistaken in this conclusion. Answering particular moral problems does not require that one first adopt and defend a general moral theory any more than (in Lawlor's example) understanding motion in physics requires that one first adopt and defend a 'unified theory of everything'. Therefore, teaching applied ethics as the application of moral theories to cases is misguided.

Lawlor's paper provoked an interesting exchange between Lawlor and David Benatar, who defended the fairly modest position that discussion of moral theory can have some place in teaching applied ethics (Benatar 2007, 2009; Lawlor 2008; Saunders 2010). There are two broad currents in the debate between Lawlor and Benatar. The first flows from Benatar's claim that paying some attention to moral theories may help participants to recognize the theoretical assumptions implicit in their own responses to practical moral problems. On this point, there does not seem to be a great distance between Lawlor and Benatar. Lawlor accepts that it might be useful when discussing an issue with a student to question whether that student assumes that consequences (for example) are all that matter in adjudicating on a moral problem, but he stops short of accepting that such a discussion should be explicitly a discussion about consequentialism as a moral theory.

On this first point, in discussions with professionals, I have found that there is merit in noting the different general types of consideration that may play into a response to a case, which include consequences, duties, rights and sometimes virtues. For example, a case study used in our training with actuaries casts the participant as the Scheme Actuary to the pension scheme of a large insurance firm. A casual conversation with a journalist friend reveals that the friend intends to publish a story about a director of the firm, alleging that the director was involved in various criminal dealings before changing his name, some fifteen years before assuming his current position. Should the actuary warn the company? Report to the regulator? Try to stop the journalist friend publishing her story?

A case of this kind has many different stakeholders and stakeholder groups, for example the company's employees, its customers, members of its pension scheme, the broader public, the accused director, the journalist and the actuary herself. The first inclination of some participants might be to enumerate these stakeholders and then seek to find a solution which results in the satisfaction of the largest possible number of them. This, of course, is to ignore the fact that one may have specific duties to specific stakeholders or groups of stakeholders, which one does not have to others. Thus, the case opens up a distinction between too broad aims that we can have in making ethical decisions: the achievement of optimal consequences versus the fulfilment of specific duties to individuals or groups. However, it would be wrong to characterize this as a conflict between a consequentialist and a deontological view of ethics. In fact, any plausible consequentialist theory would need to be able to account for such duties and it is not difficult for consequentialists to find ways to do this.

Thinking about the case in terms of consequentialism versus deontology, therefore, does not help one to respond to the case itself. However, thinking about professionalism in a more theoretical way might. For example, it might be that the participant comes to see that considerations about the apparently beneficial consequences of taking some action – trying to persuade the journalist not to publish, say – are trumped by the central importance in professional ethics of acting in the public interest, which would be a live consideration both for the journalist and for the actuary.

The second disputed claim in the debate between Lawlor and Benatar has to do with the additional benefits which, according to Benatar, can be produced by including some discussion of moral theories in applied ethics teaching. Benatar gives two examples: first, that 'students can be taught the important lesson, relevant to both theory and practice, that just because there is a disagreement – even an unresolved one – this does not mean that every view is correct', and second that 'a discussion of theory ... can introduce students to philosophical reasoning via issues about which students may be less defensive and more open-minded' than they are about the hotly contended issues inherent in their own discipline (Benatar 2007: 627). Thus, it appears that Benatar sees discussion of ethical theories partly as a 'training ground' (Lawlor 2008: 827) in which participants can hone their ethical reasoning skills. Lawlor is right to point out, in reply to Benatar, that there are many, less distracting ways of achieving these aims without discussing moral theories. On the latter point, in work with professionals, it can be helpful for precisely this reason to discuss cases drawn from other professions, or from no profession at all, in order to prompt participants to regard the issues with some critical distance.

More broadly, as is hopefully shown by the actuarial example discussed earlier, encouraging participants to reflect critically on the nature and purpose of their profession can offer a useful training ground in which participants hone their ethical reasoning skills, without distracting them with disputes with which they are unlikely to have sufficient time to engage adequately, and which are anyway unlikely to affect their answer to a specific moral issue or case. In contrast, theoretical considerations about professions generally, and their own profession in particular, are both more obviously relevant to their own practice and more likely to affect how they think about particular cases. In the putative case outlined briefly in the previous section, the tension was between the interests of large groups of stakeholders and the professional's duties to particular groups, along with the need to preserve trust in the profession. It is highly plausible that ideas about the nature and purpose of the profession will affect the professional's response to cases of this kind. Thus this approach can have the advantage identified by Lawlor of allowing us to 'abstract away from the particular case, talking at the level of moral theories, where the students would be less passionate and more considered, and then apply that to the case, demonstrating what they are committed to' (ibid). The theoretical discussion can then be a training ground without being *just* a training ground. It is also relevant to, and has implications for, the more concrete cases being discussed.

Integrity and motivation

Whenever professions attempt to articulate their core values, integrity tends to be front and centre in their thoughts.[4] Despite a strong emphasis on integrity as a centrally important value for professionals, attempts to define it can be varied and vague. Often it is associated with other value terms such as 'honesty' and 'fairness', or with a very broad willingness to 'do the right thing'. Through training and research, and drawing on existing philosophical research, I have worked with professionals to try to reach a clearer conception of what integrity is, and to investigate ways in which professions and employing organizations can effectively promote and encourage integrity, properly understood.

Integrity has been a subject of many of the conversations I have had with professionals, but the original impetus for this work came from a piece of research commissioned by the Institute of Chartered Accountants in England and Wales, whose aim was to come to a better understanding of how integrity can be encouraged and promoted within organizations (Baxter et al. 2012). This research included interviews with ninety-six individuals working in fifteen organizations in the UK and Channel Islands, eighty-four of which I carried out myself. Each interview began with the interviewee being presented with a series of short character vignettes, followed by the question, Does the person described have integrity? The vignettes – which included someone facing a difficult decision at work, a person who is selfish but not deceitful about her selfishness, and another person who is dedicated, at the expense of their own self-interest, to a set of principles which most people would find abhorrent – were intended to test the interviewee's intuitions about what integrity is. Having gone through this process, each interviewee was then able to respond to questions about how integrity plays out in their own organization on the basis of a view of integrity which has benefited from some reflection. As researchers, we were able to build up a rich data set of observations about the intuitions of the people involved.

Philosophy with Professionals

Through reflection on this work, I have come to see integrity as essentially a motivational trait: it is a matter of holding deep-seated values which are reliably motivating when making decisions (McFall 1987). On this conception, integrity will not help you to identify what the right thing to do is, but it will help you reliably to do the right thing, or what you take to be the right thing, even when doing the wrong thing would be personally or professionally expedient. In Audi and Murphy's term, then, integrity is an 'adjunctive virtue' (Audi and Murphy 2006): it is valuable when the agent's other values are good, but can be harmful when they are not (imagine a highly motivated racist politician).

If this conception of integrity is accurate, it poses problems for professions both in their training and in any attempts they might make to *assess* members' integrity. In training, participants may be presented with case studies and asked what they would do in the situation described. In a simplistic version of this type of training, the situation will be designed to illustrate the correct application of a single principle from the code of ethics; participants are then trained to identify the correct response to the situation which shows that they have understood this correct application. In more sophisticated case study-based training, case studies are developed to which multiple principles may be relevant in a way that puts them in tension, and ethical considerations external to the code of ethics may also come into play. The problem is that someone's ability to identify and justify a permissible or desirable response to either type of case study says nothing at all about how they would be motivated to behave if they encountered the situation in real life. In which case, how can such training be used to inculcate integrity in participants? A similar problem applies to attempts to use case studies to assess members' integrity. Such assessments are increasingly popular with professional bodies. Members are put through a compulsory test in which they are graded on their responses to a series of case studies. To the extent that such a test is intended to be a test of integrity it is bound to fail, since it could be passed by someone with the ability to employ reasoning skills to analyse and respond to a case, but no integrity at all.

In the first section of this chapter I outlined a 'pre-reflective' framework of professional ethics, which I suggested may be a more-or-less unarticulated assumption in the minds of some professionals. According to this framework, the primary responsibility is to the employing organization or its shareholders. The value of the professional's work lies in her ability to return a profit to the employer, and the professional's responsibility to the client is generated by the instrumental value of the professional's work for the client in returning this profit. Ethical constraints are then set by law, regulation and reputational concerns (if the professional treats her client poorly, the organization's reputation will suffer, and hence its ability to attract clients in order to generate further profits in future). Through reflecting on the nature of professionalism and of their particular profession, it is hoped that professionals will move from this framework to one which is influenced by broader concerns of the public interest and the social need for professions.

Working within this altered ethical framework also brings a different set of motivations for the professional. The professional comes to see the values of her profession, and the principles underlying its work, as derived from the broader social

140   *Philosophy and Community*

value of professional work – from its utility in fulfilling the public good. Properly taking account of the ethical concerns affecting the work, then, comes to be seen as an inherent element of doing the job *well*. A professional equipped with this new understanding of her ethical environment may thus come to be more strongly motivated by these underlying values and principles, which are now seen as having a value which is at once more direct and broader than the value to be derived from protecting the reputation of the employing organization. Moreover, because she has come to see things in this way through a process of reaching her own conclusions through dialogue with others, she has greater ownership of the resulting perspective, which is itself more strongly motivating. Perhaps most importantly, this new source of motivation does not depend for its force on the possibility that the employer's reputation will suffer as a result of unethical behaviour, or the possibility that the individual with face repercussions as a result of failing to comply with law or regulations. These three factors – that the professional is motivated directly by the values and principles, that she is motivated by what she sees as *her own* values and principles and that she is motivated regardless of external incentives – mean that this pattern of motivation is more plausibly constitutive of integrity that the pre-reflective pattern of motivation.

'No right or wrong answers?'

Much of the work that we do with professionals makes use of case studies as a basis for discussion. Participants are presented with a case and asked questions about it – most importantly, what would they do in the situation described, and why? An aspect of this work which professionals often find challenging is that cases are presented and discussed with no expectation that everyone present will be able to agree on a definitive answer to the case. Several responses may be permissible and the emphasis is on providing a justification, in the light of the facts, relevant principles and values and challenge from other participants, for a response. There are several pedagogical advantages to working with cases in this way. First, it is simply true that many situations in professional life are like this – well-informed and competent professionals, reasoning in good faith, can arrive at different conclusions about the correct response to a case. Case studies which treat ethical questions like mathematical questions – problems with only one possible correct solution, such that anyone reaching a different answer must be guilty of faulty reasoning – risk simplifying and misrepresenting ethics in a way which prepares professionals poorly for real life. Also, cases that exhibit this level of difficulty often do so because they involve a clash of two or more values or principles. One value or principle seems to be recommending one course of action and another value or principle seems to be recommending a different, incompatible course of action. Choosing between alternatives in such a scenario involves more than arbitrarily prioritizing one principle over another. As I suggested at the beginning of the chapter, examining the foundations of principles – *why* they are important – allows one better to interpret them in the context of cases and to understand their limits. Working through this process gives professionals a deeper understanding of principles

Philosophy with Professionals 141

than they would achieve by straightforwardly applying single principles to cases and churning out unambiguously correct answers.

Nonetheless, using cases of the type described raises some meta-ethical and epistemological questions. A phrase which is often heard from professionals, including those engaged in teaching ethics within the profession, and which rings alarm bells for ethicists, is the claim that 'there are no right and wrong answers in ethics'. The worst thing about hearing this phrase, for me at least, is the knowledge that I will have to try to explain why it is not quite right in a way which makes sense to professionals with no grounding in ethics, while still acknowledging that the cases to be examined will not yield unambiguous answers in the way that they might be used to from other training courses.

Consider an example: An architect is engaged by a city council to design a residential building for a housing estate. In the architect's opinion, the brief for the project constrains her to design a building which, while well within legal health and safety parameters, and not presenting an unacceptable danger to the public, is not optimally safe. Moreover, it would, in the architect's opinion, be possible to alter the brief so as greatly to improve the safety of the building, without significantly compromising the overall aims of the project, and without significantly increasing its cost. What should the architect do in this case? The difficulty of the case is due to its involving a clash of two key duties: a duty to the client to act on their instructions and a duty to the wider public (represented in prospective occupants of the building) to ensure their safety. If one takes the duty to the client to be primary, then one might suggest raising concerns with the client, trying to explain why the brief ought to be changed, and so on. One might even suggest taking one's concerns elsewhere if there is evidence that the client has still, after this discussion, failed to understand the implications of the work as described and the potential for alternatives, on the grounds that the client may be mistaken about her best interests. However, one would presumably not recommend attempting to overrule the client's informed choice, or refusing to take on the work, as long as it is legal and minimally compliant with health and safety regulations. However, if the duty to the *public* is taken to be primary, these more drastic responses might come into play.

When we say, in a case like this, that there are several justifiable responses, what are we saying about the ethical status of these responses? There are at least two possible answers to this question. One possibility is that there is in fact only one optimal response but that, given the information we have and can reasonably be expected to obtain, it is beyond our ability to know what this response is. Given these epistemic limits, it is plausibly permissible for an individual to choose whichever response seems to them to be the best one, even if this response may not be, in the final analysis, optimal. The other possibility is that there are, in fact, multiple permissible responses with nothing, ultimately, to recommend one over another, even if we were in possession of all the relevant information. This possibility might be implied by meta-ethical positions such as value pluralism or some forms of relativism.

How might we try to resolve the architectural case described earlier? One way would be to think more deeply about the nature and purpose of architecture as a profession. Should architects see their primary duty as being to the client or to the public? It could be argued in favour of the latter possibility that architecture is not like, say, criminal law, in

142   *Philosophy and Community*

which a strongly client-centred ethic can be plausibly justified by the utility of this ethic in serving the public good – the public good is served by each individual client getting the best defence available. Architecture is different in that the direct effects of decisions taken by architects are felt most strongly not by their clients but by their end users: the people who must live and work in the buildings they design, as well as the general public whose environment is shaped by their work. Therefore architecture should have a public-centric ethics rather than a client-centric ethics. A counterargument could be made on democratic grounds: at least when the client is a democratically accountable entity such as a city council, it would be wrong for an architect to impose standards beyond legal requirements. The council should make decisions about safety standards and be accountable to the public for them. The architect can register her objection, but ultimately ought not to seek to override the client's wishes.

The debate sketched here reflects a real one which is taking place within the architectural profession (Marrs and Hurst 2015). I am not seeking to resolve this debate here, but merely to point to how discussion of examples can open up these deeper debates and how, in turn, coming to a conclusion about the deeper question can affect how one thinks about the concrete examples. At least in some cases, this gives us something that we can say in reply to the claim that there are 'no right or wrong answers in ethics'. In a case such as the architectural case discussed earlier, it may be possible to resolve what seems to be a clash of incommensurable values, and hence a genuine dilemma, by reflecting more deeply on the nature of the profession, its purpose, its social context and the ethical implications of these. At this point, we still might have an impasse between two participants in a debate – it might be that one participant is now arguing for a client-centric ethics of architecture, while the other is arguing for a public-centric ethics. However, through deepening the debate in this way, the participants can perhaps start to see how there might be a possibility of a right answer to a question which might previously have seemed to be nothing more than a brute matter of opinion. They might therefore see the importance of reaching one's own conclusions about these deeper questions. More than this, they might come to see these questions as something that requires collective debate and agreement on the part of the profession as a whole, and might become a more active member of their profession as a result.

Conclusion

In this chapter, I have been able only to sketch some of the issues which are frequently raised in conversations with professionals about the ethics of their work. I have hopefully given some considerations in favour of making critical examination of the nature of professional work a central focus of such conversations. Of course, it should not be the only focus. However, I have found it to be a very useful way of finding common ground between philosophers and professionals, encouraging deeper reflection in a way that has a clear and direct impact on the way professionals work. It also teaches a more general skill, which is the skill of abstracting from problems, illuminating the deeper

Philosophy with Professionals 143

issues underlying them, applying theory if relevant and focusing back in on the original problem armed with a better understanding. This skill, as much as any particular piece of theoretical understanding pulled directly from philosophical enquiry, is something that philosophers, and particularly applied ethicists, can usefully contribute to professional communities. Critically examining professionalism itself is a way of teaching this skill while remaining firmly grounded in the reality of professional work.

As I noted at the beginning of the chapter, one of the characteristic features of a community of practice is that its members interact with each other, sharing knowledge and ideas in order to improve the practice in which the community is engaged. The kind of reflective conversation I have been describing is another example of this process. The fact that what I have described is the professional community *self-reflecting*, through critically examining the idea of professionalism itself, is part of what makes this an example of community philosophy. Many of the techniques of philosophy – crystallizing latent ideas, identifying and then critically examining one's founding assumptions, coming to a better understanding of an issue by articulating and defending a position – can be introduced to the professional community with outcomes that are of practical as well as intellectual value. This deeper self-reflection is unusual for professional communities; it is a challenge but a rewarding and illuminating one.

Notes

1 I am using 'ethical' and 'moral' interchangeably here.
2 This view, of course, is not universal, and is undoubtedly more prevalent in some professions than others. Members of the medical professions, for example, are much more likely to see the patient as the primary locus of value.
3 It may be objected that this description is something of a caricature, and that many professionals are fully aware that their primary duty is to the public, or their clients, rather than to their employer. Medical professionals, for example, are surely more closely concerned with the well-being of their patients than that of their employer. While this may be true, however, there is considerable variation among professions here and among individuals within professions. Medical professionals, partly due to the nature of their work and partly due to the relatively advanced state of ethical training in their fields, are probably somewhat unusual in this regard.
4 For example, integrity is identified as a core value by the International Federation of Accountants (2005) and the International Bar Association (2005).

References

Audi, R., and Murphy, P. E., (2006), 'The Many Faces of Integrity', *Business Ethics Quarterly*, 16 (1): 3–21.
Baxter, J., Megone, C., Dempsey, J., and Lee, J., (2012), *Real Integrity: Practical Solutions for Organisations Seeking to Promote and Encourage Integrity*, London: The Institute of Chartered Accountants in England and Wales.

Benatar, D., (2007), 'Moral Theories May Have Some Role in Teaching Applied Ethics', *Journal of Medical Ethics*, 33: 671–2.

Benatar, D., (2009), 'Teaching Moral Theories is an Option: Reply to Rob Lawlor', *Journal of Medical Ethics*, 35: 395–6.

Bennion, F. A. R., (1969), *Professional Ethics: The Consultant Professions and their Code*, London: Knight.

Friedson, E., (1994), *Professionalism Reborn: Theory, Prophecy, and Policy*, Cambridge: Polity Press.

International Bar Association (2005), *IBA International Principles on Conduct for the Legal Profession*, [Online], Available at: https://www.ibanet.org/Document/Default.aspx?DocumentUid=1730FC33-6D70-4469-9B9D-8A12C319468C, Accessed 15 October 2018.

International Federation of Accountants (2005), *Revised Code of Ethics – Completed*, [Online], Available at: https://www.ethicsboard.org/projects/revised-code-ethics-completed, Accessed 15 October 2015.

Lawlor, R., (2007), 'Moral Theories in Teaching Applied Ethics', *Journal of Medical Ethics*, 33 (6): 370–2.

Lawlor, R., (2008), 'Against Moral Theories: Reply to Benatar', *Journal of Medical Ethics*, 34 (11): 826–8.

Marrs, C., and Hurst, W., (2015), 'RIBA and ARB Ethical Codes Attacked', *Architects' Journal*, 1 July 2015.

McFall, L., (1987), 'Integrity', *Ethics*, 98 (1): 5–20.

Saunders, B., (2010), 'How to Teach Moral Theories in Applied Ethics', *Journal of Medical Ethics*, 36 (10): 635–8.

Wenger, E., (2000), *Communities of Practice: Learning, Meaning and Identity*, Cambridge: Cambridge University Press.

World Federation of Engineering Organizations, *Code of Ethics*, [Online], Available at: http://www.wfeo.org/wpcontent/uploads/code_of_ethics/WFEO_MODEL_CODE_OF_ETHICS.pdf, Accessed 1 October 2018.

10

In philosophical conversation with: New and beginning teachers

Janet Orchard, Ruth Heilbronn and Carrie Winstanley

Introduction

There is an urgent need to reassert the place for community and philosophy in the education of teachers. For, while the general value of belonging to a professional learning community has long been recognized (e.g. Bolam et al. 2005), the distinctive contribution that a philosophically informed, CoE (Community of Enquiry) -based approach can make to teachers' reflective practice has largely remained unrealized. Seminal work on the notion of a 'community of practice' (CoP) (Lave and Wenger 1991) has much to offer teacher education and 'Philosophy for Teachers', or 'P4T' (Orchard, Heilbronn and Winstanley 2016), adapted from the more familiar idea of 'P4C' (Philosophy for Children), develops that idea in specific ways appropriate to new and beginning teachers.

The impetus for P4T sprang from the recognition that teachers needed 'space' and a particular quality of time during their professional education in which to reflect on ethical matters as these arose from their practice. As Campbell (2003) has identified, the lone teacher in the classroom is frequently 'struggling to cope without much guidance with the dilemmas and tensions that unavoidably surface when one is engaged in the moral domain' (138–9), and there is little information on where ethics education appears in teacher education (Walters, Heilbronn and Daly 2017). This resonated with our own experience as teachers and teacher educators. We saw our student teachers and new teachers in school increasingly pressurized by the various technical demands of their jobs, with little or no time to reflect on ethical issues and scant opportunity for teacher educators to engage in the kinds of learning activities that support such reflection and engagement. Indeed, in our own jurisdiction (England) there is no formal requirement for teacher educators on higher education courses to teach ethics to teachers or engage in pre-service ethical preparation (Maxwell et al. 2016).

Yet teaching is fundamentally an ethical endeavour (Hansen 1995 and 2001; Carr 2006; Campbell 2003 and 2008; Papastephanou 2006; Smith 1999; Warnick and Silverman 2011). It is a relational practice, one which requires knowledge and understanding of the complexity of contingent instances, and the ability to react and interact with sound moral judgement. Teaching is 'embodied, played out in specific social-cultural contexts' (Griffiths 2013: 221). Teachers hold values in their practice as a result and generally manifest a strong vocational commitment to being good teachers (Hansen 2001; Estola and Erikkilä 2003; Campbell 2008; Higgins 2010). Where is the formal and structured opportunity to support them in developing a vocational sense of commitment that is both considered and informed?

Elements of ethics education may appear when professional codes of practice and conduct are introduced to new teachers (These are widespread in teaching internationally, for example, DET 2006; SACE 2011; TCI 2012; GTCS 2012; AAE 2015; UNESCO 2015.). Rich (1984) has argued that ethics education for teachers should be built around these. However, Davids (2016) warns of the limitations of legalistic approaches to ethics in these policy documents (e.g. in SACE 2011) which may not reflect the actual experiences of teachers. If they are to be supported in identifying ways in which to act ethically, or in how to use ethical judgement, she argues, it is important to attend to the interrelated practices of deliberation, belonging and inclusion, as manifestations in themselves of ethical teaching.

Teaching standards offer another mechanism that may trigger some limited input into professional ethics education. Such standards are now customary in most international contexts for teacher accreditation (Drury and Baer 2011) and usually carry a conceptualization of ethics for teaching. The English Teaching Standards (DfE 2011) have a separate section (Part B) relating to personal and professional conduct. Teacher educators are therefore obliged to engage their student teachers with ethics as far as they are related to professional conduct in a generalized way (DfE 2011; Ofsted 2015). Again, Davids's (2016) warnings of the limitations of legalistic approaches to ethics are pertinent. Heilbronn (2017) also raises this issue in discussing some serious implications of the regulation under Part B of the English standards that teachers must report to the police anyone they suspect of possible 'radicalization', without having opportunities to reflect on interpretations and implications of the legal guidelines and their own roles within these.

In our work as teacher educators we interpret ethics education more widely than standards and codes can capture, seeing teaching as a human practice, concerned with relationships, and as fundamentally ethical (Dewey 1909; van Manem 1991; Noddings 1992; Hansen 1995 and 2001; Dunne 2003). We concur with the assumption that 'ethics and teaching seem inherently compatible and unavoidably intertwined' (Campbell 2008: 357). Furthermore, the limited amount of research dealing with children's attitudes to their teachers confirms the importance of relationships in teaching. Children's voices confirm teaching as a human practice. They think that 'good' teachers are those who respect them, care if they learn, know them well and know how they learn (e.g. Kutnick and Jules 1993; Beishuizen et al. 2001).

Codes of practice and teaching standards are extremely limited in their affordance for supporting teachers in their ethical practice, since they outline general rules without specificity of context, although they are useful in pointing the way to professionally acceptable behaviour which can be helpful for teachers to make sense of what it is they hope to achieve through education. Todd (2001: 436) suggests that professional

Philosophy with New and Beginning Teachers

codes do at least provide some sense of 'moral ambience' for those engaged in practice. However, standardized ethical statements 'impose ethics on education from the outside' (ibid) and do not give enough guidance for teachers faced with the ambiguity, complexity and contingency of the present moment in which teaching happens (Campbell 2008; Griffiths 2013). The process of familiarizing teachers with the codes and standards does not necessarily produce the desired effect on teachers' conduct, as it is not possible to follow predetermined norms that do not reflect teachers' experiences.

The practice of P4T began as an attempt to create opportunities to address the concerns of students and early career teachers. Committed to the value of dialogical, enquiry-based pedagogy (see below and Orchard, Heilbronn and Winstanley 2016), we experimented by translating collaborative and experiential forms of teaching and learning already established in schooling, to the new context of vocational education in higher education. We were seeking to find out whether such work might help teachers in managing those difficult ethical situations in the classroom that they might otherwise experience alone and unsupported – situations for which non-standard responses are usually required. Teachers needed space in which to reflect on the actual ethical situations they encountered, and we sought ways to launch, manage and support their reflective work which were different from those limited opportunities already established in teacher education programmes. Two interlinking models of collaborative reflection informed the work we did: that of the 'community of practice' and that of work in philosophy with and for children, concerned with dialogue in a 'community of enquiry'. We discuss each of these key ideas next in more detail.

Communities of practice in teacher education

General notions of collective enquiry, reflection and self-evaluation are well established in teacher education through a number of earlier initiatives (Bolam et al. 2005), and in this regard the key principles which underpin P4T are not new. Dewey observed that educational practices may 'provide the data, the subject matter, which forms the problems of inquiry' (Dewey 1929: 16). Stenhouse (1975) argued for collective enquiry by teachers as school and classroom researchers playing an active part in the curriculum development process, and Schön (1983) was influential in advocating the notion of the 'reflective practitioner'. The specific term 'CoP' is generally attributed to Lave and Wenger (1991) and developed through the later work of Wenger (see Wenger 1998a and b; Wenger and Snyder 2000). The notion arose originally from a study of apprentice midwives in West Africa which went on to be applied to other contexts, including education.

Communities of practice have come to be defined as 'the communities through which individuals develop and share the capacity to create and use knowledge' (Wenger 1998a: 1), and there are some parallels between this and work being developed as P4T. According to Wenger, CoPs are almost always created informally and distinct from formal organizational units' (ibid: 2) such that they may not always be given names. They can exist anywhere in human activity; indeed, each of us may belong to several, in the various contexts in which we interact with others, participating in a CoP either as a core member or on its periphery. CoPs arise out of the activities which bring people in social groupings together, which might include anything from engaging in lunchtime discussions to solving difficult problems, and the learning comes from mutual engagement in activities. 'CoPs develop around things that matter to people such that as a result, their practices reflect the members' own understanding of what is important' (ibid).

Even though as a particular example of a CoP the communities we create in our workshops are short-lived, P4T is certainly organized around what matters to teachers in their daily practice. It aims to support teachers to understand and ideally to cope better with the inevitable ethical dilemmas that arise in the classroom. As Sim identifies, the CoP in which 'members have similar needs and experiences' is an 'effective structure to examine and reflect on these complex situations' (Sim 2006: 78). So far, a shared concern with 'behaviour management', common in new and early career teachers, has been the focus of pilot P4T workshops, and this is significant because standardized and codified statements about such management give little guidance in managing the complexity of various ethical demands.

Wenger (1998a) has also stated that a CoP is defined along three dimensions: what it is about, how it functions and what capability it has produced. The essence of what P4T is 'about' is the overarching objective of developing teachers' ethical awareness, sound judgement or 'practical wisdom' (Dunne 1993; Smith 1999; Carr 2006; Heilbronn 2008; Higgins 2010). The way in which P4T functions is according to principles of Socratic dialogue promoted by the 'community of enquiry', which we discuss in more detail in the later sections. The 'capability' that P4T produces lies in the development of the dispositions of participants to act ethically in the moment in classrooms.

The essence of the CoP is its continual renegotiation of aims and reaffirmation of agreement of the participation of its members and consultation on the focus of joint undertaking. Members are bound together through mutual engagement in some activity related to developing understanding about something that arises from the communal shared practice. In the case of P4T, this binding together is temporary and short-lived, but strong and intense for the time that the community of enquiry (CoE) spends together. The practices that develop out of the mutual engagement in a common endeavour reflect the members' own understanding of what is important:

> Even when a community's actions conform to an external mandate, it is the community – not the mandate – that produces the practice. In this sense, communities of practice are fundamentally self-organizing systems. (Wenger 1998a: 2)

This was illustrated in our own P4T communities, where we used the external mandate of the need for pre-service teachers to meet Part B of the Teachers' Standards (DfE 2011) to make their participation in P4T during a hectic Post Graduate Certificate of Education (PGCE)[1] programme possible, while making sure that the group had clear ownership of the issues being examined – which were not imposed by us – through a process of negotiation and discussion.

Philosophy with New and Beginning Teachers

Other initiatives in creating CoPs in teacher education are pertinent to our conception of P4T, how it functions and what it achieves. Jimenez-Silva and Olson found that where pre-service teachers have successfully engaged in a CoP with teachers in schools, they have a better understanding of the relationship of theory in practice (Jimenez-Silva and Olson 2012). Similarly, Sutherland, Scanlon and Sperring (2005) found that those CoPs that involved experience of practical issues in schools and the opportunity for reflection enabled participating pre-service teachers to 'relate the theory taught at the university to their practical needs' so that 'the theory became more meaningful for them' (ibid: 90). CoPs have also been shown to be useful for those already working in school contexts (Sim 2006; Sutherland, Scanlon and Sperring 2005). On this basis, P4T may be a useful process for teachers hoping to establish a CoP in their schools, over longer periods of time than that is currently the case with our workshops, and this could conform to the kind of professional learning community advocated by Bolam et al. (2005).

'Professional learning communities' (PLCs) are one specific kind of CoP whose benefits for in-service teachers are widely recognized (ibid). Broadly speaking, PLCs involve a group of people both sharing and critically interrogating their practice in an 'ongoing, reflective, collaborative, inclusive, learning-oriented, growth-promoting way' (Toole and Lewis 2002). Synergies with the current work we have piloted under the term 'P4T' include the emphasis on collaborative and inclusive reflection. Were P4T to develop into work undertaken predominantly with in-service teachers rather than pre-service ones, and were the work to be ongoing rather than focused on creating a temporary CoE during a twenty-four-hour period along the lines just described, the connections between these two modes of learning could be rather closer.

Communities of Practice may also make use of ICT, or blended-learning models, and run over several weeks or months (Hodgkinson-Williams, Slay and Siebörger 2008). None of this is presently the case in P4T, although one way in which to address issues raised concerning the scalability and sustainability of the ethical retreat model would be to create groups meeting over time for shorter periods, and perhaps virtually, in lieu of face-to-face twenty-four-hour encounters. For example, the notion of the virtual 'community of enquiry', established with schoolchildren in the work of Generation Global[2] but not yet formalized in an HEI setting, sets up the further specific possibility of inter- and transnational dialogue exploring global ethical concerns in teaching including teaching sustainably (Coles et al. 2017) or in addressing teachers' capacity to respond ethically to religious and/or cultural diversity (Orchard 2018).

Communities of enquiry and dialogue

The second strand to have influenced our work came from P4C, sometimes referred to as Philosophy with Children (PwC).[3] Following a series of discussions with colleagues, we looked to establish PwC/P4C strategies to structure and conduct the workshops we wanted to focus on professional ethics for teachers and teacher educators, and we found the model of the CoE to be particularly valuable. Numerous existing versions and iterations of CoE can be found in the P4C/PwC[4] literature; our focus here is to explain what explicitly about these methods has proved so helpful in the pilot P4T workshops with teachers. In the UK, the organization Society for the Advancement of Philosophical Enquiry and Reflection in Education (SAPERE) is one of the largest that provides, as its website banner states, 'Philosophy for Children, Colleges, Communities'. SAPERE's definition of the CoE is helpful here, where the closeness to the CoP can be clearly identified:

> A Community of Enquiry is a group of people used to thinking together with a view to increasing their understanding and appreciation of the world around them and of each other. (SAPERE 2017)

Further detail about the practice of the CoE and P4C can be found on SAPERE's website.[5]

The origins of the CoE idea can be traced back to Peirce's notion of the community of inquiry and to Dewey's concern with education for 'democracy as associated living', that is, the creation of a consensual community in which joint enquiry is integral. The development of the CoE has also been linked to Vygotskyan social practices of 'thinking together' (Murris 2008) and back further to Socrates and Plato (ibid). P4T makes use of Deweyan notions in P4T's mode of working, particularly in the importance of reflection in problematic situations.[6] As Cam reminds us, 'Dewey's standard substitute for 'think' is 'inquire' (Cam 2018: 59).

The CoE is not the only element of P4C practice that we have used: we also adapted other activities that help to build positive community relationships from the outset, including techniques for setting the tone of the workshop, agreeing shared aims and ways of working, as well as sharing ideas and techniques for framing questions together. These link back to common features of the CoP. The various strategies for creating the most conducive setting are frequently discussed in the literature around P4C, and for a systematic review it is worth exploring the work of Trickey and Topping (2004). However, since this publication other developments have emerged, taking the notion of philosophical enquiry with children in different directions and reconsidering how it can be used. Examples of this include 'narrative ethical enquiry' ideas (Robinson 2014) and ways of engaging children in using philosophy to help them to learn how to 'live well' (Cassidy 2012).

Running through all these modes of P4C is the idea of dialogue, as distinct from discussion. As Wolfe and Alexander (2008) attest, there is a clear difference:

> Discussion: the exchange of ideas with a view to sharing information and solving problems. Dialogue: achieving common understanding through structured, cumulative questioning and discussion which guide and prompt, reduce choices, minimize risk and error, and expedite 'handover' of concepts and principles. (ibid: 3)

During their teacher education (or 'training'), students do tend to engage in 'discussion', as described in the previous sections, but the opportunities for dialogue are more limited. P4T allows space and expertise to help develop the skills of dialogic work, and the experience of being part of a group striving for common understanding.

SAPERE is one of many advocates of P4C that reference the notion of the '4c's in dialogue: critical, creative, caring and collaborative. Emphasizing the importance of these elements and the notion of a dialogic approach, Wolfe and Alexander assert that 'dialogue is not simply a precondition for learning but essential for knowledge construction and human development generally' (ibid: 4). Ideas around dialogue are taken further by other thinkers, such as Freire (1972), who emphasizes a different aspect: *praxis*. Freire considered dialogue to be indispensable in education as it formed a basis for people to take action. *Praxis* is action informed by values, and the role of dialogue is to make this action central for learners, to enable them to make a difference and to change and improve their situations. To enact these positive values requires dialogue undertaken with a backdrop of respect, within a cohesive community in which people are working together towards common aims.

By way of illustration we include a list of elements that are essential for dialogic teaching. They are helpful in imagining the nature of the conversations in the P4T sessions, which were characterized by the following:

- interactions which encourage students to think, and to think in different ways;
- questions which invite much more than simple recall;
- answers which are justified, followed up and built upon rather than merely received;
- feedback which informs and leads thinking forward as well as encourages students;
- contributions which are extended rather than fragmented;
- exchanges which chain together into coherent and deepening lines of enquiry;
- discussion and argumentation which probe and challenge rather than unquestioningly accept;
- professional engagement with subject matter which liberates classroom discourse from the safe and conventional; and
- classroom organization, climate and relationships which make all this possible.

(Alexander 2017).

In the next section we give some concrete examples of P4T work with teachers.

P4T in practice

P4T developed from a series of seminars, supported consistently by the generosity of the Philosophy of Education Society of Great Britain (PESGB). The first was a twenty-four-hour residential weekend for twenty-one teacher educators, led by researchers from the Centre for Research Ethics and Ethical Deliberation (CREED) and the Centre for Learner Identity studies (CLIs) at Edge Hill University (2011). CREED research had evidenced the tension around ethical issues arising in practice

(Shortt et al. 2015). The event was structured around four previously piloted themes: the ethics of a prescribed curriculum; power and accountability in the classroom; the ethics of responding to learners; and the ethical teacher. Role-play was used to develop scenarios as the basis for interaction with one another. However, the role-play process became complicated and artificial, stimulating a proposal from participants whose own P4C training and experience led them to believe that more meaningful and productive reflection on ethical dilemmas might arise from incidents identified and experienced by the participants themselves. This became the cornerstone of P4T practice.

A seminar for teacher educators, funded by The Higher Education Academy (HEA) and PESGB, followed in 2013. Participants took part in workshops exploring the values and dispositions of 'the good teacher' and the theme of professional formation and ethical uncertainty. This allowed us to share cases and experiences of pre-service teaching and together explore how we might foreground essential ethical dimensions of teacher education despite the existing rather hostile conditions of training provision. It was a natural development then to involve pre-service teachers, education students and their tutors with philosophers of education, and this was the essence of what became the P4T approach. With continued funding from HEA and PESGB we organized two 24-hour residential workshops, with two further workshops, one in England and one in South Africa, funded by the PESGB and the South African National Research Foundation respectively.

The stated aims of the workshops have been to

- create space and time for critical reflection away from the 'busy-ness' of schools;
- create a community of practice in a residential 'safe-space' conducive to this kind of work, where potentially confidential concerns could be aired;
- develop independence and confidence among student teachers in how to manage examples of ethically complex and potentially challenging classroom situations;
- address existential concerns which arise typically among beginning teachers when dealing with challenging behaviour by their pupils, including burnout, and sustaining motivation and a sense of moral purpose; and
- offer teacher educators a form of professional development in the methods of dialogic teaching and learning, and in the value and possibilities of such engagement.

The activities over twenty-four hours have been steered by an experienced SAPERE trainer, who is also a philosopher of education, and included other invited philosophers of education. When we borrowed some of the P4C strategies, it was vital for us to work with an experienced facilitator. The coordinator acted as co-enquirer, helping the group in many ways, such as building a collaborative, reflective ethos which meant instilling a cooperative and caring culture, grounded in mutual respect, and which functioned as a safe space for the expression of ideas in the group search for understanding, meaning and values – always supported by reasons. This is no mean feat to achieve in a short time span but is essential to the P4T practice as it has emerged. As Murris notes, a CoE has to be able to respond to the thoughts of its members in ways that are 'genuinely

Philosophy with New and Beginning Teachers

open-ended, critical and self-reflective' (Murris 2008: 671). This requires a facilitator who is, in Murris's words, 'actively seeking opportunities to be perplexed, numbed and open to change through reflection and self-reflection' (ibid), emphasizing the need for them to be enabling and attentive to the needs of others.

Having learnt that role-play was unhelpful, we ensured that the ethical dilemmas explored in the workshop were based on participants' own direct classroom experience. We worked to develop deep consideration of ethical issues, building on CoE practices, as the following example from the P4T seminars illustrates. An experience a pre-service teacher on a practicum initially shared with another participant, highlighted the kinds of dilemmas and ways of working through them. When shared in the CoP/CoE as a whole, the group voted to work on her narrative. The teacher recounted the experience as one in which she had been lenient with a child who had broken some school rule. She did so, she explained, because she was sympathetic to the pupil's circumstances, which she knew about, but the other children did not. She reported some pupils complaining vociferously that overlooking the rule-breaking was unfair, and she realized that they had interpreted this as an instance of the teacher failing to apply rules consistently. It was difficult for her to regain the confidence of the class as a result. She still believed that her actions were the right ones in the circumstances and yet she could also understand the children's point of view. She was left feeling troubled, concerned that she could have handled the situation better and perplexed about what she could have done otherwise.

In the large group discussion this personal classroom story led to a substantive dialogue in which the concepts of fairness, equitable treatment and equality were discussed and examined in some depth. Questions were posed about what might be done in similar circumstances. Participants went on to explore concerns such as 'How can we treat people equally when different responses would be helpful?' 'What does it mean to be fair?' and 'How can compassion be squared with equity?' These discussions were thoughtful and stimulated engaged and sustained contributions, demonstrating both elements of dialogic work (Alexander 2017) and the power of the CoP).

In a follow-up session building on the group discussion, key words and concepts in the questions that were raised were interrogated to find a hierarchy of the concepts being generated, since some concepts are more generalized and generalizable than others. For example, on the discussion of rules, fairness and differential treatment, an overarching theme was 'justice'. Highlighting these complex and principal ideas is a P4C practice in which participants are able to see how their own more specific issues and questions would fit within the umbrella concept – 'justice' in this example. Through exploring the concept and related practical concerns, clarificatory and specific further questions arose, using a P4C strategy known as 'concept stretching'. This helped participants to think about ways forward in other situations when reflection was needed to articulate reasons for actions. In this the philosophers of education were helpful in guiding clarification, demonstrating how P4T operates typically as philosophical enquiry in the community. In summary, both the content of the discussion, and the dialogical and iterative methods used, engage everyone to build on their own experience of practice. Everyone contributes, and these contributions form the basis of the community learning.

154   *Philosophy and Community*

Critical reflections

What does this work reveal about the nature and value of community and philosophy in the professional formation of teachers at the pre- and early career stage? What does working in this field have to teach philosophers? What do these practices offer to the members of the CoP/CoE which they would not have benefited from otherwise? Are there wider points of learning from the P4T experiment that we can take into future work?

A different learning experience

Participants identified a number of factors that made up the distinctive experience of inquiry and deliberation, which was not one that they had habitually experienced in their pre-service courses and which were typical of pre-service teacher education programmes in Wales and England. These factors were a particular sense of time, of space and of ways of working.

The pace of the sessions gave them time for 'slow learning' (Smith 2017), through the deliberation on concerns about their work in schools. In schools, their roles often revolved around having too many time-consuming duties, a problem compounded because the purpose of the duties was unclear. Many participants felt that even when the value and purpose of those duties had become clearer to them, they had insufficient time to undertake them well. In the P4T workshops they could consider issues at a pace which enabled their concerns to be uncovered and explored in some detail.

The second factor that contrasted to being in school and working on the PGCE was the provision of a safe space for participants' concerns to be aired and shared with the group as a whole and the environment was important in the success of P4T to date. For example, an early workshop took place at Gladstone's Library, near Hawarden in north Wales, where participants reported the powerful positive impact that the chosen location had exercised on them. Another took place in a Quaker retreat centre in the Oxfordshire countryside, which has a long history and association with ethical and reflective practice and afforded the opportunity for time outside and some gentle strolls around the grounds. The character of the building and the sense of history it engendered proved amenable to reflection. The atmosphere contributed to the participants' positive sense of well-being and eating communally allowed for discussion to flow continuously, ensuring the different sessions linked together smoothly and momentum was maintained.

The mode of working proved significant too, as the iterative nature of the process of discussion led to a deepening of inquiry as the workshop progressed, which participants appeared to find satisfying. It allowed deep reflection on issues which student teachers considered disturbing and unsettling One person described the experience as being like a 'safety valve' that helped them manage the complexity of their work. Time was spent drawing connections, clarifying meanings and going deeper into the issues raised. Values were explored allowing insights and thoughts to be shared, leading to new perspectives, disparate directions and a deepening of understanding. Participants reported that they enjoyed the experiences despite finding them challenging.

Philosophy with New and Beginning Teachers

In addition, other educational professionals who were present thought they could take away specific actions from the workshops. Having seen the value of carving out time and creating a safe space for dialogue, teacher educators stated their intentions to take the ideas into their work with head teachers (establishing inquiry-based approaches), to use dialogical enquiry methods and to introduce students and colleagues to this mode of reflection. This emphasizes the value of identifying and exploiting what we have described elsewhere as 'leaky spaces' (Orchard, Heilbronn and Winstanley 2016), or spaces in a formal agenda, like a meeting or curriculum time which are not completely defined and can therefore be open to innovation and afford an opportunity to try out some elements of the work we describe.

Reflections on community

As already established in this chapter, there are different types of CoPs/CoEs and they have various pros and cons. For our purposes it was helpful to build and use the CoP quickly and intensely, in a context divorced from daily regular activity, so as to lend an immediacy to the discussions. The benefits included students being able to engage in depth in complex discussions about knotty ethical issues, and in these conditions they were very good at analysing the intricacies and nuances of the various scenarios they considered (as also found by Bauml 2009). However, a clear disadvantage is the 'one off' nature of the community which would need to be sustained on a different basis, were this to be wished for by participant members.

In an ideal world, moreover, the conveners should have limited if any professional connection to the students or teachers participating in the community, in terms of grading their work or performance, given the potential impact of power relationships and issues around motivation that typically arise in regular university classroom settings. This was not possible in the less than optimal conditions in which the workshops operated. However, we did create a context where student participants were free to disagree with facilitators and other staff 'without fear of reprisal' (Jimenez-Silva and Olson 2012: 342); and as far as we are aware by operating 'Chatham House' rules[7] this was possible in the workshops undertaken thus far. Sim concurs, noting:

> Establishing strong and supportive 'communities of practice' within teacher education programmes should be an effective strategy in enabling tensions to be examined in safe and non-threatening environments. (Sim 2006: 79)

In two cases, however, the stories shared of problems identified in classroom practice were potentially compromising for teacher educators involved because they revolved around allegations of poor (in one case illegal) practice by qualified school teachers. This again raises the question of whether tutors should be involved with their own student teachers in the CoP/CoE. Adding a further note of caution, in the use of CoP practice and theory (in our P4T work one of the central tenets is to problematize the terms we are using ourselves): while it makes it easier to discuss our project by referring to CoP and P4C, we are not necessarily advocating all the different and various ways in which these concepts can be used. Moreover, we tend to use the terms 'dialogue' and 'deliberation' interchangeably when we describe our work, exposing us to the challenge that we are not entirely clear what P4T practice entails.

Watson also expresses concerns about clarity around the nature and purpose of a professional learning community. While she emphasizes their 'potentially significant role in ... destabilising the rigidities with which the school as institution surrounds itself' (Watson 2014: 27), she also expresses disquiet about the ubiquity of such communities, calling for a re-examination of the underpinning concepts and meanings. We have similar concerns for both CoPs and P4C, but having noted that striking similarities can be seen between CoP and key features of some types of P4C/PwC practices, we found both sets of practices useful as models for building effective CoPs in very limited time frames. It is also worth noting that one criticism of the CoP model as it has developed is how aligned with systems theory and instrumental concerns it now is. It has become 'managerialist' (e.g. Cox 2005) and lost its more radical edge (e.g. Huzzard 2004; Contu and Willmott 2003). We believe that P4T offers an important corrective to that.

Reflections on philosophy

For philosophers of education, P4T provides a means by which to communicate key principles and ideas within the discipline to a professional audience in ways that are both relevant to their practice and accessible. Making relevant connections is important in the case of teachers who are not philosophically trained since this helps to make the philosophy interesting and applicable. Reflecting philosophically through a CoE approach avoids the difficulties inherent to the traditional mode of delivering the educational foundations programme to teachers on vocational training programmes such as the PGCE, which is so short. (This seems not to be so pressing for those on Education Studies degrees, who have more time to spend developing ideas.) We have organized the workshops deliberately to take place towards the end of the PGCE, when participants have a reasonable amount of practical experience in the classroom on which to reflect and to relate to the experiences shared by their peers in the community.

The presence of participants within the community who have some formal knowledge and understanding of philosophy is significant: they are able to make pertinent philosophical observations in the moment, related to the participants' experiences and in language they can understand. The philosophers might be the tutors/ teacher educators but could also be the beginning teachers themselves. For example, one participant who had both a first degree and a doctorate in moral philosophy made a significant positive contribution to the first P4T workshop and this was made possible by the collectivist, non-hierarchical approach to professional learning.

Concluding remarks

This experiment established, for the brief time we were together, an open-ended, critical and self-reflective CoE focused on shared ethical concerns. The factors

Philosophy with New and Beginning Teachers 157

contributing to its success included time dedicated to a form of ethical deliberation based on real experiences; making use of P4C models of Communities of Enquiry, led by an experienced facilitator; and creating an appropriate space for deliberation, in which philosophers of education contributed.

Ethical deliberation on matters arising in practice for teachers has proved an important element in their professional practice, and the model we have built up has worked well for these teachers. We now need to think about the sustainability of the initiative. We are confident of its success but aware how dependent it has been on 'one off' research grants. One issue in the sustainability of the model is the pivotal role played by an independent facilitator with a specific and 'niche' set of knowledge, professional skills and competencies. Another is that of scalability. Clearly there is a need for some kind of preparation for ethical decision-making in teacher education – how much philosophy might all teachers reasonably expect to experience during their initial teacher education if this is such a priority? How might this initiative be repeated year on year with new cohorts? Such questions need addressing at the level of policy as well as in the practice of individual teacher educators.

Nonetheless, it is equally clear that the programme made a considerable, potentially transformative, difference for many of the participants. Regardless of context, teachers will always be confronted by particular ethical challenges for which they are unprepared. The P4T format presents a space for navigation of these challenges, through a unique opportunity for self-reflection with others, albeit briefly, through this particular form of professional learning community.

Notes

1   The Post Graduate Certificate of Education (PGCE) in England is a thirty-three-week programme leading to the award of Qualified Teacher Status (QTS). Courses are available across all phases; that is, Primary, Secondary and Post-Compulsory Education PGCEs are available. It is the most common route of all the possible routes into teaching.
2   See https://generation.global/
3   The discussion about the use of 'for' or 'with' has obvious implications, not particularly relevant to this article. Users of both terms come from a common foundational literature and practice.
4   For example, Trickey and Topping (2007) conducted a major empirical study into P4C, but for readers of this chapter, it serves as a useful guide and summary of the field, referencing the work of key people in the international field, such as Matthew Lipman, as well as those who have influenced practice in the UK, like Robert Fisher and Joanna Haynes.
5   'P4C focuses on thinking skills and communal dialogue ("philosophizing") and aims to build "communities of enquiry" where participants develop the 4C's: creative, critical, caring and collaborative thinking skills.'

- Caring = listening (concentrating) and valuing (appreciating) (e.g. showing interest in, and sensitivity to, others' experiences and values

- Collaborative = responding (communicating) and supporting (conciliating) (e.g. building on each other's ideas, shaping common understandings and purposes)
- Critical = questioning (interrogating) and reasoning (evaluating) (e.g. seeking meaning, evidence, reasons, distinctions, and good judgements)
- (P4C Cooperative)
- Creative = connecting (relating) and suggesting (speculating) (e.g. providing comparisons, examples, criteria, alternative explanations or conceptions).'

6 For Dewey, reflection arises in a problematic situation: it starts from 'a felt difficulty' (1910: 72). Some 'felt difficulties' can be settled by observation and reasoning but some cannot. In order to understand the problematic situation some kind of action is necessary, a process that Dewey names 'inquiry'.

7 The rule states that participants are free to use the information received, but neither the identity nor the affiliation both of the speaker(s) and of any other participants may be revealed.

References

AAE (2015), 'AAE Code of Ethics for Educators', [Online], Available at: http://www.aaet eachers.org/index.php/about-us/aaecode-of-ethics, Accessed 22 November 2015.

Alexander, R., (2017), 'What Is Diaologic Teaching?', [Online], Available at: http://www .robinalexander.org.uk/dialogic-teaching/, Accessed 10 July 2017.

Bauml, M., (2009), 'Examining the Unexpected Sophistication of Preservice Teachers' Beliefs about the Relational Dimensions of Teaching', *Teaching and Teacher Education*, 25 (6): 902–8.

Bolam, R., McMahon, A., Stoll, L., Thomas, S., and Wallace, M., (2005), *Creating and Sustaining Professional Learning Communities*. Research Report Number 637. London: General Teaching Council for England (GTC).

Burgh, G., (2018), 'The Need for Philosophy in Promoting Democracy: A Case for Philosophy in the Curriculum', *Journal of Philosophy in Schools*, 5 (1): 38–58.

Beishuizen, J. J., Hof, E., Van Putten, C. M., Bouwmeester, S., and Asscher, J. J., (2001), 'Students' and Teachers' Cognitions about Good Teachers', *British Journal of Educational Psychology*, 71 (2): 185–202.

Burstow, B., (2014), 'Teachers Need Quality Time Set Aside to Keep Learning', *The Conversation*, [Online], Available at: http://theconversation.com/teachers-need-qual ity-time-set-aside-to-keep- learning-28412, Accessed 11 August 2015.

Cam, P., (2018), 'The Generic Argument for Teaching Philosophy', *Journal of Philosophy in Schools*, 5 (1): 59–75.

Campbell, E., (2003), *The Ethical Teacher*, Maidenhead: Open University Press.

Campbell, E., (2008), 'Teaching Ethically as a Moral Condition of Professionalism', in L. Nucci and D. Narvaez (eds), *Handbook of Moral and Character Education*, 601–17, New York: Routledge.

Carr, D., (2006), 'Professional and Personal Values and Virtues in Education and Teaching', *Oxford Review of Education*, 32 (2): 171–83.

Carter, A., (2015), 'Carter Review of Initial Teacher Training', [Online], Available at: https://www.gov.uk/government/uploads/system/uploads/attachment_data/file/3999 57/Carter_Review, Accessed 11 August 2015.

Cassidy, C., (2012), 'Philosophy with Children: Learning to Live Well', *Childhood and Philosophy*, 8 (16): 243–64.

Coles, A., Dillon, J., Gall, M., Hawkey, K., James, J., Kerr, D., Orchard, J., Tidmarsh, C., and Wishart, J., (2017), 'Towards a Teacher Education for the Anthropocene', in P. Corcoran, J. Weakland and A. Wals (eds), *Envisioning Futures for Environmental and Sustainability Education*, 73–85, Wageningen: Wageningen Academic Publishers.

Contu, A., and Willmott, H., (2003), 'Re-Embedding Situatedness: The Importance of Power Relations in Learning Theory', *Organization Science*, 14 (3): 283–96.

Cox, A., (2005), 'What are Communities of Practice? A Comparative Review of Four Seminal Works', *Journal of Information Science*, 31 (6): 527–40.

Davids, N., (2016), 'Deliberation, Belonging and Inclusion: Towards Ethical Teaching in a Democratic South Africa', *Ethics and Education*, 11 (3), 274–85.

Davis, M., (1999), *Ethics and the University*, London: Routledge.

Demos, (2009), 'Leading from the Front', [Online], Available at: http://www.demos.co.uk/ publications/ leading-from-the-front, Accessed 21 May 2015.

Denscombe, M., (2008), 'Communities of Practice: A Research Paradigm for the Mixed Methods Approach', *Methods Research*, 2 (3): 270–83.

Department for Education (DfE), (2011), 'Teachers' Standards 2011, Updated 2013', [Online], Available at: https://www.gov.uk/ government/publications/teachers-standards, Accessed 10 June 2018.

Department for Education and Training (DET), (2006), *Teachers' Code of Professional Practice*, Canberra: Department for Education and Training.

Dewey, J., (1909), *The Moral Principles in Education. The Middle Works of John Dewey, 1899–1924, Volume 4: Essays, 1907–1909*, Carbondale and Edwardsville: Southern Illinois University Press.

Dewey J., (1910), *How We Think, The Middle Works of John Dewey, 1899–1924, Volume 6: The Collected Works of John Dewey, 1882–1953*, Carbondale, IL: Southern Illinois University Press.

Dewey, J., (1916), *Democracy and Education. The Middle Works of John Dewey, 1899–1924 Volume 9: The Collected Works of John Dewey, 1882–1953*, First release, electronic edition 2003.

Dewey, J., (1929), *The Sources of a Science of Education*, New York: Horace Liveright.

Drury, D., and Baer, J., (2011), *The American Public School Teacher: Past, Present, and Future*, Cambridge, MA: Harvard Education Press.

Dunne, J., (1993), *Back to the Rough Ground*, Notre Dame, IN: University of Notre Dame Press.

Dunne, J., (2003), 'Arguing for Teaching as a Practice: A reply to Alisdair MacIntyre', *Journal of Philosophy of Education*, 37 (2): 353–71.

Estola, E., and Erikkilä, R., (2003), 'A Moral Voice of Vocation in Teachers' Narratives', *Teachers and Teaching: Theory and Practice*, 9 (3): 239–56.

Freire, P., (1972), *Pedagogy of the Oppressed*, Harmondsworth: Penguin.

Griffiths, M., (2013), 'Critically Adaptive Pedagogical Relations: The Relevance for Educational Policy and Practice', *Educational Theory* 63 (3): 221–36.

General Teaching Council for Scotland (GTCS), (2012), *Code of Professionalism and Conduct (COPAC)*, [Online], Available at: http://www.gtcs.org.uk/standards/copac.a spx, Accessed 22 November 2015.

Hansen, D., (1995), *The Call to Teach*, New York: Teachers College Press.

Hansen, D., (2001), *Exploring the Moral Heart of Teaching*, New York: Teachers College Press.

Heilbronn, R., (2008), *Teacher Education and the Development of Practical Judgement*, London: Continuum.

Heilbronn R., (2017), 'Dewey and Culture: Responding to Extreme Views', *Journal of Philosophy of Education*, 51 (1): 89–101.

Higgins, C., (2010), 'The Good Life of Teaching: An Ethics of Professional Practice', *Journal of Philosophy of Education*, 44 (4): 479–602.

Hodgkinson-Williams, C., Slay, H., and Siebörger, I., (2008), 'Developing Communities of Practice Within and Outside Higher Education Institutions', *British Journal of Educational Technology*, 39 (3): 433–42.

Hopkins, D., and Reid, K., (1985), 'Introduction: Rethinking Teacher Education', in D. Hopkins and K. Reid (eds), *Rethinking Teacher Education*, 1–7, Beckenham: Croom Helm.

Huzzard, T., (2004), 'Communities of Domination? Reconceptualising Organisational Learning and Power', *The Journal of Workplace Learning*, 16 (6): 350–61.

Jimenez-Silva, M., and Olson, K., (2012), 'A Community of Practice in Teacher Education: Insights and Perceptions', *International Journal of Teaching and Learning in Higher Education*, 24 (3): 335–48.

Kutnick, P., and Jules, V., (1993), 'Pupils' Perceptions of a Good Teacher: A Developmental Perspective from Trinidad and Tobago', *British Journal of Educational Psychology*, 63 (3): 400–13.

Lave, J., and Wenger, E., (1991), *Situated Learning*, Cambridge: University of Cambridge Press.

Maxwell, B., Tremblay-Laprise, A.-A., Filion, M., Boon, H., Daly, C., van den Hoven, M., Heilbronn, R., Lenselink, M., and Walters, S., (2016.), 'A Five-Country Survey on Ethics Education in Pre-service Teaching Programs', *Journal of Teacher Education*, 67 (2): 135–51.

Murris, K. S., (2008), 'Philosophy with Children, the Stingray and the Educative Value of Disequilibrium', *Journal of Philosophy of Education*, 42 (3–4): 667–85.

Noddings, N., (1992), *The Challenge to Care in Schools: An Alternative Approach to Education*, New York: Teachers College Press.

Ofsted (2015), 'Initial Teacher Education Inspection Handbook', [Online], Available at: https://www. gov.uk/government/publications/initial-teacher-education-inspection-handbook, Accessed 11 August 2015.

Orchard, J., (2018), 'Practical Judgement, Religious Education Research and the Professional Formation of RE Teachers', Paper presented at the twenty-first session of the International Seminar on Religious Education and Values, Friedrich-Alexander University, Erlangen-Nürnberg, 29 July–3 August 2018.

Orchard, J., Heilbronn, R., and Winstanley, C., (2016), 'Philosophy for Teachers (P4T): Developing New Teachers' Applied Ethical Decision-Making', *Ethics and Education*, 11: 42–54.

P4C Cooperative (2015), [Online], Available at: http://p4c.com/, Accessed 15 August 2015.

Papastephanou, M., (2006), 'Education, Risk and Ethics', *Ethics and Education*, 1 (1): 47–63.

Rich, J. M., (1984), *Professional Ethics in Education*, Springfield, IL: Charles C. Thomas.

Robinson, G. C., (2014), 'You Live and Learn: Narrative in Ethical Enquiry with Children', *Childhood and Philosophy*, 10 (20): 305–30.

Schön, D., (1983), *The Reflective Practitioner: How Professionals Think in Action*, London: Temple Smith.

Shortt, D., Reynolds, P., McAteer, M., and Hallett, F., (2015), 'To Believe, to Think, to Know – To Reach? Ethical Deliberation in Teacher-Education', in R. Heilbronn and L. Foreman-Peck (eds), *Philosophical Perspectives on Teacher Education*, 89–108, Oxford: Wiley Blackwell.

Sim, C., (2006), 'Preparing for Professional Experiences: Incorporating Pre-service Teachers as Communities of Practice', *Teaching and Teacher Education*, 22 (1): 76–83.

Smith, R., (1999), 'Paths of Judgement: The Revival of Practical Wisdom', *Educational Philosophy and Theory*, 31 (3): 327–40.

Smith, R., (2017), 'Slow Learning and the Multiplicity of Meaning', in M. Peters and J. Stickney (eds), *A Companion to Wittgenstein on Education: Pedagogical Investigations*, 101–15, Singapore: Springer.

Society for the Advancement of Philosophical Enquiry and Reflection in Education (SAPERE), (2017), *Philosophy for Children, Colleges*, Communities, [Online], Available at: www.sapere.org.uk, Accessed 2 July 2017.

South African Council for Educators (SACE), (2011), '*The Code of Professional Ethics*', [Online], Available at: https://www.sace.org.za/pages/ethics-department, Accessed 22 May 2018.

Stenhouse, L., (1975), *An Introduction to Curriculum Research and Development*, London: Heinemann.

Sutherland, L., Scanlon, L., and Sperring, A., (2005), 'New Directions in Preparing Professionals: Examining Issues in Engaging Students in Communities of Practice through a School-University Partnership', *Teaching and Teacher Education*, 21 (1): 79–92.

Teaching Council Ireland (TCI), (2012), *Code of Professional Conduct*, [Online], Available at: http://www.teachingcouncil.ie/en/Fitness-to-Teach/Code-of-Professional-Cond uct/, Accessed 22 May 2018.

Thornberg, R., (2006), 'Hushing as a Moral Dilemma in the Classroom', *Journal of Moral Education*, 35 (1): 89–104.

Todd, S., (2001), '"Bringing More than I Contain": Ethics, Curriculum and the Pedagogical Demand for Altered Egos', *Journal of Curriculum Studies*, 33 (4): 431–50.

Toole, J. C., and Louis, I. S., (2002), 'The Role of Professional Learning Communities in International Education', in K. Leithwood and P. Hallinger (eds), *Second International Handbook of Educational Leadership and Administration*, 245–78, Dordrecht: Kluwer.

Topping, K. J., and Trickey, S., (2007), Impact of Philosophical Enquiry on School Student's Interactive Behavior, *Thinking Skills and Creativity*, 2: 73–84. http://dx.doi.o rg/10.1016/j.tsc.2007.03.001

Trickey, S., and Topping, K., (2004), 'Philosophy for Children: A Systematic Review', *Research Papers in Education*, 19 (3): 365–80.

UNESCO (2015), *Teacher Code of Practice for the Philippines*, [Online], Available at: http: //teachercodes.iiep.unesco.org/teachercodes/codes/Asia/Philippines.pdf, Accessed 22 November 2015.

Van Manen, M., (1991), *The Tact of Teaching: The Meaning of Pedagogical Thoughtfulness*, Albany: State University of New York Press.

Walters, S., Heilbronn, R., and Daly, C., (2017), 'Ethics Education in Initial Teacher Education: Pre-service Provision in England', Professional Development in Education, [Online], Available at: https://www.tandfonline.com/doi/abs/10.1080/19415257.20 17.1318773, Accessed 4 April 2018.

Warnick, B. R., and Silverman, S. K., (2011), 'A Framework for Professional Ethics Courses in Teacher Education', *Journal of Teacher Education*, 62 (3): 273–85.

162 *Philosophy and Community*

Watson, C., (2014), 'Effective Professional Learning Communities? The Possibilities for Teachers as Agents of Change in Schools', *British Educational Research Journal*, 40 (1): 18–29.

Wenger, E., (1998a), 'Communities of Practice: Learning as a Social System', *The Systems Thinker*, [Online], Available at: https://moo27pilot.eduhk.hk/pluginfile.php/415222/mod_resource/content/3/Learningasasocialsystem.pdf, Accessed 4 April 2018.

Wenger, E., (1998b), *Communities of Practice: Learning, Meaning, and Identity*, Cambridge: Cambridge University Press.

Wenger, E., and Snyder, W. M., (2000), 'Communities of Practice: The Organizational Frontier', *Harvard Business Review*, 78: 139–45.

Wolfe, S., and Alexander, R. J., (2008), *Argumentation and Dialogic Teaching: Alternative Pedagogies for a Changing World*, [Online], Available at: http://www.robinalexander.org.uk/wp-content/uploads/2012/05/wolfealexander.pdf, Accessed 22 May 2018.

11

In philosophical conversation with: Learning-disabled performers

Nick Wiltsher and Aaron Meskin

Academic philosophy is an anxious discipline. Two things about which the discipline has been anxious recently are diversity and impact. Philosophy has an internal diversity problem: much soul-searching has been dedicated to the question of whether the way in which academic philosophy is often done has a tendency to marginalize people who aren't white, male, non-disabled and so forth. Philosophy also has an external impact problem: how can an often abstract and abstruse discipline demonstrate the concrete effects on wider society so beloved of those holding the purse-strings?

It might seem that philosophical aesthetics – the branch of philosophy devoted to studying the issues raised by art, beauty and related matters – is particularly well placed to address these anxieties. On the one hand, art and the appreciation of beauty are, as best as we can tell, human universals, found in every culture and at every time. Since philosophical aestheticians tend to be interested in what is essential to – or at least standard in – the aesthetic domain, and not merely contingent to particular times and places, one might expect them to investigate art in an inclusive fashion. If one wants to understand what art, beauty and artistic expression are, then surely one needs to study them wherever they are found, not just when they are the products of non-disabled white European males. Philosophical aesthetics, then, might be expected to be one of the least marginalizing branches of philosophy.

On the other hand, aesthetics also seems as if it should be one of the least abstract and abstruse sub-disciplines of philosophy. After all, philosophical aestheticians are not focused on esoteric issues about the existence of numbers or the ultimate nature of reality. Their focus is on such things as works of art and beautiful (or unattractive) natural environments. These do not appear to be rarefied matters – at least not in the first instance. While it might not be obvious how a metaphysician, concerned with non-existence or nature's fundamental structure, could have an impact on wider society, it seems clear that philosophers of art should be able to have such an impact – after all, their domain of focus is an important part of that wider society.

We think that, broadly, this is right in theory: aesthetics is a philosophical sub-discipline that is especially well suited to inclusiveness and impact. However, in practice, philosophical aesthetics has not been any more inclusive or impactful than any other sub-discipline in the past hundred years or so. Aestheticians have concentrated on forms of 'high' art from the European tradition, and works produced by white, non-disabled men.[1] And they have done no more than any other sub-discipline to pursue opportunities for engagement and impact outside the academy.

There's much to be said about the reasons for these failings, and about whether they're specific to aesthetics or general to philosophy, but we won't be saying much about those topics in the present piece.[2] Instead, we want to reflect on how things go when aestheticians try to rectify the failings. We are philosophical aestheticians with significant interests in inclusiveness and impact. In this chapter, we describe and reflect on our experiences of working with the learning-disabled performers of the Mind the Gap theatre company, and examine ways in which those experiences interact with the two issues described.[3] The project involved us collaborating with Mind the Gap and Thinking Space, a not-for-profit company in the UK which focuses on philosophical education, projects and training. The initial impetus was provided by Mind the Gap, who wished to take advantage of a collaborative grant scheme and bring in experts in aesthetics to help its performers sharpen their critical relations to their own practices.

For academics, the project presented practical problems of approach: How might, or should, we adapt our practice as researchers and teachers to this new context? What challenges would we face working with people who were not academically trained, and in some sense disabled? It also presented opportunities to learn: How might what we do in such a context feed back into our everyday practice, and how might that feedback improve the climate of our departments? How might the project indicate ways in which philosophy can demonstrate impact and be more inclusive? This chapter describes what we did, what we learned and how we have benefited. Our reflections include some tentative suggestions regarding how aesthetics, and philosophy more broadly, might do better in the domains of impact and inclusiveness.

Introduction to the context of the work

The project was a collaboration between three parties. First, Mind the Gap, a professional theatre company based in Bradford, a large city in the north of England. Almost all of its performers identify as 'learning-disabled'; that is to say, they have Down's syndrome, autism or other such conditions. The company's work encompasses a range of theatrical styles (promenade, proscenium, site-specific) and performance media (stage, screen, music and dance). The company as a whole, and performers individually, has enjoyed considerable successes, including performances at the 2012 London Paralympics and roles in television programmes such as *Coronation Street*, a long-running British soap opera. (American readers might imagine a less fantastical version of *Days of Our Lives*.)

The second, and leader of the collaboration, was Grace Lockrobin, director of Thinking Space. Based in Yorkshire, England, Thinking Space comprises a small team of philosophers, educators and academics. Their aim is to create opportunities for people to think philosophically together. These opportunities include workshops, events, training courses and research projects. Lockrobin had previously explored the intersection of philosophical inquiry and theatre through partnerships with various UK-based theatre companies: West Yorkshire Playhouse, Wakefield Theatres, Unfolding Theatre, Theatre Blah Blah Blah and Theatre Cap-a-Pie. She had also explored the use of philosophical inquiry with learning-disabled people through work with Beacon Hill Arts/Beacon Films (a UK-based production and training organization working with learning-disabled film-makers). The third collaborators were the two of us: philosophers, who were at the time of the project employed at, or associated with, the University of Leeds, UK. We both have expertise in aesthetics and the philosophy of art, and interests in impact, outreach and diversity.

The collaboration was instigated by Mind the Gap. They sought to take advantage of a competitive grant scheme offered by The Exchange, a pilot programme run by The Cultural Capital Exchange and funded by Arts Council England and the Higher Education Funding Council for England. The scheme offers small awards to artists, small- and medium-size enterprises, and early career academics. These awards are designed to create collaborative projects and encourage interdisciplinary investigation.[4] Mind the Gap saw an opportunity to explore questions about the value of their work, what they might do to improve it, and how they might reflect more critically on it during its development. In part, this was driven by Arts Council England's interest in assessing the quality of the work it funds.[5] The Resident Director for Mind the Gap had worked with Meskin in community theatre, where they had informally discussed the potential for collaboration. Wiltsher was brought in as the primary early career academic. Thinking Space, who have an affiliation with the School of Philosophy, Religion and History of Science at Leeds, were brought on board owing to their expertise in facilitating this kind of project.

The aims and parameters of the project were quickly established. Over a series of five half-day sessions, a Leeds philosopher and a Thinking Space practitioner would work with several Mind the Gap performers and their artistic director to explore questions of artistic value, theatrical quality, critical reflection, and response to such reflection. The project outcomes would be presented to the full company and invited guests in a sharing session at the project's end.

Each of the parties undoubtedly had different hopes, expectations and questions going into the project. But we will concentrate on our own. As philosophers experienced in teaching undergraduates, we had several expectations, or questions, about how the project might go. On the practical side, some of these concerned, in general, the way in which people might respond to philosophical prompting outside an academic context. Some concerned, specifically, the challenges and the potential of working with learning-disabled people: whether their particular disabilities might affect such things as the issues they were concerned with, or the sort of exercises that were suitable. For example, would less confrontational exercises be better? Others concerned the status of the participants as artists. Would they care about the philosophical issues that we worry about? Or is aesthetics really about as useless to the artist as ornithology is to the bird? A further question concerned the stated aim that the project be run as a collaboration rather than a programme of tutorial sessions: How would this affect the context of learning, and how would we help to make the project a collaboration? On the more theoretical side, we were interested to find out whether the performers' status as learning-disabled people made any difference to their judgements of what was valuable about their work and what was important about art in general.

The reflective outcomes that we will detail later (in the section Critical Reflections) do not all straightforwardly respond to these hopes and expectations. Nonetheless, it is interesting to compare what we were thinking about before the collaboration, to what we got out of it in the end. Before we come to reflections, though, we need to describe the collaboration.

Description of the work

The five half-day sessions were divided into three phases. The first session was introductory, and set the agenda for the remainder. Sessions two to four consisted of workshops, led by Lockrobin, during which the research questions established in the first session were explored. Our role in these workshops was partly to assist with the running of the activities and partly to contribute specific expertise in aesthetics. For most of the sessions, Wiltsher was the philosopher in attendance, since the grant was for work with an early career researcher. Meskin attended some sessions and was involved in the fifth and final session, which was a sharing with the rest of the company, other Leeds philosophers and other interested parties. We will now describe in more detail the content of these sessions.[6]

Session one

The main aims of this session were to introduce the participants to each other and to establish the questions to be collectively pursued during the workshops. The meeting began with a showcase of Mind the Gap's work, including examples of traditional theatre pieces, site-specific pieces, classic performances and new works. In return, and rather more briefly, Lockrobin and Wiltsher introduced themselves, outlining their backgrounds, interests and thoughts about the collaboration. The rest of the workshop session was spent establishing and pursuing the questions in which the group was interested. A primary set of interrelated research questions, both central to philosophical aesthetics and of particular interest to the participants, were identified: What is good art? On what basis can art be judged?[7] And, in what ways could Mind the Gap's performers evaluate the quality of their own work at different stages of the creative process? A set of secondary questions of interest were also identified, concerning whether Mind the Gap's work is artistically good, whether it is socially good, what the relation between those two forms of goodness might be,[8] and what the purposes of Mind the Gap are.

Session two

As per the research questions, the first workshop started with activities designed to establish vocabulary for talking about the value of art generally, before moving on to

Philosophy with Learning-Disabled Performers   167

talking about theatre specifically. The first activity involved participants selecting a picture postcard they liked and explaining why they liked it. In so doing, participants naturally picked up on features of the pictures such as their colours, simplicity, realism or emotional impact. Wiltsher's main contribution during this exercise was to point out the commonalities and differences among the various features being picked up on (formal, expressive, representational and so on) and relate those to wider ways of talking about aesthetic matters.

The next exercise introduced the idea of offering and debating reasons for liking art, with specific application to theatre, by creating situations in which participants were asked to argue for one side or another of a binary position. Issues addressed included the question of whether happy artists or happy audiences should be the aim of theatre companies, and whether Mind the Gap was preferable as a company to the Royal Shakespeare Company (RSC). The following exercise was a more nuanced version of the same, involving physical movement. With locations in the room designated as ends of a spectrum, participants positioned themselves according to their view – right at the RSC end, all the way with Mind the Gap, somewhere in the middle – and then changed their position if debate moved them to do so.

Besides the content of the activities concerned with exploring such things as critical vocabulary, part of their point was to develop practical ideas. Some of these were just to do with embedding the practice of giving reasons, but some were more generally about the practice of philosophizing about things: for example, letting everyone speak or assuming positions for the sake of argument or to see their force. Aspects of the activities, such as literal movement to indicate change of position, reinforced these ideas. These activities reflect a general conception of what it is to do philosophy. While we are sceptical about the prospects for sharply delimiting the boundaries of philosophical inquiry, we do think that central aspects of that practice can be identified. Among these are a commitment to taking justifications for views as far as they can be taken, and a norm of thoroughgoing engagement with views and their justifications that are contrary to those that one holds oneself. By encouraging the participants to pursue reasons for their views, and consider thoroughly the views of others, we were encouraging the development of these key philosophical capacities and values.

Session three

The aim of this session was to start developing ideas about how to deal with and respond to criticism of work by Mind the Gap, using examples provided by the Resident Director of genuine feedback from Mind the Gap shows.

In the first activity, participants watched clips of a Mind the Gap performance, and then tried to imagine how various characters, such as friends, parents or performers, might respond. The activity made salient the fact that different kinds of responses could be given to the same performance, and also raised the question of the distinction between helpful and unhelpful feedback and criticism. The group at this stage had a preference for feedback which was positive, whether or not it was credible or objective.

In the next activity, participants were presented with a fictional situation in which the Resident Director and Meskin, acting in the role of the director of a company similar to

168   *Philosophy and Community*

Mind the Gap, and her interlocutor, articulated a number of critical 'post-performance' comments about a Mind the Gap performance – that the actors lacked discipline, that the music was cheesy and that the mood was lazily upbeat. Participants were invited to act out how they might respond. Perhaps because this was an opportunity for the performers to perform, the Mind the Gap artists were extremely engaged with this exercise.

Session four

This session was partly continuation and partly preparation. The first part of it was spent building on the previous session's activities. Critical comments from those activities were sorted into groups according to how helpful they were. In this process, with help from Wiltsher and Lockrobin, several of the participants were able to consider and articulate the idea that positive and negative comments might not line up with helpful and unhelpful comments: for example, the idea that a parent saying 'that was perfect' might not actually be very helpful for developing one's practice. The second part of the session was given over to a review of the earlier sessions, reflections on them, and collaborative establishment of a format for the sharing event and a plan of things to be done by participants in preparation for it.

Session five

This was the sharing event. It was attended by many members of Mind the Gap, including performers, directors, administrators and technicians; by philosophers from the University of Leeds; and by Thinking Space practitioners. The event included a description of the project activities and exercises, as well as examples of those exercises led by the performers and involving audience members. It also involved a rerun of the critical comments exercise, in which, interestingly, one of the participants gave differently formulated and nuanced responses to the critical comments. This demonstrated the development of his thinking over the course of the sessions. The event ended with a question and answer session, in which members of the collaboration discussed its outcomes and what they might do with the results.

Critical reflections

In reflecting on the collaboration, we find ourselves revisiting the thoughts and worries we had in mind when it started, and the issues of inclusion and impact we outlined at the start of this chapter. Relative to our thoughts at the time, it's surprising how few of our reflections concern issues or challenges surrounding engagement with learning-disabled people. There were, in fact, few such challenges or issues to be surmounted. If we learn anything about inclusiveness from that observation, it's that it's not so difficult to work with people who differ from those we typically encounter in academia: we can promote inclusiveness just by pursuing impact. Accordingly, while both inclusiveness

Philosophy with Learning-Disabled Performers 169

and impact are thematic in the reflections that follow, much of what have to say is more obviously pertinent to the latter topic.

The nature and value of philosophy

Our reflections on the nature and value of philosophy come in three parts: the first is about the nature of philosophy, the second is about how philosophy might be done, and the third is about the relevance of philosophical aesthetics to the practice of actual artists.

The first thing to say was that it was not at all difficult to engage with the performers in broadly philosophical discussion about some of the central issues in aesthetics: the value of art, the nature of reason-giving in the aesthetic domain, and the value of art criticism. On the contrary, it was easy. Working with artists who had, by and large, no previous exposure to philosophy did not present a challenge at all. (In fact, their lack of preconceptions might have been a bit of an advantage.) And this, we suspect, is because philosophy is not actually an abstruse discipline, but rather one that significantly connects with the lives of ordinary people. There are certainly perfectly respectable bits of philosophy which are quite rarefied – paraconsistent logic, anyone? Nonetheless, we suggest that philosophical issues, broadly speaking, are never far away from everyday thought and talk.

But again, it is not just the philosophical nature of the issues addressed that made our collaboration with this community philosophical. The discussions in which the performers engaged were also philosophical because they adopted some of the key tools and methods of philosophy: interrogation of ideas and concepts, the search for bedrock justifications of views, the serious consideration of views opposed to one's own. And, again, it was not just easy to engage the performers with the issues; they also took quickly to the methods. Just as the issues philosophers address are not far from the surface of the everyday, the methods by which they do so, or perhaps the reasons for why they do – the sense that better justifications can be uncovered through hard work – are likewise not far removed from ordinary thought and practice. These are some of the reasons why philosophy is so well suited for outreach activities and public engagement.

It could also be that some of the specific methods employed in the collaboration were especially well suited to the context. A notable aspect of the collaboration was the alacrity with which the Mind the Gap performers engaged with exercises in which they were required to perform: to assume positions, to get into character, to take on and argue from perspectives outside their own. While all the exercises we undertook added to the collaboration, these were the exercises that the company seemed to get most from.

This answers, quite positively, our initial worry about whether exercises that involved confrontation or arguing would be suitable for the collaboration. If anything, it seemed to us that the performers were *more* ready to argue or to confront than undergraduates typically are. Where seminars can sometimes be uncomfortably silent as students hesitate to participate, the performers were immediately, actively and audibly engaged.

Speculatively, one might think that this is because performers are comfortable with, and adept at, the practice of adopting for the sake of some project a position, character or view that is not in fact their own. Undergraduates are often not this way, and can be reluctant to explore positions or views as if they are ones they actually hold – almost as if doing so would commit them somehow to those positions.

Whether this reveals anything about the nature of philosophy as such is debatable. It could be argued that philosophy has some essentially performative element, but it is not obvious that this is the case. Although lecturing and presenting certainly have performative elements, writing philosophy need not be performative in any substantive sense. (And if all writing is performative, then there need not be anything distinctively performative about philosophical writing.) On the other hand, it does seem to us that the practice of 'trying on' alternative perspectives, even if those perspectives are not performed, is pretty central to doing good philosophy. After all, a very good way to construct a convincing philosophical argument is to imagine oneself in the position of a critic. Hence, when we think about the implications of our project for teaching philosophy, and for getting students to do philosophy, there are some potential lessons. It may well be that a way to get students, and people more generally, to engage better with philosophical arguments is to emphasize, and if necessary to model, the performative and role-taking aspects of the practices we are trying to inculcate.

Regarding the significance of aesthetics, one might worry that the issues that aestheticians address are not ones that are close to the surface for working artists – again, that aesthetics is to artists as ornithology is to birds. And this, perhaps, proved partially true and partially false during the collaboration. As we said earlier, we found that the performers were very ready and able to engage in philosophical inquiry, both in terms of method and in terms of topics, and the issues that were of central importance to them were issues about the value of their art: about what was good about it, about how it could be improved, about ways in which it could be described and understood and critiqued. While philosophical aestheticians do address more rarefied and abstruse questions, they also pay great attention to those very questions. In that sense, the relevance of aesthetics to artists was clear.

But in another sense, it was less clear. A good number of the things that Mind the Gap's performers thought were valuable in their work, and in art more generally, were not things that contemporary Anglo-American aestheticians tend to emphasize. The performers placed a high value on realism; they thought that good theatre was true to life. Moreover, they thought that this realism was valuable because it assisted with the social, educational role of the company, which the artists thought was central and valuable to their practice. Good theatre, and good art, in their eyes, plays a crucial social function, and can educate people about important social issues.

Now it is quite likely that the performers felt this way in part because of the very nature of their company, and their work; it is reasonable for performers belonging to groups that have suffered marginalization and discrimination, to want to use their work to discuss, criticize and change the social context. But this observation does not give a reason to ignore their opinion on what makes art valuable. Quite the opposite. It suggests, perhaps, that if aestheticians want to think about how their field could be more inclusive, they might do well to consider more deeply the links between art and social functions, and the roles that art can play in advancing social justice.[9] These are issues that have arguably not been at the forefront of philosophers' discussions of the value of art in recent times, and perhaps, if philosophical aesthetics is to be truly relevant and have impact, they should be.

What philosophers can learn

We have just mentioned something we learned from the collaboration regarding attitudes towards the value of art. We now wish to concentrate more closely on several other things we learned. The first concerns omissions in philosophy and philosophical aesthetics; the second has to do with practical matters regarding university education; the remainder are about how we practise philosophy and outreach.

On the subject of philosophy's omissions, it is certainly the case that philosophy generally, and aesthetics specifically, have been ignorant or dismissive of philosophical issues concerning disability and of the salience of disability and the experiences of disabled people to philosophical problems. For example, discussions of the conditions under which abortion might be permissible or even desirable have often proceeded on the basis of unexamined and objectionable assumptions and prejudices concerning the value of the lives of disabled people, and about the kinds of experiences they have.[10] Thankfully, this pattern of omission and ignorance is being challenged by a growing body of work.[11]

This work is admirable, and we have no wish to criticize it. In a nascent literature, there is only so much that can be done. Nonetheless, it is notable that the discussion of disability in philosophy has often been concerned with *physical* disability.[12] To take a recent example, Elizabeth Barnes makes an explicit choice to focus her excellent book on disability, *The Minority Body*, on physical disability (2016: 2–4). Comparatively little has been said about learning disabilities like those of the Mind the Gap performers. Working with learning-disabled people obviously made salient to us this omission. It could be that there are, in fact, no issues or problems that are particular to this kind of disability, but this is a hypothesis that needs examining, and if there are distinctive philosophical issues, they need to be addressed.

Whether there are indeed *philosophical* issues raised by learning disabilities is not a question we can address here. But we do wish to gesture towards a practical point about inclusiveness in universities made salient to us by the collaboration. The range of learning disabilities and learning differences with which universities are currently prepared to engage is fairly limited. Universities seem, in general, quite willing to accept students with conditions such as dyslexia, dyspraxia or attention deficit hyperactivity disorder (ADHD), for which accommodations are fairly easily found – such thing as extra time on exams are low-cost, low-hassle interventions. Universities do not seem to be prepared to deal with more challenging learning disabilities, ones which would require substantial changes – not just changes of pedagogy but changes in how students are recruited, and how promise and preparedness for academia are assessed.[13]

Now, one might think that the sort of disabilities we are talking about are simply not the kind that can be accommodated in an academic environment. Against this, and returning this discussion to the collaboration in question, we wish to emphasize how few problems we encountered working with Mind the Gap's performers. It would be an exaggeration to say that there were no differences compared with the experience of working with other people lacking a philosophical or academic background, but such differences were minor, and presented no impediment to fruitful, collaborative philosophical work. Further, the willingness of schools and universities to do more to help students with dyslexia, dyspraxia, dyscalculia and so on is a relatively recent phenomenon. Although dyslexia, for example, was identified as a condition in the late nineteenth century, the British government gave it little attention until the 1980s (despite a 1978 report recommending action authored by no less a philosophical authority than Mary Warnock).[14] Dyslexia was named in the 1995 Disability Discrimination Act as a condition requiring accommodation by employers and educational institutions. Schools and universities are now better at accommodating dyslexia and similar conditions, and at finding ways to recognize talents and achievements that might be obscured by them. So, in the case of dyslexia, a condition that was for a long time treated by relevant authorities and institutions as an insuperable impediment to learning is now not seen as such. Similarly, it is possible that, with sufficient imagination and attention to what learning-disabled people actually say and want, universities could become environments in which they too can succeed. It would require a large shift of attitude and approach in several key institutions, and some imaginative thinking about recruitment, teaching and retention. But there is no reason to think it cannot be done.

We now wish to turn to a more general lesson we learned about modes of engagement. When philosophers think about impact and engagement, they tend to do so in ways that are related to the modes in which they teach. Teaching at the university level is often research-led; this means, in broadest terms, that academics often teach on subjects that they also research, and use their research to drive their teaching. This encourages a model on which teaching is a form of dissemination: one does the research, and then one tells one's students about it.

This is of course a very crude way of describing university teaching, one that does not fit the actual practice of many academics, and there is much to be said about whether it is a desirable mode of pedagogy. Nonetheless, the prevalent assumption about public engagement is that dissemination is the model. One does the research, and then one tells the world about it. The problem is how to get the world to listen, or to be interested.

This project had a different mode, and suggests an alternate and potentially more profitable way in which philosophers can pursue engagement and impact.[15] As we have emphasized throughout, the project was a collaboration. The work being done was done together, in a spirit of joint inquiry. While we might have had more idea than our partners did in advance of how the work might go, it remains the case that the model of the project was not one where we told the performers what we knew; rather, we explored the issues and questions together, and (as we hope we have indicated) we all learned things from it.

The extent to which this collaboration was symmetrical can be overstated. We were, after all, present qua experts in the field, and we were kindly thanked during the final sharing session for passing on things we knew. However, the moral we wish to draw is that collaborative enterprises such as this one, where philosophers' expertise helps to structure a joint inquiry, may be more rewarding and fruitful ways to seek engagement and impact than the typical research-then-report mode.

A further point follows regarding the distinction between *public* engagement and *community* engagement. The 'public' with whom philosophers and academics try to engage is frequently, implicitly, treated as a homogeneous mass of people, distinguished as a group only by their status outside academia. A community, on the other hand, is a subgroup of the public, distinguished in some significant way from other groups. There are various different kinds of communities, but for our purposes, it is worth pointing to the category of 'psychological communities', which Daniel Bell characterizes as follows:

> Communities of face-to-face personal interaction governed by sentiments of trust, co-operation, and altruism ... group[s] of persons who participate in common activity and experience a psychological sense of togetherness as shared ends are sought. Such communities, based on face-to-face interaction, are governed by sentiments of trust, cooperation, and altruism in the sense that constituent members have the good of the community in mind and act on behalf of the community's interest. (Bell 2016)

We are not claiming that all community engagement does, or should, focus on psychological communities to the exclusion of other kinds of community. But we do claim that psychological communities are interesting and worthwhile communities with which to engage and that, in this particular case, we were engaging with one.

Furthermore, the fact that a community of this sort involves shared ends, cooperation and trust suggests that *engaging with*, as opposed to *merely interacting with*, a community might involve intentionally adopting some of the norms and practices of that community, and sharing some of the norms and practices of one's own community. This, we think, is a fruitful way to see the collaboration we are discussing: we shared some of the norms and practices of academic philosophy, and we adopted some of the norms and practices of the community of performers with whom we were engaged. For example, we engaged in a lot more physical movement than when we usually philosophize. And our philosophizing does not typically involve specifically theatrical activities – as was the case in the critical comments exercise. So the joint inquiry we discussed earlier might usefully be thought of as interaction between communities, structured by the sharing of practices and norms. We might even see such collaborations in terms of the construction of a new, temporary community united by trust, cooperation and the shared goal of collaborating on a joint project of inquiry. This conception of community engagement might be more productive than the implicit idea of engagement with an undifferentiated public.

What do philosophers offer?

This brings us on to the final point we wish to make, about what philosophers have to offer the wider world in terms of engagement and impact. As we said at the start of this chapter, philosophers do worry about the appeal and impact of their work, and are in some ways right to do so; contemporary work in some areas of philosophy may be hard to relate to everyday interests and concerns. But this collaboration reminded and reassured us that aestheticians, at least, have expertise that can make a positive contribution to institutions like Mind the Gap. If funders such as Arts Council England are interested in assessing 'the quality of work produced' by funded organizations to inform their funding decisions,[16] then aesthetic inquiry may be crucial to the success of an arts organization. There are, then, opportunities for engagement and impact awaiting those with the imagination to find them.

Conclusion

When we reflect on this collaboration, we can see a number of lessons and ideas, for philosophers, for universities and for those wishing to collaborate with them – ideas about impact, inclusiveness, the role and value of philosophy and so forth. But we would like to conclude by emphasizing something that has perhaps not been given its due in our discussion. This collaboration was, above all, *fun*. It was worthwhile in all sorts of other ways, but the overriding memory is of thoroughly enjoyable sessions doing entirely pleasurable work with highly amenable and collegial collaborators. If that's not a reason to get out of the classroom and into the community, we don't know what is.[17]

Notes

1 For discussion of the focus on high art, see Carroll (1998) and Wolterstorff (2015). For a recent investigation of black aesthetics, see Taylor (2016).

2 Wiltsher (2017) discusses some of the reasons why aesthetics has been fairly narrow in its pursuits and offers some prescriptions for doing better.

3 A note on vocabulary. One of the first things we asked in the preliminary stages of the collaboration was how our collaborators prefer to be described. 'Learning-disabled' was the immediate and clear answer, and so we have used this descriptor throughout the chapter. They also preferred 'performers' rather than 'actors' or 'artists', but we have used the latter occasionally for the sake of variety.

4 See https://www.wearetheexchange.org/ (permanently archived version available at https://perma.cc/9757-DWTR).

5 See https://www.artscouncil.org.uk/quality-metrics/quality-metrics (permanently archived at https://perma.cc/FN4S-8HCJ); for discussion, see https://www.the guardian.com/culture/2016/oct/04/quality-metrics-arts-council-england-funding (permanently archived at https://perma.cc/YZ6E-9PC5).

6 Much of the material in this section was adapted from Grace Lockrobin's contribution to the final project report.

7 See Budd (1995) and Kieran (2001) for discussion of these questions.

8 The relationship between artistic goodness and other forms of goodness is a central question in philosophical aesthetics. See, for example, Budd (1995, chapter 1) or Kieran's discussion of aestheticism and cognitivism in Kieran (2001).

9 For efforts in this direction, see Wolterstorff (2015), Taylor (2016) and Irvin (2016).
10 See, for example, Singer (1983).
11 See Hartley (2011), Silvers (2016) and Wasserman et al. (2016) for overviews of recent scholarship. Barnes (2016) is a notable recent work in this area. See Hall (2018) for a very recent discussion of dance and disability.
12 'Although there are several important exceptions, a high proportion of philosophical writing on disability, as well as social policy, has concentrated on physical disability, and within physical disability reduced mobility' (Wolff 2009: 404).
13 See https://www.theatlantic.com/education/archive/2016/09/there-is-no-right-way -to-learn/501044/ for a useful discussion about this in the US context (permanently archived at https://perma.cc/TR5H-HCJA).
14 See Kirby (2018) for a short history of dyslexia in the UK. A similar story can be told in the United States.
15 For another example of a public engagement philosophy project not built around dissemination, see Meskin and Liao (forthcoming).
16 See https://www.artscouncil.org.uk/national-portfolio-organisations/artistic-and-qua lity-assessment for discussion (permanently archived at https://perma.cc/Q9D7-8HF4).
17 Thanks to Nadia Mehdi and the editors of this volume for helpful comments on earlier drafts of the paper. And thanks to The Cultural Capital Exchange for funding the project. Grace Lockrobin, Joyce Lee and the Mind the Gap performers were fabulous collaborators.

References

Barnes, E., (2016), *The Minority Body: A Theory of Disability*, Oxford: Oxford University Press.
Bell, D., (2016), 'Communitarianism', in *The Stanford Encyclopedia of Philosophy*, [Online], Available at: https://plato.stanford.edu/archives/sum2016/entries/communitarianism/, Accessed 15 January 2019.
Budd, M., (1995), *Values of Art: Pictures, Poetry and Music*, London: Penguin.
Carroll, N., (1998), *A Philosophy of Mass Art*, Oxford: Clarendon Press.
Hall, J. M., (2018), 'Philosophy of Dance and Disability', *Philosophy Compass*, 13 (12): e12551.
Hartley, C., (2011), 'Disability and Justice', *Philosophy Compass*, 6 (2): 120–32.
Irvin, S., (ed.), (2016), *Body Aesthetics*, Oxford: Oxford University Press.
Kieran, M., (2001), 'Value of Art', in B. Gaut and D. Lopes (eds), *The Routledge Companion to Aesthetics*, 293–304, London: Routledge.
Kirby, P., (2018), 'A Brief History of Dyslexia', *The Psychologist*, 31: 56–9.
Meskin, A., and Liao, S., (forthcoming), 'Experimental Philosophical Aesthetics as Public Philosophy', in S. Réhault and F. Cova (eds), *Advances in Experimental Philosophy of Aesthetics*, New York: Bloomsbury.
Silvers, A., (2016), 'Feminist Perspectives on Disability', in *The Stanford Encyclopedia of Philosophy*, [Online], Available at: https://plato.stanford.edu/archives/win2016/entries/ feminism-disability/, Accessed 15 January 2019.
Singer, P., (1983), 'Sanctity of Life or Quality of Life?' *Pediatrics*, 72: 128–9.
Taylor, P. C., (2016), *Black Is Beautiful: A Philosophy of Black Aesthetics*, Malden, MA: Wiley Blackwell.

Wasserman, D., Asch, A., Blustein, J., and Putnam, D., (2016), 'Disability: Definitions, Models, Experience', in *The Stanford Encyclopedia of Philosophy*, [Online], Available at: https://plato.stanford.edu/archives/sum2016/entries/disability/, Accessed 15 January 2019.

Wiltsher, N., (2017), 'Lonely Arts: The Status of Aesthetics as a Sub-discipline', *Metaphilosophy*, 48 (5): 798–812.

Wolff, J., (2009), 'Cognitive Disability in a Society of Equals', *Metaphilosophy*, 40 (3–4): 402–15.

Wolterstorff, N., (2015), *Art Rethought: The Social Practices of Art*, Oxford: Oxford University Press.

12

In philosophical conversation with: People in prison – beyond rehabilitation

Andy West and Kirstine Szifris

Introduction

This chapter provides an insight into the relevance of teaching philosophy to prisoners. Here, we take an interest in the role of philosophy in the rehabilitation process, and question whether philosophical dialogue with people who happen to be in prison takes on a particular and distinct meaning. To do this, we describe our philosophical practice, followed by a critical dialogue about the purpose of our work. In particular, we draw on research from Schwitzgebel and Rust (2013) into the ethical behaviour of ethics professors, asking whether becoming more attuned to our own 'moral' character relates to our 'moral' behaviour. The fact that we present our ideas in a dialogue format is not incidental, since our classes are mostly dialogue-driven, as opposed to content-driven.

In this chapter, I and my colleague Kirstine Szifris will outline what a philosophy class in prison looks like. We will do this by sharing our own practice and also the practice of some of our colleagues. The dialogue that follows considers whether it is either ethical or apposite to do philosophy with people in prison. This means that as well as describing what our practice looks like, we will also carry out some conceptual analysis of our practice.

What do the classes look like?

Both Szifris and I have facilitated philosophy sessions in men's prisons, and often with people who are long-term prisoners, people at the 'deep' end of the system. Most of Kirstine's work focused on two prisons that catered to men serving long sentences. I mostly work in London prisons, often in collaboration with Mike Coxhead (King's College London) and Andrea Fassolas (Guild of Psychotherapists) on King's Philosophy in Prison project and with The Philosophy Foundation. In writing this chapter, we have taken care to protect the identities of our participants and the prisons in which we worked. Any names have been changed and identifying features altered. Furthermore, during the course of our work, participants have been fully informed of any research aspects to the work we do (particularly Szifris).

So what does a typical session look like? The first thing to say is that it is an enquiry rather than a class. That means that the facilitator presents students a question fertile with philosophical directions. For example, one question might be, 'If Theseus changes all the parts of his ship over ten years then is it the same ship?' (Worley 2010). Students are then invited to take the class in their own direction. Participants then engage in a dialogue, guided by a facilitator, on the topic at hand. This is distinct from content-driven course where we might teach participants about different theories of identity. We favour the enquiry method of philosophy in prisons because it starts with discussion and therefore offers immediate engagement.

However, while the class is discussion-based, the facilitator is there to make sure that particular norms and values are at play in the discussion. It is not the case that any type of conversation will do. The facilitator is there to allow participants the opportunity to find out what they think, for students to test their own assumptions and appreciate the implications of their ideas (Hannam and Echeverria 2009). Philosophy, as we envisage it, is not about the mere sharing of opinions but being able to think about one's own opinion (Worley 2016). The fact that we use a dialogical approach in prisons is not insignificant. As we discuss further later, it may be a key part of the benefit of doing philosophy with people in prison (see also Lien 2007; Kennedy 1999).

Although sessions are at first discussion-based, we also cover ideas from professional philosophers. After talking about the Ship of Theseus, we would give the perspective of famous philosophers on the subject. For example, what does Locke or Hume say about identity, and do we agree with them or not? Often philosophy classes happen the other way around. Students hear what Locke thought and then respond. However, what I notice is that these classes can often fail to engage students because the teacher sets out to teach the students answers to questions that students have not asked. In my experience, by covering content after the enquiry stage, students are desperate to know what Locke or Hume thought. The subjects we tend to cover in the class are from the side of philosophy directly concerned with the human condition rather than problems in predicate logic, and so on. Questions would be as following: What makes me who I am? How are our identities formed? What does it mean to be free? Should I always believe what is true? What does it mean for something to be true? Is happiness the same as pleasure? Do we suffer because we want things? Am I the same person I was yesterday? Can we change the past? What is 'madness'? What makes an action morally 'right' or 'wrong'?

The ethos with which the facilitator delivers the session is important. It's essential that they don't try to push their own agenda to get the students to come away with a certain position about why we suffer or what makes an action good or bad (Hannam and Echeverria 2009). More is said about this later. The facilitator must allow for and engage with intellectual disagreement and conflict between participants while maintaining an environment of trust and values of respect and care between the people attending (Daniels 2008; Splitter 2011; Worley 2016). A whole paper could be written on just this aspect, as conflict and escalation are very relevant to the prison setting (see Szifris 2018 for further discussion). We touch more on this again in the later sections.

Our classes require no reading from students (though we often give out optional reading materials at the end of a class). The lack of reading is a deliberate inclusion-based decision, given that people in prison *tend* to have lower than average levels of literacy (see Creese 2016). Every prison will require a different kind of class. Prison populations can vary from short-term prisoners from exclusively white-British populations, to long-term prisoners, to people who speak English as a foreign language.

Philosophy in prisons isn't just happening in the UK but also in the US, among other places. Nancy McHugh, a professor at Wittenberg University, has delivered philosophy in prisons, and even co-wrote a paper with her students titled 'An Epistemology of Incarceration: Constructing Knowing on the Inside' (The LoCI and Wittenberg Writing Group 2016). In Chicago, the Prison and Neighbourhood Arts Project run classes on the philosophy of punishment in Stateville prison. One of the people on this project is Jessica Bird, Assistant Professor in the Department of Criminology, Law and Justice at the University of Illinois. Szifris and I tend to avoid philosophical issues relating too closely to the criminal justice system for fear that it will make it harder for the learners to enter into abstraction. That is to say, it is useful in philosophy to be able to analyse dispassionately your opinion from outside of yourself. My worry was that prisoners might find questions about the criminal justice system too close to home to be able to abstract. (Szifris says more about this in the next section.) However, Bird tackles these sorts of issue head on. Sometimes she does this by discussing theories of justice, or sometimes she selects, very astutely, the more salient features of prison as a topic and as a lived reality. For example, in the maximum security prison where she works, it is forbidden for there to be any touch between staff and prisoners. So Bird holds enquiries on touch. She draws upon Nussbaum's work on emotions (Nussbaum 2003) and the students discuss what touch is and what role it might play in an emotional and ethical life.

This brief overview should go part of the way towards showing the diversity of approaches currently at work in doing philosophy in prisons. A key point is that each prison is very much its own ecosystem and calls for its own approach. The materials and emphasis one might give to a class composed solely of men going through substance rehabilitation might be very different to a class delivered to a group of men serving time for sex offences. Some prison regimes give you hour-long classes; others can give you no less than three hours due to security schedules. Each class inside prison is intensely particular and this chapter makes no pretence to universal claims on how philosophy is or ought to be done in prisons.

The ambiguous impact of philosophy and rehabilitation

Andy West: When I tell people I run philosophical enquiries in prison, they often ask if it helps make prisoners into 'better people'. They wonder if I'm there serving a rehabilitation agenda. I always have to re-orientate myself when I hear this. I'm not in the habit of thinking of my students in prison as 'bad people' who need to be made 'better'. They are just my students. The fact they are in jail doesn't necessarily mean they are immoral. Gang culture, for example, seems to involve a strong sense of ethics, relative to its own context (Cohen 1971). When I hear the idea that philosophy might make prisoners better people, I think of my students who had extensively studied philosophy before their incarceration.

It's not uncommon to suppose that doing philosophy makes you a morally better person. For example, some have argued that the widespread teaching of philosophy might save us from another Donald Trump (see Sarajlic 2016, for example). So if one thinks philosophy makes people morally better, then one can see why one might teach philosophy to prisoners to make them better people. However, there is evidence to suggest that philosophical training might not make you 'a better person'. Schwitzgebel and Rust (2013) conducted research into the ethical behaviour of ethics teachers. The results might have big implications on why, if at all, Kirstine and I should be doing philosophy with people in prison. I'll say more about this once I first explain Schwitzgebel and Rust's experiment and how they did it.

Schwitzgebel and Rust gave questionnaires to ethics professors and non-philosophy professors. They asked the professors if they thought it was wrong to eat the meat of a mammal. Sixty per cent of ethics professors said meat eating was wrong, whereas 19 per cent of non-philosophy professors said it was wrong. Then they asked both groups if they had eaten the meat of a mammal in the last week. Around half of the 19 per cent of non-philosophy professors said they had. Significantly, around half of the 60 per cent of ethics professors said they had too. So, whether someone was an ethics professor or not had no bearing on whether they practised what they argued for. Similar results also held for voting, giving blood, responding to student emails, calling their mothers, cleaning up after themselves at a conference and charity giving. There was no case where ethics teachers did better than non-philosophers with regard to actually doing the things they said were right.

Ethicists were no more likely to practise their expressed values than any other type of professor. So what implications does this have for the ethics of doing philosophy in prisons? Schwitzgebel and Rust's research show us that the ethical impact of doing philosophy is ambiguous. Therefore, the ethical justification for doing philosophy with people in prison becomes uncertain. Philosophy might not make 'better people' of prisoners or, at least, might not make people behave more consistently with their views. We have to ask a question: What remit do Kirstine or I have to deliver the philosophy classes if we aren't contributing directly to moral development?

Kirstine Szifris: Andy concludes by stating that the impact of doing philosophy upon one's ethical life is ambiguous. The question for this chapter is, If the impact on ethical life is ambiguous, why then do philosophy with people in prison? If philosophy does not make us more ethical, or at least more consistent in our behaviour, what relevance can or does it have to rehabilitation? There are two responses to this: the first relates directly to Schwitzegebel and Rust's research and the second relates to the role of education in prison more generally. I will address both in relation to criminological theories and research.

In terms of Schwitzgebel and Rust's research, we would need to think about a few things when applying it to people in prison. If we were to assume that it is possible to have a direct equivalence between a person's expressed morality and their behaviour, there are a range of assumptions to explore on this point. Here, I would like to consider two of them:

1. That the individual knows what their moral principles are and has the capacity to express them.
2. The individual thinks before they act.

As regards the first, I recall one of my own philosophy classes where one of the men stated that is was wrong to smoke in a car with a child. I asked him to explain why he felt that way. Eventually, after some dialogue, we came to discuss rights and the harm principle. However, it took time for the individual to express his reasons for this. He could be clear about the rights and wrongs of a particular action, but struggled to articulate the principles that he held that lead to this opinion. It is difficult, therefore, to know if this individual has sufficient grasp of his own moral principles to be able to apply them consistently.

As to the second assumption, the complex question of whether a person thinks before they act raises a number of issues. The role of habitual or instinctive behaviours, (Kahneman 2011), the role of self-control (Gottfreddson and Hirschi 1990) and the role of the culture or environment (Wikström et al. 2012) all affect people's day-to-day decision-making. In particular, to assess whether someone acts in accordance with their ethics, we must also consider whether circumstances have challenged their ethics. Someone might state that it is wrong to smoke in a car with a child, but this might be challenged if they find themselves in a seven-hour traffic jam. If the assertion is never challenged by circumstances (and the individual never smokes in a car with a child), can we state with assurance that they have acted in accordance with the morality?

Circumstances in prison could challenge the most restrained person's ethics. In the context of a prison, behaviour is predicated on the need for 'survival' (Cohen and Taylor 1972; Liebling, Arnold and Straub 2011). Research has shown that the prison environment can breed a toxic, hyper-masculine environment that encourages the development of an identity that is based on physical prowess, one that shows no fear, that does not back down and can stand up to threats and bullying (Liebling 2012; Crewe 2009; Jewkes 2005). I conclude in my own research:

> The fear, expressed by some of my participants, is that this cultivated 'macho' self gradually becomes who they are; no longer a front but an expression of the fundamental self, because, after ten, fifteen, twenty years in prison without spaces in which they can present different, more pro-social, versions of the self, this macho front becomes all they know. (Szifris 2018: 199)

Andy West: That's interesting. It makes me think about what would happen if people in prison took Schwitzgebel and Rust's test. You'd have to factor in the fact that not everyone can easily articulate justifications for what they think. And that maybe prison compromises your ability to act as ethically as you would like to. The need not to appear weak can change if people can act on their expressed values or not. Those considerations are important when discussing ethics and rehabilitation with prisoners. So what do these considerations mean for our question? Why should we do philosophy with prisoners? Particularly if philosophy has little to no bearing on rehabilitation. (I am assuming here that a more ethical life is a less criminal life, though of course this is not uncontroversial.)

Kirstine Szifris: Of course, we could question the role of morality in criminal activity (see Wikström et al. 2012, for a full discussion of this). My research indicates that the strength of philosophy lies in its abstraction (Szifris 2016). This is particularly relevant to the prison context. In an environment where much of the activity relates to offending behaviour, engaging in activity that addresses the whole person takes on a particular meaning. In philosophy classes, I did not ask them to reflect on *their* actions in particular, but instead on how we, as people and members of society, ought to act. By *not* focusing on the crimes of the participants and discussing philosophies that bore no direct relation to their pasts, the philosophy class provided a sense of freedom and a potential 'hook' for participants to engage in learning. When my students do philosophy, they discuss topics like responsibility, consequences and meaning without being required to talk about themselves, or at least not about their 'offending' selves. This is not to say that the conversations could not be deeply personal but to emphasize that in philosophy we meet the learner as a whole person. In doing this, we discuss what this means, how environments, beliefs and interactions have shaped and will shape our understanding of ourselves. We do this *together* as a collaborative dialogue.

Herein lies a contradiction. Is it possible that the philosophy course is relevant to rehabilitation precisely because it is not relevant to rehabilitation? In other words, because we, as philosophy facilitators, approach our students as people and as learners (as opposed to prisoners in need of correction, or offenders who have done something wrong), we might have a profound impact? As the philosophy technique allows learners to take dialogue in the direction that suits them and to work with the material and express their thoughts and opinions without fear of reprisal, it could be inherently more rehabilitative than other more prescriptive courses. This, of course, remains to be seen.

Andy West: Now that's a paradox. Philosophy might help with rehabilitation because it doesn't seek to help with rehabilitation. I expect this depends a lot on the motivation of the facilitator delivering the philosophy. You might have a facilitator who is moralistic in their approach. They may wish to 'help people to get better' and nudge the student's thinking towards the 'better way'. If you have a good facilitator, they will be neutral in the discussion and be able to suspend their own judgement on the issue at hand. For example, if the facilitator has strongly held preconceptions about the issue of, say, justice, while facilitating an enquiry on justice, and they are – consciously or unconsciously – nudging the students towards that view, then philosophy becomes an insidious means of moral instruction.

Kirstine Szifris: I agree. To try to guard against this, I have focused on philosophy as an 'activity of thought' (Law 2007) or 'thinking about thinking' (Honderich 1995). This helps me keep in mind the idea of collaborative dialogue that sought to understand and develop *how* people think, as opposed to *what* people think. For me, this is a subtle, but key, distinction. It lies at the heart of the idea of *collaborative* (as opposed to adversarial) dialogue; we are not there to make people think the way *we* think. (I would argue that we should not enter philosophical dialogue with such an agenda.) Instead, we look to enter dialogue with the intention of taking an interest in our fellow participants' world views and seeking to understand the reasoning and principles that lie behind them.

Is it unethical to do philosophy with prisoners?

Andy West: I can see how some people might think that philosophy is good for prisoners. A high number of prisoners lack basic literacy (Creese 2016), so there might be an assumption that engaging prisoners in just about any education is good for them. But one thing I found when I started working in prison was how many clever people were inside. Planning for my first ever class in a prison, I stripped down the content of the materials I had planned to the lowest common denominator. Then twenty minutes in to a three-hour lesson, I was starting to run out of material, and I had students talking to me about Rousseau and Hobbes. I had one guy who'd just finished an Open University degree in criminology, and I had to up my game. The fact is, there are some intelligent people in prison. For example, the novelist and former UK Conservative Party chairman, Jeffery Archer, was in Belmarsh, a South London maximum security prison.

There are so many different kinds of people in prison that I wonder if it is 'good' to do philosophy with all of them. I'm thinking about certain types of paedophiles whose crimes might have involved careful and premeditated grooming of their victims: crimes that involve persuasion and manipulation. Philosophy helps sharpen our instruments of persuasion. Should we teach philosophy to people who might use it to repeat their crimes? Do we want a world with more persuasive sexual predators?

It shouldn't be underestimated that philosophers delight in topsy-turvying things. Zeno tells us that the arrow will never hit the target (Kirk and Raven 1984). Hume thinks we are irrational to believe that the sun will rise tomorrow (Hume 1910). Nietzsche believes that it is the gentle who are most worthy of our moral contempt (Nietzsche 1967). Might doing philosophy with a highly manipulative offender mean that that offender becomes better at telling us and themselves that they did nothing wrong?

It could be morally negative to teach philosophy to some prisoners. I'm not the only one to have had this thought. One of my students in prison also voiced a similar concern. To paraphrase, he said something like the following: 'A thug is less dangerous than an educated thug.' His idea was that if you have someone who is part of a gang, terrorist group or a far-right group, and they are a thug, then that is one thing. If they are an educated thug, then that's another. An educated thug knows how to talk and justify what they do. They know how to recruit more people by talking them into joining their group. So whether it's predatory sex offenders, gang leaders or terrorists, do you think that doing philosophy with certain prisoners can ever be unethical?

Kirstine Szifris: I'm familiar with the question. The first time I presented my early findings to an audience, a postgraduate researcher posed the question of whether psychopaths might be able to use educational courses such as these to gain skills in manipulating others. However, having conducted more extensive research into the role of philosophy in the lives of men in prison, it seems that the research does not suggest that this is a likely outcome. Instead, my research suggests that philosophical dialogue provides opportunity for men to self-reflect, to engage with others and to think more deeply about the world (Szifris 2017b; Szifris 2018). I should say that, to date, there has been no research that includes a long-term follow-up with participants, and only limited research into the experience of engaging in philosophy while in prison. There remains, therefore, a range of unknowns about the effect of philosophy for adults in prison that only further research, reflection and scrutiny can answer. Until there is positive evidence to suggest that doing philosophy with people who have committed sexual offences, terrorism or crimes involving gangs is harmful, then we can't say anything further on the subject.

It is an interesting observation, Andy, that you say you don't think of the men in prison with whom you work as criminals, but rather as students. This is a mantra I have heard from teachers in a range of prisons. As a rule, teachers tend not to know, and do not wish to know, the crimes for which their learners have been convicted. While they are in the education department, the men are learners, not offenders or prisoners.

Does imprisonment create the need for philosophy?

Andy West: A student of mine had a quotation on his cell wall. It was by Dostoyevsky (another man who spent time in prison): 'There is only one thing that I dread: not to be worthy of my sufferings' (Frankl 2004: 75). He said he didn't know exactly what it meant but, if he stuck with it, the answer might reveal itself. Such sincerity of enquiry isn't common, even among people for whom philosophy is a profession.

I wonder if criminal transgression and subsequent imprisonment gives rise to the philosophical impulse. The French novelist Jean Genet, another prisoner, who was something of a philosopher of the underworld, is eloquent on this idea:

> [Those who have] indifference to the rules of loyalty and rectitude ... saying of them 'They're false' softened my heart. Still softens me sometimes. They are the only ones I believe capable of all kinds of boldness. Their sinuousness and the multiplicity of their moral lines form an interlacing which I call adventure. They depart from your rules. They are not faithful. Above all, they have a blemish, a wound. ... In short, the greater my guilt in your eyes, the more whole, the more totally assumed, the greater will be my freedom. The more perfect my solitude and singleness. By my guilt I further gained the right to intelligence. Too many people think, I said to myself, who have not the right to. They have not paid for it by the kind of undertaking which makes thinking indispensable *to your salvation*. (Genet 1964: 84)

Philosophy in Prison – Beyond Rehabilitation　　　185

If we go with Genet here, then we have to ask if it could be that those who have transgressed have access to the deepest forms of enquiry. Many people are surprised to hear that prisoners have the education or temperament to do philosophy well. But I wonder: Is there something about the prisoner's condition that makes doing philosophy firstly, a matter of urgency, and second, something prisoners might be especially well positioned to do?

Kirstine Szifris: I have found that prisoners are natural philosophers. I primarily worked with men serving long, and sometimes very long, sentences. They either had spent at least a decade in prison or were at the start of their sentences facing a possible lifetime inside. Despite discussions of violence and intimidation behind bars, the overwhelming feeling of incarceration is one of boredom and stagnation (O'Donnell 2014). People in prison have a lot of time to think, to think about how they have ended up in prison, to consider the path they wish to take while inside, to work out who they are. When it comes to the meaning of life, I have found that the most profound thinking can come from those who have had a portion of their life controlled, or taken away from them, through imprisonment.

In criminology, 'desistance' theory is currently holding sway (see Maruna 2017). The desistance paradigm has, arguably, paid the most attention within criminological literature to people (who have committed an offence) as active agents in their own lives. Desistance research is interested in how people move away from a criminal lifestyle. A branch of this field focuses on identity and the need for identity change.

Modern desistance theories also recognize the role of both internal processes and structural opportunity for change (Giordano 2016). While desistance involves a re-conceptualization of the self and a move towards compliance to social norms (see Bottoms 2002, for more on compliance), 'the extent to which ex-offenders can achieve their desires and goals is partly dependent on the availability of legitimate identities' (Farrall 2016: 201). Opportunity, therefore, plays a key part in successful identity change. Identity change, and, in turn, identity-related desistance, involves the individual asking, and answering, two key questions: 'Who do I want to be?' and 'How do I want to live?' These two questions are fundamental to developing a personal philosophy and a sense of self (Szifris 2018).

Further to this, prison has been described as a 'radical shattering' of routine (Liebling 1992) involving isolation from friends and family (Cohen and Taylor 1972), loss of autonomy and agency (Sykes 1958), loss of personal safety (Jewkes 2005), and boredom and stagnation (O'Donnell 2014). The prison environment is such that prisoners rarely feel like they can be themselves or relax. It can induce an 'existential crisis' leading to a need for prisoners to find activities that provide opportunities for 'meaning making' with some research suggesting that meaning-making is essential to survival in prison (see, for example, Leibling, Arnold and Straub 2011).

So, does prison promote philosophical urgency? In a sense, yes. It encourages introspection, providing people with time to contemplate themselves and their actions.

Andy West: Your analysis of hyper-masculine survival identities concurs with my experience. Prison survival is about keeping yourself to yourself and not crossing anyone's boundaries. This is why it's good to do philosophy, because it's about talking to each other in non-superficial ways.

At the beginning of courses, I meet students who sleep three cells away from each other, and they don't know each other's names. Prison life isn't very conducive to making connections with people. Lockdowns keep people in their cells and unable to mix. When there's not a lockdown, 'association' time is limited. In some prisons, people are kept on remand for a few weeks while others are there for years. So the prison population is often transitory, physically isolated and emotionally aloof (Cohen and Taylor 1972). This is why it becomes important that prisoners attend education or activities – to interact with people. Philosophy, in particular, is about personal exchange: meeting people on the level of their ideas, beliefs and values. My students see one of their classmates on the house block and say hello and shake hands. In prison, just learning someone's name and something about them is significant.

I like what you say about contemplation and introspection. It makes me think of *Discipline and Punish: The Birth of the Prison* (Foucault 1977). Foucault says that what we now understand as the modern prison was, at the time of its invention, not 'at first a deprivation of liberty to which a technical function of correction was later added; it was from the outset a "legal detention" entrusted with … reforming individuals' (Foucault 1977: 237). Foucault reminds us that before modern prisons, there were public floggings and humiliations. Modern prisons were first thought to be progressive. They were based on principles of the monastic ideal. They were a place where, through solitude and hard work, the soul could be purified. Foucault paraphrases prison pedagogy by Beaumont and Tocqueville written in 1831: 'Thrown into solitude, the convict reflects … it is in isolation that remorse will come to assail him' (Foucault 1977: 237). But history has shown that prison has limited success in reforming individuals (Foucault 1977: 237). It tends to make the lives of people who are often already disadvantaged even harder to cope with. Forced solitude doesn't often lead to the moral detox that was hoped for.

What Foucault's ideas remind us of is that the modern prison was supposed to be a place to foster contemplation. But it turned out that surviving prison requires people to shut off so much of themselves that they can't reflect. 'Prolonged segregation does not reduce violence, but may contribute to it and leads to poor mental and physical health' (Shalev 2018: 11–17). If the modern prison was supposed to be a place of contemplation, then maybe more modern prisons should be doing philosophy with their inmates.

However, I still have some questions about the suitability of doing philosophy in prisons. I worry it might increase the vulnerability of prisoners. I told a group of prisoners the story of Pandora's Box. I said that seven evil spirits came out of the box and then hope followed. I asked, 'Imagine if you could put one evil back into the box. Which would you pick?' Some students picked hope.

The central part of the philosophical process is the aporetic moment – the state of loss or confusion, when everything comes undone. Yet prison is a place where the imperative is to hold things together. To live in prison is to be dropped into a battle: it can be a battle against the system, one's own impossible desires (say for sex or the world outside), guilt, shame and a battle against physical violence itself (Sykes 1958).

Surviving that battle necessitates wearing a psychological armour (Goffman 1969). I worry that my students doing philosophy take off that armour, and afterwards I send them back into that battlefield. Am I leaving them exposed? Maybe I am not; or maybe I am and that's irresponsible on my part; or maybe I am and that's part of respecting the agency of my students. I don't know the answer. But this is something I will carry on asking. I'd be curious to know what my students make of the question of what philosophy does for their sense of safety while in jail; perhaps I will ask them.

References

Bottoms, A., (2002), 'Morality, Crime, Compliance and Public Policy', in A. Bottoms, and M. Tonry (eds), *Ideology, Crime and Criminal Justice: A Symposium in Honour of Sir Leon Radzinowicz*, 39–42, Cullompton: Willan Publishing.

Cohen, A. K., (1971), *Delinquent Boys: The Culture of the Gang*, New York: Macmillan.

Cohen, S., and Taylor, L., (1972), *Psychological Survival: The Experience of Long-term Imprisonment*, Harmondsworth: Penguin.

Creese, B., (2016), 'An Assessment of the English and Maths Skills Levels of Prisoners in England', *London Review of Education*, 14 (3): 13–30.

Crewe, B., (2009), *The Prisoner Society: Power, Adaptation and Social Life in An English Prison*, Oxford: Oxford University Press.

Daniel, M.-F., (2008), 'Learning to Philosophize: Positive Impacts and Conditions for Implementation: A Synthesis of 10 Years of Research (1995-2005)', *Thinking: The Journal of Philosophy for Children*, 18 (4): 36–48.

Farrall, S., (2016), 'Understanding Desistance in an Assisted Context: Key Findings From Tracking Progress on Probation', in J. Shapland, S. Farrall, and A. Bottoms (eds), *Global Perspectives on Desistance: Reviewing What We Know and Looking to the Future*, 187–204, Oxford: Routledge.

Foucault, M., (1977), *Discipline and Punish: The Birth of the Prison*, London: Penguin Books.

Frankl, V., (2004), *Man's Search for Meaning*, London: Rider.

Genet, J., (1964), *The Thief's Journal*, New York: Grove Press.

Giordano, P. C., (2016), 'Mechanisms Underlying the Desistance Process: Reflections on "A Theory of Cognitive Transformation"', in J. Shapland, S. Farrall, and A. Bottoms (eds), *Global Perspectives on Desistance: Reviewing What We Know and Looking to the Future*, 11–27, Oxford: Routledge.

Goffman, E., (1969), *Asylums*, London: Penguin.

Gottfredson, M. R., and Hirschi, T., (1990), *A General Theory of Crime*, Stanford, CA: Stanford University Press.

Hannam, P., and Echeverria, E., (2009), *Philosophy with Teenagers: Nurturing a Moral Imagination for the 21st Century*, London: Network Continuum.

Honderich, T., (1995), *The Oxford Companion to Philosophy*, Oxford: Oxford University Press.

Hume, D., ([1748] 1910), *An Enquiry Concerning Human Understanding*, New York: P.F. Collier and Son.

Jewkes, Y., (2005), 'Loss, Liminality and the Life Sentence: Managing Identity Through a Disrupted Lifecourse', in A. Liebling and S. Maruna (eds), *The Effects of Imprisonment*, 366–90, Cullompton, Devon: Willan Publishing.

Kennedy, D., (1999), 'Philosophy for Children and the Reconstruction of Philosophy', *Metaphilosophy*, 30 (4): 338–59.

Kirk, G. S., and Raven, J. E., (1984), *Presocratic Philosophers: A Critical History with a Selection of Texts*, 2nd edn, Cambridge: Cambridge University Press.

Law, S., (2007), *The Great Philosophers: The Lives and Ideas of History's Greatest Thinkers*, London: Quercus Publishing.

Liebling, A., (1992), *Suicides in Prisons*, London: Routledge.

Liebling, A., (2012), *Can Human Beings Flourish?* Prison Phoenix Trust Lecture, 29 May 2012, London, UK.

Liebling, A., Arnold, H., and Straub, C., (2011), *An Exploration of Staff-Prisoner Relationships at HMP Whitemoor: 12 Years On*, London: National Offender Management Service, Ministry of Justice.

Lien, C., (2007), 'Making Sense of Evaluation of P4C', *Thinking: The Journal of Philosophy for Children*, 17 (1 and 2): 36–48.

The LoCI and Wittenberg Writing Group (2016), 'An Epistomology of Incarceration: Constructing Knowing on the Inside', *philoSOPHIA*, 6 (1): 9–25.

Maruna, S., (2017), 'Desistance as a Social Movement', *Irish Probation Journal*, 14: 5–20.

Nietzsche, F., (1967), *On The Genealogy of Morals*, New York: Vintage Books.

Nussbaum, M., (2003), *Upheavals of Thought: The Intelligence of Emotions*, Cambridge: Cambridge University Press.

O'Donnell, I., (2014), *Prisoners, Solitude and Time*, Oxford: Oxford University Press.

Sarajlic, E., (2016), 'How to Prevent Another Trump in the Future? Teach Kids Philosophy', *The Huffington Post*, 17 November 2016.

Schwitzgebel, E., and Rust, J., (2013), 'The Moral Behavior of Ethics Professors: Relationships Among Self-Reported Behavior, Expressed Normative Attitude, and Directly Observed Behavior', *Review of Philosophy and Psychology*, 27 (3): 293–327.

Shalev, S., (2018), 'Can Any Good Come out of Isolation? Probably Not', *Prison Service Journal*, 236: March 2018, 11–16.

Splitter, L., (2011), 'Identity, Citizenship and Moral Education', *Educational Philosophy and Theory*, 43 (5): 484–505.

Sykes, G.M., (1958), *The Society of Captives. A Study of a Maximum Security Prison*, Princeton, NJ: Princeton University Press.

Szifris, K., (2016), 'Philosophy in Prison: Opening Minds and Broadening Perspectives through Philosophical Dialogue', *Prison Service Journal*, 225: 33–8.

Szifris, K., (2017a), 'Philosophical Dialogue', in Crane P. (ed.), *Life Beyond Crime: What do Those at Risk of Offending, Prisoners and Ex-offenders Need to Learn?*, 153–60, London: Lemos and Crane.

Szifris, K., (2017b), 'Socrates and Aristotle: The Role of Ancient Philosophers in the Self-Understanding of Desisting Offenders', *Howard Journal for Crime and Justice*, 56 (4): 419–36.

Szifris, K., (2018), *Philosophy in Prisons: An Exploration of Personal Development*. Unpublished thesis, Cambridge University.

Wikström, P.-O. H., Oberwittler, D., Treiber, K., and Hardie, B., (2012), *Breaking Rules: The Social and Situational Dynamics of Young People's Urban Crime*, Oxford: Oxford University Press.

Worley, P., (2016), 'Ariadne's Clew: Absence and Presence in the Facilitation of Philosophical Conversations', *The Journal of Philosophy in Schools*, 3 (2): 51–70.

Worley, P., (2010), *The If Machine: Philosophical Enquiry in the Classroom*, London: Continuum.

13

In philosophical conversation with: Philosophy Ireland – Building a national P4C network

Charlotte Blease

Ireland's president might be regarded as a modern-day Philosopher King. 'The teaching of philosophy in schools', he claimed in 2016, 'is one of the most powerful tools we have at our disposal to empower children into acting as free and responsible subjects in an ever more complex, interconnected and uncertain world' (Higgins 2016). On national and international platforms, the figurehead of the fastest growing economy in the European Union has also underscored the importance of the pedagogy 'philosophy for children'.

Today (2019) philosophy is a new school subject in Ireland bolstered by growing interest among teachers and pupils, and supported by centralized curricular training programmes. Yet just three years ago it was still not an examinable option for pupils. Beyond this, only scattered, pockets of enthusiasts promoted its value in education. In this chapter I describe how, over a period of two years, unique circumstances catalysed by the efforts of 'philosophy activists' created an independent, national network – Philosophy Ireland[1] (hereafter PI)– that gained national and international recognition, and continues to earn attention from the highest echelons of Irish society (Higgins 2017; Blease 2017; Freehill-Maye 2018).

The story I'm about to unfold is personal, reflecting my experience of helping to initiate this organization. Seneca's maxim about luck – 'preparation meets opportunity'[2] – may be considered overused; then again some clichés earn their well-worn stripes. As a description of the origins of PI, it fits. Opportunity was in abundance. In what follows, I outline a brief history of philosophy developments in Ireland. Delving into my beginner's exploration of community outreach ('the preparation'), I move on to describe the recent events and incipient local conditions that enabled the seeding of this network ('the opportunities'). In the second part of this chapter I share three personal lessons that I hope impart suggestions about how individuals or interested parties might maximize opportunities to launch their own philosophy networks.

This account comes with two disclaimers. First, it takes many committed and energetic individuals to forge a national network. We were a twelve – then fourteen-person team during the formation of the organization. To list all of the contributions of every one of these individuals would do them greater justice; and conceivably each person would emphasize different aspects of the PI journey. I have done my best to sketch a portrait of PI and to give an accurate portrait of its formation, but apologize in advance for shortcomings and omissions. Relatedly, striking a balance between the accidental personal encounters which are elemental aspects of this story, while avoiding too much history in miniature, is tricky. Much of what follows describes deeply personal ambitions and a desire to see philosophy rooted in my own community. Perhaps inevitably these events are told through a first-person lens: I hope the reader will pardon these indulgences.

Second, this chapter aims to be equal part narrative, equal part guidance. Risking that most disreputable blend of genres – self-help and philosophy – if any of what follows stirs interest or assists philosophy enthusiasts and educational activists, whatever their stage or seniority, and regardless of where they hail from, then, in some measure, the purpose of this chapter will be fulfiled.

Background to PI

An accidental detour

At the outset, a caveat emptor: I am not a teacher. Nor am I experienced as a practitioner in philosophy for children (P4C) or as an academic whose specialism is philosophy of education. In fact, my initial involvement in philosophy for children was, first, financial and, second, shamelessly expedient – as a sought-after antidote for classroom humiliation.

Completing a PhD in philosophy of science in 2008, I immediately took up a post as an adjunct lecturer. Hitting a minor existential crisis – the desirability of working in a philosophy department long-term – I fell into school teaching purely by accident. An advertisement for philosophy postgraduates to introduce the subject to teenagers appeared in my email. Handsomely paid, the scheme, run by the Royal Institute of Philosophy, in London, was an opportunity to surpass my hourly lectureship rate. The role seemed to me to be undemanding – How difficult could teaching a bunch of teenagers be? Not trained in crowd control, I promptly set about writing to the poshest grammar schools in the Belfast area, advising them to contact the Royal Institute to apply for this excellent scheme. Five principals replied and I would soon return to school.

My preparation for these classes was admittedly minimal. The requirement was to teach ten-week introductory courses, for one or two hours per week. Planning the course, I decided to introduce a new theme each week. On the first week, 'What is philosophy?'; in week two, the focus would be metaphysics and 'Does God exist?'; in week three, epistemology and Descartes's *Meditations on First Philosophy*; in week four, philosophy of art; week five, ethics; week six, jurisprudence; and so on. Entering the classroom full of pride at my newly minted prefix, delighted by the prospects of an easy financial boost, I imagined the pupils reminiscing, years from now, about the luminary who brought them philosophy.

The reality was disarmingly different, though it could have been worse. Faced with thirty intelligent, diligent school girls – politely expressionless, their well-meaning teacher looking on in puzzlement – I found my syllabus was clearly failing to kindle much interest. Diffident teenage-hood was not wholly responsible. Reflecting now on what went wrong, three observations occur. First, I lectured the students: telling them what to think, without getting them to think; my teaching style, amounted to the relatively futile exercise of philosophy dictation. Second was the curse of expertise. Immersed in concepts of philosophy, I developed amnesia about first forays into the field. Paying scant attention to the procedural knowledge of *doing philosophy* – of recognizing philosophical puzzles, getting into the habit of asking questions, and of occupying that heady, vertiginous space that constructs answers with more questions – my teaching overlooked the importance of acclimatizing students to enquiry.

Third was 'the generalization of expertise'. This blunder arises when an individual who has skills in one domain assumes that their expertise is a green card permitting entry into foreign fields. It happens when clerics assume that they are experts on all things moral, when physicians believe a biomedical degree encompasses people management, or when PhDs think they can teach without being taught how. Beyond these errors was the fear of squandering a rare opportunity to introduce philosophy to young people.

So, how *should* one teach philosophy in schools? The path of least resistance involved seeking out advice rather than face fifty weeks' worth of philosophy classes and the comeuppance of zombified teenagers. Within weeks I was enrolled on a SAPERE two-day course in philosophy for children. With renewed enthusiasm I returned home, not just to teach schoolchildren, but to roll out introductory courses for adult learners. Results, in the form of engagement and classroom dialogue, were instantaneous. Pinpointing when I saw the value of philosophy outside ivory towers, I would date it to this introduction to P4C.

Reignited, my passion for philosophy crackled with born-again intensity. Generous funding from the Royal Institute of Philosophy paid for an introductory philosophy conference organized at my home university. The delegates were one hundred local schoolteachers and their pupils; the speakers included a philosopher experienced in educational outreach and a well-respected Northern Irish journalist who spoke about the benefits of his philosophy degree in his career. Eager to spread the word, I penned articles for local newspapers and in-house teaching magazines, taking up every invitation to speak about the importance of philosophy in schools (Blease 2011).

The most important facet in this new-found fervour was initiating a philosophy outreach campaign at Queen's University, in 2010. The goal was to build a self-sustaining programme in the university's philosophy department which involved training undergraduate students in the same two-day P4C course I had taken. Equipped with this training, the students would work in pairs to run philosophy sessions in Belfast primary schools for six weeks, to facilitate philosophical dialogue with pupils aged ten to eleven years. The idea is to bring philosophy out of the academy to pupils and their teachers. And asked in their first job interviews what use philosophy was, graduates would have an answer: They'd have 'real world' experience of encouraging serious

192   *Philosophy and Community*

classroom enquiry, gaining confidence and responsibility in the process. A 'win-win' for the university, to date, is that the 'Philosophy, Citizenship, and Schools Program' in Queen's University, Belfast, is still going strong.

These strides were narrow. Children in socially deprived areas of Belfast deserved access to philosophy just as much as kids in schools in the middle-class, university area. Northern Ireland, a tiny country infamous for identity politics and cultural tribalism, arguably needed a stronger dose of classroom philosophy than anything mustered within these schemes (Blease 2011). Although acutely aware of these shortcomings, as fresh opportunities were presented I moved away from philosophy outreach to pursue academic research.

The Republic of Ireland – Pivotal recent events

While these activities were taking place in the North, a number of crucial developments in the Republic of Ireland ('the South') were unfolding. In January 2015 the minister of education and skills announced that Philosophy would be included as a new short course in proposed changes to the Junior Cycle (JC) [the equivalent to GCSE level examinations in the UK]. The announcement was the result of several antecedent factors that contributed to growing pressure to embed philosophy in Irish schools.

Historically, at a primary education level, there have been few opportunities to train in philosophy for children in Ireland. However, since the 1970s, two prominent educationalists – professors Joe Dunne and Philomena Donnelly – successfully bucked this trend by introducing P4C pedagogies into teacher training programmes at Dublin City University.[3] Although these strides were limited, they helped to seed the pedagogy among generations of primary school teachers and learners. Second was the role of the Royal Irish Academy (RIA). One of the oldest, and most prestigious academic institutions in the country, the RIA continues to act as a lively policy and ideas forum in Irish cultural life. Organized into over a dozen academic committees, each group is tasked with promoting subject-specific policy and research issues of public concern. The Academy's National Committee for Philosophy and Ethics, which comprises representatives from university philosophy departments from the whole island (North and South) played an influential role in campaigning for philosophy in schools. During a period of five years its members tirelessly lobbied the Irish Government's Department of Education and Skills in a bid to create curricular space for the subject. These efforts ensured that philosophy was within earshot of politicians and the public.

Third, perhaps surprisingly, was the role of the quality press in keeping the issue on the radar. Notably, the former Education Correspondent for *The Irish Times*, Joe Humphreys single-handedly embedded philosophy into mainstream media with the launch of his 'Unthinkable Column' – now a fixture in the paper. Every Tuesday, since World Philosophy Day, November 2013, *Irish Times* readers are invited to a research-led dialogue on philosophy featuring local, and visiting, philosophers. Humphreys's indwelling media support undoubtedly played a major role in prioritizing coverage of

Building a National Philosophy for Children (P4C) Network in Ireland 193

the schools' campaign within the paper's education pages, while also maintaining the visibility of philosophy among readers.

Finally, in the wake of the financial crisis in 2008 Michael D. Higgins unveiled his 'Ethics Initiative'. Initiated in early 2013, it was described by Higgins as 'an invitation to the public to explore our values as society' (Higgins 2015). At its launch, he inaugurated a programme of over fifty nationwide events to stimulate public discourse on ethics. This programme culminated with an address at the President of Ireland's National Seminar at the Áras an Uachtaráin (the Irish presidential residence in Phoenix Park, Dublin) on 28 March 2015. Here, Higgins reiterated that

> our schools' curricula and pedagogical methods reflect the kind of humanity our society seeks and nurtures. The society we so dearly wish for will not take shape unless we acknowledge the need for an education of character and desires, the need to encourage and support critical reflection and a more holistic approach to knowledge. (ibid)

In a speech that, given recent political events, appears strikingly sagacious, Higgins closed by explicitly referencing 'the value of teaching philosophy in our schools' (ibid) as a direct means of enhancing the quality and inclusiveness of democratic debate among the country's citizenry.

Precipitating events ('Preparation Meets Opportunity')

Numerous factors, not least the good fortune of an erudite head of state, converged to bring about the decision to include philosophy as a new (albeit optional) school subject in (Southern) Irish schools. This announcement also marked the beginning of a new set of problems and fresh opportunities. The need for an organized network became apparent. Recognition of this fact, however, only arose after two serendipitous events that directly resulted in the idea to launch a public meeting about philosophy in schools.

First was a chance meeting. Working in a vibrant and supportive philosophy community in University College Dublin (UCD), I contributed to a Society for Women in Philosophy in Ireland seminar which aimed to showcase the 'use' of philosophy beyond the academy. Among the speakers was Sabina Higgins (spouse of Michael D. Higgins) – a philosophy graduate and political activist in her own right. As everyone attending the meeting quickly realized, Mrs Higgins was an enthusiast for the importance of philosophy in education – not least for its role in fostering civilized, civic debate.

As a result of lively discussion at this seminar, and newly forged connections, close colleagues teamed up to set about organizing a one-day, public forum on philosophy in schools. Our aim was to focus attention to the new short course and discuss the importance of philosophy in primary level education. Scheduling the public meeting for a Saturday in late August we expected no more than thirty people to attend.

194   *Philosophy and Community*

Nonetheless, thanks to generous funding we were able to bring together a formidable panel of speakers which included education policy-makers (drawn from Northern Ireland and the Republic); Prof Keith Topping, an educational psychologist who led major studies of P4C in Britain; and Marelle Rice, a highly experienced teacher and leading P4C trainer, to facilitate a taster session of classroom philosophy. Invited contributors also included Joe Humphreys and Dr Philomena Donnelly. Titling the meeting 'Philosophy and the Irish School' we publicized the event in *The Irish Times* (Humphreys 2015); by email; and via our own social media networks – Twitter proved indispensable. Our aim was inclusiveness – parents, teachers, students – anyone with any level of interest should feel welcome to attend. Such was the demand for tickets that the venue was changed, and (again) tickets quickly sold out. Crammed into the largest room we could book, on 22 August 2015 were over eighty delegates drawn from all over Ireland (The Irish Times 2015).

Word of mouth and generosity struck a second lucky break. Hearing about the conference, a senior philosopher and member of the RIA taskforce, Dr Brian O'Connor, invited me to stand in for him at a meeting with the National Council for Curriculum and Assessment (the government body responsible for publishing national curricula in Irish schools). Forwarding his draft for the content of the new short course – which opened with classical logic, topics in epistemology and metaphysics – it was apparent that it fell into some of the same pitfalls into which I had earlier stumbled. High standards and rigour are essential in school curricula, but these needed to be guided by pedagogical expertise.

The meeting with education authorities would be a unique chance to influence the new philosophy curriculum and to promote the value of P4C in primary schools. Ahead of the meeting I drafted my own unperfected 'philosophy in schools' white paper, laying out what philosophy was; why it mattered in education; what it was 'good for'; why pupils (and parents) should welcome it; and why embracing a pedagogy such as P4C would be pivotal to the success of the short course.

Two important outcomes emerged from the meeting. First, the executives were highly responsive to the importance of philosophy. Wholeheartedly, they committed to the value of a public event and agreed to speak at the August forum. Second was the need for someone experienced to author the course curriculum, placing P4C at its heart. Marelle Rice was especially well equipped for this task, and further discussions with Prof Keith Topping were a valuable opportunity to learn more about the educational outcomes of P4C.

Where we're at

While the short course has only recently been launched, and take-up is expected to be slow until the new JC curriculum takes root, a new philosophy movement has undoubtedly emerged in Ireland. Over the past two years, around two hundred teachers and trainers have received Continuing Professional Development training in P4C. To date, four universities across the whole of Ireland now include P4C as part of their

Building a National Philosophy for Children (P4C) Network in Ireland   195

degree courses – including within philosophy and education degrees. In 2018, national curricular authorities have appointed Marelle Rice as philosophy consultant to help shape up their primary and secondary school education. And during the last academic year (2017/18) a new national competition, hosted by University College Dublin – the Young Philosophy Awards[4] – was unveiled, with an impressive two hundred entries from primary and secondary schools (Humphreys 2018). PI – a relatively small network – was undoubtedly the force that sparked these projects forging alliances, fresh opportunities and new perspectives on education.

Lessons learnt

Drawing generalizations from the particulars of experience is fraught with challenges. However, distilling three themes, this part of the chapter aims to provide ideas that may be helpful, or at least of interest, to those considering launching their own philosophy networks.

A strong vision

To begin, PI was launched with a clear-cut vision. Unquestionably, this aided our mission to deliver – what we deemed to be – an urgent message to multiple stakeholders. At the meeting held in August 2015, we were precise about these goals and bold in our outlook. Philosophy was a right in education that should not just be afforded to the privileged few. Numeracy and literacy are not the exclusive possession of university professors, nor should skills in thinking be. *Philosophy is for all*, we argued.

Several points flow from the claim that philosophy should be accessible to everyone. Our aim was to go beyond supporting the secondary school short course, and to embed philosophy at every level of Irish education and society – including, and perhaps most importantly, in primary schools. When it comes to examinable school subjects, evidence of knowledge acquisition is required among teachers – as should be the case for any secondary school subject. Nonetheless, our message was – and remains – that it is possible and desirable to instil the dynamics and building blocks of philosophical thinking and dialogue among young children. Therefore, teachers of all levels can and should be trained to build these core skills and to facilitate philosophical dialogue in the classroom. A new network would embrace the goal to train all teachers in P4C. In the short term, then, any supporting organizations must support teacher training and engage interest in the new short course; but taking the long view, philosophy – again, like numeracy and literacy – we argued, must be a basic, cross-curricular teaching competence.

The mission statement also underlined another important message. Acknowledging individual proponents of P4C and of community philosophers across Ireland, a key objective was to unite these groups under a shared national network. Identifying a gap, the ambition was to fill it. Where the UK has well-recognized P4C training organizations such as SAPERE, and the Philosophy Foundation, our explicitly stated

196   *Philosophy and Community*

aim was to create an Irish equivalent. For want of a better phrase: good artists copy, great artists steal. And in this respect, we openly – and unashamedly – looked to outstanding models of P4C for inspiration. It seemed to us both an imperative and a matter of practicality, that such a network be seeded in Ireland. Why outsource expertise – inevitably at greater cost – if excellence in training can be obtained locally and – even better – embedded in centralized teacher training programmes?

Besides, the opportunity to build something original and unique presented an exciting prospect. We explicitly identified a need to build grass-roots philosophy communities, and to nurture a national organization built on locally sourced talent and interest. At the get-go, however, the aim was to be internationalist – not inward looking – and collaborative, to partner with other philosophy in education organizations. In the spirit of P4C, numerous international philosophy organizations (to date: SAPERE and The Philosophy in Education Project in the UK, Brila in Canada, and the Institute for the Advancement of Philosophy for Children in the United States) have responded with warmth and munificent support for PI's mission.

Finally, we were also conscious of indirect opposition to the idea of philosophy in schools. The new course would be part of a wider curricular overhaul that was already meeting strong resistance from teachers' unions. Philosophy was proposed as one of a number of new subject options in the JC reform. Under the proposed changes, pupils would be able to choose up to four out of nine short courses, including coding, digital media, and Chinese languages and culture. So, even if reforms occurred, philosophy would be in a precarious position. How many teachers in secondary school have philosophy as a component of their university degree? Worse still, given the option to prepare a new syllabus (and a short course at that), overworked and stressed out teachers might pick the path of least resistance. Concerns about its usefulness among pupils and parents might also render it niche interest. In short, we were alert to the fact that philosophy might fail to get a foothold in schools – and teachers (not to mention pupils and parents, and even curricular authorities) – might care less. Keeping our message simple, on point, and upholding a bold vision, aided our case.

Diverse collaborators

At the first public event we unofficially launched what we hoped would become a new community philosophy network. We made a direct appeal to recruit and involve other likeminded people to help with its formation. This approach was less a strategy than a plea. To get anywhere in achieving our goals, we needed manpower. We were still unsure about what form this new organization would take, though one thing we were clear about was the need for diversity – both in expertise and in experience. A homogenous group of academic philosophers would be undesirable. We needed teachers, parents, students, as well as academics, and people with sound organizational skills.

Fortunately, during preparation for the August event such individuals began to step forward. And immediately after the public meeting, a consolidated group of around eight gathered in the kitchen of a new colleague's home in central Dublin. Our aims

Building a National Philosophy for Children (P4C) Network in Ireland   197

were to plan the organization and solidify our goals, as well as to get to know each other.

Conversations and meetings in the months to come were marked by openness and friendly directness. More women than men, we were a mix of individuals in our thirties and forties. As volunteers with busy jobs – drawn from all over Ireland, with two of us based in England – we determined to meet on a monthly basis though some of us corresponded daily. Hackneyed as it sounds, diversity was indeed our strength: we were school teachers, students, parents, philosophy researchers, lecturers in philosophy of education, and enthusiasts with philosophy backgrounds who wanted to use our learning. All of us wore more than one of these hats, and around half of us had experience of teaching philosophy in the community including primary and secondary schools, prisons, art galleries and among adult learners. Only three of our members had extensive – that is, at least five years' worth of – experience of school and community philosophy. A range of experience, interests and personalities would prove essential: enthusiasm, big ideas and teaching experience may be necessary to launch a new organization, but they are not sufficient. As a collective, we had skills in website design, marketing, and prior experience of running committees. Last but not least we had individuals who excelled at listening and reorienting the group to practicalities.

Designating ourselves the 'steering committee' we described our organization as democratic, with a flat and fluid leadership. Early on, and to remain as inclusive as possible in our meetings, we introduced the idea of a rotating chair – each month someone different would act as chairperson while another individual took minutes. The hope was to spread the labour, and to give everyone a voice. The chairperson sent an agenda in advance to which everyone could add additional issues.

In reality, and as might be expected, governance and management were vital to make progress. As a relatively large and diverse group of individuals, each brimming with ideas, diversity was a strength that also invited challenges. In the early days, especially, pre-determined agendas sometimes got lost in wider discussion that once or twice became impassioned. Perhaps inevitably, there was also disorientation about what P4C meant. Some individuals had strong views, some had none.

Monthly meetings fly by quickly. If we were to get organized, we could not squander time; on the other hand, dialogue (philosophical dialogue, no less) was important to fine-tune our mission. Additionally, we were growing in size. New members, introduced via our own networks, were always welcome, but new blood brought new opinions. The group expanded to around fourteen members.

At least three decisions were successfully enacted – some tacitly – to advance our purpose. First, we limited the group size – no more members would be admitted to the steering committee. Second, we admitted that the group was already too large to navigate key decisions. The judgement was made to organize into subcommittees of between three to five individuals. These subcommittees included organizing the official launch; designing the website; social media campaigns; liaising with the Irish curricular authorities on the short course; initiating P4C training; teaching philosophy in prisons. Groups would work to advance these agendas. And with smaller working groups we became more efficient. This also diffused some of the more negative aspects

198   *Philosophy and Community*

of that inescapable intra-group competition that arises among individuals of similar ages who share similar career paths. Insider competition can propel an organization forward, but too much rivalry can also kill it.

Third, reflecting these dynamics and the voluntary nature of the group, we would need understated leadership – something like P4C's 'guide on the side'. Pragmatic management would be crucial to get things done: to answer emails from members of the public, and to resolve group tensions. Many members have families, and all of us had savage schedules. Leadership had to hit the right note – respectful but implicit, and forthright in acknowledging the value of each person's contributions. At times it would be necessary to remind everyone of our vision – what bonded us, and brought us together as a unit.

In the first year we agreed to prioritize three items: (i) develop resources and training programmes to support the new short course; (ii) publish our website as a virtual hub for the organization; and (iii) organize an official launch date, which would be set for the following August (2016). We also aimed to secure small pots of funding from universities, and educational organizations (which we successfully obtained). These priorities would occupy the majority of discussion at meetings, while other activities were pursued via smaller online and offline get-togethers. Building trust was essential, and we organized a Dropbox file to share resources among members, and to facilitate collaboration.

Commitment to attendance at meetings would be varied – we accepted that. Some core members shouldered more work than others. With the formation of any society, and with the passage of time, dynamics fluctuate before they stabilize. Yet, in the two years of setting up PI, however, the group remained remarkably fixed and resolute.

Vigorous marketing

Philosophy has a reputation for being abstruse, technical and dry. Thus many might believe that the subject ought to remain confined to the ivory tower along with academic philosophers. Philosophy's image problem isn't helped by philosophers. Some appear to view the field as *cosa nostra* – 'our thing'. Cloistered off, philosophy is typically considered fit only for the very brightest and best. Reassuringly *recherché*, a philosophical education thereby serves as intellectual insignia, a status symbol. Our aim was to challenge the crasser elements of elitism, while promoting educational excellence.

Promotion and marketing are often regarded as distinctively corporate ideals with no place in academia. Though, contrary to what scholars might say, self-aggrandizement certainly plays a motivational role in university life, perhaps especially in the 'me-against the world' humanities where teamwork – and therefore sharing the spoils – is rarer than in science. Regardless, and in spite of this, fearless promotion of philosophy with a clear and simple message would be crucial to improve public awareness.

As with any advertising campaign, knowing one's audience is imperative. We recognized the importance of a website, replete with basic information about philosophy, its value, and PI members. A website – and an organization – would need a name. Various ideas were mooted – Should we call ourselves a society? A collective? A network? After some discussion, we recognized that anyone who wanted to find out about philosophy in Ireland would probably do one thing: they'd google some combination of 'Philosophy' and 'Ireland', so that would be our name.

In small but spikey measure, we experienced prickly push-back from one or two academic philosophers who failed to see the bigger picture. The whisper was that a faculty member deemed it impertinent to call our group 'Philosophy Ireland' – after all 'there was no Professor of Philosophy on our committee'.[5] 'Academic politics', Henry Kissinger once observed, 'is so bitter because the stakes are so low'. In the same spirit, perhaps it bears repeating that occupying a Chair of Philosophy is neither necessary nor sufficient for doing philosophy nor being a philosopher.

For the most part, however, we were met with bounteous encouragement from our host universities and schools, and when possible, offered financial support.[6] In part this was because we conveyed our mission successfully to different stakeholders. If community and schools' philosophy was to get off the ground in Ireland, diverse groups needed to know this was something they needed. And in order to seed the importance of P4C within the short course in philosophy, Irish curricular authorities would need support in training teachers to take up the course. PI aimed to drive interest while working with centralized government agencies to provide accredited teacher training courses. Marketing would take on various guises.

First, P4C has not *yet* been embedded in any centralized national curriculum in the world – so why not point this out to curricular authorities? As a tool for persuasion it was useful. Here was a chance to do something distinctive and great, and for Ireland to lead the way. Closer to home, it was also an opportunity to surpass the UK which has experienced setbacks in launching Philosophy GCSE,[7] and where A-level philosophy – introduced in the 1990s – has plateaued at an annual take-up of around 3,000 pupils, regrettably biased towards privileged pupils.[8] Again, competitively spurred, Ireland might seize a unique (if smug) opportunity to lead by example.

Second, in order for a new subject is to take hold, it must perform favourably in a cost-benefit analysis. What was the trade-off for schools of disruption to timetables and financial outlays? Head teachers manage tight budgets; if they can get something of value for free, there is a chance they will take it. University-undergraduate partnerships, for example, would be one mutually beneficial way to help roll out P4C, and promote the value of philosophy in primary schools thereby exposing the benefits of the pedagogy to teachers. Similarly, a healthy circulation between schoolchildren, undergraduates and university departments could only appeal to hungry scholars eager to exploit research angles and secure 'impactful', interdisciplinary funding.

Another 'marketing' strategy in dealings with schools and curricular authorities was to emphasize that P4C training is relatively inexpensive, and far below the cost of purchasing laptops or tablets for every child, at around £8.00 per child (Gorard, Siddiqui and See 2017). Moreover this investment is one that can grow year on year. So much the better if the curriculum was centralized and P4C could become a core feature of tertiary-level teacher training.

But what would be the *point* of any initial outlay or efforts for teachers or schools? Published, peer-reviewed evidence played a significant role here. To illustrate, in the initial meeting with curriculum executives, it was helpful to research and then appeal to the 'Key Skills' embedded in the Framework for the JC (National Council for Curriculum and Assessment 2015). Philosophy ticked many of the requisite boxes, but an evidence-base for some of these outcomes was more persuasive than dialogue. Handing over copies of scientific papers with key empirical findings highlighted in yellow, made life easier for busy executives. Indeed, even if schools, or indeed parents, cared not a jot for philosophy, here was evidence that doing philosophy would likely advance their kids' English and maths, not to mention their articulacy and behaviour in the classroom; in a Christmas-come-early for education officials, improvements were even greater for children from lower socio-economic brackets (Trickey and Topping 2004, 2006). Finally, thanks to – albeit highly dubious – 'Leprechaun economics', Ireland is the tech hub of Europe. With daily headlines about robots filching jobs, it was important to showcase the integral role of philosophy to the design, regulation, and ethical use of emerging technologies (Vickers 2017). Evidence that philosophy graduates are sought after by financial and information technology sectors for their analytical skills, and that critical thinking would be last frontier for automation, also helped support our case (Hartley 2018). As with any school or university subject choices, clarifying the benefits of options – including philosophy – is worthwhile. Why be demure?

An 'edge' in employability might appear to be the 'wrong reason' to pursue philosophy. Plenty of cultural commentators have scorned the suggestion that philosophy (or more broadly, the humanities) be debased as a means to an end (Newman 1854/2015; Leavis 1962/2013; Macneill 2011). Re-enacting older debates, it is claimed that these fields are intrinsically valuable 'for their own sake', the idea that they might be perceived as servile to other goals greeted with flamboyant nose-holding. Elsewhere I have interrogated the bifurcation between instrumental versus intrinsic values and concluded that it rests on unsupported dichotomies (utility versus non-utility, theoretical versus applied, educated versus trained) (Blease 2016a). Space does not permit exploration here but I suggest that the aims of a philosophical education always involve goals (e.g. to seek the truth; to foster a questioning attitude, to advance judgement and improve skills in communicating abstract ideas). The thrust of these sentiments was communicated in teaching magazines, newspapers and public presentations (Blease 2015; 2016b).

Other marketing strategies included 'PI Ambassadors' whom we listed on the website. Figures from media, academia and public life were invited to endorse and lend support to our cause. Last but not least, we were delighted to name Sabina Higgins as our Patron. Mrs Higgins inaugurated our official launch: formidable yet approachable, she represents what PI has set out to achieve. And no doubt she helped us to secure the presidential seal of approval (Humphreys 2016).

Conclusion

Philosophy *in* Ireland – like PI – is very much a work-in-progress. In a short period of time, committed individuals collaborated to improve the visibility of philosophy and its value. Undoubtedly happenstance and a unique microclimate created opportunities

Building a National Philosophy for Children (P4C) Network in Ireland   201

to seed our network. Not every country is fortunate to have a progressive head of state. Nonetheless, teamwork and trustful alliances were essential to turn political ethos into action. A pragmatic capacity to work together and showcase the mutual value of *philosophy for all* enabled us to partner, successfully, with different stakeholders – schools, curricular authorities and universities. It is easy to get things done when you believe in the message. Like Michael D. Higgins, we continue to urge that 'an exposure to philosophy is vital if we truly want our young people to acquire the capacities they need in preparing for their journey in the world' (Higgins 2016).

Notes

1   See www.philosophyireland.com
2   The maxim is often attributed to Seneca although the origin is likely to be a quotation from Demetrius the Cynic: 'The best wrester', he would say, 'is not he who has learned thoroughly all the tricks and twists of the art, which are seldom met with an actual wresting, but he who has well and carefully trained himself in one or two of them, and watches keenly for an opportunity of practicing them'. Seneca, *On Benefits*, vii. 1.
3   More correctly, professors Dunne and Donnelly preferred the phrase 'philosophy with children'. While I do not wish to detract from important pedagogical disputes, I retain 'P4C' throughout for brevity and to avoid unfortunate acronyms 'PwC'.
4   See http://youngphilosopherawards.ucd.ie
5   In fact, the judgement-call was invalidated as one member of our group (Aislinn O'Donnell) was soon appointed Professor of Philosophy of Education at Maynooth University.
6   Notably, leadership in the Philosophy Department, University College Dublin – in particular professors Maria Baghramian and Jim O'Shea – provided unwavering support for PI.
7   I should point out that I'm privileged to have been involved in supporting the UK's *The Philosophy in Education Project* directed by Dr John Taylor, an organization which is vigorously striving to establish a Philosophy GCSE.
8   Thanks due to Dr Michael Lacewing for this information.

References

Blease, C., (2011), 'Empowering Young Minds of the Future', *The Irish News*, 19 July 2011.
Blease, C., (2015), 'Philosophy is a Right', TEDx University College, Dublin, [Online], Available at: https://www.youtube.com/watch?v=neRk9NOip4c, Accessed 19 September 2018.
Blease, C., (2016a), 'In Defense of Utility: The Medical Humanities and Medical Education', *Medical Humanities*, 42 (2): 103–8.
Blease, C., (2016b), 'Is This on the Exam? The Pressing Need for Philosophy in Schools', *The Irish Times*, 2 May 2016.
Blease, C., (2017), 'Philosophy Can Teach Children What Google Can't', *The Guardian*, 9 January 2017.

Freehill-Maye, L., (2018), 'Going Beyond the STEM Trend: Ireland Pushes Philosophy', *Pacific Standard*, 2 March 2018.

Gorard, S., Siddiqui, N., and See, B. H., (2017), 'Can "Philosophy for Children" Improve Primary School Attainment?' *Journal of Philosophy of Education*, 51 (1): 5–22.

Hartley, S., (2018), *The Fuzzy and the Techie: Why the Liberal Arts Will Rule the Digital World*, London: Penguin Random House.

Higgins, M. D., (2015), 'Speech at the President of Ireland's Ethics Initiative National Seminar', Áras an Uachtaráin, 28 March 2015, [Online], Available at: https://www.president.ie/en/media-library/speeches/speech-at-the-president-of-irelands-ethics-initiative-national-seminar, Accessed 19 September 2018.

Higgins, M. D., (2016), 'Speech at Reception for Philosophy Ireland', Áras an Uachtaráin, 19 November 2016, [Online], Available at: https://www.president.ie/en/media-library/speeches/speech-at-a-reception-for-philosophy-ireland, Accessed 19 September 2018.

Higgins, M. D., (2017), 'Speech by President Higgins at a Reception to Launch Irish Young Philosopher Awards', Áras an Uachtaráin, 17 November 2017, [Online], Available at: https://www.youtube.com/watch?v=Os2oUivqNBI, Accessed 19 September 2018.

Humphreys, J., (2015), 'Philosophy: The Subject that Improves Children's Literacy, Numeracy and Conduct', *The Irish Times*, 15 August 2015.

Humphreys, J., (2016), 'Sabina Higgins Backs Campaign for Teaching Philosophy in Schools', *The Irish Times*, 28 August 2016.

Humphreys, J., (2018), 'Meet Ireland's Young Philosopher', *The Irish Times*, 3 June 2018.

The Irish Times (2015), 'Education for What? The Compelling Case of Critical Thinking', *Editorial*, 22 August 2015.

Leavis, F. R., ([1962] 2013), *The Two Cultures: The Significance of C. P. Snow*, Cambridge: Cambridge University Press.

Macneill, P. U., (2011), 'The Arts and Medicine: A Challenging Relationship', *Medical Humanities*, 37: 85–90.

National Council for Curriculum and Assessment (2015), *Framework for Junior Cycle*, [Online], Available at: https://www.ncca.ie/en/junior-cycle/framework-for-junior-cycle, Accessed 19 September 2018.

Newman, J. H., ([1854] 2015), *The Idea of a University*, London: Aeterna Press.

Trickey, S., and Topping, K. J., (2004), '"Philosophy for Children": A Systematic Review', *Research Papers in Education*, 19 (3): 365–80.

Trickey, S., and Topping, K. J., (2006), 'Collaborative Philosophical Enquiry for School Children: Socio-Emotional Effects at 11 to 12 Years', *School Psychology International*, 27 (5): 599–614.

Vickers, H., (2017), 'Philosophy Essential for All', 20 April 2017, [Online], Available at: http://edtechnology.co.uk/Article/philosophy-essential-for-all, Accessed 19 September 2018.

14

In philosophical conversation with: A diverse group of adults – 'Dwelling Together in Diverse Spaces'

Darren Chetty, Abigail Bentley and Adam Ferner

Introduction to the context of the work

This chapter offers reflections on a community philosophy project undertaken at University College London, UK (UCL) in July 2017. The project was undertaken by Darren Chetty and Abigail Bentley, both PhD researchers at UCL with an interest in issues around multiculturalism and racism. Darren was a contributing author to the book *The Good Immigrant*, and after reading the book and discovering that Darren was also based at UCL, Abigail contacted him with an interest to collaborate on a project. The UCL Grand Challenges scheme – the funder of the project – aims to promote cross-disciplinary working within the university and explores six areas related to matters of pressing societal concern, with one of the six strands being 'Cultural Understanding'. Under this strand, a call was put out in February 2017 for a small grant of £2,500 with the theme of 'Growing up Multicultural', to which Darren and Abigail submitted a project proposal.

Given the restricted funding, Darren and Abigail wanted to try and do something that might have a lasting impact, but that would be achievable within the time and budget restraints – something that would satisfy the requirements of the funding while deepening their own understanding of issues relating to multiculturalism and racism. A key concern was that the project be non-exploitative for the participants and, ideally, something they could view as a positive, useful experience. Darren and Abigail wanted it to result in an output that would be widely accessible, and of interest to educators in particular. It was decided that a film would be the most effective and efficient way of documenting the process and disseminating the findings.

Description of the work

The aim of the project was to explore experiences of UCL students and London residents living in a multicultural society by investigating the interplay between race,

204 *Philosophy and Community*

identity, self-esteem and interaction with the education system. The project was titled 'Dwelling Together in Diverse Spaces', and it was decided that discussion circles with a group of eight to sixteen people would be the most interesting way to explore these aims. The discussions were facilitated by Darren and informed by his practice and study of Philosophy for Children (P4C). While Darren and Abigail provided a clear statement of aims in order to satisfy the conditions for funding, they also aimed to be responsive to the discussions in each session.

The sessions were structured into four group discussions of one hour, each followed by small group interviews in which the participants could reflect on the group discussion and expand on individual experiences and viewpoints. The sessions took place on a Monday and Tuesday evening over a two-week period in July 2017. In total, thirteen people participated in the project, although not everyone attended every session. The participant ages ranged from twenty-four to forty-six, and consisted of eleven women and two men. An invitation for participants was shared by email at the UCL Institute for Education, UKHipHopEd[1] and the UCL Institute for Global Health. Darren also advertised on his Twitter account.

The wording of the advert for participants was as follows: 'Are you interested in discussions about race, racism and identity? We are seeking a diverse range of participants for a series of discussion circles and interviews focusing on the broad theme of "growing up multicultural". These will be filmed and made into an educational documentary … [followed by further project details]'. As part of the recruitment process, applicants were asked to fill in a short survey. Those who responded were sent a copy of the participant information sheet and given two days to think about whether they would like to take part, after which they were contacted for follow-up by Abigail. In total, twenty-eight people expressed interest in the project. Out of these, sixteen agreed to participate, with the remaining twelve unavailable due to time or geographical constraints. Of the sixteen who agreed to take part, three did not turn up to the sessions, leaving thirteen participants who consented to the study and took part in at least one session. Consent forms were signed at the beginning of the first session. The project was granted full ethics approval on 21 June 2017 from the UCL Institute of Education.

Darren and Abigail decided in advance that the sessions would be video recorded and edited into a short film documenting the process of the project and summarizing the discussions. A discussion plan would also be developed to go alongside the film. The film would then be screened at a public event with a panel discussion afterwards.

Due to time and budget constraints, Darren and Abigail decided to film two of the four discussion sessions. Session one was not filmed in order to give the group a chance to get to know one another before the cameras were turned on. Participants were asked to introduce themselves and, if they wished, to comment on what had brought them to the project and to express any hopes, concerns or questions they might have. This was followed by a discussion exercise. Darren read out a series of statements based on ideas he had encountered in classroom and public dialogue. Participants were asked to position themselves along a spectrum in the room, ranging from 'strongly agree' to 'strongly disagree'. Participants were then encouraged to talk to the group about their position on the spectrum, to respond to what others had said, and at times to consider

In Philosophical Conversation With: A Diverse Group of Adults   205

what someone positioned differently might say. Darren offered very little commentary on what people said beyond drawing the group's attention to the broad range of positions within the group and inviting them to consider what that meant for future discussions.

The statements were as follows:

1. Before we talk about multiculturalism and racism, we need to establish ground rules.
2. Talking about racism can make people feel uncomfortable.
3. Our attitude to racism is shaped in our childhood.
4. We should always aim to find areas of commonality in our discussions.
5. It is important that we stay calm when discussing racism.
6. Black people cannot be objective about racism.
7. White people cannot understand what it feels like to experience racism.
8. If someone becomes upset, we should stop the discussion.
9. Discussion spaces reserved for people of a particular racialized identity are a bad idea.
10. Multiculturalism has affected my life in a significant way.
11. Racism has affected my life in a significant way.

Session two was filmed. In this session Darren used an email – based on one that was sent to him – as a starting point, or as it is often described in P4C literature 'stimulus for discussion'. After reading the email, participants were asked to formulate questions about anything they found interesting or puzzling about the starting point. These questions were then used as a way into philosophical inquiry. The text ran as follows:

Dear Darren,

I read and greatly enjoyed your essay in 'The Good Immigrant'. I am running a series of lunchtime seminars at Prestige University on the theme of immigration, multiculturalism and racism. I think the students would learn a great deal from you. Would you be willing to come and give a talk on your work this term? Unfortunately we don't have a budget to pay a speaker's fee but we can pay for your travel. We can also offer you a free lunch with our highly motivated students.

I look forward to hearing from you.

Kind regards,

A.N. Organizer

In session three, which was not filmed, Darren attempted to ask participants to share an experience from their own lives, similar to the email, to talk about potentially problematic scenarios. There was some unwillingness to do this from participants; this in itself became the question for inquiry for the session.

The final session was filmed and, as a starting point for inquiry, used three short readings (provided in advance of the session). They focused on the topic of cultural appropriation. The first was a newspaper article reporting on comments made by

Amandla Stenberg about Kylie Jenner (Eleftheriou-Smith 2015). The second was an online article by Adam Elliott-Cooper arguing for the importance of a structural critique of cultural appropriation (Elliott-Cooper 2015). The third was an online article by Kenan Malik, in which he argues that 'cultures do not, and cannot, work through notions of "ownership". The history of culture is the history of cultural appropriation – of cultures borrowing, stealing, changing, transforming' (Malik 2016). At the end of sessions two and four, participants were asked to reflect on that session and the previous one in groups of between two and four and to expand on their thoughts as they saw fit. These sections were also filmed.

In order to produce the film, Darren and Abigail worked with the filmmaker, Meghna Gupta. Meghna did an initial edit of the material, and Darren and Abigail subsequently added to it. The material was amended iteratively to create the final version. Voice-overs and an introduction were recorded after the initial editing process. A time was then arranged to screen the film privately to the participants. It was screened in a neutral setting and time was allowed for feedback afterwards. On the basis of the feedback, some further edits were made.

'Dwelling Together' was screened publically to an audience of around 200 people on 16 November 2017 and was followed up with a panel discussion. The panellists consisted of Dr Joanna Haynes, associate professor of Education Studies at the University of Plymouth, UK; Lesha Small, senior associate at LKMco and teacher; Sundeep Lidher, researcher at the Runnymede Trust; and Steve Williams, a P4C practitioner and trainer. The panel was chaired by Jack Bicker, a philosopher and senior teaching fellow at the UCL Institute of Education. The film has since been posted on YouTube, and there is a corresponding WordPress page.[2]

Critical reflections

What follows is a 'conversation', conducted over email, between Adam Ferner and Darren Chetty. Adam, racialized as white, is an academic philosopher and practical philosopher working with young people. Darren and Adam met through a reading group at UCL Institute of Education organized by Adam and Judith Suissa on philosopher Barbara Applebaum's *Being White, Being Good: White Complicity, White Moral Responsibility, and Social Justice Pedagogy* (Applebaum 2010).

Adam: Watching the 'Dwelling Together' film encouraged me to think a lot more about how the dynamics in a room can depend on my being racialized as white. I've worked in academic philosophy in the UK and France, and in youth centres and schools, but – like a lot of postgraduate philosophy educators – I've had no official pedagogical training (aside from a couple of cursory, non-compulsory workshops) and certainly nothing that's focused on how my whiteness may affect uptake of ideas and facilitation. Seeing the film has reinforced my view that this is a significant and troubling oversight. Could you begin by briefly outlining some of the logistical issues of the 'Dwelling Together in Diverse Spaces' project as you and Abigail saw them?

In Philosophical Conversation With: A Diverse Group of Adults   207

Darren: The time frame for completing the project set by the funders was relatively short, which led to our recruitment period also being quite short. We advertised through UCL as well as through other networks we were involved in. A number of participants heard about the project through my twitter account. As a couple of participants mentioned having read something I'd written as part of the reason they felt willing to get involved, it is entirely possible that this was also the reason other people chose not to get involved! In the first session one of the participants pointed out that there were no white men among participants. In fact, three white men had expressed an interest in being involved but were unable to commit to the dates we had. All three were scholars involved with research into racism.

The fact that the project was being filmed made it quite unusual and in all likelihood impacted on who was, and was not, willing to be involved. Abigail and I went beyond the requirements of the funding ethics committee with regards to consent for the film. We decided early on, in discussion with the participants, that we would screen the film for them first, and take into account their comments. We were as upfront as possible about having planned the project, thus exerting some control over it, while at the same time trying to be responsive to the participants' needs. We tried to stay alert to the risks the participants were taking in having potentially difficult conversations filmed for public viewing. Where and when we made mistakes, we tried our best to own them, to apologize and to do what we could to rectify the situation. I think the result is a film that can be read as a jointly authored text.

Participants were offered refreshments, but were not paid for their time. Abigail and I did not receive any payment for the project, although we undoubtedly benefit from the institutional position of leading the project and indeed in authoring this chapter. Our hope was that participants would find the project useful. A few have informally reported that the project impacted upon them positively.

Adam: In a recent joint report by the British Philosophical Association and the Society for Women in Philosophy, UK, Helen Beebee and Jennifer Saul (2011) describe the ways that cultural norms – within academic philosophy – exclude certain voices while privileging others. Among other things, they focus on the 'macho' environment fostered in seminar rooms (with participants 'going for the jugular', 'shooting down their opponents', etc.). This oppositional, symbolically masculine environment is clearly something you tried to avoid in the 'Dwelling Together' project. Could you explain how you went about doing that?

Darren: In the first instance, my approach to the facilitation of philosophical inquiry is informed by my study and practice of Philosophy for/with Children (P4C/PwC) and the idea of the 'community of inquiry', described by Matthew Lipman, Ann Margaret Sharp and Frederick S. Oscanyan (1980) as a community 'committed to the procedures of inquiry, to responsible search techniques that presuppose an openness to evidence and to reason' (Lipman et al. 1980: 45). Lipman's original P4C programme – and a great deal of the work it has inspired – has children as its focus. However, the training offered for teachers usually involves them participating in a community of inquiry together, and P4C seminars and conferences for practitioners and scholars regularly feature all-adult communities of inquiry.

Rather than thinking of dialogue as the means by which we arrive at solutions, I took the view that it figures as a problem, and one that's worth engaging with. I think Nicholas Burbules's 'The Limits of Dialogue as a Critical Pedagogy' (2000) is very useful in pointing out that some people find themselves outside the agreed norms of a particular dialogic encounter. I've written elsewhere how encouraging participants to adopt positive body language (like smiling at each other) will minimize opportunities to talk about racism (Chetty 2014). Alternatively, it may well encourage what psychologists have described as an 'affective-cognitive incongruity' (see, for example, Laing and Esterson 2016), often associated with poor mental health. In the opening session Abigail and I chose not to work towards ground rules that everyone had to sign up to in order for the dialogue proceed. Instead, I read out the series of statements about racism, multiculturalism and dialogue. I think this approach worked well for the group – which is not to say it would work well for all groups in all circumstances. The effect, I think, was to (further) sensitize participants to the complexities of dialogue and to demonstrate that while I would consider myself to have some responsibility for 'holding' the space, we all had a continuing responsibility to negotiate the way in which our conversations would take place.

However, I think that a focus on avoiding what you term an 'oppositional' environment, while important for discouraging the kind of macho behaviour that I too have witnessed in seminar rooms, can sometimes become an obstruction to open inquiry about racism. There is a growing literature bearing witness to the phenomenon of people racialized as white experiencing discomfort with conversations about racism and consciously or unconsciously employing a broad range of 'tools' in order to change the focus of the conversation (see, for example, Picower 2009; DiAngelo and Sensoy 2014; Chetty and Suissa, 2016). Where this is the case in conversations, it may require one or more people to either draw the group's attention to what is going on, or else to bring the conversation back to the topic of racism – and in doing so be potentially interpreted as making an 'oppositional' move – or more strongly, being 'oppositional'. This too is well documented in the literature. The 'angry Black woman' stereotype is one that is often employed in public discourse to locate the cause of an interpersonal dynamic shaped by a culture of racism and sexism, or more specifically to use Moya Bailey's term 'misogynoir' (Bailey 2010), in an individual at the receiving end of that dynamic.

Amy Reed-Sandoval (2019) has argued that in response to what she sees as important and valid critiques about the coloniality, eurocentricity and 'Whiteness' of P4C practices (Chetty 2014; Rainville 2000; Kohan 1995; Reed-Sandoval and Sykes 2017), P4C should be 'reformed rather than abandoned' (Reed-Sandoval 2018: 39). My own sense is that these critiques themselves remain marginal in P4C discourse, which may well suggest a more fundamental problem in the field of P4C, and a resistance even to the types of reform she proposes. Rather than seeing the failure of P4C scholars to engage with philosophical thinking about racism and colonialism as caused by the lack of People of Colour within the global P4C community, I have proposed that the problem may lie considerably deeper with the concept of 'reasonableness' and how it is understood by practitioners. Cultivating 'reasonableness' is regarded by Lipman as the primary aim of P4C (see Chetty 2018), but I have suggested that 'P4C practices

In Philosophical Conversation With: A Diverse Group of Adults   209

that fail to historicise, examine and challenge prevailing notions of reasonableness establish a "gated community of inquiry"' (Chetty 2018: 39). By this I mean that certain articulations come to be outside the norms, values and procedures of the community of inquiry given that it is regulated by an, often unproblematized, notion of what constitutes reasonable speech and action. That said, Dwelling Together can be read as an early experiment in reforming P4C.

Adam: How so?

Darren: Well I'd suggest the following factors add up to practice sufficiently distinct from common P4C practice among adults (i.e. on training courses, at conferences and seminars) to constitute a kind of reform of P4C:

1. Foregrounding racism and multiculturalism in the call for participants.
2. Not establishing ground rules, but rather viewing dialogue as a problem rather than a solution (Lefstein 2006) and keeping the question of how we engage with each other open to the community of inquiry rather than something to be agreed at the outset.
3. Beginning with the experiences and philosophical thinking of People of Colour.
4. Including the actions of people racialized as white towards People of Colour in the starting points/stimuli.
5. Having a facilitator who is racialized as other than white.
6. Having a facilitator who has a grounding in P4C literature and literature pertaining to racism, whiteness and dialogue.

All of these 'reforms' are replicable for other P4C projects, and only Point 5 is beyond the grasp of people racialized as white. I am not suggesting that these are factors that should feature in all P4C practice. However, I would suggest P4C practitioners consider their reasons for not adopting in them in particular circumstances.

In engaging in this project, I felt it was vital that we had an opportunity to listen to each other as best we could before we made the typical philosophical moves of asking for reasons, making distinctions, and looking for alternative explanations. These are all suggested as moves facilitators might make; and they can enrich philosophical inquiry. However, I think facilitators need to appreciate that the kind of questions asked by philosophers: 'Are you sure about that?'; 'What is your evidence?'; 'What is your justification?'; 'Could it be caused by something else?'; 'Is it necessarily the case?', appear to be remarkably similar to the dialogic moves People of Colour often encounter when being disbelieved, or experiencing testimonial injustice or being 'gaslit'. The Dwelling Together group helped me appreciate this fact. In session three, I suggested that participants share instances from their own experience that might be useful starting points for inquiry, like the email I had shared in session two. I felt this was a useful move because many people in the group had commented on the high level of trust in the room, and I wanted to ensure the material for inquiry was not only coming from my own personal experience. The proposal, however, was resisted by participants who felt they were being asked to share painful experiences of racism in a space where others might raise doubts as to the accuracy of their interpretation. This was not my intention, but I could understand the concerns, and these concerns subsequently became the subject of our inquiry for that session. I think that productive philosophical dialogue about racism should make space for People of Colour to bring their lived experience to bear on the conversation but should not be dependent upon them doing so, or it ends up coercing them to share often painful information in order to ensure the conversation continues. At the same time, philosophizing about racism is unlikely to be productive if the starting point is too removed from the realities of racism, for example, if it is portrayed only in metaphor (see Chetty 2014) and through the kind of abstracted thought experiments popular among some ethics teachers. As Grace Robinson puts it: 'Ethically educative experiences, which may also be philosophically rigorous, are more likely to be found in rich "flesh and blood" narratives full of character, complexity, and contingency – since these are the factors at play in moral life' (2016: 49).

In order to arrive at 'flesh and blood narratives' in our philosophical conversations, I tried to 'slow down' my facilitation so that others would also resist the 'rush to judgment'; and in recognition of the possibility that the stories people shared might well contain philosophical insight. This departs from some schools of thought within P4C that advise against people in the community of inquiry using narrative rather than clearly articulated rational justification for their thinking.

Adam: To my mind, one of the brilliant things about the project is the way you and Abigail managed to discuss the conceptual issues, while simultaneously exploring them in practice. In the second session, you focus on what Nora Berenstain, building on the work of Audre Lorde (2007), Toni Morrison (1975) and Kristie Dotson (2011), calls 'epistemic exploitation' (Berenstain 2016: 569). 'Epistemic exploitation occurs when privileged persons compel marginalized persons to educate them about the nature of their oppression.' At one point, there is an exchange between a white participant and Black participant:

'I'm just wondering … and I don't know if this is a question or not … but if this is about facilitating conversations about multiculturalism, and this is about making, you know, people understand more … how am I going to make sure that I hear what you're saying? How are we going to make sure that I can hear what you're saying, if I'm going to mess up, because I inevitably will?'

'Let me ask you a question in return. … How can you demonstrate to me that you've invested in the survival of my daughter, the young man just killed in Stratford by the police? … When you can demonstrate to me that you have a serious investment in my survival, and that you see my survival and my thriving as essential to your own survival and thriving – when you see those two things as compatible, then we can have a conversation.'

'What would that look like though? What would my investment…'

'I throw the question back to you. What would that look like?'

In Philosophical Conversation With: A Diverse Group of Adults   211

I could imagine this kind of conversation creating a certain amount of discomfort; how did this play out in the room and how did you manage it as a facilitator?

Darren: Well, first of all, thank you on behalf of everyone involved for the kind words about the film. I think that we did manage to some extent to begin to engage with the complexities of racism and how they were not merely 'out there' but also present in the room, in our conversations and our interactions.

A number of people referred to the exchange you mention in conversations with me after the screening of the film. One P4C facilitator expressed the opinion that 'throwing a question back' at someone was not in the spirit of philosophical dialogue. They argued that if we agree to engage in dialogue, we implicitly agree to answer any reasonable question asked of us. I'm not sure how representative that opinion is, but my sense is that it is an opinion that others share. It would be easy to interpret 'Let me ask you a question in return …' as a move that dodges the question, particularly as we may associate it with a politician who, when asked a question they would rather avoid, responds with another question. However, when I was facilitating this dialogue, that wasn't how I understood the comment. The politician worries about how the answer may make them look. However, in the film the concern, as I understood it, was with how the question, however well intentioned, shifted the burden of tackling racism onto a Black woman. To some viewers this may seem very subtle. To others it may seem very obvious. And if it is a move that you have experienced repeatedly it may well be one that you have found important to resist.

'Common sense' in philosophical inquiry suggests we should demonstrate our own reasonableness by being willing to answer reasonable questions asked of ourselves. But what if we have a very clear sense that what is being asked of us is not *reasonable* in our own understanding of the word? What if we recognize the way that common notions of reasonableness have been invoked in courts and public discourse as ways of legitimizing racially unjust actions (Armour 1997; Chetty 2018)?

I did not understand the move to throw back the question as shutting down dialogue (another criticism I encountered). Rather, I interpreted the move as keeping the inquiry open by negotiating how it might proceed. I think the discomfort arose from the fact that such a negotiation is relatively rare in conversations around racism. The point for me is not that the initial question was one that cannot be asked but rather that where we create a philosophical environment in which it cannot be resisted, through the enforcement of norms and ground rules, we create a subtly but powerfully coercive atmosphere. In the simplest terms, we create the conditions whereby victims of oppression find themselves tasked with the job of educating others about their oppression. I would see this as one of the ways that dialogue is a problem – and I attempted to be alert to how discomfort was distributed in our conversations. I can't say with any certainty that I always got this right. I do think the small group interviews and regularly 'checking in' with people in the breaks was helpful in this regard.

Adam: I realize that the sessions didn't all go 'according to plan', and that they sometimes moved quite far from the topics you and Abigail had originally aimed to discuss. This can be a mark of a good conversation, but were there ever times you thought the discussions were unhelpfully sidetracked, or became overly recursive? If so, did you try to redirect them?

Darren: I think this is a difficult question! As mentioned earlier, session three didn't go according to plan and the result was a conversation that I found very useful – and which I think and hope others found useful too. I think it was good that I came to the session *with* a general plan – but also I tried to present this as a proposal rather than an instruction. I've been a participant in communities of enquiry where participants have muttered about not wanting to go along with the facilitator's opening activity. But I've not experienced, as far as I can recall, a group pushing back and saying that they don't wish to do the activity. One of the norms of P4C practice, I suggest, is that we 'play along' and place our trust in the facilitator (and the same is true more broadly, in philosophy seminars, etc.). However, we may have good reasons for not wishing to do so, for retaining a hermeneutics of suspicion – even as the norms inherent in the practice promote a hermeneutics of faith (see Lefstein 2006).

As you say, changes of direction might indicate a good conversation is happening. 'Sidetracked' would seem to imply a sense of direction in the inquiry, and while that is a common notion in P4C literature, as a facilitator I was trying to suspend my judgement as to what the 'main-track' of the inquiry should be. There were occasional moments where participants commented that 'we keep coming back to …' and at those moments I would try to help the group consider why that was, whether we had attended sufficiently to the thing we returned to and where else we might go.

While facilitating, I sensed that, in session four, the participants had not given as much consideration to the article by Adam Elliot Cooper as they had to the other two articles. In retrospect, I think I may have provided too many texts as a starting point. However, my own position as a non-Black man may also have contributed to my not fully appreciating the strength of feeling that the article quoting Amandla Stenberg's comments about the appropriation of Black features and culture would generate – and the need to give space for articulations of those feelings. So while I may have understood the discussion to be recursive at points, it might be that my understanding was informed by my desire to make some sort of 'philosophical progress', rather than to stay with articulations of upset. Despite my best efforts, I may well have failed to attend sufficiently to the affective dimension of our discussion and how each participant experienced this.

Adam: Final question: Given the way the Dwelling Together project panned out, the funding dynamics and the film's reception, do you think it's the kind of thing you'd consider doing again? The project is hugely valuable, but is it the kind of thing that you, as an educator and researcher, can viably incorporate into your practice?

Darren: In some ways the issue of epistemic exploitation that you identify in the email we used and in the interaction in the film extends to the premise of the film itself. To what extent can it be said to portray philosophical conversations featuring People of

Colour for the educational benefit of a white audience like yourself? A philosophical community of inquiry in the P4C tradition, featuring mostly People of Colour and facilitated by a Person of Colour, is a rare thing – it is not something I have observed at P4C conferences nationally or internationally or seen in the few videos available of P4C practice. Indeed, 'Socrates for Six Year Olds', the BBC documentary (1990) that brought P4C to the attention of the first P4C practitioners in the UK featured Matthew Lipman working with an apparently all-white group of philosophers and then following one of them into an apparently all-Black school in New Jersey where he uses Lipman's materials that make almost no reference to racism. So to some extent the Dwelling Together film addressed a lacuna in the literature, training materials and resources on P4C – but I am opening myself to the charge of positioning People of Colour as educators for white people, in virtue of filming the project.

The film screening was very well attended and the discussions that followed the panel showed that many of those present saw the film as a potentially valuable resource, just as we had hoped. We screened the film on World Philosophy Day 2017, the same day that SAPERE (Society for the Advancement of Philosophical Enquiry and Reflection in Education) held a conference in London. Two of my fellow SAPERE trainers were on the panel and a number of SAPERE trainers were in the audience. All those I spoke to reported that the film gave them plenty to think about. A number of them remarked that they heard ideas expressed that were very new to them and that the film raised questions they had never before considered.

However, take-up since then has been less than the participants, Abigail and I had hoped. Adam, you are a rare example of someone who watched the film and then contacted one of us to respond to it in detail. I think this suggests that we are some way off the theoretically achievable reforms that I identify above. It has led me to consider where I devote my energies with my work in philosophy and dialogue. I have worked on other philosophy projects with highly diverse communities and am confident that philosophical inquiry of the type we attempted in the project holds some promise. I am less confident that many of my P4C colleagues are interested in this work. That may be for any number of reasons – it is far harder to attract funding for work of this kind and it requires a willingness to put even dearly held principles (ground rules, stimuli, suitable content and reasonableness to name just a few) that we hold as P4C practitioner-advocates into question. Working on the project was emotionally demanding as lengthy conversations about racism almost inevitably are. But I think the decision to *film* the project probably added to the emotional demands on all of us – and I remain uncertain as to whether those additional demands were worth it for the participants, for Abigail, and for myself. As Kristie Dotson writes of academic philosophy: 'One has to examine closely who has the burden of destabilizing norms at any given time and whether this is a worthy activity for the targeted populations. Diverse practitioners may disproportionally shoulder it' (Dotson 2012: 15).

It is important to acknowledge that the project benefited me intellectually, giving me an opportunity to philosophize with a more diverse group of adults than I usually encounter in my P4C work and with fewer institutional restrictions. I am sometimes asked by P4C colleagues what can be done to make P4C more inclusive, or diverse or representative of the population. I feel that I have shouldered enough of the burden for now answering that question and I don't feel the slow pace of change is due to a lack of viable solutions. Therefore the next time I am asked 'What can we do?', I shall respond by quoting one of the participants from 'Dwelling Together' – 'I throw that question back to you'.

Acknowledgements

Meghna Gupta, Judith Suissa, UCL Grand Challenges, the panellists for the film screening. Special thanks to all of the participants in the 'Dwelling Together in Diverse Spaces' project.

Notes

1 The UK #HipHopEd Seminar Series was founded by Darren Chetty who co-convenes with PoetCurious. The seminars take the shape of 'dialogic cyphers' involving teachers, hip-hop artists, students, youth-workers and scholars, all with an interest in exploring the intersections of hip hop and education.
2 See https://dwellingtogetherfilm.wordpress.com

References

Applebaum, B., (2010), *Being White, Being Good: White Complicity, White Moral Responsibility, and Social Justice Pedagogy*, Plymouth: Lexington Books.
Armour, J. D., (1997), *Negrophobia and Reasonable Racism*, New York: New York University Press.
Bailey, M., (2010), 'They Aren't Talking About Me ....' *The Crunk Feminist Collection*, [Online], Available at: http://www.crunkfeministcollective.com/2010/03/14/they-arent -talking-about-me/, Accessed 10 January 2019.
Beebee, H., and Saul, J., (2011), 'Women in Philosophy in the UK: A Report by the British Philosophical Association and the Society for Women in Philosophy UK', [Online], Available at: https://www.bpa.ac.uk/uploads/2011/02/BPA_Report_Women_In_Ph ilosophy.pdf, Accessed 10 January 2019.
Berenstain, N., (2016), 'Epistemic Exploitation', *Ergo: An Open Access Journal of Philosophy*, 3 (22): 569–90.
Burbules, N. C., (2000), 'The Limits of Dialogue as Critical Pedagogy', in P. Trifonas (ed.), (2002), *Revolutionary Pedagogies: Cultural Politics, Education, and Discourse of Theory*, 251–73, London: Routledge.
Chetty, D., (2014), 'The Elephant In The Room: Picturebooks, Philosophy For Children And Racism', *Childhood and Philosophy*, 10 (19): 11–31.
Chetty, D., (2018), 'Racism as "Reasonableness": Philosophy for Children and the Gated Community of Inquiry', *Ethics and Education*, 13 (1): 39–54.
Chetty, D., and Suissa, J., (2016), 'No Go Areas' Racism and Discomfort in the Community of Inquiry', *The Routledge International Handbook of Philosophy for Children*, 11–22, London: Routledge.

DiAngelo, R., and Sensoy, Ö., (2014), 'Getting Slammed: White Depictions of Race Discussions as Arenas of Violence', *Race Ethnicity and Education*, 17 (1): 103–28.

Dotson, K., (2011), 'Tracking Epistemic Violence, Tracking Practices of Silencing', *Hypatia*, 26 (2): 236–57.

Dotson, K., (2012), 'How is this paper philosophy?', *Comparative Philosophy*, 3 (1): 3–29.

Eleftheriou-Smith, L. M., (2015), 'Kylie Jenner Criticised by Hunger Games actress Amandla Stenberg for "Appropriating Black Culture" with Cornrows Selfie', [Online], Available at: https://www.independent.co.uk/news/people/kylie-jenner-criticised-by-h unger-games-actress-amandla-stenberg-for-appropriating-black-culture-10384632.ht ml, Accessed 10 January 2019.

Elliott-Cooper, A., (2015), 'Towards a Structural View of Cultural Appropriation', [Online], Available at: https://mediadiversified.org/2015/07/17/beyond-iggy-azalea/, Accessed 10 January 2019.

Kohan, W., (1995), 'The Origin, Nature and Aim of Philosophy in Relation to Philosophy for Children', *Thinking: The Journal of Philosophy for Children*, 12 (2): 25–30.

Laing, R. D., and Esterson, A., (2016), *Sanity, Madness and the Family*, Abingdon: Routledge.

Lefstein, A., (2006), 'Dialogue in Schools: Towards a Pragmatic Approach', *Working Papers in Urban Language and Literacies*, 33, London: King's College London.

Lipman, M., Sharp, A. M., and Oscanyan, F. S., (1980), *Philosophy in the Classroom*, Philadelphia: Temple University Press.

Lorde, A., (2007), *Sister Outsider: Essays and Speeches*, Berkeley: Crossing Press.

Malik, K., (2016), 'The Bane of Cultural Appropriation', Aljazeera, 14 April, [online], Available at: https://www.aljazeera.com/indepth/opinion/2016/04/bane-cultural-a ppropriation-160414080237198.html, Accessed 10 January 2019.

Meghna, G., (2018), 'Dwelling Together', [Online], Available at: https://www.youtube.com/watch?v=y7HMHt6LNu0&t=337s, Accessed 4 January 2019.

Morrison, T., (1975), 'A Humanistic View' in Public Dialogue on the American Dream Theme, Part 2, Panel conducted by the Portland State Black Studies Center, [Online], Available at: https://pdxscholar.library.pdx.edu/orspeakers/90/, Accessed 25 January 2019.

Paul, A., (Director), (1990), *Socrates for Six Year Olds*, [TV programme], BBC, 1990.

Picower, B., (2009), 'The Unexamined Whiteness of Teaching: How White Teachers Maintain and Enact Dominant Racial Ideologies', *Race Ethnicity and Education*, 12 (2): 197–215.

Rainville, N., (2000), 'Philosophy for Children in Native America: A Post-Colonial Critique', *Analytic Teaching*, 21 (1): 65–77.

Reed-Sandoval, A., (2019), 'Can Philosophy for Children Contribute to Decolonization?' *Precollege Philosophy and Public Practice*, 1 (1): 27–41.

Reed-Sandoval, A., and Carmen Sykes, A., (2017), 'Who Talks? Who Listens? Taking Positionality Seriously in Philosophy for Children', in G. Maughn, J. Haynes and K. Murris (eds), *The Routledge International Handbook of Philosophy for Children*, 219–16, New York: Routledge.

Robinson, G., (2016), 'Feeling the Pull: Ethical Enquiry and the Tension It Creates for Teachers', *Analytic Teaching and Philosophical Praxis*, 36 (1): 44–54.

Ukhiphoped, (2018), 'Dwelling Together', Dwelling Together: A Film Talking about Racism, [Online], Available at: https://dwellingtogetherfilm.wordpress.com/, Accessed 4 January 2019.

15

In philosophical conversation with: Undergraduate students and a local school community

Elizabeth Watkins

Introduction

This chapter focuses on the contribution to community philosophy made by undergraduate philosophy students. Most of the chapter will focus on the activities of one cohort of students working in the community of a local primary school as part of the Philosophy Exchange programme at the University of Leeds, UK. On the programme, philosophy students learn to run philosophical enquiries in community settings, including planning and delivering a semester of philosophy sessions while on placement in a Leeds primary school. In this chapter, I will use Leeds Philosophy Exchange as a way of bringing to light a small number of general claims that we can make about undergraduate students' distinct contribution to community philosophy.

I will begin by describing the context in which this takes place, giving the reader an overview of the module, its provenance, aims and structure. Then, through a series of detailed illustrations of the work that students do in this setting, I will explain what I take the main contributions of students to be in the field of community philosophy. Lastly, I will offer a series of critical reflections that touch on why we might think there is an onus on students to do community philosophy, on what philosophical work in the community reveals about philosophy, and its value for both the community and for philosophers.

For the avoidance of confusion, I will explain a few terms that I will use throughout the chapter. First, I use the word 'students' to refer only to university students, and I will typically refer to the schoolchildren involved as 'pupils'. Second, I will often refer to the 'philosophical enquiries' that students run in the classroom. This is shorthand for the 'Community of Philosophical Enquiry', a methodology informed by philosopher John Dewey, and later developed by Mathew Lipman, Ann Sharp and Gareth Mathews in the 1960s and 1970s – and, in this case, given a distinctive form through the module's course leader. These enquiries seek to address a wide range of philosophical issues through caring, collaborative, critical and creative dialogue between peers. The means by which issues are explored in an enquiry is not through teaching the canonical texts, or the positions that famous philosophers took, but by participants exploring their own responses within an open and equal facilitated dialogue with others.

The context of this example of community philosophy

All the experiences related in this chapter stem from the four years I spent as a tutor on the Leeds Philosophy Exchange module. This module for second year undergraduate joint-honours and single-honours philosophy students was designed and led by Grace Lockrobin, Teaching Fellow at the University of Leeds and founder of Thinking Space – a Community Interest Company in the UK. The practice that the course develops reflects the methodology for philosophical enquiry that the course leader has developed through her work with Thinking Space, with a distinct emphasis on using open-ended stimuli to begin an enquiry, and pupils influencing the philosophical content of the sessions, sometimes by formulating questions themselves or by identifying issues they find interesting during the discussion. Another distinctive element of the programme is its breadth: it involves the majority of the school community, with teachers and teaching assistants planning and delivering sessions – both with students and independently – as well as participating in twilight training sessions delivered by the course leader. Therefore, the 'exchange' part of the module title should be understood as a three-way sharing of knowledge and skills between pupils, students and teaching staff.

Course aims and structure

The Leeds Philosophy Exchange module evolved over time in conversation with the staff at the school, with students, tutors and the course leader's own reflections. The aims of the module, however, have remained broadly the same. First, students are expected to be able to understand and articulate key questions, positions and defences within community philosophy – and philosophy with children in particular. These are questions such as 'Can children do philosophy?', 'What is the appropriate role of the facilitator?' and 'What counts as a good stimulus for philosophical enquiry?' Second, they should be able to formulate their own judgements on these issues, and to be able to argue for these in ways that are clear, persuasive and philosophically grounded. Third, students are expected to be able to sustain a semester of planning and delivering weekly philosophical enquiries in the classroom, working reflectively and collaboratively with both their peers and teaching staff throughout the placement. What is more, this practice should be informed by the theoretical questions that students have discussed and on which they have formed positions, as well as by their general understanding of key philosophical issues. And their planning and delivery of philosophical enquiries should explore creative ways to approach philosophy in the classroom that are age-appropriate. In addition to these already weighty objectives, students on the module have also had to weave school curriculum topics into their planning, enabling their philosophical enquiries in the classroom to enhance teaching elsewhere in the pupils' timetables.

As may already be clear, by comparison to most philosophy modules, Philosophy Exchange involves a demanding workload that bridges theory and practice, and requires a high level of professionalism. The course's structure reflects this complexity, being composed of seminars on theory and modelling, observations in the school, weekly placements in the classroom and extended reflection on these, and assessment. In what follows, I briefly outline these aspects of the module.

Seminars

The weekly or bi-weekly seminars serve two main functions: they introduce key issues within community philosophy and philosophy with children via readings and discussion, and they offer an opportunity for the module leader and tutors to model facilitation techniques, and to exemplify the relationship between theory and practice using the students as participants. The seminars are often themed (sometimes via a question), with readings selected to provide a range of perspectives on that theme. The modelling in each seminar is designed to give students a range of basic facilitation skills, an embodied experience of the role of the participant and, importantly, to exemplify how issues within that seminar's theme can arise in the classroom. For example, the theme for a given week might be 'How should philosophical enquiry with children be facilitated and by whom?' The readings include papers such as Karen Murris's 'The Role of the Facilitator in Philosophical Enquiry' (2000) and Samuel Scolnicov's 'Truth, Neutrality and the Philosophy Teacher' (1978). These explore issues including the kind of neutrality facilitators should exhibit, the extent to which the facilitator should interpret pupil responses, and when it is permissible to introduce both procedural and substantive questions. The modelling for this seminar might (among other things) show how summarizing pupils' responses can lead to misinterpretation and how asking simple questions such as 'Can you connect your comment back to the enquiry question?' can develop a discussion, while preserving neutrality.

Observations

Typically scheduled in among the weeks of seminars, students would visit the school to observe the course leader or one of the tutors running an enquiry in a classroom. The enquiry would last up to an hour, and be followed by a reflective discussion where students are asked to identify elements of the enquiry, including identifying the component parts of the session, mapping the philosophical territory covered, and itemizing the facilitation techniques employed, their rationale and effects. Often the questions would focus on making connections to the previous week's seminar question or theme, enabling students to see how the techniques modelled and issues discussed play out in practice.

Placements

The student placements occur in the second semester of the module, and are the point at which students are expected to facilitate, or co-facilitate, their own enquiries in the classroom. Students will be assigned half a class of pupils (around fifteen individuals) and a postgraduate tutor. They will be introduced to the teacher and/or teaching assistants of the class who will work in partnership with them to plan and deliver sessions. For younger pupils, students may only need to plan for twenty-minute enquiries; for the oldest pupils (aged ten or eleven), students will need to cover an hour in the classroom. The placements typically run for eight weeks, with students delivering or co-delivering enquiries with school staff once a week.

To support this process and to ensure the quality of experience for pupils and the students, tutors and the designated teaching staff read through the planning in advance, and reflective discussions are held for half an hour before and after each enquiry. These discussions are an essential part of the placement, as it is here that students are most acutely able to hone their abilities to accurately recall and critically respond to their own facilitation, enabling them to develop as community philosophers.

Assessments

Students are assessed in a variety of ways that reflect the range of emphases in the module. The majority of their marks come from completing an extended essay that combines an account of how they have made progress as a philosophy facilitator (and, of course, what constitutes progress in this field) in ways that make reference to both their practice and the theory. In addition, students are expected to give a presentation that argues for a position on one of the module's key issues, such as 'Should children do philosophy?' Students are also assessed on their classroom practice and planning, though this represents the smallest proportion of their marks to reflect the vagaries of running enquiries with children. Having given an overview of the module, I now turn to consider the precise nature of the work done by students, and the value of this contribution to community philosophy.

The contributions of undergraduate philosophy students to community philosophy

I now explore how undergraduate philosophy students do community philosophy while they are involved in Leeds Philosophy Exchange, and the contribution to community philosophy that this work represents. First, I focus on the 'exchange' part of the module, highlighting the ways in which students develop with, and benefit from, their interaction with the different layers of the school community (pupils, teachers, teaching assistants). Second, I comment on what might be unique about students' contribution to philosophy.

Exchange

The philosophical community with which this chapter is concerned comprised three main groups of people: students, teachers/teaching assistants and pupils. While there is a transmission of knowledge and skill between the course leaders and tutors and these three groups throughout the course, the second semester in the school is particularly oriented towards building connections between the students and the school community, specifically the teaching staff and the pupils.

From their contact with students, pupils develop in ways that we might expect from a little knowledge of what the aims of philosophy with children are, and what an enquiry looks like. They learn new behaviours conducive to having philosophical discussions, such as putting their hands in front of them to express their desire to speak, sitting still, careful listening and making eye contact. Of course, these are behaviours that their teachers expect in every other part of the school day, but there is a greater emphasis on them in philosophical enquiry, as these behaviours are prerequisite for getting a discussion off the ground. In addition, new cognitive demands are made of pupils: they must make connections between their ideas and those of the speakers after them in the discussion; they must be able to explicitly acknowledge and explain the ways that their opinions differ or agree with those of their peers; and they must be able to disagree in ways that are respectful. Pupils' work with students also seeks to introduce a questioning disposition, and provides pupils with opportunities to question everyday concepts like happiness, 'pet-ness' (what makes a pet, a pet) and knowledge. And student-led enquiries offer new ways for pupils to interact with their peers, involving, for instance, a substantial amount of pair- and group-working on subjects such as what it is permissible to do when one is invisible.

The exchange from pupils to students is perhaps more surprising. Some of this transmission comes just by virtue of students working with unfamiliar children, and therefore it is not obviously unique to running philosophical enquiries. For instance, students develop a social intelligence that detects restlessness, a lack of comprehension or emotional sensitivity, and they learn how to appropriately adapt their sessions to cope with these responses. Students also have to become exemplars of the behaviour they seek to foster in their participants, such as careful listening and making eye contact. However, parts of the pupil–student exchange do arise by virtue of students doing *philosophy* in the community. It is important to recognize that the students are only in the second year of their undergraduate philosophy degree – just over halfway through the three years to graduation – and that some of the philosophical problems they are discussing will have come up only recently in their academic study. The relative inexperience of the students in philosophy generally creates a paradoxical effect whereby students are both the 'expert' in the room, while also discovering new positions and new approaches to their subject that can challenge the rules and methods of the academic setting. One example of this would be insights into the value of using personal experience, or the emotions, to inform a response to, or imaginative explorations of, a philosophical scenario. The unorthodox responses of pupils to canonical problems that are traditionally presented (such as running the Ship of Theseus thought experiment) encourages students to critically engage with philosophy as it is taught in the academy, and to make careful judgements as to which philosophical approaches are helpful and to be valued in community and academic settings. This can lead students either to adapt their methods, for instance, by using role-play to explore the trolley problem, or to abandon their lecture content in favour of discussions that relate more directly to pupils' experiences, such as how we know that the tooth fairy doesn't exist.

The range of responses from pupils can also challenge facilitators' assumptions and reveal the value of thorough planning. For instance, a session on gender that was premised on pupils having strong intuitions about the different personality traits, hobbies and career choices of women and men, found the children argued vehemently from the outset that there were no such distinctions to be drawn: that football was for girls as much as it was for boys, and that boys should be allowed to wear dresses if they liked. This overturned the students' expectations of the pupils' understanding of, and investment in, gender issues, forcing the students to think on their feet and to improvise appropriately.

Another important channel of exchange is between students and the teacher or teacher assistant with whom they are paired. Here students benefit from the classroom experience of teachers, who in their interventions during philosophical enquiries demonstrate key insights into reading children's behaviour and behaviour management. Perhaps more substantially, students are able to consult with their teacher or teaching assistant on how to pitch their sessions in ways that relate to their group's experience and understanding, and how to draw on the more able members of the group in ways that support, rather than shut out or discourage, the contributions of other pupils. Through their planning conversations with teachers, students also develop a sense of whether or not a subject is too sensitive (e.g. death or the existence of God), too advanced or too basic. Teachers are also able to shed light on their curriculum and to help students develop an angle on a topic that will complement their teaching and be interesting to pupils. For example, when pupils were studying the Egyptians, students devised a session that centred on the ethics of archaeology (as this practice was understood at the time of discovering Tutankhamen's tomb), focusing on the question: 'Was Howard Carter a grave robber?' And when it was run in the classroom, the teaching assistant was able to introduce key characters, their actions and facts that the children had studied, and that motivated and made specific some of the more abstract philosophical questions the session explored.

Since the module's pilot in 2011, teachers at this particular school have been independently practising as community philosophers in their school setting. This considerable experience has made them exemplars in a range of ways, including good philosophical behaviour on the part of the facilitator and developing appropriate philosophical content. One teacher in particular was exemplary for students in his ability to combine neutrality – the asking of concise questions that expanded the discussion – and a caring manner.

The exchange from students to teachers and teaching assistants takes four main forms. First, prior to their involvement with Leeds Philosophy Exchange, many teachers will typically have had no formal training in philosophy. Therefore, one obvious, but important, form of transmission is a general understanding of how to get onto philosophical terrain, or what makes something philosophical, as well as knowledge of particular canonical problems. This occurs through involvement in students' planning, exploration of philosophical issues in the classroom and the twilight training they attend with students. For example, the nature of time and epistemological questions about testimony will be new to many teachers, as will the idea that one can have a philosophical discussion about whether or not a teapot can be a pet, or whether ants should have more rights than chimpanzees. The teachers' and teaching assistants' input into connecting curriculum topics and student enquiries enables them to help discern the philosophical potential in their curricula, revealing philosophy in a piecemeal way that can also introduce new approaches to their topics.

Second, the particular language, techniques and desired outcomes of effective facilitation can help refine and develop teachers' own methodologies for pupils' learning in the classroom. Of course, teachers and teaching assistants are already aware of many different methodologies they can employ in the classroom and through which their pupils can learn – the considered self-effacement that facilitation involves is unlikely to be a new idea to them. However, the degree to which neutrality on the part of the facilitator is required, and the consistency with which this should be exercised, can extend teachers' insight. The presence of students can also introduce a new language for facilitation. Questions such as 'Can you expand on that?'; 'Could you tell us what made you think of that?'; 'How does that connect to the previous comments?' and 'Can you connect that thought to the question?', as well as the emphasis on giving examples, counterexamples and drawing distinctions, are essential parts of the students' philosophical toolkit. These can illuminate new methods of opening up pupils' engagement in the classroom without overly directed interventions on the part of the teacher or teaching assistant.

Third, through sharing the planning and delivery of student enquiries, as well as leading their own enquiries independently, teachers are better able to run an effective philosophy session. This includes how to choose an appropriate concept and stimulus; how to structure the session; how to anticipate responses and keep attention on the philosophical issue. In co-delivered sessions, teachers get to witness and contribute to the students' on-the-job training, as the latter group wrestles with the choices they have to make for the delivery of any one enquiry. And while teachers bring a huge amount of insight and knowledge to this process – particularly about what will best engage pupils and about behaviour management – they also learn, through discussing and developing students' materials, as well as creating their own, about the different phases through which an enquiry can pass. They come to appreciate how you might justify the choice of a given storybook above a thought experiment for getting at the concept of happiness, for instance, and they see how the planning plays out in practice. In this last sense, teachers get to learn through their own mistakes and through the students' successes and mistakes in co-delivered sessions. For instance, a well-structured session that focused on the concept of compassion failed to generate much response because the pupils did not have a sufficiently well-developed understanding of this term; this was not recognized in time for the students to explore its definition and generate examples in ways that could have rescued the enquiry.

Philosophy with School and University Students 223

In some cases, what teachers gain from their involvement in Leeds Philosophy Exchange is the opportunity to see their pupils in a setting that reveals new facets of their character and abilities. Because philosophical enquiry offers opportunities for pupils to interact in ways that may be different to normal classroom practice, it can reveal confidence, shyness, new opinions and team-working abilities that were disguised or hidden from the teachers up to that point.

Effects

The exchanges detailed earlier had a variety of effects on the school community, and I note in the later sections a few of the most prominent changes. Teachers have remarked that the behaviours demanded of pupils in philosophy sessions bleed out into their everyday encounters with pupils and school staff. For instance, one teacher commented that when he is having a conversation with pupils to settle disputes among them, pupils will put out their hands to register their desire to contribute to the discussion in the same way that they do in philosophy sessions. A further outcome of running the programme in the school has been the development of some exceptionally strong philosophy facilitators among the teaching staff. Through their training and exposure to students over many years, some teachers have mastered what makes a discussion philosophical, as well as how to be a good philosophy facilitator. This enables teachers not just to be exemplars in using social intelligence and behaviour management (among other techniques), but also to demonstrate best practice in facilitating philosophy in ways from which students can directly learn. While it is impossible to quantify the effect on pupils of this sustained presence of philosophy within their school community, it is simply a fact that pupils have had exposure, across their primary school life, to some of the substantive issues that are of import to humans, and, to varying extents, have cultivated a range of dispositions conducive to philosophical discussion.

The distinctiveness of students' contribution to community philosophy

Students engage in community philosophy on the Leeds Philosophy Exchange programme from a unique perspective. For the majority of individuals, they will be only a year or two into their undergraduate education in philosophy, and have experienced the majority of this learning through the standard university methods (seminars, lectures and essays). The Philosophy Exchange programme demands that they develop new approaches to philosophical problems with which they may have only recently become familiar, and that they are willing to explore new philosophical territory in ways that are engaging for children.

In spite of these considerable challenges, one of the key contributions that students make is in demonstrating the range of philosophical issues that can be meaningfully tackled through dialogue in the community. In many years of the programme, students have chosen their own concepts, stimuli and questions, and structured these into session plans in ways that reveal new territory for philosophical work in the community. Students have revealed the possibilities for dialogue on ideas including the place of robots in human society; what makes an ideal school; gender theory; making sport fair; and the difference between humans and other animals.

I think there is something distinct in students' contribution by virtue of them being both students and students of philosophy. And it cuts both ways in the sense that some students' relative inexperience of philosophy can lead to their increasing enthusiasm and confidence with the course sessions plans or, in some cases, creating and testing their own materials, as well as finding it deeply rewarding when they get profound and surprising responses from pupils. In other cases, this inexperience can lead to insufficiently well-formed ideas on what philosophy is, and what it ought to do in the community setting, as well as an understanding of the material insufficient for handling the often unphilosophical and tangential responses that working with non-philosophers typically (and understandably) forces you to negotiate. On the whole, being a philosophy student in a community setting lends itself to a sense of collaborative learning of myriad kinds. Students develop their understanding of philosophy, and what this could look like in a community setting, simultaneously with pupils and teaching staff. Of course, the students have a head start here that can enable them to steer the sessions with more confidence.

Students get to see issues that have been thoroughly covered in their lecture halls and seminar rooms come to life in surprising ways through the minds of people much younger than themselves. This enables them to develop and refine well-grounded perspectives on what might distinguish academic and community philosophy. Relatedly, assumptions about the methodology of philosophy that are often implicit or poorly argued for within academic departments of analytic philosophy are constantly challenged by pupils' responses in the classroom. The use of subjective experience, including the imagination and emotions ('But I would feel closer to my sister than I would do to the person drowning in the pond'), as well as moving from specific examples to general claims ('My computer is intelligent because it remembers all the things I tell it') are such commonplace occurrences in the community setting that an appraisal or re-appraisal of their place in philosophical study more generally is almost inevitable. More so than those philosophers who have not worked in community settings, Philosophy Exchange students are excellently positioned to challenge and reformulate the dominant claims about how philosophy ought to be done.

Critical reflections: The onus on philosophy students

The conclusion of this chapter brings together the various strands of the preceding sections through an exploration of the question, 'To what extent is there an onus on students to apply their academic training in philosophy to the community setting?' I argue that there is an onus on students to share the skills and knowledge they have acquired – through their academic training in philosophy – with the non-academic community. I explore three grounds for this: the egalitarian approach to education,

Philosophy with School and University Students 225

preventing obsolescence in philosophy, and the rehabilitation of philosophy into public life. A demand for outreach opportunities can also be made to philosophy departments on similar grounds, and I will touch on the differences and similarities between these cases.

The egalitarian approach to education

Currently philosophy is only studied, practised and experienced by a minority of people. This is particularly true in the UK, which does not have a strong tradition of teaching philosophy in schools, unlike countries where it is a mandatory part of the curriculum. That philosophy ought to be made open to more people can be argued for as a variant on equal access to opportunities for all, as inspired by the second part of John Rawls's principle:

Social and economic inequalities are to be arranged so that they are both:

a) such as to offer the greatest benefit to the least advantaged, consistent with the just saving principle, and

b) *attached to offices and positions open to all under conditions of fair equality of opportunity* (1971: 302, italics added).

My approach is premised on three claims:

1. That part of satisfying the idea that opportunities (jobs, hobbies and social roles) can be open to anyone is that we all have access to the same levels of education. That's to say, it is an important facet of creating more equal access to opportunity that everyone has access to more or less the same core skills and other educational resources that enable them to thrive in the life they have chosen.
2. That philosophy represents a unique and powerful contribution to any set of educational resources. At the foundational level, philosophy teaches you to think more clearly, and to be able to communicate this thought well. It gives you the confidence to stand back from the many issues that life throws at you and to consider them fully. In addition, it offers frameworks that can guide us in very particular and important scenarios, such as when we consider starting a relationship, choosing a job, having children, or getting treatment for an illness. No other subject gives such foundational skills that can be utilized in so many different circumstances, and that offer substantive ways of structuring our options on how to live.
3. That currently philosophy is only enjoyed by a minority of people, therefore giving them an advantage in thinking about their lives.

Philosophy students are in the position of understanding the subject sufficiently to begin imparting their knowledge to others, while having the time to do this. It is a

226   *Philosophy and Community*

ripe opportunity to share these essentials skills with others who may have not had the
chance to develop these skills or to consider philosophical issues. Another facet to
consider is that university students still represent a privileged group of people among
the population at large, and that this creates an onus based on their relative life chances
by virtue of having studied at university, relative to those who did not.

Preventing obsolescence in philosophy

Philosophy is often accused of concerning itself with abstract issues that bear little or
no connection to ordinary life, and that no one other than academic philosophers care
about. There may be some truth to this claim, though the subject is rapidly changing
as the demographic of philosophers becomes more diverse, and the funding bases for
university research shift to encourage research that has a well-defined application.
There are two ways in which students help create and maintain strong links between
philosophy and the choices faced by most people in the world we live in. First, this
can happen by working in the community and introducing philosophy to new people
– in this case, children and the school staff the students work alongside. The work
of students enables non-philosophers to feel the pull of philosophical issues, and
to explore these using examples from their own lives. In doing so, students build
intellectual bridges between the academic subject and the wider world. This comes
from getting into the classroom and running engaging philosophical enquiries with
people who would otherwise probably not have encountered the subject in any
substantial way. Philosophy becomes relevant to them through its power to engage
them both emotionally and cognitively. Second, students will explore a wide range of
issues over the course of their placement, many of which will have strong bearing on
the participants' and facilitators' everyday experience. The work in the classroom may
lead to a progressively more philosophical approach to everyday issues. But it can also
enable pupils, students and staff to realize the philosophical nature of choices that they
may have already made, or thoughts they may have had (e.g. the grounds for their
family becoming vegetarian or why they always trust the internet more than Dad to
help them with geography homework).

Philosophy's image problem

Another charge that is often levelled at academic philosophy is that it is dominated
by white men, in the matter of both who teaches the subject and what is taught.
There is much truth to this claim as only 19 per cent of UK philosophy professors are
female, lower than the 45 per cent of female undergraduates (British Philosophical
Association 2011), and, as an example, only 3 per cent of authors listed in the Stanford
Encyclopaedia of Philosophy are of a non-white racial background (Schwitzgebel
2014). In the United States, only 0.32 per cent of US authors of research publications in
top philosophy journals are black (Bright 2016), with only 1.32 per cent black faculty

staff in philosophy departments (Botts et al. 2014). This has led to recent student-led campaigns for greater diversity in philosophy departments, both independently of and within the wider 'Why Is My Curriculum White?' campaign run by the National Union of Students in the UK. International student organizations such as Minorities and Philosophy have also sought to increase the diversity of what is taught in the academy and of who it is taught by and the range of people who benefit from it.

Students working in the community, many of whom will be under twenty-five, female and of non-white races, can sow the seeds for a different perception of philosophy in ways that encourage a greater diversity of people to engage with the subject throughout their life. Students can pre-emptively stamp out the perception that the doors of philosophy departments are only open to white men. Just through their presence as philosophers in the classroom, they have the power to shape children's first impressions of philosophers, and to create positive role models that encourage a greater diversity of people to pursue the subject. In addition, the pupils of the school at the centre of this chapter are very diverse in terms of income, race and religion. Therefore, this diversity of young people experiencing philosophy in a sustained and inclusive manner can help disturb any perception – existing or potential – that philosophy is not for them, and to generally foster an empowered positive perception of the subject.

Conclusion

This chapter has focused on one group of adults – undergraduate students in philosophy at the University of Leeds – and their contribution to community philosophy, focusing in particular on the community within a primary school in Leeds. In addition to giving an overview of the module's aims, structure and the input of the school as well as the university, this chapter laid out the complex forms of knowledge and skills exchanged between the course leader and tutors, the students, teachers, teaching assistants and pupils. The chapter has also explored what I take to be the distinctiveness of the students' contribution to community philosophy, in particular the way that they are able to develop new approaches for doing philosophy in community settings, and how philosophical work in a school community enables students to take a critical stance on the nature of both community and academic philosophy generally. My conclusion is that there are strong reasons for philosophy students to do this work in the community. Despite the academic discipline of philosophy being often perceived as largely irrelevant to modern life, as well as the preserve of those who have long dominated our society, my contention is that that philosophy in community settings is a vital resource from which everyone could benefit.

References

Botts, T. M., Bright, L. K., Cherry, M., Mallarengeng, G., and Spencer, Q., (2014), 'What Is the State of Blacks in Philosophy?', *Critical Philosophy of Race*, 2 (2): 224–42.

Bright, L., (2016), 'Publications by Black Authors in Leiter Top 15 Journals 2003–2012', [Online], Available at: https://schwitzsplinters.blogspot.co.uk/2016/01/publications-by-black-authors-in-leiter.html, Accessed 31 January 2019.

British Philosophical Association (2011), *Women in Philosophy in the UK*, London: British Philosophical Association.

Murris, K., (2000), 'The role of the Facilitator', *Thinking: The Journal of Philosophy for Children*, 15 (2): 40–6.

Rawls, J., (1971), *A Theory of Justice*, Cambridge, MA: Harvard University Press.

Schwitzgebel, E., (2014), 'Citation of Women and Ethnic Minorities' in the Stanford Encyclopaedia of Philosophy', 7 August 2014, [Online], Available at: https://schwitzsplinters.blogspot.co.uk/2014/08/citation-of-women-and-ethnic-minorities.html, Accessed 31 January 2019.

Scolnicov, S., (1978), 'Truth, Neutrality and the Philosophy Teacher', in M. Lipman and A. M. Sharp (eds), *Growing Up with Philosophy*, 392–405, Philadelphia: Temple University Press.

16

In philosophical conversation with: Adolescents in a behavioural health unit

Alissa Hurwitz Swota and Michael De La Hunt

The death of curiosity is not inevitable.

(Fisher 2011)

The practice of medicine is a deeply ethical one. Complex philosophical issues permeate every unit of the hospital with increasing regularity. Not only are healthcare providers faced with difficult ethical issues; patients and families confront such vexing issues as well. On the adolescent behavioural unit at our hospital, we have developed a group called 'Thinking Together', dedicated to exploring some of the deep philosophical issues our patients grapple with both in and out of the hospital setting.

Adolescent behavioural health unit

Prior to exploring our Thinking Together group, it is important to understand the structure and composition of our adolescent behavioural health unit. We have both an inpatient and a partial hospitalization programme (or alternatively called Day Stay; hereafter PHP). Our inpatient unit is a fourteen-bed unit, while PHP can have as many as ten patients at a time. Participants generally range in age from twelve to seventeen years old, though younger patients have been admitted to the inpatient part of the unit. Patients are male, female and transgendered; come from urban, suburban and rural homes; and have varying religious, ethnic and cultural backgrounds, leading to a wide variation in psychosocial diversity. We feel that such diversity enhances the community dynamic of the Thinking Together group discussions.

Patients on the two units (inpatient and PHP) typically have one or more of the following diagnoses:

1. Mood and/or anxiety disorders.
2. History of self-injurious and/or suicidal symptoms.
3. Substance use.

4. Trauma history.
5. Parent–child relational problems.
6. Adjustment disorder in response to various psychosocial stressors.
7. Autism spectrum disorder.
8. Eating disorder.
9. Psychotic disorder.
10. Disruptive behaviour disorder.
11. Co-morbid significant medical illness.

We may exclude patients who are not felt to be appropriate based on the severity of their illness; ability to tolerate group interactions; age; immaturity; degree of developmental delay; or due to safety concerns. Interestingly, Fisher notes that 'what a child lacks is experience, not the capacity to think about and discuss things. But children need very little experience to be able to discuss some of the important issues of life' (Fisher 2011). In our group, unfortunately, it is often the case that the children have experienced things with which no one should ever become acquainted. These experiences provide the children in our group privileged insights and unique perspectives on the issues we discuss. It is these experiences that create an environment in which the children are, in large part, the teachers. In this chapter we will describe how Thinking Together fits within the overall adolescent behavioural health programme, provide detailed examples of what we discuss in our group, and explore possible ways to enhance our current programme as we move forward.

Group philosophy

Driving this group is the idea that children and adolescents are naturally very insightful, and ought to be given the opportunity to wonder and engage with seemingly common concepts on a deeper level. The foundation of the group is built, in large part, on the same basis as that of philosophy for children. It is built on the goal of carving out a space where children and adolescents are encouraged to ask 'why?'. They are encouraged to ask and explore philosophical questions, 'questions ... about our ideas or concepts of the world – about what we think and believe ... questions about what we think about the way we make sense of life as human beings' (Fisher 2011). By exploring issues that are relevant to the participants, the group provides a space for members to think together, to ask questions of one another, and hopefully, to gain greater awareness of, and appreciation for, the difficulties they may be facing. Extended, thoughtful wondering, requests for reasons to support claims, and critical engagement with peers is the landscape for Thinking Together.

Thinking Together creates an atmosphere of intellectual stimulation and challenges the adolescent patients to think of their life issues in ways foreign to many of the participants. We have found that teenagers are very responsive to, and engaged in, our group discussions. Often, in the discussions, teenagers find direct applications to the issues that they struggle with by virtue of being a teen, including issues of existentialism,

Philosophy with Adolescents in a Behavioural Health Unit 231

resiliency, trust, anger, personal identity, heroism, loneliness, variations on the issue of power, and many other topics. These discussions not only serve as a means of drawing out the patients to become involved in a lively group discussion but actually give voice to many of the issues with which they struggle. As Matthew Lipman notes in the context of education:

> We expect the pupil to find clear and unambiguous meanings in contexts which are rich in indirection and allusiveness. ... But we do not teach him to think about thinking, although he is capable of doing so and would be interested in doing so. We do not sufficiently encourage him to think for himself, to form independent judgments, to be proud of his personal insights, to be pleased with his prowess in reasoning ... the fashion is now to encourage the child to feel, to be sensitive – having first armored him against feelings and anesthetized him against sensations. But we do not trust him to think. (Lipman 1976: 7–9)

We have discovered that our discussions during Thinking Together prompt thoughtful responses from participants and validate the struggles they have experienced. Thinking Together not only is useful in engaging with patients but actually augments their acceptance of other therapeutic interactions, and their response to psychotherapy and treatment interventions. In short, the discussions help patients to feel 'proud of [their] personal insights, [and] to be pleased with [their] prowess in reasoning' (Lipman 1976: 9).

Group structure

Thinking Together is held once a week in both the inpatient and outpatient adolescent behavioural health units. Attendance is optional, but strongly encouraged for appropriate patients as part of their unit programming and overall treatment plan. Although their attendance is strongly encouraged, out of respect for their burgeoning autonomy and in an effort to create a natural dynamic of community participation based upon each attendee's level of comfort, their participation in the discussion is completely voluntary. Participants sit around a table in a circular group arrangement that encourages each participant to feel comfortable and of equal status. Discussion is initiated by the group leader who introduces a topic. As the session progresses, the group leader monitors participation in the discussion and makes attempts to elicit comments from each of the group participants in a non-threatening, non-forceful manner, respecting the patient's degree of comfort, autonomy and self-awareness. Efforts are made to redirect the focus to other patients if a particular individual begins to monopolize the discussion, or if a patient is noted to be withdrawing from active participation.

During our one-hour meetings, the group leader begins by introducing herself. She lets the group know that she is not a therapist, and that the primary goal of the group is to have a good discussion. The group leader identifies herself to the group as

232 *Philosophy and Community*

a 'co-inquirer', guiding them in their Thinking Together discussion. Next, the group leader asks the patients to introduce themselves, and to name their favourite band or musician as a means of encouraging participants to participate. Having the group members feel comfortable engaging with one another is crucial to creating momentum for furthering the discussion.

The group leader then introduces the topic for discussion. This may be done by the group leader simply stating that she has been wondering about an issue lately. For instance, the group leader may begin a conversation on anger by noting, 'I noticed a woman in a store the other day who seemed to get really angry at another woman nearby for no apparent reason; I began to wonder if anger is always a bad thing? If not, when would anger be a good thing? Is it both a bad and good thing, and if so, how can that be?' Topics may also be introduced by the group leader (or chosen member) reading out loud a quotation or a passage relevant to the day's discussion After this introduction, the group leader prompts responses from the group on what the passage or quotation means to them. To progress the discussion, additional quotations, stories or passages may be introduced. Throughout the hour, the group leader steps in and out of the discussion to introduce new quotations, add comments, deflect the discussion to various participants to ensure their engagement, or sometimes to highlight relevance to philosophical theories. The group leader may also remain silent to encourage the patients to talk among themselves with limited interference or commentary, all while being mindful of the time left of the session.

About five to ten minutes before the end of the hour, the group leader starts the process of winding down the discussion, identifying that time is almost up, and encouraging any final comments. A question posed by the group leader at the end of almost every session to all participants is 'What is one thing you might remember or that really struck you from our discussion?' During this brief 'wrapping up' the group leader may sometimes add a thoughtful commentary, but will always thank the participants both for engaging in discussion and for trusting one another enough to share what are often difficult, personal stories.

Topics

In an effort to give perspective to the reader on how a Thinking Together group works, we provide the following examples of actual session topics that we have held on our units. There are numerous examples that could be used, but we have selected several concept topics that are not only appropriate for philosophy for children in general, but are also especially well suited as topics for discussion with adolescents in a mental health programme. The discussions are illustrative of philosophy for children in terms of methodology and content. With regard to the former, the group leader builds discussions around clarifying complex concepts, pressing participants to provide and weigh reasons for their various claims, and teasing out different perspectives in order to gain a robust understanding of the topic at issue.[1] In terms of content, discussions aim to better understand vexing concepts, helping participants

Resilience

In our group we focus on topics that are relevant to the group members. Members of our groups have come to hospital after facing some of the most difficult times of their young lives. Resilience is one of the most popular topics to discuss in group. We begin discussion by asking if anyone in the group has ever heard of the word 'resilience', and then proceed to tease out what the word means. Ages of patients can range from twelve to seventeen years. As such it is not uncommon for some members to be unfamiliar with the concept. Beginning with conceptual clarification – a starting point that is often employed in philosophical writings – the group works together to come up with a working understanding of the concept 'resilience'. Patients familiar with resilience often describe it as 'bouncing back', usually after facing a difficult time or situation. After establishing a working definition of the concept, the discussion has often centred on whether or not the individuals in the group consider themselves to be resilient. This part of the discussion focuses on self-awareness, and pushes participants to do the difficult philosophical work of articulating their own conception of themselves with particular regard to the characteristic of resilience.

In light of the context in which the discussion takes place, it is fascinating to listen to group members self-report on this issue. Keeping in line with a philosophical discussion, instead of stopping at the level of self-reporting, we go on to explore why they do or do not consider themselves to be resilient. That is, participants are pressed for reasons to support their self-conceptions, engaging in a sort of meta-analysis of themselves. Interestingly, some participants have noted that they think that, by definition, they are resilient because they faced a difficult time (i.e. the issue(s) that brought them to the behavioural health unit) and have come to the programme for help. At the same time, participants have noted that they do not consider themselves resilient precisely because they are in our programme. Pointing out how the same situation can be interpreted in different ways lends itself well to exploring how difficult issues can take on new meaning when viewed from a different perspective. In addition to asking if group members consider themselves to be resilient, the group leader presses group members further by asking them if they believe that others would consider them to be resilient. Probing in this way pushes group members to try and see themselves as others might see them, testing the limits of their capacity for abstraction. If differences are noticed in how individuals see themselves, as opposed to how others might view them, these are then explored. Group members are asked why they reached the conclusions they did, and are encouraged to be reflective about their conclusions. Making thoughtful, clear assertions and then backing them up with reasons is a mainstay in philosophy. It is also a consistent component of our group practice. Rather than getting frustrated when pressed for rationales, or when asked to clarify a thought, patients have typically

234 *Philosophy and Community*

risen to the occasion, asking for more time to reflect instead of 'passing' on providing such insights.

This interaction between leader and participants is meant to convey to the group participants the importance not only of one's own perspective but also of a larger community, through both deeper introspection and consideration of potential alternative viewpoints. It is akin to other therapeutic group activities in which a person's viewpoint is challenged with reality-testing; but it is different from individual therapy and traditional group therapy in that the topic has philosophical content rather than focusing on psychopathology issues and concerns. It encourages group attendees to contribute their viewpoints to the discussion, providing a more comprehensive democratic community perspective in an effort to have individuals further develop their own thinking skills, as well as appreciating the opinions and perspectives of other participants with differing developmental, psychosocial, ethnic and cultural backgrounds.

A question commonly asked by the group leader is, 'What do you think the trajectory of resilience looks like?' or 'What does it look like to be resilient?'. The group leader then goes on to clarify by asking whether, in order to be considered resilient, one faces a difficult time and then 'bounces back' quickly on a constant, upward slope. Can one rightfully be considered resilient if their path rises and then flattens out before continuing to rise again? Might one's trajectory include some valleys amid an overall upward rise? The group leader often uses questions, poems and short stories during discussions. The following quotation is one used when wondering about resilience and what a resilient trajectory might look like:

> For many years a tree might wage a slow and silent warfare against an encumbering wall, without making any visible progress. One day the wall would topple – not because the tree had suddenly laid hold upon some supernormal energy, but because its patient work of self-defense and self-release had reached fulfillment. The long-imprisoned tree had freed itself. Nature had had her way. (Douglas 1999: 294)

Examining this quotation allows group members to examine resilience in terms of the speed at which one 'bounces back' after a difficult situation. That is, is resilience something on which there is a time limit of sorts? If 'progress' in the bouncing back process is slow in coming, is one no longer to be considered resilient? Even more, it presses participants to think about how they understand progress and what 'bouncing back' looks like in their own lives. When discussing what progress looks like on the way to bouncing back, participants often note that when progress is measured with a large yardstick, one is deemed to have progressed only when leaps and bounds have been accomplished. Such a long perspective can be disheartening. Instead, we think about reframing our understanding of what constitutes progress. Rather than viewing progress as attending and enjoying a party, or making it through an entire year at school, for some participants simply getting out of bed in the morning is a big step. For others, making it into school is a monumental feat. Understood in this way, progress is more attainable,

Philosophy with Adolescents in a Behavioural Health Unit 235

and the idea that participants may in fact be making progress and may be more resilient than they first thought, provides a tincture of hope and a seed of confidence.

Self-identity

One of the most well-received topics we discuss in Thinking Together centres on the complex philosophical concept of self-identity. After introductions of group members and group leader, the discussion begins with the following quotation from a well-known children's book, *The Velveteen Rabbit*:

> 'Real isn't how you are made,' said the Skin Horse. 'It's a thing that happens to you. When a child loves you for a long, long time, not just to play with, but REALLY loves you, then you become Real.'
>
> 'Does it hurt?' asked the Rabbit.
>
> 'Sometimes', said the Skin Horse, for he was always truthful. 'When you are Real you don't mind being hurt.'
>
> 'Does it happen all at once, like being wound up', he asked, 'or bit by bit?'
>
> 'It doesn't happen all at once', said the Skin Horse. 'You become. It takes a long time. That's why it doesn't happen often to people who break easily, or have sharp edges, or who have to be carefully kept. Generally, by the time you are Real, most of your hair has been loved off, and your eyes drop out and you get loose in the joints and very shabby. But these things don't matter at all, because once you are Real you can't be ugly, except to people who don't understand.' (Williams 1991: 5–6)

After reading the quotation the group leader asks the rest of the group what they think about it. Often group members note that they liked the passage. They are then pressed to say why they liked it and what part they liked the best. This again demonstrates the need for, and importance of, providing reasons for claims that are made. More often than not, group members note that they like the last part of the quotation best, 'But these things don't matter at all, because once you are Real you can't be ugly, except to people who don't understand.' Questions surrounding whether or not group members have anyone in their lives who knows the 'Real' them are broached. If a group member says that there is someone in his/her life that knows the 'Real' him/her, then they are pressed to try and articulate how that person would describe them. Some group members find the words come easily when thinking of how others perceive their true, Real self. Other group members struggle, getting stuck on how to engage their capacity for abstraction and determine how someone else might view the Real them.

A frequent follow-up question is, 'Do you know the Real you?' Wondering if you know yourself, truly know yourself, is a profound, deeply philosophical activity. One of the most interesting things that come up during this discussion is when a group member maintains that someone knows who she *really* is, but then goes on to claim that she herself does not. Epistemological questions emerge, such as 'How can you maintain that someone else knows the Real you if you do not know the Real you?', and 'How do you know if someone is correct about how they would describe the Real you, if you claim not to have knowledge of the Real you?' Group members are then lead to grapple with complex philosophical issues such as how one knows something. Further, if they believe that someone else knows the Real them, does it follow that they must have at least some insight into their true selves as well? Rather than meeting such difficult questions with frustration, group members – with rare exceptions – rise to the challenge. A common response from participants is that they are continually getting to know who they Really are; that figuring themselves out is a work in progress. Such insights are astute and lead to questions such as 'If you had to describe the Real you at present, what would you say?' Prompting participants again, especially after recognizing that their understanding of themselves can and likely will change over time, usually produces additional responses.

As participants are working through the difficult identity questions posed by the *Velveteen Rabbit* quotation, we often begin to consider why it is that there are so few others who know the Real us. Often a question arises as to whether others don't know the Real us because we are slow to reveal who we truly are, or because it takes a lot of time to get to know who someone truly is, or simply because others may not invest the effort to make such a determination. Might it be some combination of these factors, or something altogether different? Another hypothesis that group members have proposed is that it takes courage to reveal your Real self to others. When this hypothesis comes up, the group leader takes the opportunity to introduce this short poem by Shel Silverstein:

> She had blue skin,
> And so did he.
> He kept it hid
> And so did she.
> They searched for blue
> Their whole life through,
> Then passed right by –
> And never knew. (Silverstein 2011: 20)

Using this poem helps to get group members to wonder what their 'blue skin' might be. Responses to the question 'What is your "blue skin"?' have included everything from 'Everyone thinks I am really tough on the outside, but I am really scared about what others think of me' to 'People think I am so funny and really happy, but I use humor to cover the fact that I am really sad'. These responses came from participants who interpreted 'blue skin' to be something about themselves that they hid from others. These participants talked about how tiresome it was to keep their 'blue skin', hidden, to keep their 'mask' up. Comfort was found by recognizing that others in the group felt similarly: others in the group had 'blue skin' as well.

Philosophy with Adolescents in a Behavioural Health Unit

Discussions about 'blue skin' allow us to explore notions of self-acceptance, and the long, hard process of allowing yourself to open up and reveal your 'blue skin'. Putting oneself in a position of being vulnerable is a frightening proposition. For someone who has an anxiety disorder or trauma history, beginning the hard work of allowing others to get to know the Real them, to be vulnerable, is even more complex.

Teasing out an awareness of the potential payoffs of opening themselves up to others, such as true friendship and finding someone who 'gets you', is a wonderful realization to come to during our discussion. It also opens the participants to consider defining themselves beyond their own skin colour. The teenage years are an important stage of developing one's personal identity. Given today's societal cultural emphasis on ethnicity, and identity based upon skin colour, this discussion introduces a theme of self-identity using hypothetical 'blue skin colour' as an abstract metaphor for something a person identifies with, rather than how one actually appears or what one is born with. This allows more general considerations, and a greater sense of community based on personal identification, rather than phenotypic appearance or group assignment based upon cultural norms.

Moving forward

Our discussions in Thinking Together may focus on the concept of trust, using the Lemony Snicket quotation, 'Deciding whether or not to trust a person is like deciding whether or not to climb a tree because you might get a wonderful view from the highest branch, or you might simply get covered in sap, and for this reason many people choose to spend their time alone and indoors where it is harder to get a splinter' (Snicket 2005: 14–15). They may focus on the concept of loneliness, using the Robin Williams quotation, 'I used to think that the worst thing in life was to end up alone. It's not. The worst thing in life is to end up with people who make you feel alone.'[2]

Regardless of the topic, Thinking Together has provided a time and space where patients can learn from one another and engage in deep, thoughtful, reasoned discussions about a wide variety of topics. Patients are pressed to identify and question their assumptions, be mindful of what follows from their statements, and grapple with concepts they may have thought straightforward at one time. Such activities and ways of working to understand oneself and the world are at the heart of philosophical inquiry. The work that is done in group is difficult, making the fact that it is ranked as one of the favourite groups by patients even more impressive. Thinking Together helps patients gain self-confidence speaking in a group of their peers, something not often come by in the age group at issue. Another important consequence of our group is the realization that one often learns more from disagreement than agreement. Emerging out of the group is a sense of community among participants, an awareness that they are not alone in their struggles, and a recognition that the difficult work of engaging with others around complex issues is extremely beneficial. Ultimately, during almost every group, the group leader walks away with the privilege of having gained valuable insights from the group members.

Limitations

Not infrequently, group members disagree with one another. It is imperative that group members are aware of and appreciate that disagreement is something that will make the discussion better. Hopefully, participants gain an appreciation of the fact that disagreement is not synonymous with, nor does it entail, disrespect. While disagreement is looked on favourably, disrespectfulness is not tolerated. It is incumbent upon the group leader to create a space where wondering and questioning can occur, and members don't feel threatened when faced with opposition. This is difficult to do in a setting where group members have mental health issues, including trauma histories, mood disorders, self-esteem issues or disruptive behaviours disorders. It is critical to the functioning of the discussion that the group leader learns how to manage the tone of the discussion – avoiding disagreements turning into conflict. This can be done by the group leader modelling good listening techniques for the patient-participants, including quiet listening, respectful reflection and positive participation as a co-inquirer (diminishing their authoritative role). But it is also done by demonstrating their leadership when necessary. At times, it may become expedient for the group leader to take over control of the session, and potentially expel a participant whose behaviours are considered too inappropriate, or disruptive, for continued participation. It is also important that the group leader has a close working relationship with the nursing staff who can assist if a participant is having a crisis, needs to be expelled from the discussion, or for other reasons cannot continue and needs to leave the group.

An additional complication of working in a hospital setting is the frequently changing census on the unit. Because of the progressively shorter lengths of stay on acute care units in recent years, it is uncommon for a patient to be on such a unit for longer than five to seven days. Consequently, the make-up of the group is constantly in flux, thus necessitating that each session begins with an introduction of the purpose, framework and expectations of Thinking Together. In addition, not only does the constantly changing census impede a cohesiveness often arising out of longer term relationships among participants; it also stands in the way of the group leader building on past discussions. Such disadvantages would not be nearly as prominent in longer term residential hospital facilities, further supporting the claim that Thinking Together groups would be ideally suited for longer term care services.

Wrapping up

It has been our experience that our Thinking Together groups on the inpatient and PHP units have been an important addition to the complement of various therapeutic groups provided. It is our impression, especially in the light of patient participant comments, that patients feel the Thinking Together group opens them up for discussion in other groups, improves their self-esteem and self-confidence in group discussion and participation, and creates a lively atmosphere of interaction, bonding and mutual respect. We feel that they quickly grasp the function and purpose of these sessions, and are eager to discuss their thoughts and feelings to a greater extent than in more traditional group therapy sessions. They seem enthusiastic in expressing themselves in ways that many adults rarely do through more traditional therapy approaches. We try and provide them with an awareness of the sense of freedom and joy that comes with allowing oneself to wonder. Some participants have told us that their experience in Thinking Together has made them want to explore philosophy further. Lastly, we hope that by participating in the sessions, the participants learn to appreciate themselves and their ideas – as well as those of others – as valuable and meaningful. Patients frequently comment, after they have adjusted to being on the unit and have met other patients, that they are no longer afraid, dysphoric or ashamed of being admitted. They come to accept that they are not so different from the other patients and vice versa. It is our hope that through Thinking Together participants come to accept that others from differing backgrounds have had similar issues and experiences, and that by learning from the ideas and experiences of others, they may come to learn and understand more about themselves.

In considering our experience with facilitating Thinking Together groups in our unit programming, we have come to appreciate the value of using community philosophy in drawing out thoughts, ideas, interpersonal interactions and self-exploration among the diverse population of participants we uniquely have in our psychiatric settings. Rather than creating an identity based on their diagnoses, psychosocial stressors or personal psychopathology, Thinking Together allows participants to identify and appreciate the importance of how they think in the context of their community. We feel that philosophy groups are a useful and thought-provoking means of creating engagement; encouraging 'thinking out of the box'; incorporating a greater community awareness and a broader perspective in the context of the larger group. It creates a unique dynamic that allows for identifying similarities with others from distinctly differing backgrounds, as well as personal differences from others from similar backgrounds. In contrast to traditional group therapy – in which the attendees and discussions tend to focus on the participants' similarities around a specific issue or psychopathology (substance abuse, trauma, mood disorder, etc.) – group philosophy creates discussions around topics that focus on their thoughts and viewpoints, despite their diagnoses. There are obvious challenges in facilitating a group with teenagers in psychiatric settings, and in creating a democratic discussion including participants with such diversity. However, we consider that the strength of these group sessions comes from the diverse nature of the participants and the varying viewpoints that each contributes to the topic, as well as the comprehensive perspective their participation provides.

Notes

1 Thanks to Jonathan Matheson for helping with this point.
2 The quotation is taken from the 2009 film written and directed by Bobcat Goldthwait, *World's Greatest Dad* (Magnolia Pictures, USA).

References

Douglas, L. C., (1999), *The Robe*, New York: Houghton Mifflin.
Fisher, R., (2011), '"Can Animals Think?" Talking Philosophy with Children', *Philosophy Now*, 84: 6–8.
Lipman, M., (1976), 'Philosophy for Children', *Metaphilosophy*, 7 (1): 17–33.
Silverstein, S., (2011), 'Masks', in *Every Thing on It: Poems and Drawings*, 20, New York: HarperCollins.
Snicket, L., (2005), *The Penultimate Peril*, New York: HarperCollins.
Williams, M., (1991), *The Velveteen Rabbit, or How Toys Become Real*, New York: Bantam Doubleday Dell Publishing Group.

Part Three

Philosophy and Community: Possibilities

17

Coda

Amanda Fulford and Richard Smith

In the preface to this volume, we stated that the central concepts with which this volume would be concerned were, as its title suggests, 'philosophy' and 'community'. The reader does not have to look too far into any chapter to find that the terms occur with unsurprising regularity. But at the end of this volume, we return to these central terms, reflecting on them in the light of our colleagues' contributions. We ask ourselves whether our understanding of them might have changed, or whether we now have better reasons for sticking with our initial thoughts on these concepts.

To those who have read to this point in the volume, especially the chapters in Part Two, such an activity will sound entirely familiar. Trying to make progress in understanding concepts through dialogue together with others is, as this volume has shown, a practice very commonly used in different forms of public philosophy. It is as if the writing of this volume has itself been a form of dialogue among the various authors – a philosophical conversation about the concepts which were important to us: 'community' and 'philosophy'.

So what progress have we made? What are the possibilities for thinking about the concepts of philosophy and of community? This is not a case of summarizing our colleagues' contributions, and coming to some decision based on the majority view. It does mean taking seriously all the ideas that have been written about – even those with which we might disagree. It also means being open to changing our minds, an attribute that is important, though often frowned upon in modern politics which tends to see it as a sign of weakness or of not possessing sufficient conviction about the matter in hand.

To focus on better understanding the concepts of philosophy and community through attention to the practices of public philosophy was indeed one of our aims in this volume. But far from settling these concepts – in the sense of coming to a particular understanding – this volume has further *un*settled them. What the practices of our colleagues show is that we simply cannot understand 'philosophy' solely in terms of the *particular* practices of philosophy undertaken by professional philosophers in the academy. But equally, the practices of public philosophy may extend our understanding of what 'counts' as philosophy; but they do not settle it. David Barton, writing about what literacy 'is', stated simply that it is 'what people do with it' (Barton, Hamilton and Ivanič 2000: 7). We might say the same of philosophy: it happens when

244 *Philosophy and Community*

people engage in reasoned dialogue together over any issue that concerns them. It is not defined by a set of texts that must be read; ideas that must be understood; beliefs that must be held; or methods of argumentation that should be followed. If this is the case, then philosophy can be done in prisons, community centres and pubs, and with trainee teachers, learning-disabled performers, patients in health settings and with professionals. But what such a broader conception of philosophy allows is an openness to possibilities not only in terms of the location of philosophy but also in terms of those who practise it, and what the focus of the practices might be.

To talk of 'community philosophy' suggests work with particular groups of people. Indeed, some of the chapters in this volume critically reflect on work with such discrete communities (such as new and trainee teachers). But often public philosophy takes place with groups of people who do not have any such common identity. The Philosophy in Pubs movement (PIPs) operates with diverse groups of adults, and philosophy in museums and art galleries takes place with any visitors who wish to engage in the conversation. In these examples, the community itself is not the starting point for the philosophy. It is rather that the community is *created* by the shared practice of philosophy. It is not that, through philosophy, diverse groups necessarily come to an agreement, or a common understanding about a particular issue; indeed, they may disagree strongly. But being with others is mediated through communication, and leads to communion – to community.

The Preface to this volume ended with a quotation from the American philosopher, Stanley Cavell, who wrote that we are 'educations for one another' (1990: 31). In this Coda, we return to Cavell again. His philosophy is richly interwoven with references to, and detailed examples from, opera, Shakespeare, literature and Hollywood film from the 1930s and 1940s. His style of writing and approach to the concepts and ideas with which he is concerned often differs from those of other philosophers. Perhaps this makes his work all the more interesting for thinking about community philosophy since its style and approach differentiates it from philosophy as it tends to be practised in the academy. Cavell's work has extraordinary resonance for the ideas with which this volume has been concerned, in particular with how community is created and maintained through language. For Cavell, language and community are ineluctably linked.

Cavell is interested in the way in which we understand the words and concepts we use in our everyday lives. This seems remarkably similar to some of the practices of public philosophy that also begin from the concepts that are of interest to communities – justice, identity and resilience are just some examples from our colleagues' work in the chapters in Part Two of this volume. For Cavell, when we ask about the specific circumstances in which we would say a particular thing, we are talking about what he calls criteria. For example, what are the criteria that determine whether we use the term 'imagination or 'fantasy' to describe a particular way of thinking? To use another example, what constitutes a satisfactory distinction between the concepts of 'autonomy' and 'freedom'? Again, our colleagues provide numerous examples from their public philosophy work of this same attention to our words which allows us to understand each other, and to go on together.

But Cavell goes further. He argues that if language is to be a means of communication, then there must be agreement in criteria. Such agreement signals community; as Cavell puts it in his seminal work, *The Claim of Reason*: 'The philosophical appeal to what we say, and the search for our criteria on the basis on which we say what we say, are claims to community' (1979: 20). But there is a note of caution here: Cavell is not saying that we should push aside our own strong feelings and go along with the majority view for the sake of the community. It is not that we should pursue some kind of generalization based on a majority view. Nor is it the case that we should come together on a particular occasion and arrive at an agreement. The same might be said of public philosophy where dissenting views are not sidelined, but rather are taken seriously, and those who find sound reasons for continuing to hold such views must be respected.

The search for criteria and the creation of community are, in Cavell's account, a matter of consent. We can choose to give our consent to the community, and in so doing we say that the world seems this way for us too. In this sense the community speaks for us, and we also speak for the community. We agree in criteria – or as Cavell puts it, we are 'mutually attuned top to bottom' (ibid: 32). But where we disagree (over a concept, an idea, a word), we dissent from community; the community no longer speaks for us, and we cannot speak for it.

There is a great deal at stake in Cavell's ideas of criteria and community. The same might be said of the practices of public philosophy, especially given the politically and socially turbulent times in which we live. This should not mean that we avoid the opportunities and responsibilities that being part of a community of language users brings. To be in community entails embracing the responsibility of how to go on together. As Cavell writes:

> What I require is a convening of my culture's criteria, in order to confront them with my words and life as I pursue them and as I may imagine them; and at the same time to confront my words and life as I pursue them with the life my culture's words may imagine for me: to confront the culture with itself along the lines in which it meets in me. ... This seems to me a task that warrants the name of philosophy. It is also the description of something we might call education. (Cavell 1979: 125)

*   *   *

Philosophy has often been thought of as a kind of therapy. Socrates's interlocutors, in Plato's dialogues, tend to have problems that are rooted less in weakness of the intellect than in defects of character. Euthyphro is supremely confident that he knows the difference between right and wrong; Theaetetus assumes that philosophical analysis must proceed smoothly and sequentially, like the geometry in which he shows such promise; Phaedrus seems to think that sitting at the feet of Socrates under a plane tree by the banks of the river Ilissus makes him a philosopher like Socrates himself. These and other characters in the dialogues need, more than anything, to approach philosophical questions with a little more humility. It is notable that the dialogues to which each of the three young men above gives his name end with little achieved in this respect. Therapy takes time.

Wittgenstein writes that there is no single philosophical method, 'though there are indeed philosophical methods, like different therapies' (*Philosophical Investigations* § 133). The clarity that philosophy seeks is not some kind of purified, crystalline language, of the sort that Michael Dummett (above, p. 109) seems committed to find: it consists simply in philosophical problems disappearing altogether (ibid). This, when it happens, 'makes me capable of stopping doing philosophy when I want to' (ibid). Philosophy can even cure us of philosophy. Wittgenstein writes of how pictures hold us captive (*Philosophical Investigations* § 115): one of the pictures that enthrals us is the picture of science. So impressive have been the advances of science in the last hundred years in particular, and so enormous the benefits that it has brought to our lives, that anything that looks or sounds 'scientific' risks being venerated uncritically. This naturally applies to philosophy itself, where what Dummett (in Midgley 2018: 10) calls 'the modern logical and analytical style of philosophizing' cast a spell over academic, Anglophone philosophy for many decades, and still fascinates many.

Here is Clare, a fourteen-year-old girl in Penelope Lively's novel *The House in Norham Gardens* (Lively 1974). Clare's teacher, Mrs Cramp, is criticizing – not unkindly – Clare's essay for containing phrases like 'sort of' and 'or anything', and generally being 'messy': 'So what I really wanted to say was that you must remember that language is an instrument, Clare. An instrument to be used precisely'.

Later the same day Clare is back at home. Her friend Liz has come to tea. Clare muses over her conversation with Mrs Cramp:

> 'Language', said Clare to Liz, 'is an instrument. You have to use it precisely. Like a
> screwdriver or something. Not just bash around vaguely?'
> 'What *are* you on about?'
> 'But the trouble is that people don't. They say things like "quite" and "rather" and
> "ever so many" and "by and large" and "much of a muchness" and "quite a
> few". Now what do you suppose a person means when he says "quite a few"?'
> Liz said, 'It would depend what he meant quite a few of. Bananas, or miles, or
> people living in Manchester'.
> 'Years'.
> 'Then it could mean anything'.
> 'Quite', said Clare. (pp. 60–2)

It is not the purpose of this Coda, any more than it is of the book as a whole, to set up binaries: community philosophy against analytic or academic philosophy, philosophy indoors against philosophy outdoors, philosophy as conversation against philosophy as text. But what the lovely vignette above reminds us is that philosophy can return us to the ordinary world of the imprecise and the messy just as it can remove us from it to the realm of sharply delineated abstract ideas. The different kinds of philosophy need each other, not least to cure us of the distortion that exclusive attachment to any one philosophical school, style or fashion can bring.

*   *   *

References

Barton, D., Hamilton, M., and Ivanič, R., (2000), *Situated Literacies: Reading and Writing in Context*, Abingdon: Routledge.

Cavell, S., (1979), *The Claim of Reason: Wittgenstein, Skepticism, Morality and Tragedy*, Oxford: Oxford University Press.

Cavell, S., (1990), *Conditions Handsome and Unhandsome: The Constitution of Emersonian Perfectionism*, Chicago: University of Chicago Press.

Lively, P., (1974), *The House in Norham Gardens*, London: Heinemann.

Midgley, M., (2018), *What is Philosophy For?* London: Bloomsbury.

Wittgenstein, L., (1972), *Philosophical Investigations*, trans. G. E. M. Anscombe, Oxford: Blackwell.

Afterword: Thoughts on moving philosophy outside

Graeme Tiffany

Introduction

In considering future possibilities for Community Philosophy, we might reflect on the diversity of stimuli used to initiate dialogue. Typically, these stimuli are introduced to a group, by the facilitator. In this sense, the facilitator has a good deal of control over what that stimulus is and, to some extent, how it is received. As such (and as argued earlier in this volume in my chapter 'Community Philosophy and Social Action'), there are questions about protecting the process of philosophical enquiry from manipulation, and these questions deserve attention. I also argued that the settings and spaces in which philosophical enquiry takes place exert varying, and sometimes extraordinary, levels of influence on how the process of philosophical enquiry pans out. This includes whether or not social action occurs. In seeking to escape from these constraints, we might consider the possibility of escaping, quite literally, from the spaces and places implicated, thereby lessening concerns about manipulation. What if we were to trust the wider world to provide the stimulus for our enquiries? The logic then is to consider spaces and places beyond the building-based settings typically used – so often 'inside'. What if public philosophy took place *outside*? That said, care is needed to resist interpreting 'outside' too narrowly in terms of 'outdoors', and then implicitly 'The Great Outdoors', with all the connotations of outdoor and adventure education that these terms – beloved of some, but hated by others – bring. To talk of 'outside' (in preference to 'outdoors') is to articulate something altogether more accessible, which is a theme I also emphasized in Chapter 5 on social action. In its stead, simply stepping outside the buildings that so many of us inhabit for great swathes of our lives creates the potential to come into contact with myriad stimuli. This also means such stimuli are more likely to be chosen by the group rather than the facilitator, and this seems important. Hence the urban environment, with its roads and streets, and the fringes of towns and cities, become as valuable a trigger for thinking as what lies beyond, whether the countryside or hills and mountains.

And to 'step out' is surely to walk, a universal activity if ever there was one, and accessible to all but a small minority. Furthermore, few if any of us are raised without cultural references to walking, and, intriguingly, to references that invoke the capacity of walking (outside) to stimulate thinking. Consider the many who say, 'I'm going for a walk to clear my mind'; for them a simple trip round the block will often do. Or as

Afterword 249

Gros puts it, invoking Henry David Thoreau's ideas: 'Walking, as they say, "empties the mind". In another way, walking *fills* the mind with a different sense of purpose' (2014: 97). Indeed, many philosophers, way back to the Ancient Greeks, have made reference to walking. We have, then, a veritable history to draw upon that provides a stimulus for philosophical enquiry 'outside'. Indeed, there appears to be great potential in combining walking with philosophical enquiry, and as such, this practice deserves further scrutiny.

Walking technologies

We might start by considering the many 'walking technologies', the ways in which walking is used for a wide variety of purposes. For example, there has been a growing interest in walking for health reasons, whether to aid weight loss and counteract obesity, or for the general promotion of physical activity and well-being (Public Health England 2017; HM Government 2018). Walking is now also prescribed by General Practitioners and other health care professionals to mitigate social isolation and support improved mental health (France et al. 2016; South et al. 2017). It is pertinent again to note that walking becomes a proxy for being outside (and that this is valued as much as the physical act of walking). This view is routinely articulated not only in the narrative of 'social prescribing' but also in 'Green Prescribing' (Bloomfield 2014). Very often, the suggestion is also to walk with others; it's presumed that walking together supports talking together, with all the benefits which that brings. There may be more: in my experience, influenced by work with French street social work colleagues, I've come to value walking with others in a deeper way – as an expression of solidarity. Likewise, those with a similar job in Spain speak of *acompañamiento*, or 'accompaniment'. Think of the symbolism of being 'alongside', and 'side-by-side'. Fanon, in his advocacy for a decolonized psychology where the emphasis is on dialogue, mutual respect and the empowerment of those marginalized, writes: 'What we want is to walk in the company of man, every man, night and day, for all times' (2004: 238). That this contests the value commonly ascribed to 'face-to-face' conversations again seems significant. I remember well having to discuss sensitive issues with the young people with whom I worked, and how many said very little when sat on the other side of a desk. Few resisted my suggestion that we might walk together; and when we did they invariably talked. It is as if walking with others renders it a political act.

Many others have recognized that walking together supports talking together. In the corporate world, 'networking' has morphed into 'netwalking',[1] and has become a means to build and develop teams. 'Walking meetings' are increasingly common. Pared back, walking in and of itself seems to constitute a stimulus for conversation, which is where its resonance for public and Community Philosophy comes in. It's also worth noting that science appears to be on its side: there is growing evidence that when we move there are cognitive benefits – arguably that we think better (Suzuki and Fitzpatrick 2015). Walking is easily co-opted into a wider contestation of the Cartesian Dualism, that an interrelationship between mind and body *does* exists.

250   *Philosophy and Community*

Then there are the geographers, who, within so many sub-disciplines, have long since recognized the value of walking as a tool for research, as a means to find out more about people and the spaces and places they inhabit. Importantly, they've realized that walking with others, say with residents of an area, enables an understanding of it through local eyes – which chimes again with philosophical enquiry as a form of participatory research. I did this as a new street-based youth worker. I asked young people to guide me around the estates in which they lived. This helped enormously in my community profiling activities, in understanding and contextualizing where folk were 'coming from'. This elicits a further memory of walking with children, whose pace is often extremely slow. And yet, committing to walk at their pace means we see things that ordinarily we wouldn't, and understand time differently. Together we illuminate an understanding of place.

Psycho-geography particularly resonates with such philosophical endeavour; here walking is deliberately constituted as a process of de-familiarization, and research is conceptualized – as in the French *chercher* – as searching. This encourages experimentation and ultimately the potential of rethinking; thoughts and opinions are revealed as merely habitual, re-evaluated and removed. For Guy Debord (1956) and other Situationists, walking helped 'express not subordination to randomness but total insubordination to habitual influences' (ibid: 26); it becomes an *active* effort to change perspective. Walking becomes a *dérive*, or 'drift', a playful and yet purposeful attempt to consider the influence of the environment on how we think and behave, and capable of 'provoking sharp emotional reactions' (ibid: 50); such reactions are stimuli, if you like, for enquiry into things other than the taken for granted. Conversely, we might aim deliberately to 'problematize' the world (Freire 1970), critiquing the very things we take for granted and assume unchallengeable. Thus walking becomes a means to come into contact with, and develop, new ideas, particularly when (in the form of the *dérive*) there is an intention to head off in new and unpredictable directions with the aim of opening up new forms of awareness. Thoreau's (1862) notion of 'sauntering' resonates also: he advocates walking without a particular purpose, both physically and metaphorically being (and moving) 'off the beaten path', *sans terre* – without any particular home. And happy to be so, given the thoughts it inspires and the quality of the dialogue that ensues. In this sense, walking, when combined with enquiry-based philosophical practices, become propositional – capable of showing us new ways of thinking, acting, being and becoming.

Walking as a philosophical proposition

Conceptualizing walking as a propositional activity, and a philosophical one at that, constitutes it as capable of suggesting – proposing – to us where we might go, both physically and philosophically. Walking then becomes an embodied philosophical practice. We might look to 'sense walks' and synaesthesia[2] walks, which deliberately encourage a focus on a specific sense, in recognition that (for example) a particular smell can trigger, say, thoughts of times past. Thereafter, a walk leader with philosophical inclinations might use the idea of synaesthesia to ask participants to describe what they hear as if it were a smell. This use of a linguistic descriptor from a different sense modality can spark creative thinking and nourish dialogue; it connects again with the idea of walking as de-familiarization. As Braidotti (2013: 88–9) writes, involving 'the loss of familiar habits of thought and representation in order to pave the way for creative alternatives'; in finding ways of knowing and communicating through movement, new modes of subjectivity are generated, and we learn to think differently. Our experience of moving symbolically resists pre-determination, contests the idea that thought is already *realized*. It keeps assumptions at bay. In a Deweyan sense, it becomes uncertainty-appreciative, which, surely, all good philosophical practice strives to be. Methodologically then, these propositions connect actual experience with *what could be*: they are also *speculative*. Again, this impacts on our understanding of philosophy as a form of politics; when we think of *what could be*, there is the potential to break out of conformity, to destroy order, to think in non-binary ways: 'walking becomes a "lure for feeling"' (Whitehead 1978: 25) that can 'pave the way along which the world advances into novelty' (ibid: 187). Walking, in this sense, is steadfastly *not* technical, something we are *instructed* in doing; it becomes something related to the *unforeseen* – we're never quite sure what will happen. This again makes it an ideal medium for philosophizing. We might think of this as of the flight of an aeroplane (ibid: 5); as walkers we have a starting point, a point we see or observe from; then, as we move, we 'take flight in the thin air of imaginative generalization' (ibid); and then we land again, having been stimulated to reflect/think again. 'Such thought supplies the differences which direct (static) observation lacks' (ibid).

Walking as Community Philosophy: Examples from practice

How to turn all this into practice? How to connect public and Community Philosophy with walking? First, there is a need to embrace a community dimension, to realize that in all that has been said thus far, there is more to be had from the stimulus of walking if it takes place in a social context, where experiences and the ideas that flow from them can be shared in support of mutual learning. A specific intention of my own work has been to bring people together who don't know one another – or at least not very well – to walk and talk together. The aim is to create or further develop a community, even if only for the duration of the walk. This makes walking and thinking a collaborative affair; what's created is a product of our 'entangled inter-relating' (Barad 2007: ix). As individuals, we are also shaped by this: our actions, our agency, are products of the same entanglement. And this adds to the sense that this is also a political act: entangled practices are *productive*: 'Different *intra*-actions produce different phenomena' (ibid: 58). 'Philosophy Walks'[3] typically begin with a brief invitation to participants to say what appeals about the idea of bringing walking together with philosophy. These contributions, and other 'getting to know' activities, set the foundations for the walk to be a collaborative endeavour. While trusting the environment to stimulate discussion, use is often made of the many things philosophers have said about walking. Participants are frequently amazed (as was I when I started researching this connection), how many philosophers have invoked walking as a means to think philosophically. This tends to resonate with those present, who often express similar sentiments and desires, if not necessarily experiences. Such references can, and often do, act as powerful stimuli for dialogue, and, in their everyday nature, support participants' identification with philosophy. Of these, Socrates's preference for encounters in the street (and the legacy of Socratic dialogue that has so influenced Community of Enquiry methodologies) is particularly apt, as is the significance of movement within the *agora* – a non-institutional, public, space: literally, a 'gathering place' where conversations could take place. The Platonic dialogue where Socrates encounters Phaedrus, who convinces him to go for a walk in the countryside (this being the only dialogue in which we find Socrates outside of Athens' city walls), consolidates the idea that Philosophy Walks can take place in both urban and rural areas. In this, the experience of leaving the city unsettles Socrates, but nonetheless provokes him to abandon some of his customary assumptions: 'You must forgive me, dear friend; I'm a lover of learning, and trees and open country won't teach me anything, whereas men in the town do. Yet you seem to have discovered a drug for getting me out' (*Phaedrus* 230d-e, in Verdenius 1955).

Other philosophers also employ the device of walking (again both physically and philosophically) to get 'outside civilization', in order to garner different perspectives and think anew. Frédéric Gros (2014: 20) describes Friedrich Nietzsche's belief that thinking actually necessitates walking as his 'eulogy of the foot'. Indeed, Nietzsche proclaimed: 'It is our habit to think outdoors' (1974: 322). Another stimulus I have used is Henry David Thoreau's view, enshrined in his proposal of a 'new economics' ([1854] 2016), that walking teaches us the distinction between profit and benefit (which is surely an enquiry into values). In Gros's account of Thoreau, walking produces 'nothing saleable' (2014: 89); nevertheless the benefit is immense. More adventurous Philosophy Walks tend to take place in hilly and mountainous terrain. This creates the opportunity to connect with the origins of the word 'summit', which, quite literally, saw people walking to the top of a hill in order to gain a different perspective in and on their conversations and meetings. While Philosophy Walks are principally directed at those who are attracted to the idea of walking and philosophizing *for its own sake*, wanting to 'stretch their minds as well as their legs' – for personal reasons, and often for no more than the joy of the endeavour – the earlier analysis suggests a combination of walking and philosophical enquiry can have more specific aims. In this sense, walking can make a significant contribution to the process whereby Community Philosophy informs social action. Indeed, Philosophy Walks I've led with the residents and the staff of a range of statutory and voluntary agencies have been used to research community needs and to inform strategies to meet those needs. For example, the staff of a community housing association walked from its inner-city office, through residential areas for which they were responsible, to the urban fringe and beyond. The diversity of environments stimulated reflection and enabled the team to take stock of aims and purposes, and to review and evaluate the work they were doing. Ultimately, they were able to think critically and creatively about the organization's future. Similarly, walking is found to have the capacity to promote community development and community

Afterword 253

cohesion. The 'Step-into-Dialogue' Project in Kirklees, UK, works with the leaders of community organizations to support them in learning the practical and philosophical skills needed to lead walks with the communities with which they are engaged, but also to bring members of different communities together to walk and talk together in order to aid that cohesion.

Concluding remarks

It seems then, in considering future possibilities for Community Philosophy, that the idea of 'moving philosophy' – as in movement-catalysed philosophy – constituting it as an embodied philosophical practice, has great potential. Rather than seeing walking as a novelty, perhaps it has the capacity to advance a new orthodoxy, in which the starting position for all philosophical activity is outside. There is a wealth of argument from the history of philosophy, and in valuable accounts from practice, that suggests this is precisely what we should do.

* * *

Notes

1 A quick internet search reveals numerous initiatives which use walking to promote discussion and networking. See, for example, TeamWalking: https://www.teamwalking. co.uk/. The Twitter feed @netwalking, and hashtag #netwalking, provide links to many more.
2 Synaesthesia is a condition in which one sense (e.g. hearing) is simultaneously perceived as if by one or more additional senses, such as sight. Other forms join objects such as letters, shapes, numbers or people's names with a sensory perception such as smell, colour or flavour.
3 For an account of a 'Philosophy Walk', see Hallisey (2018).

References

Barad, K., (2007), *Meeting the Universe Halfway: Quantum Physics and the Entanglement of Matter and Meaning*, Durham: Duke University Press.
Bloomfield, D., (2014), *A Dose of Nature*, Evidence Report, [Online], Available at: http://www.health.govt.nz/our-work/preventative-health-wellness/physical-activity/green-pr escriptions/green-prescriptionresearch/green-prescription-patient-survey, Accessed 29 January 2019.
Braidotti, R., (2013), *The Posthuman*, Cambridge: Polity.
Debord, G., (1956), *Theory of the Dérive*, trans. Ken Knabb, Situationist International Online, [Online], Available at: https://www.cddc.vt.edu/sionline/si/theory.html, Accessed 29 January 2019.

Fanon, F., (2004), *The Wretched of the Earth*, New York: Grove Press.

France. J., Sennett, J., Jones, A., Fordham, R., Williams, J., Burke, A., Meierkord, A., Fong Soe Khioe, E., and Suhrcke, M., (2016), *Evaluation of Walking for Health*. Final Report to Macmillan and the Ramblers, London: Walking for Health.

Freire, P., (1970), *Pedagogy of the Oppressed,* trans. Myra Bergman Ramos, New York: Herder and Herder.

Gros, F., (2014), *A Philosophy of Walking*, London: Verso.

Hallisey, N. (2018), 'Solvitur Ambulando', *Country Walking Magazine*, August 2018, [Online], Available at: https://www.teamwalking.co.uk/uploads/Walking%20Philoso phy%20North%20York%20Moors.pdf, Accessed 29 January 2019.

HM Government (2018), 'Focus on Brisk Walking, Not Just 10,000 Steps', [Online], Available at: https://www.gov.uk/government/news/focus-on-brisk-walking-not-jus t-10000-steps-say-health-experts, Accessed 29 January 2019.

Nietzsche, F., (1974), *The Gay Science*, trans. Walter Kaufmann, New York: Vintage.

Public Health England, (2017), 'Ten Minutes Brisk Walking Each Day in Mid-Life for Health Benefits and Towards Achieving Physical Activity Recommendations – Evidence Summary', [Online], Available at: https://assets.publishing.service.gov.uk/ government/uploads/system/uploads/attachment_data/file/639030/Health_benefits_o f_10_mins_brisk_walking_evidence_summary.pdf, Accessed 29 January 2019.

South, J., Giuntoli, G., Kinsella, K., Carlessa, D., Longa, J., and McKenna J. (2017), 'Walking, Connecting and Befriending: A Qualitative Pilot Study of Participation in a Lay-Led Walking Group Intervention', *Journal of Transport and Health*, 5: 16–26.

Suzuki, W., and Fitzpatrick, B., (2015), *Healthy Brain, Happy Life*, New York: Harper Collins.

Thoreau, H. D., ([1862] 2006), *Walking*, New York: Cosimo Classics.

Thoreau, H. D., (2016), *Walden*, London: Penguin.

Verdenius, W. J., (1955), 'Notes on Plato's *Phaedrus*', *Mnemosyne*, Fourth Series, 8 (4): 265–89.

Whitehead, A. N., (1978), *Process and Reality: An Essay in Cosmology*, New York: Free Press.

Index

Adult Learning Project (ALP)   71
aesthetics   163–4
Alcibiades   105–6
Alexander, R.   151
applied ethics   135–8
Archer, J.   183
Aristotle   xii, 21
art galleries   118–29
Arts Council England   165, 174
Augustine of Hippo, St   92
Austin, M.   91
authenticity   124

Bakkioui, S.   10
Barnes, E.   171
Bell, D.   173
Benatar, D.   136–7
bioethics   24
Bird, J.   179
Birmingham Midland Institute   109–10
Briggle, A.   19, 25
Brila Youth Project   16
Brown, S.   80
Buber, M.   92
Burbules and Rice   40
Burnett, K.   98

Café Philo   16
Cameron, D.   42
Cashio, J.   ix
Cavell, S.   xv, 49–51, 93–4, 244–5
Cicero, Marcus Tullius   3, 5
citizenship   44–7
communities of practice   131
Community of Philosophical
      Enquiry   216
Coxhead, M.   177

Darani, L.   10
Davies, B.   86
Debord, G.   251
Demetrius the Cynic   201 n.2

De St Croix, T.   81–2
Dewey, J.   vii–x, 8, 31, 56, 58, 59, 98,
      118, 150, 158 n.6
Donnelly, P.   192
Dostoyevsky, F.   184
Douglas, L. C.   234
Dummett, M.   109, 246
Dunne, J.   192
Dwelling Together (project and film)
      206, 207, 212
dyslexia   172

Echeverria, E.   7, 178
Enroth, H.   43
environmental ethics   24
Epictetus   95
epistemic exploitation   210–12
Esmée Fairbairn Foundation   79
Evans, J.   25, 30

Fanon, F.   250
Farrell, F.   65
Fassolas, A.   177
Federation of Australasian Philosophy in
      Schools Associations (FAPSA)   16,
      33 n.2
Field Philosophers   24
Fisher, R.   229, 230
Foucault, M.   96–7, 186
Frega, R.   59
Freire, P.   7, 71, 72, 81, 83–4
Frodeman, R.   19, 25

Genet, J.   184
Gros, F.   97, 253
Gupta, M.   206

Haack, S.   65
Hand, M.   20, 30
Hannam, P.   7, 178
Harris, P.   83–7
Heilbronn, R.   7

256   *Index*

Higashi, K.   10, 80
Higgins, H. D. (President of Ireland) 189, 193, 201
Higgins, S.   193, 200
Hobbs, A.   98
Hodgson, N.   40
Holloway, J.   81
hooks, b.   7
Humphreys, J. (*The Irish Times*)   192
Husserl, E.   92

Institute for Philosophy in Public Life   24
Institute for the Advancement of Philosophy for Children (IAPC)   16, 33 n.2
integrity   138–40

James, W.   58
Joseph Rowntree Foundation   99

Kaplan, D.   91
Kennedy, D.   30, 98, 100
Kumar, S.   86
Kwak, D.-J.   40, 43, 47, 48

Lachs, J.   vii
Latour, B.   51–2
Lawlor, R.   136–8
Lipman, M.   xiii, 8, 9, 21, 118, 119, 126, 207, 208, 213, 216, 231, 253
Lively, P.   246
Llanera, T.   61
Lockrobin, G.   164–6, 217
London Philosophy Club   25
Lowry, R.S.   124
Lucas, S.   124

McHugh, N.   179
Magee, B.   18, 19
Malik, K.   206
Masschelein, J.   44–8
Matthews, G.   8, 20
Maudsley Philosophy Group   16
Meager, S.   15, 126
Midgley, M.   108–109
Mind the Gap (theatre company) 164–74
Monbiot, G.   87–8
Moses, M.   99

Mostert, P.   7
Murris, K.S.   31, 150, 152–3
museums   118–29

National Institute of Adult and Continuing Education (NIACE) 71
Nisbet, R.   38
Noddings, N.   38
Novalis (Friedrich von Hardenberg)   viii
Nussbaum, M.   18, 25, 95, 129, 179

Oakeshott, M.   108
O'Brien, D.   91
O'Donnell, A.   52
O'Donnell, I.   185
Ofili, C.   124
Orchard, J.   7

Peirce, C.S.   58, 118, 150
Peters, M.   92
Phelan, S.   38
Phillips, C.   4, 56
Philosophy
    academic   213
    demographic of   226–7
    professionalization of   22–3
Philosophy Breaks Bread podcast   ix–x
Philosophy Exchange (University of Leeds) 216–27
Philosophy for Children (P4C)   xiii, 7–9, 69, 70–5, 190–8, 201 n.3, 204, 207–9, 211–14
Philosophy for Teachers (P4T)   7, 16, 145–62
Philosophy Foundation   16, 177
Philosophy in Pubs   16
Philosophy in the City/Archer Project 16
Philosophy Ireland (PI)   189–90, 195–6, 200
Picasso, P.   121–2
Plato   18, 49, 94–7, 104–7, 113, 245, 253
Powell-Cotton Museum   80–1
pragmatism   63
praxis   151
Presocratic philosophers   103
Princeton Universities Prisons Teaching Initiative   16

Index

Prison and Neighbourhood Arts Project (Chicago)   179
prisons   75, 177–87
professionalism   133–5
Public Philosophy Network   24

Rawls, J.   225
Reed-Sandoval, A.   208
resilience   233–4
Rice, M.   194, 195
Rorty, R.   56, 58–67
Rose, N.   38, 42, 43
Royal Institute of Philosophy   191
Royal Irish Academy   192
Russell, B.   26–7
Rust, J.   180, 181

Sandel, M.   viii, 16, 24
SAPERE, *see* Society for the Advancement of Philosophical Enquiry and Reflection in Education
Sautet, M.   4
Schopenhauer, A.   19
Schwitzgebel, E.   180, 181
Seal, M.   83–7
self-identity   235–7
Seneca, Lucius Annaeus   95–7, 189, 201 n.2
Sgarbi, F.   91
Shakespeare, W.   103
Shalev, S.   186
Sharp, A.   8
Sidebottom, K.   10
Silverstein, S.   236
Sim, C.   155
Simons, M.   44–8
Smith, A.   61
Smith, B.   91
Smith, M.   71–2
Smith, R.   92, 97
Snicket, L.   237
Society for the Advancement of Philosophical Enquiry and Reflection in Education (SAPERE)   9, 16, 79, 150, 151, 191, 196, 213
Society of Philosophers in America (SOPHIA)   vii–ix

Socrates   ix, 3, 5, 6, 18–19, 25, 94, 97, 104–7, 245, 253
Socrates Café   4, 16, 56, 57, 62, 64
Spendiff, K.   10
Standish, P.   93
stoicism   94
Stuhr, J.   64–5
Sutcliffe, R.   8
synaesthesia   254 n.2

Tent City University   16
Thatcher, M.   41, 113
Thinking Space   16, 118, 164–8, 217
Thinking Together group   229–39
Thinking Village   16, 76–9
Thoreau, H. D.   251–3
Thucydides   105
Tiffany, G.   7, 10
Topping, K.   194
Touch Project   82–3
Tripodi, V.   126
trolleyology   22

University College London (UCL) Grand Challenges   203

Van Dyck, A.   119
Vansieleghem, N.   99
The Velveteen Rabbit (Williams, M.)   235–6
Vlieghe, J.   40

walking   250–4
Warnock, M.   17, 24, 172
Warwick Commission on the Future of Cultural Value   117
Watson, C.   156
Weistein, J.   15
Wenger, E.   131, 148
White, J.   20
Why is My Curriculum White? campaign   227
Williams, R.   237
Wilson, J.   124
Wilson, L.   124
Winstanley, C.   7
Wittgenstein, L.   110, 246

Zamojski, P.   40

CPSIA information can be obtained
at www.ICGtesting.com
Printed in the USA
LVHW111912031221
705203LV00004B/96